Film Review

1998-99

James Cameron-Wilson became a committed film buff when he moved to London at the age of seventeen. After a stint at the Webber Douglas Academy of Dramatic Art he joined *What's On In London* and took over from F. Maurice Speed as cinema editor. Later, he edited the trade newspaper *Showbiz*, was commissioning editor for *Film Review*, was consultant for *The Movie Show* on BSkyB TV and was a frequent presenter of the Radio 2 *Arts Programme*. He is also author of the books *Hollywood: The New Generation*, *Young Hollywood*, *The Cinema of Robert De Niro* and *The Moviegoer's Quiz Book*. His film reviews are currently syndicated in the *What's On* magazines distributed in Birmingham, Manchester, Liverpool and Stratford, and he has a regular column in *Film Review*, Britain's longest-running film magazine. He has also written frequently for *The Times*, as well as contributing to *The Sunday Times*, the *Guardian*, *Flicks*, *Mensa Quest*, *Movies*, *Photoplay*, *Film Monthly*, *Xpose*, *Exposure*, *Midlands Zone*, *Ritz*, *London MAG*, etc. etc. He was also Britain's resident dial-a-film critic for more than two-and-a-half years and on television has made 100 appearances on *The Movie Show* (as critic and quizmaster) and regularly popped up on CNN, Channel One and BBC Worldwide Television. Besides the cinema, James Cameron-Wilson's academic interests include beer, ball lighting and beavers.

F. Maurice Speed was born on 18 October, 1911, and helped establish London's first entertainment guide – *What's On In London* – in 1937. After the war, while still editing *What's On*, he founded the first edition of this annual, which he dedicated to his wife, the actress Lorenza Harris. His other publications included *The Western Film Annual*, *Movie Cavalcade* and *Star Parade*. He died peacefully on the morning of 28 August, 1998 in London.

Film Review

1998-99

Including Video Releases

James Cameron-Wilson

Founding father: F. Maurice Speed
1911-1998

TO MY BROTHER CHRISTOPHER,
FOR HELPING TO EASE ME INTO
THE 21ST CENTURY

Acknowledgements

The author would like to express his
undying gratitude to the following,
without whom this book would not have
been possible: David Aldridge, Charles
Bacon, Ewen Brownrigg, Christopher
Cameron, Michael Darvell, Marianne
Gray, Anne Heche, Wendy Hollas,
Karen Krizanovich, my mother, Frances
Palmer, Virginia Palmer, Fred Price,
David Quinlan, Philip Rose, Simon Rose,
Lorna Russell, Mansel Stimpson and
Derek Winnert. Till next year …

Founding father:
F. Maurice Speed, 1911-1998

First published in Great Britain in 1998 by
VIRGIN BOOKS
an imprint of Virgin Publishing Ltd,
Thames Wharf Studios, Rainville Road,
London W6 9HT

A catalogue record for this book is available
from the British Library

ISBN 1-85227-767-X

Designed and typeset by Fred Price

Printed in Great Britain by
Butler & Tanner Ltd

Contents

Introduction

James Cameron-Wilson

I have a bone to pick. While the trailer for *Godzilla* – the one in which the old fisherman loses his rod – generated the best must-see buzz since the White House exploded, it was a glaring exception to the rule. Filmmaking, for all its secondary pretensions, is first and foremost about storytelling. Yet critics insist on picking over the bones of the narrative as if it were their sole proviso to ruin the film for their readers. But, given a little time, any reviewer worth his or her canapes should be able to scrape together enough background information both to satisfy his or her word count and shed fascinating light on a film.

The point is not that *Emma* Woodhouse really loves George Knightley, but that director Douglas McGrath caught the essence of Jane Austen's original novel. Interesting, too, is that the maker of such a quintessentially English subject was born in Texas (near Austin?) and, of all things, began his career writing material for the satirical TV revue *Saturday Night Live*. It may also be

Just an excuse to show a picture of Gwyneth Paltrow

worth mentioning that McGrath chose the California-born Gwyneth Paltrow to play his aristocratic English rose when he heard her white-trash Texan accent in *Flesh and Bone*. 'Once I knew she had that ear,' McGrath explained, 'I knew she could handle Emma.'

All such background information – for me, at least – brings colour and substance to the film I am watching. Knowing that Jaye Davidson in *The Crying Game* is really you-know-what just destroys my enjoyment. Films are predictable enough without journalists exploring the storyline with the morbid attention of a proctologist.

Which brings me back to trailers. While I appreciate that a trailer is designed to lure an audience to the cinema, that does not mean it has to kill the meal. A good trailer – like the one for *Godzilla* and, a year earlier, *Men in Black* – should put over the flavour of the product, not disclose the recipe. Like a first date, it can hint at things to come without bedding down with the viewer.

The trailer for *Forrest Gump* crammed in all of the best bits in a frenzied three-and-a-half minutes – and more or less spelt out the entire story. The formula obviously worked, as *Gump* went on to rake in more money for Paramount Pictures than any other film. But that doesn't mean that large sections of the movie-going public weren't damned let down. Likewise, such narrative-driven pictures as *Mad City*, *Red Corner* and *Hope Floats* were completely sabotaged by their trailers, while the promo reel for *Deep Impact* negated the suspense of the film's first 100 minutes by showing the comet actually colliding with earth. Sorry to blow the ending, but you'd have to be sensorially deprived not to have got there first.

Like readers who turn to the last page of a mystery novel first, trailers have turned disappointment into an art form. With so much celluloid flotsam storming our multiplexes, the deepest impact has to be made in the shortest amount of time. That's marketing, folks. But, for the long haul, it's not very smart marketing. How much disappointment can an audience take?

Top Twenty UK Box-Office Hits

1 Titanic
2 The Full Monty
3 Men in Black
4 The Lost World: Jurassic Park
5 Tomorrow Never Dies
6 Bean
7 Batman and Robin
8 Sliding Doors
9 Hercules
10 Spiceworld The Movie
11 Deep Impact
12 Flubber
13 As Good As It Gets
14 My Best Friend's Wedding
15 Scream
16 Scream 2
17 Good Will Hunting
18 MouseHunt
19 Alien Resurrection
20 L.A. Confidential

Sink and swim: Leonardo DiCaprio and Kate Winslet float to the top of the box-office charts in James Cameron's record-vaporising *Titanic*

Show-offs: William Snape, Mark Addy, Robert Carlyle, Steve Huison and Tom Wilkinson in *The Full Monty*, the top-grossing British film in Britain

Scary monsters and super creeps: Will Smith and Tommy Lee Jones protect the universe as our *Men in Black*

The halitosis nightmare: Julianne Moore and Jeff Goldblum on the receiving end in Steven Spielberg's *The Lost World: Jurassic Park*

Gone today: Jonathan Pryce blackens the media's name in *Tomorrow Never Dies*

Top Ten Box-Office Stars

Star of the Year: Leonardo DiCaprio

Let's get one thing straight: people didn't queue round the block to see *Titanic* because of Leonardo DiCaprio. However, millions of schoolgirls queued round the block *again* to see *Titanic* because of Leonardo DiCaprio. To mangle an old adage: once smitten, twice buy me another goddamn ticket! To prove his precipitant box-office appeal, the Oscar-nominated star went on to turn the plodding *Man in the Iron Mask* into a commercial success. Thus, with extreme reluctance, we have to acknowledge the 23 year old's box-office supremacy.

So where was Tom Cruise, last year's box-office champ? Well, he was holed up in England shooting endless retakes on Stanley Kubrick's perpetual *Eyes Wide Shut*, an erotic drama that has gone down in history as the Hollywood film with the longest production schedule ever (running from 4 November 1996 to July 1998!). Anyway, with Cruise's future schedule shunted somewhere into the 21st century, it's unlikely we'll see him on this page again for a year or two.

Meanwhile, we can marvel at the continuing success of Will Smith who, rated tenth last year, has vaulted to second place on the back of the phenomenal takings of *Men in Black*. And as for Rowan Atkinson, few commentators can deny that the extraordinary popularity of *Bean* was due principally to the TV comic with the constipated posture.

What's so gratifying about this chart are the glaring anomalies. While both sides of the pond embraced the spectacular melodrama of *Titanic*, other such American triumphs as *Contact*, *Conspiracy Theory*, *I Know What You Did Last Summer* and *Michael* performed relatively slowly here. Conversely, the less indigenously successful *MouseHunt*, *Alien Resurrection*, *The Borrowers* and *One Fine Day* did considerably better.

For the record, the runners-up this year include John Travolta, Harrison Ford, Keanu Reeves, Pierce Brosnan and, er, the Spice Girls.

2 Will Smith

3 Rowan Atkinson

4 Robin Williams

5 Nicolas Cage

6 Bruce Willis

7 Gwyneth Paltrow

8 George Clooney

9 Jack Nicholson

10 Julia Roberts

Releases of the Year

In this section you will find details of all the films released in Great Britain from 1 July 1997 to the end of June 1998 – the period covered by all the reference features in the book.

The normal abbreviations operate as follows: Dir – for Director; Pro – for Producer; Assoc Pro – for Associate Producer; Ex Pro – for Executive Producer; Co-Pro – for Co-Producer; Ph – for Photographer; Ed – for Editor; Art – for Art Director; Pro Des – for Production Designer; M – for Music; and a few others which will be obvious.

Abbreviations for the names of film companies are also pretty obvious when used, such as Fox for 20th Century-Fox, and UIP for Universal International Pictures. The production company is given first, the releasing company last.

All films reviewed by James Cameron-Wilson unless otherwise specified.
Additional contributors: Charles Bacon, Ewen Brownrigg, Marianne Gray,
Karen Krizanovich, Mansell Stimpson and Derek Winnert.

Addicted to Love ★★★★

Sam, a small-town astronomer, has stars in his eyes. An incurable romantic, he lives for the sight of his childhood sweetheart, Linda, and for the sky at night. So, when Linda falls under the spell of a charismatic French restaurateur on a sojourn to New York, Sam sets up an elaborate, clandestine observatory to keep an eye on her. However, Sam hadn't planned on the intervention of Maggie, the Frenchman's spurned fiancée, whose spying tactics are altogether more sinister... With a cast headed by Meg Ryan and Matthew Broderick and with a title like *Addicted to Love*, you'd be forgiven for expecting a romantic comedy. Well, this contrived, predictable yet oddly touching film *is* very funny and inescapably romantic, but it also borders on farce and displays an unexpectedly wicked nature. Like life itself, it is sweet, funny and frequently very nasty. Marking the directorial debut of actor/producer Griffin Dunne, the film is also remarkably stylish. Seldom have Hollywood comedies displayed such visual ingenuity, exemplified by the scene in which Broderick whitewashes his wall to reveal the emerging image of his errant girlfriend, reflected by his camera obscura. FYI: The director's father, the distinguished writer Dominick Dunne, plays the restaurant critic Howard Matheson.

Cast: Meg Ryan (*Maggie*), Matthew Broderick (*Sam*), Kelly Preston (*Linda*), Tcheky Karyo (*Anton*), Maureen Stapleton (*Nana*), Nesbitt Blaisdell (*Ed Green*), Remak Ramsay, Lee Wilkof, Dominick Dunne, Susan Forristal, Larry Pine.

Dir: Griffin Dunne. Pro: Jeffrey Silver and Bobby Newmyer. Ex Pro: Bob Weinstein and Harvey Weinstein. Co-Pro: Caroline Baron and Johanna Demetrakas. Assoc Pro: Susan E. Novick. Screenplay: Robert Gordon. Ph: Andrew Dunn. Pro Des: Robin Standefer. Ed: Elizabeth Kling. M: Rachel Portman; numbers performed by The Left Banke, Us3, Luscious Jackson, Ry Cooder, Los Lobos, Serge Gainsbourg and Jane Birkin, Stephane Grappelli, MC Solaar, etc; 'Addicted To Love' sung by Neneh Cherry. Costumes: Renee Ehrlich Kalfus. (Outlaw Prods/Miramax–Warner.) Rel: 1 August 1997. 100 mins. Cert 15. USA. 1997.

Afterglow ★★★¹⁄₂

Montreal; today. Although the light in their marriage may have long dimmed, there is still a glow that binds Lucky and Phyllis Mann together. An all-round 'Mr Fix-it', Lucky 'never got past having fun and not feeling crappy' about what he does. On the other hand, Phyllis, a faded B-movie actress, has resorted to the bottle and resides in her tortured past. Together, they share a

Cuckold cruelty: Meg Ryan shoots from the hip in Griffin Dunne's wicked *Addicted to Love* (from Warner)

Fanning the embers: Nick Nolte and Julie Christie revisit their past in Alan Rudolph's densely textured *Afterglow* (from Columbia TriStar)

terrible secret, a secret that's about to be blown out of the closet as their lives cross with a young couple also suffering major marital problems... Skilfully weaving a number of moods and motifs into a complex, powerful and stylish tapestry, *Afterglow* once again shows what an accomplished and individual talent writer-director Alan Rudolph is (cf. *The Moderns*, *Choose Me*). A terrific cast rises to the material (Julie Christie received her third Oscar nomination for her part), attacking Rudolph's dialogue with gusto (Nolte: 'I don't know what I like, but I know what art is'). Rich in nuance, *Afterglow* is a classy comedy empowered by a steel thread of pathos.

Nick Nolte (*Leland 'Lucky' Mann*), Julie Christie (*Phyllis Mann*), Lara Flynn Boyle (*Marianne Byron*), Jonny Lee Miller (*Jeffrey Byron*), Jay Underwood (*Donald Duncan*), Domini Blythe (*Helene Pelletier*), Yves Corbeil (*Bernard Ornay*), Alan Fawcett (*Count Falco/Jack Dana*), Genevieve Bissonnette (*Cassie*), Michele-Barbara Pelletier (*Isabel Marino*), France Castel, Claudia Besso, Ellen David, Ivan Smith.

Dir and Screenplay: Alan Rudolph. Pro: Robert Altman. Ex Pro: Ernst Stroh and Willi Baer. Co-Pro: James McLindon. Assoc Pro: Rebecca Morton. Ph: Toyomichi

Kurita. Pro Des: Francois Seguin. Ed: Suzy Elmiger. M: Mark Isham; numbers performed by Tom Waits, Fausto Leali, and Gilbert Becaud. Costumes: Francois Barbeau. (Moonstone Entertainment/ Sand Castle 5/Elysian Dreams–Columbia TriStar.) Rel: 29 May 1998. 114 mins. Cert 15. USA. 1997.

Un Air de Famille ★★★

Gathering for its weekly ritual dinner, the Menard clan – matriarch, two middle-aged sons, rebellious daughter and one tipsy daughter-in-law – is in for some rude awakenings. Henri's wife has just left him, so he is in a particularly scratchy mood. Philippe, his brother, is preoccupied with his family's approval rating, having just made a two-minute appearance on TV. And their sister, Betty, has decided to end her dead-end relationship with Denis, who works in Henri's cafe as general dogsbody. The family is meant to be celebrating the 35th birthday of Yoyo, Philippe's wife, but there's just not enough good will to go round... Adapted by co-stars Jean-Pierre Bacri and Agnes Jaoui from their own play, *Un Air de Famille* is like Alan Ayckbourn marinated in garlic. Yet, in spite of some strong flavour, the nuances of character are subtly drawn, eliciting smiles of recognition in favour of knee-jerk guffaws. And the acting is uniformly excellent. F.Y.I. Bacri and Jaoui

Family appearance: Co-writer and co-star Jean-Pierre Bacri in Cedric Kaplisch's wry *Un Air de Famille* (from Metro Tartan)

previously adapted Ayckbourn's *Smoking/No Smoking* for director Alain Resnais.

Jean-Pierre Bacri (*Henri Menard*), Agnes Jaoui (*Betty Menard*), Jean-Pierre Darroussin (*Denis*), Catherine Frot (*Yolande Menard*), Claire Maurier (*la mère*), Wladimir Yordanoff (*Philippe Menard*), Cedric Kaplisch (*la père*), Tuesday (*Caruso, the labrador*).

Dir: Cedric Kaplisch. Pro: Charles Gassot. Ex Pro: Jacques Hinstin. Screenplay: Jean-Pierre Bacri, Agnes Jaoui and Kaplisch. Ph: Benoit Delhomme. Art: Francois Emmanuelli. Ed: Francine Sandberg. M: Philippe Eidel; numbers performed by Dalida, Patti Smith, and Enrico Caruso. Costumes: Corinne Jorry. (Telema / Le Studio Canal Plus / France 2 Cinema–Metro Tartan.) Rel: 6 March 1998. 110 mins. Cert 15. France. 1996.

High melodrama: Gary Oldman greets the President of the United States (Harrison Ford) in Wolfgang Petersen's familiar *Air Force One* (from Buena Vista)

Air Force One ★★

Posing as a crew of TV journalists, a gang of terrorists from Kazakhstan take over the world's most protected aeroplane, the presidential 747 Air Force One. Led by the utterly ruthless, idealistic Ivan Korshunov, the rebels mow down the plane's secret service brigade before taking the First Lady, her 12-year-old daughter and several members of the Oval Office hostage. Unless the Kazakhstan rebel leader Alexander Radek is released from prison, the terrorists promise to execute one hostage every 30 minutes. But then they hadn't bargained on the heroic intervention of one man hiding in the hold – the president of the United States... While the concept of a US president who can handle himself in the action department is a good one, *Air Force One* suffers from comparison with too many similar airborne thrillers (*Executive Decision*, *Con Air*, *Turbulence*). The effects, too, are below average for this sort of thing (particularly considering the $85 million budget), and the direction surprisingly pedestrian for the man who brought us *Das Boot* and *In the Line of Fire*. The effect is of extreme *déjà vu* tempered by a sneaking admiration for Gary Oldman's Russian accent.

Harrison Ford (*President James Marshall*), Gary Oldman (*Ivan Korshunov*), Wendy Crewson (*Grace Marshall*), Paul Guilfoyle (*Chief of Staff Lloyd Shepherd*), William H. Macy (*Major Caldwell*), Liesel Matthews (*Alice Marshall*), Dean Stockwell (*Defence Secretary Walter Dean*), Glenn Close (*Vice President Kathryn Bennett*), Xander Berkeley (*Agent Gibbs*), Tom Everett (*NSA Advisor Jack Doherty*), Jurgen Prochnow (*General Alexander Radek*), Donna Bullock (*Press Secretary Melanie Mitchell*), Michael Ray Miller, Carl Weintraub, Esther Latham, Elya Baskin, Levani Outchaneichvili, David Vadim, Andrew Divoff, Bill Smitrovich, Philip Baker Hall, Willard Pugh, Dan Shor, Glenn Morshower.

Dir: Wolfgang Petersen. Pro: Petersen and Gail Katz, Armyan Bernstein and Jon Shestack. Ex Pro: Thomas A. Bliss, Marc Abraham and David Lester. Screenplay: Andrew W. Marlowe. Ph: Michael Ballhaus. Pro Des: William Sandell. Ed: Richard Francis-Bruce. M: Jerry Goldsmith and Joel McNeely. Costumes: Erica Edell Phillips and Nino Cerruti. Visual effects: Richard Edlund. (Beacon Pictures / Columbia Pictures / Radiant Prods–Buena Vista.) Rel: 12 September 1997. 124 mins. Cert 15. USA. 1997.

Albino Alligator ★★★★

New Orleans; today. When three petty criminals bungle a robbery, they inadvertently kill three cops during their getaway. Hiding out in a basement bar ('Dino's Last Stand'), they take five hostages – aggravating a situation that, unbeknownst to them, didn't even involve them in the first place... A tense heist thriller that ripples and banks with the nuances of its protagonists, *Albino Alligator* has the structural discipline of a play but the texture and in-your-face immediacy of pure cinema. Marking the directorial debut of the actor Kevin Spacey (*The Usual Suspects*, *Swimming With Sharks*), the film heralds a major new filmmaking talent. Spacey not only exhibits an extraordinary command of the minutiae of his visual canvas, but knows how to manipulate silence and has extracted outstanding performances from an exciting cast (Dunaway hasn't been this good since the Ice Age). P.S. In the South, albino alligator is a term used to describe 'a deliberate sacrifice for deliberate gain'.

Matt Dillon (*Dova*), Faye Dunaway (*Janet Boudreaux*), Gary Sinise (*Milo*), William Fichtner (*Law*), Viggo Mortensen (*Guy Foucard*), Skeet Ulrich (*Danny 'The Kid' Boudreaux*), John Spencer (*Jack*), M. Emmet Walsh (*Dino*), Joe Mantegna (*G.D. Browning*), Frankie Faison (*Marv Rose*), Melinda McGraw (*Jenny Ferguson of Action News, Channel 7*), Brad Koepenick, Willie C. Carpenter.

Dir: Kevin Spacey. Pro: Brad Krevoy, Steve Stabler and Brad Jenkel. Line Pro: Barbara Hall. Screenplay: Christian Forte. Ph: Mark Plummer. Pro Des: Nelson Coates. Ed: Jay Cassidy. M: Michael Brook. Costumes: Isis Mussenden. (Motion Picture Corporation of America / UGC DA International–Electric.) Rel: 22 August 1997. 97 mins. Cert 18. USA / France. 1996.

Alien Resurrection ★★½

Cloned from a blood sample she left behind before nose-diving into a vat of molten lead, Ellen Ripley finds that her rebirth has left her with a mix of alien genes. It's 200 years later and a renegade outfit of intergalactic scientists are seeking to exploit the potential of the mother of all aliens. Just then the craft is boarded by a band of pirates with their own nefarious agenda... As distinct in tone from the earlier films as they

White heat: William Fichtner in Kevin Spacey's tense *Albino Alligator* (from Alliance Electric)

were from each other, this is the comic-strip edition of the series, complete with wisecracks, strutting caricatures and fantastic picturesque flourishes. Yet for all its visual panache, this fourth edition of the *Alien* franchise is still about a lot of people running down a lot of corridors followed by a lot of goo. There are, however, a few marvellous moments, such as when Brad Dourif taunts the alien by pushing his face against the glass that separates them. Otherwise, this banquet for the eyes is nothing but a lot of sound and fury

Mommie Dearest: Sigourney Weaver mothers Winona Ryder in Jean-Pierre Jeunet's picturesque *Alien Resurrection* (from Fox)

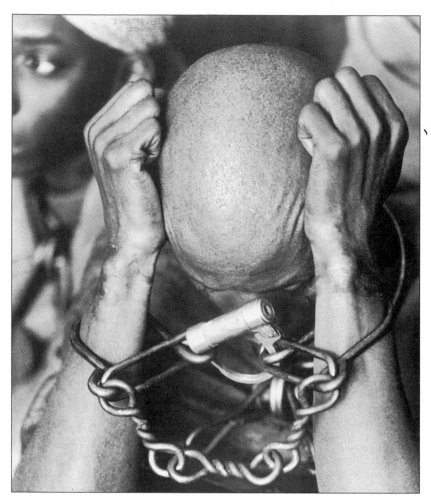

and smoke and mirrors leading to a famine of emotion.

Sigourney Weaver (*Ellen Ripley*), Winona Ryder (*Annalee Call*), Ron Perlman (*Johner*), Dan Hedaya (*General Perez*), J.E. Freeman (*Dr Wren*), Brad Dourif (*Gediman*), Michael Wincott (*Elgyn*), Dominique Pinon (*Vriess*), Gary Dourdan (*Christie*), Kim Flowers (*Hillard*), Raymond Cruz (*Distephano*), Leland Orser (*Purvis*).
    Dir: Jean-Pierre Jeunet. Pro: Bill Badalato, Gordon Carroll, David Giler and Walter Hill. Co-Pro: Sigourney Weaver. Screenplay: Joss Whedon. Ph: Darius Khondji. Pro Des: Nigel Phelps. Ed: Herve Schneid. M: John Frizzell. Costumes: Bob Ringwood. Sound: Leslie Schatz. Visual effects: Pitof and Erik Henry. Alien effects: Alec Gillis and Tom Woodruff. (Fox/Brandywine–Fox.) Rel: 28 November 1997. 105 mins. Cert 18. USA. 1997.

An American Werewolf in Paris ★

A trio of American graduates visit Paris to scare up a little action with some serious European babes.

Slave laboured: A scene from Steven Spielberg's sincere but cumbersome Amistad *(from UIP)*

Climbing to the top of the Eiffel Tower one night, they witness a French girl throw herself off the balcony, saved seconds later by a heroic bungee jump from Andy. With just her shoe as a keepsake, Andy tracks down his distressed damsel to a house of ominous secrets... The success of John Landis's *An American Werewolf in London* (1981) – to which this affront bears no relation – was its canny mix of the comical and unsettling. Here, the humour is both limp and adolescent and the thrills of a tedious, formulaic nature. The dialogue is dumb, the plotting simplistic and the digital computer effects less convincing than the prosthetic make-up employed by Rick Baker in the original.

Tom Everett Scott (*Andy*), Julie Delpy (*Serafine*), Vince Vieluf (*Brad*), Phil Buckman (*Chris*), Julie Bowen (*Amy*), Pierre Cosso (*Claude*), Thierry Lhermitte (*Dr Pigot*), Tom Novembre (*Inspector Leduc*), Maria Machado, Ben Salem Bouabdallah, Charles Maquignon, John Waller, Nicholas Waller, Anthony Waller (*metro driver*).
    Dir and Ex Pro: Anthony Waller. Pro: Richard Claus. Co-Pro: Alexander Buchman. Screenplay: Waller, Tim Burns and Tom Stern. Ph: Egon Werdin. Pro Des: Matthias Kammermeier. Ed: Peter R. Adam. M: Wilbert Hirsch; Ravel; numbers performed by Dany, Louisa's Choice, Under Pressure, Phil Buckman, and Jonathan Richman and the Modern Lovers. Costumes: Maria Schicker. Sound: Hubert Bartholomae. Visual effects: John Grower. (Hollywood Pictures/Cometstone Pictures/J&M Entertainment–Entertainment). Rel: 31 October 1997. 102 mins. Cert 15. UK/Netherlands/Luxembourg. 1997.

Amistad ★★

1839-1841. Following weeks of unspeakable cruelty, 53 African natives take command of the Spanish slave ship *La Amistad* and order the two remaining crew members to steer them back to Africa. However, when the ship is apprehended by an American naval vessel, the Africans are put on trial in Connecticut for murder... Having caricatured blacks in his shameful *The Color Purple*, Steven Spielberg, now twelve years wiser (and the adoptive father of two African-American children), has gone to great pains to compensate with this incredible slice of little-known American infamy. But in his rush to bestow dignity on the proceedings, Spielberg has hurled all the drama out of the window and left us with a turgid, unwieldy and phenomenally boring historical tract. Furthermore, while stressing the authenticity of his approach – casting genuine Mende-speaking Africans in the parts of the mutineers – why did he then go and hire such British actors as Hopkins, Hawthorne, Postlethwaite, Ralph Brown and Jeremy Northam to play Americans? John Williams' omnipresent and irritating music is another major minus. FYI: Amistad is Spanish for 'friendship'.

Morgan Freeman (*Theodore Joadson*), Nigel Hawthorne (*Martin Van Buren*), Anthony Hopkins (*John Quincy Adams*), Djimon Hounsou (*Cinque*), Matthew McConaughey (*Roger Baldwin*), David

Foster children: local kids taunt Rachel Weisz as *Amy Foster* (from Columbia TriStar)

Paymer (*U.S. Secretary of State Forsyth*), Pete Postlethwaite (*Holabird*), Stellan Skarsgard (*Lewis Tappan*), Razaaq Adoti (*Yamba*), Anna Paquin (*Queen Isabella*), Tomas Milian (*Calderon*), Peter Firth (*Captain Fitzgerald*), Jeremy Northam (*Judge Coglin*), Arliss Howard (*John C. Calhoun*), The Honorable A. Blackmun, Associate Justice (Ret.) (*Associate Justice Joseph Story*), Abu Bakaar Fofanah, Chiwetel Ejiofor, Derrick N. Ashong, Geno Silva, John Ortiz, Ralph Brown, Darren Burrows, Allan Rich, Paul Guilfoyle, Xander Berkeley, Austin Pendleton, Daniel Von Bargen, Rusty Schwimmer, Pedro Armendariz, Frank T. Wells, Kevin J. O'Connor, Leon Singer.

Dir: Steven Spielberg. Pro: Spielberg, Debbie Allen and Colin Wilson. Ex Pro: Walter Parkes and Laurie MacDonald. Co-Pro: Tim Shriver. Co-Ex Pro: Robert Cooper. Assoc Pro: Bonnie Curtis and Paul Deason. Screenplay: David Franzoni and (*uncredited*) Steve Zaillian. Ph: Janusz Kaminski. Pro Des: Rick Carter. Ed: Michael Kahn. M: John Williams; Viotti. Costumes: Ruth Carter. (DreamWorks/ HBO Pictures–UIP.) Rel: 27 February 1998. 155 mins. Cert 15. USA. 1997.

Amy Foster ★★★½

Enraptured by the vast vista of the open sea and the relentless caress of the rain, Amy Foster has always been considered something of an outsider. Speaking seldom and keeping herself to herself, the farmer's servant girl is never happier than when collecting 'gifts from the sea' and decorating her beachside hideaway with them. Then the ocean offers up the most tempting keepsake of all: the handsome Ukrainian survivor of a local shipwreck who, like Amy, is immediately branded an unsavoury misfit... By transplanting the original setting of Joseph Conrad's 1901 short story from Kent to Cornwall, Beeban Kidron's best film to date has gained an inordinate power as the stark remoteness of the community of Colebrooke is accentuated, as are the aquatic elements that Amy Foster is so much a part of. At a time when outstanding photography is almost commonplace, the lighting and locations here are really quite exceptional, yet they never dwarf the fine playing from the cast. Squarely occupying its own place and time, *Amy Foster* is an exemplary example of the powerful symbiosis of cinema and the short story format. Previously known as *Swept By the Sea*.

Vincent Perez (*Yanko Gooral*), Rachel Weisz (*Amy Foster*), Ian McKellen (*Dr James Kennedy*), Joss Ackland (*Mr Swaffer*), Kathy Bates (*Miss Swaffer*), Tom Bell (*Isaac Foster*), Zoe Wanamaker (*Mary Foster*), Tony Haygarth (*William Smith*), Fiona Victory (*Mrs Smith*), William Scott Masson, Eve Matheson, Dave Hill, Roger Ashton-Griffiths, Matthew Scurfield, Janine Duvitski, Willie Ross, Janet Henfry, Paul Whitby, Angela Morant.

Dir: Beeban Kidron. Pro: Kidron, Polly Tapson and Charles Steel. Ex Pro: Garth Thomas and Tim Willocks. Assoc Pro: Devon Dickson. Screenplay: Willocks. Ph: Dick Pope. Pro Des: Simon Holland. Ed: Alex Mackie and Andrew Mondshein. M: John Barry. Costumes: Caroline Harris. (Phoenix Pictures/Greenlight Fund/ Tapson Steel/National Lottery/Arts Council of England/Canal Plus/British Screen Finance–Columbia TriStar.) Rel: 8 May 1998. 113 mins. Cert 12. UK/USA/ France. 1997.

Anastasia ★★★½

When the royal family of Russia is overthrown by the evil machinations of Rasputin, the tsar's eight-year-old daughter, Anastasia, is left unconscious in the mêlée. Ten years

Tsar wars: Rasputin exercises his wrath in Don Bluth and Gary Goldman's visually sumptuous *Anastasia* (from Fox)

Praise the Lord: Robert Duvall experiences an epiphany in his extraordinary *The Apostle* (from UIP)

later, a handsome conman and his affable sidekick are auditioning suitable candidates to impersonate the missing Anastasia in order to collect a handsome reward from the princess's grandmother. Just then a beautiful eighteen-year-old orphan girl called Anya stumbles into their midst... Muscling in on Disney's virtual monopoly of the animation market, Twentieth Century Fox's first venture from its own animation studios is a sophisticated, sweeping tale fashioned after the tried-and-tested Disney formula. And while the film's historical background sets it off on a turgid foot, once the story gets under way it reaps its own emotional rewards – even if the heroine herself is not as beguiling as the actress who voices her (Meg Ryan, of all people). And what the film lacks in wit it more than makes up for with some splendid visuals and numerous effective touches. FYI: *Anastasia* is the first cartoon to be presented in CinemaScope since Disney's 1959 *Cinderella*.

Voices: Meg Ryan (*Anya/Anastasia),* John Cusack (*Dimitri*), Kelsey Grammer (*Vladimir*), Christopher Lloyd (*Rasputin*), Hank Azaria (*Bartok*), Bernadette Peters (*Sophie*), Kirsten Dunst (*young Anya/ Anastasia*), Angela Lansbury (*Dowager Empress Marie*), Liz Callaway (*singing voice of Anya/Anastasia*), Lacey Chabert (*singing voice of young Anya/Anastasia*), Jim Cummings (*singing voice of Rasputin*), Jonathan Dokuchitz (*singing voice of Dimitri*), Rick Jones, Andrea Martin, Debra Mooney, Arthur Malet, Charity James.
   Dir and Pro: Don Bluth and Gary Goldman. Ex Pro: Maureen Donley. Screenplay: Susan Gauthier & Bruce Graham, and Bob Tzudiker & Noni White. Animation adaptation: Eric Tuchman. Pro Des: Mike Peraza. M: David Newman; songs: Lynn Ahrens (*lyrics*), Stephen Flaherty (*music*). (Fox–Fox.) Rel: 27 March 1998. 94 mins. Cert U. USA. 1997.

The Apostle ★★★★½

Texas/Bayou Boutte, Louisiana; the present. A passionate Pentecostal preacher, Euliss 'Sonny' Dewey takes life by the scruff of the neck and doles out compassion and censure in equal measure. Indeed, Sonny is as likely to initiate a shouting match with God as take a loving woman to his bed. But when his wife sleeps with a 'puny-assed youth minister', Sonny lets his temper get the better of him. And now his sin, his crime of passion, looks set to obliterate the selfless philanthropy that spills out of him... Employing a mix of professional and non-professional actors, writer-producer-director Robert Duvall has created an extraordinarily authentic portrait of rural American life that is almost documentary-like in its realism. By eschewing the gimmicks of mainstream narrative cinema, the filmmaker brings home the scariness of a people reliant on their church, whether for good or for bad. Furthermore, the film takes no sides, showing both the benevolence of a simple people and the duality of an impassioned man like Sonny himself. A number of scenes, simply and unobtrusively caught by Barry Markowitz's camera, make a profound impact: Sonny's meeting with a one-legged fisherman (played by the preacher Brother William Atlas Cole), Sonny's awkward date with a mousy secretary (Miranda Richardson) and his confrontation with a racist troublemaker (Thornton).

Robert Duvall (*Euliss 'Sonny' Dewey aka The Apostle E.F.*), Farrah Fawcett (*Jessie Dewey*), Billy Bob Thornton (*troublemaker*), June Carter Cash (*Mrs Dewey Sr*), Miranda Richardson (*Toosie*), Todd Allen (*Horace*), John Beasley (*Brother Blackwell*), Walter Goggins (*Sam*), Billy Joe Shaver (*Joe*), Rick Dial (*Elmo*), James Gammon (*Brother Edwards*), Zelma Loyd, Sister Jewell Jernigan, Brother William Atlas Cole, Jan Fawcett.
  Dir, Ex Pro and Screenplay: Robert Duvall. Pro: Rob Carliner. Co-Pro: Steven Brown. Ph: Barry Markowitz. Pro Des: Linda Burton. Ed: Steve Mack. M: David Mansfield; numbers performed by Storyville, Robert Duvall, June Carter Cash, Patty Loveless, Lyle Lovett, Dolly Parton, etc. Costumes: Douglas Hall. (Butchers Run/October Films–UIP.) Rel: 12 June 1998. 133 mins. Cert 12. USA. 1997.

L'Appartement ★★★★

Paris; today and yesterday. Max Mayer is a high-flying businessman engaged to Muriel, the daughter of his employer. Stopping off at a cafe on his way to the airport, he overhears a familiar voice in the phone booth adjacent to the gents' loo. He is convinced the voice belongs to Lisa, the love of his life who inexplicably disappeared two years earlier. Discovering a hotel key by the pay phone, Max abandons his business trip to Tokyo and doubles back to Paris after Muriel has dropped him off at the airport. At the hotel, he uncovers more clues to the identity of the mysterious woman and embarks on a wild goose chase around Paris that is never entirely what it seems... Stylish, densely plotted and uncompromisingly unsentimental, *L'Appartement* is a romantic thriller that teases the little grey cells as it assaults the heart strings. And yet even beyond these ambitions the film tosses out more nutrition for contemplation, blending classical mythology and fairy tale (*A Midsummer Night's Dream, Cinderella*) into a haunting, dream-like scenario that folds in on itself as the spiralling plot tightens its grip. All the more amazing is that this is the first full-length feature from writer-director Gilles Mimouni.

Romane Bohringer (*Alice*), Vincent Cassel (*Max Mayer*), Jean-Philippe Ecoffey (*Lucien*), Monica Bellucci (*Lisa*), Sandrine Kiberlain (*Muriel*), Oliver Granier (*Daniel*), Nelly Alard, Bruno Leonelli, Vincent Nemeth.
  Dir and Screenplay: Gilles Mimouni. Pro: Georges Benayoun. Ph: Thierry Arbogast. Pro Des: Philippe Chiffre. Ed: Caroline Biggerstaff and Francoise Bonnot. M: Peter Chase; 'Le Temps' performed by Charles Aznavour. Costumes: Laurence Heller. (IMA Films/UGC Images/La Sept Cinema/M6 Films/Canal Plus–Artificial Eye.) Rel: 5 September 1997. 116 mins. Cert 15. France/Spain/Italy. 1996.

As Good As It Gets ★★★★

Downtown Manhattan, New York; the present. Melvin Udall is a novelist suffering from obsessive-compulsive disorder. Meticulous to a fault, he will use two new bars of soap to wash his hands (and then bin them), circumnavigate the cracks in the sidewalk and bring his own cutlery to restaurants. He also has little time for ethnic minorities, homosexuals or animals and will be the first to put them in their place – with corrosive wit. In fact, Melvin is the most obnoxious bachelor in Manhattan. But that is not going to stop him coming to the aid of the one waitress willing to serve him...

Circle of deceit: Monica Bellucci in Gilles Mimouni's haunting, dream-like L'Appartement (from Artificial Eye)

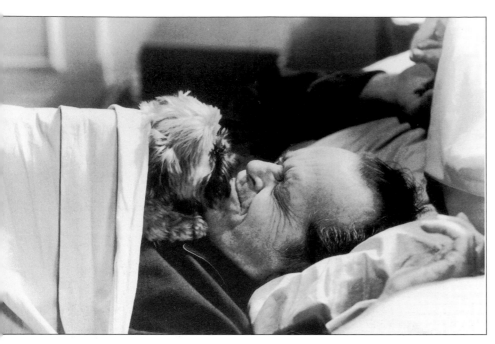

Dog days: Jill gives Jack Nicholson a wake-up call in James L. Brooks' priceless *As Good As It Gets* (from Columbia TriStar)

Braving the hardest of genres to pull off – black romance – *As Good As It Gets* achieves its objective thanks to a priceless screenplay and two stellar turns from Jack Nicholson and Helen Hunt. Resembling *Jerry Maguire* in structure and format – glossy production values, great dialogue, romantic showdowns (followed by emotional fall-out) and a cute kid – it may come as no surprise that director Brooks produced the former. However, this is only Brooks' fourth film as director in 14 years, reminding us what an underused talent he is. FYI: Nicholson took over the role of Melvin when Kevin Kline dropped out. Formerly known as *Old Friends*.

Jack Nicholson (*Melvin Udall*), Helen Hunt (*Carol Connelly*), Greg Kinnear (*Simon Bishop*), Cuba Gooding Jr (*Frank Sachs*), Skeet Ulrich (*Vincent*), Shirley Knight (*Beverly*), Yeardley Smith (*Jackie*), Jesse James (*Spencer Connelly*), Lawrence Kasdan (*Dr Green*), Julie Benz (*publisher's receptionist*), Harold Ramis (*Dr Martin Bettes*), Jill (*Verdell*), Lupe Ontiveros, Bibi Osterwald, Ross Bleckner, Brian Doyle-Murray, Kristi Zea, Shane Black, Randall Batinkoff, Jamie Kennedy, Chloe Brooks, Cooper Brooks, Linda Gehringer, Jimmy Workman, Todd Solondz, Tom McGowan, Matt Malloy, Paul Greenberg.

Dir and Pro: James L. Brooks. Pro: Bridget Johnson and Kristi Zea. Ex Pro: Richard Sakai, Laurence Mark and Laura Ziskin. Co-Pro: John D. Schofield and Richard Marks. Assoc Pro: Aldric Porter and Maria Kavanaugh. Screenplay: Brooks and Mark Andrus. Ph: John Bailey. Pro Des: Bill Brzeski. Ed: Marks. M: Hans Zimmer; 'Always Look On The Bright Side Of Life' performed by Art Garfunkel; other numbers performed by Jane Siberry, Judith Owen, Spin Doctors, Shawn Colvin, Village People, Van Morrison, The Drifters, Danielle Brisebois, and Nat King Cole. Costumes: Molly Maginnis. (TriStar Pictures/Gracie Films-Columbia TriStar.) Rel: 13 March 1998. 138 mins. Cert 15. USA. 1997.

Austin Powers International Man of Mystery ★★

Cryogenically preserved for 30 years, 1960s superspy Austin Powers is thawed out in 1997 by British Intelligence. His mission: to combat the bald, scarred, cat-stroking Dr Evil, who has returned from his own cryonic hiatus to wreak fresh havoc on earth. Discarding his plans to blackmail Prince Charles over a fabricated case of adultery and abandoning his design to punch a hole in the ozone layer, Dr Evil goes for the old nuclear threat routine. It's up to Austin 'Danger' Powers to thwart Evil's dastardly plan, to resist the charms of his nemesis's deadly female entourage and to figure out why sex is not what it used to be... Taking the concept of *The Brady*

Bunch Movie – characters from a previous era faced with 1990s cynicism – writer/producer/star Mike Myers has fashioned a funny James Bond spoof that should have been a lot funnier. Pushing gags way beyond their natural lifespan and encouraging the supporting cast to overact outrageously, Myers and director Jay Roach largely botch a wonderful opportunity. Still, a number of sequences are truly inspired, not least Myers' nude scene in which his privates are constantly obscured by Elizabeth Hurley obliviously waving objects about in the foreground.

Mike Myers (*Austin 'Danger' Powers/Dr Evil*), Elizabeth Hurley (*Vanessa Kensington*), Michael York (*Basil Exposition*), Mimi Rogers (*Mrs Kensington*), Robert Wagner (*Number Two*), Seth Green (*Scott Evil*), Fabiana Udenio (*Alotta Fagina*), Mindy Sterling (*Frau Farbissina*), Burt Bacharach (*himself*), Paul Dillon, Charles Napier, Will Ferrell, Clint Howard, Elya

The shag machine: Mike Myers hides behind Mike Myers in Jay Roach's occasionally inspired *Austin Powers International Man of Mystery* (from Guild)

Baskin, Neil Mullarkey, Patrick Bristow, Robin Gammell, Tom Arnold (*Texan in loo*), Lois Chiles (*John Smith's mother*), Carrie Fisher (*father-son counsellor*), Rob Lowe (*John Smith's mourning friend*), Christian Slater (*brain-washed guard*).

Dir: Jay Roach. Pro: Suzanne Todd, Demi Moore, Jennifer Todd and Mike Myers. Ex Pro: Eric McLeod and Claire Rudnick Polstein. Screenplay: Myers. Ph: Peter Deming. Pro Des: Cynthia Charette. Ed: Debra Neil-Fisher. M: George S. Clinton; Johann Strauss; numbers performed by Quincy Jones, Strawberry Alarm Clock, Ming Tea, Wondermints, The Mike Flowers Pops, Mike Myers, Burt Bacharach, The Lightning Seeds, Susanna Hoffs, Nancy Sinatra, The James Taylor Quartet, Dr Evil, The Cardigans, Edwyn Collins, etc. Costumes: Deena Appel. (New Line/Capella International/KC Medien/Moving Pictures/Eric's Boy–Guild.) Rel: 5 September 1997. 95 mins. Cert 15. USA. 1997.

Bang ★

Evicted from her apartment for not paying the rent, a young Asian-American woman finds herself stranded on the streets of Hollywood. Homeless and penniless, she auditions for the female lead in a movie opposite 'Dustin' but is humiliated by the producer. She is then forced to perform oral sex on a motorcycle cop, gains the upper hand, handcuffs him to a tree and steals his uniform and bike. For the remainder of the day she drives around LA impersonating a police officer and becomes increasingly distraught by what she encounters... They *released* this? Devoid of style, plausibility or even the rudiments of technical expertise (and saddled with the acting standards of a porn film), this low-budget slice-of-lifer is a real downer. Shot without permits over a five-week period, *Bang* does reveal an interesting mind at work but is castrated by a laboriously one-note performance from Darling Narita – an aspiring actress and bartender – in the central role. Deeply depressing. US title: *The Big Bang Theory*.

Darling Narita (*Girl*), Peter Greene (*Adam*), Michael Newland (*Officer Rattler*), David Allen Graf (*Peter Fawcette*), Everlast, Art Cruz, Luis Guizar, Noble James, Stephanie Martini, David Conner, Eric Kilpatrick, Stanley Herman.

Dir and Screenplay: Ash. Pro: Daniel M.

Bean There: The simple fool (Rowan Atkinson) gets up Burt Reynolde' nose in Mel Smith's *Bean* (from PolyGram). Peter MacNicol and Harris Yulin look on

Berger and Ladd Vance. Ex Pro: Jude Narita and Sean Kelly. Assoc Pro: Marc Wilkinson and Marilyn Vance. Ph: Dave Gasperik. Pro Des: Daniel M. Berger. Ed: Ash and Daniel M. Berger. M: Bill Monte. Costumes: Dana Woods. (Renegade Film/Eagle Eye/Asylum–PolyGram.) Rel: 11 July 1997. 100 mins. Cert 18. USA. 1995.

BAPS ★

Visiting LA to audition for a music video, two incredibly stupid babes from smalltown Georgia are duped into carrying out an audacious sham. Accepting $10,000 apiece, the girls pose as the granddaughter and her friend of the lost love of a sickly billionaire. Going along with the plan out of the goodness of their hearts, the girls bring the old codger back to life – much to the initial disapproval of his manservant... A black female take on Laurel and Hardy, the Bambiesque Halle Berry and Thumperesque Natalie Desselle reveal a total incomprehension of what comedy is about. This fact is reliably revealed by such highlights as the old 'let's find out what a bidet is' routine (which is stretched to new lengths) and Desselle knocking her boyfriend into a swimming pool. Not to put too fine a point on it,

BAPS is a movie of such straight-faced ineptitude that it beggars belief. Can this really be from the director of *The Five Heartbeats*?

Halle Berry (*Nisi*), Martin Landau (*Mr Blakemore*), Ian Richardson ('*Alfred*' *Manley*), Natalie Desselle (*Mickey*), Troy Beyer (*Tracy*), Luigi Amodeo (*Antonio*), Jonathan Fried (*Isaac*), Pierre (*Ali*), A.J. Johnson (*James*), Bernie Mac, Darrel Heath, Vince Cooke, Faizon Love, and as themselves: Downtown Julie Brown, Heavy D, LL Cool J, Leon, Dennis Rodman.

Dir: Robert Townsend. Pro: Mark Burg and Loretha Jones. Ex Pro: Michael De Luca and Jay Stern. Screenplay: Troy Beyer. Ph: Bill Dill. Pro Des: Keith Brian Burns. Ed: Patrick Kennedy. M: Stanley Clarke; numbers performed by Veronica and Craig Mack, Kool & The Gang, Gyrl, Kinsui, Alex Brown, etc. Costumes: Ruth Carter. Wigs: Kimberly Kimble. (New Line Cinema/Island Pictures–Entertainment.) Rel: 1 August 1997. 92 mins. Cert 15. USA. 1997.

Bean ★★★★

Desperate to rid themselves of lowly employee Mr Bean, the board of the National Gallery send their 'force ten disaster area' to the US to oversee the unveiling of 'Whistler's Mother' at the Grierson Gallery in California. There, the well-meaning but accident-prone 'art historian' systematically destroys the confidence, marriage, job prospects and Thanksgiving turkey of his host,

Bent on survival: Clive Owen, Lothaire Bluteau and their rocks in Sean Mathias's powerful, touching _Bent_ (from Film Four)

before setting his sights on Los Angeles... Boasting the same writer, producers and co-star of _Four Weddings and a Funeral_ (not to mention a song by Wet Wet Wet), _Bean_ is in good hands. A feature-length adaptation of the semi-silent TV sitcom, the film panders to the American _Dumb & Dumber_ market, but does so with common sense and wit – for Mr Bean's outrageous antics can only work if acted out within a realistic context. Here, the supporting cast conducts itself with admirable restraint, with only Burt Reynolds nudging the surrealism of camp (he obviously doesn't get it). Aiming for a slightly older, more sophisticated audience than it did on TV, this _Bean_ offers a cohesive storyline and many inspired moments as it plunges courageously into nightmarish black comedy. P.S. Had Hollywood made this, it wouldn't have dared heap such defilement on to a beloved masterpiece.

Cast: Rowan Atkinson (_Mr Bean_), Peter MacNicol (_David Langley_), Pamela Reed (_Alison Langley_), Harris Yulin (_George Grierson_), Burt Reynolds (_General Newton_), Larry Drake (_Elmer_), Tricia Vessey (_Jennifer Langley_), Andrew Lawrence (_Kevin Langley_), Richard Gant (_Det. Brutus_), Chris Ellis (_Det. Butler_), Peter Egan (_Lord Walton_), John Mills (_Shairman_), Johnny Galecki, Danny Goldring, Peter Capaldi, June Brown, Peter James, Tom McGowan, Dakin Matthews.

Dir: Mel Smith. Pro: Peter Bennett-Jones, Eric Fellner and Tim Bevan. Ex Pro: Richard Curtis. Co-Pro: Rebecca O'Brien. Screenplay: Curtis and Robin Driscoll. Ph: Francis Kelly. Pro Des: Peter Larkin. Ed: Christopher Blunden. M: Howard Goodall; Handel; numbers performed by Louise, Katrina and the Waves, Susannah Hoffs, 10CC, Blair, The Beach Boys, Wet Wet Wet, Randy Newman, Boyzone, Alisha's Attic, and Thomas Jules Stock. Costumes: Hope Hanafin. (Working Title/Tiger Aspect–PolyGram.) Rel: 8 August 1997. 90 mins. Cert PG. UK. 1997.

Bent ★★★

Prior to the grip of Fascism in Germany, decadence had a long leash in the Berlin of the early 1930s. Yet while Max enjoyed a life of promiscuity and debauchery, his excesses were nothing compared to the immorality of his persecutors. Captured by the SS, he is shipped off to a detention camp where his instinct for survival almost betrays his worth as a man... Based on the 1979 play by Martin Sherman, _Bent_ displays an arresting visual style even as it fails to escape the claustrophobia of its theatrical origins – or, indeed, succeeds at conveying a sense of time and place. But then this is a powerful play and first-time director Sean Mathias draws on its strengths as compelling theatre. He certainly pulls no punches in depicting the degeneracy of the homosexuals' lifestyle nor the uncompromising sadism inflicted on them later. Yet when one has stripped away all the chintz and shock value, what is left is an ineffably touching love story.

Lothaire Bluteau (_Horst_), Clive Owen (_Max_), Brian Webber (_Rudy_), Ian McKellen (_Uncle Freddie_), Mick Jagger (_Greta/George_), Nikolaj Waldau (_Wolf_), Rupert Graves, Rupert Penry Jones, Paul Kynman, Paul Bettany, Suzanne Bertish, David Meyer, Johanna Kirby, David Phelan, Charlie Watts, Jude Law, Sadie Frost, Geraldine Sherman, Rachel Weisz.

Dir: Sean Mathias. Pro: Michael Solinger and Dixie Linder. Ex Pro: Sarah Radclyffe and Hisami Kuroiwa. Co-Pro: Mathias and Martin Sherman. Screenplay: Sherman. Ph: Yorgos Arvanitis. Pro Des: Stephen Brimson Lewis. Ed: Isabel Lorente. M: Philip Glass; 'The Streets Of Berlin' performed by Mick Jagger. Costumes: Stewart Meacham. (Channel Four Films/NDF Inc/Ask Kodansha/The Arts Council of England/National Lottery/Nippon Film–Film Four.) Rel: 6 March 1998. 116 mins. Cert 18. UK/USA/Japan. 1996.

Best Men ★★

The day Jesse Chandler finishes his three-year jail term is the day he has decided to walk up the aisle with his long-suffering, appropriately named girlfriend, Hope. It is also the day that his groom, Billy, decides to rob a bank, embroiling Jesse and his other grooms Buzz (an ex-green beret), Sol (a strait-laced lawyer) and Teddy (a henpecked nerd) in a media-grabbing siege. And the fact that the town's sheriff also happens to be Billy's estranged father doesn't exactly help matters... An uneven hotchpotch of concepts embezzled from other sources (_Robin Hood, Hamlet, Reservoir Dogs, Butch Cassidy and the Sundance Kid_), _Best Men_ constantly works against itself. Demanding its cake and gagging on it, the film lunges from male-bonding farce to siege thriller with wilful disregard for its audience's expectations.

Dean Cain (*Sgt Buzz Thomas*), Andy Dick (*Teddy Pollack*), Sean Patrick Flanery (*Billy Phillips*), Mitchell Whitfield (*Sol Jacobs*), Luke Wilson (*Jesse Chandler*), Drew Barrymore (*Hope*), Fred Ward (*Sheriff Bud Phillips*), Raymond J. Barry (*FBI Agent Hoover*), Brad Dourif (*Lt John G. 'Gonzo' Coleman*), Tracy Fraim (*Cuervo*), Biff Yeager, Art Edler Brown, K.K. Dodds, Brad Jenkel.
    Dir: Tamra Davis. Pro: Brad Krevoy, Steve Stabler, Brad Jenkel and Deborah Ridpath. Ex Pro: Jeffrey D. Ivers and Christopher Buchanan. Co-Pro: Sheryl Schwartz. Line Pro: Jeanne Van Cott. Screenplay: Art Edler Brown and Tracy Fraim. Ph: James Glennon. Pro Des: Toby Corbett. Ed: Paul Trejo. M: Mark Mothersbaugh. Costumes: Arianne Phillips. (Orion Pictures/Rank–Film Four.) Rel: 27 March 1998. 89 mins. Cert 15. USA/UK. 1997.

The Big Bang Theory
See *Bang*.

The Big Lebowski ★★★½
Los Angeles; 1991. Jeff Lebowski likes to be known as The Dude and more or less lives up to the monicker. Entrenched in the 1970s, he's an unemployed amateur bowler and pothead who lives in a run-down bungalow on Venice Beach. However, he is *not* the crippled Pasadena millionaire of the same name and he does not take kindly to the intrusion of two thugs who break into his house, piss on his beloved rug and demand the money owed by the other Lebowski's trophy wife... Following the success of *Fargo*, the expectation surrounding the Coen brothers' next film was bound to lead to disappointment. Yet, like Danny Boyle's *A Life Less Ordinary* (which it strangely resembles), *The Big Lebowski* offers many delights. In fact, after a terrific opening, the film keeps up steam well into the second hour, until it finally loses direction, sense and comic momentum. Still, the comedy should delight Coen enthusiasts even if it is unlikely to win the brothers any new converts. Favourite sequence: where The Dude literally takes on the point of view of his own bowling ball. P.S. Note the numerous contemporary references, including allusions to the Baader-

Meinhof gang, Saddam Hussein, Prince Philip's cricket bat gaffe and Mike Tyson's ear-biting stunt.

Jeff Bridges (*Jeff Lebowski aka The Dude*), John Goodman (*Walter Sobchak*), Julianne Moore (*Maude Lebowski*), Steve Buscemi (*Donny*), John Turturro (*Jesus Quintana*), David Huddleston (*The Big Lebowski*), Philip Seymour Hoffman (*Brandt*), Tara Reid (*Bunny Lebowski*), Peter Stormare (*Uli*), David Thewlis (*Knox Harrington*), Sam Elliott (*The Stranger*), Ben Gazzara (*Jackie Treehorn*), Aimee Mann (*nihilist woman*), Jerry Haleva (*Saddam Hussein*), Warren David Keith (*Francis Donnelly, funeral director*), Flea, Torsten Voges, Jimmie Dale Gilmore, Jack Kehler, Richard Gant, Christian Clemenson, Dom Irrera, Michael Gomez, Mary Bugin, Irene Olga Lopez, Leon Russom, Jon Polito.
    Dir: Joel Coen. Pro: Ethan Coen. Ex Pro: Tim Bevan and Eric Fellner. Co-Pro: John Cameron. Screenplay: Joel and Ethan Coen. Ph: Roger Deakins. Pro Des: Rick Heinrichs. Ed: Roderick Jaynes (aka the Coen brothers) and Tricia Cooke. M: Carter Burwell; Mozart; Erich Wolfgang Korngold; numbers performed by Bob Dylan, The Gipsy Kings, Booker T & MGs, Captain Beefheart, Nina Simone, Creedence Clearwater Revival, Santana, Kenny Rogers & The First Edition, Henry Mancini, etc. Costumes: Mary Zophres. Sound: Skip Lievsay. (Working Title–PolyGram.) Rel: 24 April 1998. 113 mins. Cert 18. USA/UK. 1998.

The Big Swap ★★½
Bristol, England; today. Comprising four couples – plus Sydney and whoever she's dating at the moment – The Crowd are as close as a group of thirtysomething friends can be. Then one relaxed and alcohol-fuelled evening they decide to experiment with each other's partners – 'for a bit of fun'. It could be the beginning of a beautiful meltdown... Conceived with careful deliberation and some acumen, *The Big Swap* boasts an audacious concept. However, writer-director-producer Niall Johnson has bitten off more than he can swallow as the sheer number of his characters makes it hard to differentiate between – or sympathise with – any one of them. It's not until the film's second half that the narrative trajectories begin to fall into place and the drama takes hold. Still, Johnson provides much food for thought (and some uncomfortable soul-searching), and shows enormous promise as a director of actors and as a writer of insight.

Mark Adams (*Sam*), Sorcha Brooks (*Ellen*), Mark Caven (*Michael*), Alison Egan (*Eve*), Richard Cherry (*Hal*), Julie-Ann Gillitt (*Liz*), Antony Edridge (*Jack*), Clarke Hayes (*Fi*), Thierry Harcourt (*Tony*), Jackie Sawiris (*Sydney*), Kevin Howarth (*Julian*), Alisa Bosschaert (*Barbara*), Virginia Fiol, Lucy Parker, Stig, Phil Covell, James Holloway, Luke Baker, George (*Homer, the dog*).
    Dir, Pro and Screenplay: Niall Johnson. Ex Pro: Ian Scorer. Assoc Pro: Emma Parker, Norman Brooking and Noel Cronin. Line Pro: Jenny Apps. Ph: Gordon

Bowling ally: John Turturro licks the competition in the Coen brothers' weird and wonderful *The Big Lebowski* (from PolyGram)

On a mission from God: Dan Aykroyd is Elwood Blues in John Landis's exuberant *Blues Brothers 2000* (from UIP)

Hickie. Pro Des: Craig Johnson. Ed: David Thrasher. M: Jason Flinter and Craig Johnson; numbers performed by Hinterland with Craig Johnson and Alison Egan, Connie Francis, Jason Flinter, The Big Swappers, etc. (Moonlit Pictures / Film Four / Mayfair Entertainment / Magic Box– Film Four.) Rel: 12 June 1998. 121 mins. Cert 18. UK. 1997.

The Blackout ★
A popular and handsome movie star, Matty makes the most of the privileges of his position, in particular the loose women, strong alcohol and limitless cocaine. But there's also a need to settle down, so after a night of Bacchanalian revelry, Matty proposes to his pregnant girlfriend. However, he has completely forgotten that during a previous bout of substance abuse he had ordered her to abort their child. Can Matty control his hedonistic alter ego before it pushes him too far? Continuing to explore the dark recesses of the human soul, director Ferrara (*Bad Lieutenant, Dangerous Game*) whips up a nightmarish world of sensual excess, relayed through the use of a hallucinogenic film-making style. Maddening, self-indulgent and exclusive, *The Blackout* leaves a nasty taste in the mouth that not even the prospect of seeing Matthew Modine in such experimental material (or Claudia Schiffer in her film debut) can atone for. Isn't it time Ferrara put his dirty washing on the spin cycle?

Matthew Modine (*Matty*), Claudia Schiffer (*Susan*), Beatrice Dalle (*Annie 1*), Dennis Hopper (*Mickey Wayne*), Sarah Lassez (*Annie 2*), Steven Bauer, Laura Bailey, Nancy Ferrara, Victoria Duffy.
Dir: Abel Ferrara. Pro: Ed Pressman. Ex Pro: Mark Damon and Alessandro Camon. Co-Pro: Pierre Kalfon and Michel Chambat. Screenplay: Marla Hanson, Christ Zois and Ferrara. Ph: Ken Kelsch. Pro Des: Richard Hoover. Ed: Anthony Redman. M: Joe Delia; J.S. Bach; numbers performed by Schoolly D and Joe Delia, and U2, Gretchen Mol, Harper Simon, etc. Costumes: Melinda Eshelman. (Les Films Number One / CIPA / MDP Worldwide– Feature Film Co.) Rel: 13 February 1998. 98 mins. Cert 18. USA / France. 1997.

Blues Brothers 2000 ★★★
Eighteen years after Elwood Blues was locked up for destroying half of Chicago, the blues singer is released into a brave new world. But with his brother Jake dead, Elwood is forced to find a new partner and convince his old band members that music is still a greater high than any pharmaceutical substitute. And so, pursued by the police, the Russian Mafia, a white supremacist posse and a gaggle of nuns, the all-new Blues Brothers embark on a tour of the Deep South... Other than Elwood's quest to form a new band and rout out gigs, there's little plot or structure to this amorphous vanity project conceived by writer-producer-star Dan Aykroyd. But the film's visual panache and musical exuberance more than makes up for its shortcomings, even when the humour is in drastically short supply. The musical numbers – variously set in a strip club, at a revival meeting and during a surreal rainstorm – are truly awesome, and 12-year-old J. Evan Bonifant as the all-dancing, all-singing, harmonica-playing Buster Blues is a real find. Oh, yeah, and we mustn't forget the magical feats of Elwood's $500 second-hand police car, at one point causing the biggest vehicular pile-up in cinema history.

Dan Aykroyd (*Elwood Blues*), John Goodman (*Mighty Mack McTeer*), Joe Morton (*Cabel Chamberlain*), J. Evan Bonifant (*Buster*), Aretha Franklin (*Mrs Murphy*), James Brown (*Cleophus James*), B.B. King (*Malvern Gasperon*), Shann Johnson (*Matara*), Kathleen Freeman (*Mother Mary Stigmata*), Willie Hall (*himself*), Nia Peeples (*Lt. Elizondo*), Erykah Badu (*Queen Moussette*), Frank Oz, Junior Wells, Lonnie Brooks, Igor Syyouk, Matt Murphy, Lou Marini, Alan Rubin, Jonny Lang, Murphy Dunne, Eddie Floyd, Wilson Pickett, Steve Lawrence, Max Landis, Sharon Riley and The Faith Chorale, Sam Moore, Paul Shaffer, Gary U.S. Bonds, Eric Clapton, Bo Diddley, Isaac Hayes, Dr John, Billy Preston, Lou Rawls, Joshua Redman, Travis Tritt, Jimmie Vaughan, George Washington Jr, Willie Weeks, Steve Winwood.
Dir: John Landis. Pro: Landis, Dan Aykroyd and Leslie Belzberg. Assoc Pro: Grace Gilroy. Screenplay: Aykroyd and Landis. Ph: David Herrington. Pro Des: Bill Brodie. Ed: Dale Beldin. M: Paul Shaffer; numbers performed by Taj Mahal, The Paul Butterfield Blues Band, The Blues Brothers Band, John Goodman and Dan Aykroyd, Aretha Franklin, Blues Traveler, Sam Moore, Joe Morton, Dr John, The Louisiana Gator Boys, Lonnie Brooks and Junior Wells, etc. Costumes: Deborah Nadoolman. Choreography: Barry Lather. (Universal–UIP.) Rel: 22 May 1998. 105 mins. Cert PG. USA. 1998.

Body Count ★½
The John Hancock Museum of Art, Boston, Massachusetts / North Carolina; the present. Five unpleasant low-lifes rob an art gallery, jump into a getaway car, squabble and kill each other... A good cast squanders its talents in this depressingly mediocre crime melo which proves, yet again, that there are more stars around than decent scripts.

David Caruso (*Hobbs*), Linda Fiorentino (*Natalie*), John Leguizamo (*Chino*), Ving Rhames (*Pike*), Donnie Wahlberg (*Booker*), Forest Whitaker (*Crane*), Michael Corrigan, Richard Fullerton, James Spruill.
Dir: Robert Patton-Spruill. Pro: Mark

Extreme close-up: Heather Graham snaps away in Paul Thomas Anderson's affectionate take on the porn industry, *Boogie Nights* (from Entertainment)

Burg, Doug McHenry and George Jackson. Ex Pro: Carl Mazzacone. Screenplay: Theodore Witcher. Ph: Charlie Mills. Pro Des: Tim Eckel. Ed: Richard Nord. M: Curt Sobel. Costumes: Pauline White. Sound: Barney Cabral and Kelly Cabral. (PolyGram/Island Pictures/Main Line Pictures–PolyGram.) Rel: 24 April 1998. 84 mins. Cert 15. USA/UK. 1997.

Boogie Nights ★★★¹/₂

Los Angeles; 1977-1983. Tormented by his mother, 17-year-old no-hoper Eddie Adams elects to turn his one asset into a gold mine. Endowed with a 13 inch 'Mr Torpedo', Adams changes his name to Dirk Diggler and becomes an instant star of the adult entertainment scene. But times they are a-changing, and the future of pornography looks doomed for video mediocrity – much to the artistic frustration of Diggler's mentor, Jack Horner... Embracing the multi-character/narrative format of vintage Robert Altman, Paul Thomas Anderson builds on the promise he displayed in the criminally over-looked *Hard Eight* and turns his jaundiced eye from the sin of gambling to the sins of pornography and drugs. Again, the writer-director proves what a dab hand he is at eliciting consummate performances from his cast, elevating Burt Reynolds from hammy has-been (cf. *Striptease*) to dignified veteran. Furthermore, Anderson has taken an explosive subject matter and, without resorting to sensationalism, given it humour, rationale and a very human face.

Mark Wahlberg (*Eddie Adams/Dirk Diggler/Brock Landers*), Julianne Moore (*Amber Waves*), Burt Reynolds (*Jack Horner*), Don Cheadle (*Buck Swope*), John C. Reilly (*Reed Rothchild/ Chest Rockwell*), William H. Macy (*Little Bill*), Heather Graham (*Rollergirl*), Nicole Ari Parker (*Becky Barnett*), Phillip Seymour Hoffman (*Scotty J*), Ricky Jay (*Kurt Longjohn*), Luis Guzman (*Maurice T.T. Rodriguez*), Robert Ridgely (*The Colonel James*), Melora Walters (*Jessie St Vincent*), Thomas Jane (*Todd Parker*), Laurel Holloman (*Sheryl Lynn*), Jonathon Quint (*John Doe*), Philip Baker Hall, Alfred Molina, Nina Hartley, Michael Jace, Jack Wallace, John Doe, Joanna Gleason, Lawrence Hudd, Michael Penn, Summer, Skye, Robert Downey Snr, Veronica Hart (*the judge*), Allan Graf.

Dir and Screenplay: Paul Thomas Anderson. Pro: Anderson, Lloyd Levin, John Lyons and Joanne Sellar. Ex Pro: Lawrence Gordon. Co-Pro: Daniel Lupi. Ph: Robert Elswit. Pro Des: Bob Ziembicki. Ed: Dylan Tichenor. M: Michael Penn; J.S. Bach; numbers performed by Emotions, Boney M, Silver Convention, The Chakachas, Melanie, Three Dog Night, War with Eric Burdon, Jethro Tull, Hot Chocolate, K.C. & The Sunshine Band, The Commodores, Marvin Gaye, McFadden & Whitehead, Juice Newton, Mark Wahlberg and John C. Reilly, Roberta Flack, Night Ranger, Rick Springfield, Nena, The Beach Boys, Electric Light Orchestra, etc. Costumes: Mark Bridges. (New Line Cinema/Ghoulardi Film Co.–Entertainment.) Rel: 16 January 1998. 155 mins. Cert 18. USA. 1997.

Booty Call ★★¹/₂

When Buppy Rushon decides that enough chastity is enough, he tells his girlfriend of two months, Nikki, that he expects a little action. But this being the 1990s, Nikki plays it safe and sets up a double date with her girlfriend Lysterine and Buppy's ally Bunz. Desperate for willing booty,

Booty and the beast: Tommy Davidson and Tamala Jones get down in Jeff Pollack's outrageous *Booty Call* (from Columbia TriStar)

Socket to him: Tom Felton switches to junk food in Peter Hewitt's *The Borrowers* (from PolyGram)

joke, the good humour is undeniably infectious. FYI: 'Booty' is black slang for vagina. [*Charles Bacon*]

Jamie Foxx (*Bunz*), Tommy Davidson (*Buppy Rushon*), Viveca A. Fox (*Lysterine*), Tamala Jones (*Nikki*), Art Malik (*Akmed*), Scott LaRose (*Singh*), Gedde Watanabe (*Chan*), Ric Young (*Mr Chiu*), Ammie Sin, Bernie Mac, Robert Bidaman, David Hemblen, Amy Minique Waddell, Bill MacDonald, Karen Robinson, Amanda Tapping, Bootsie.
  Dir: Jeff Pollack. Pro: John Morrissey. Co-Pro: John M. Eckert. Screenplay: Takashi Bufford and Bootsie. Ph: Ron Orieux. Pro Des: Sandra Kybartas. Ed: Christopher Greenbury. M: Robert Folk; numbers performed by 1 Accord, Squirrel, Slick Rick, Wisdom, Gerald Levert, R. Kelly, Joe, Silk, Bonne and Clyde, Backstreet Boys, A Tribe Called Quest, Babyface, Average White Band, SWV, etc. Costumes: Vicki Graef. (Columbia/ Turman/Morrissey–Columbia). Rel: 3 October 1997. 79 mins. Cert 18. USA. 1997.

The Borrowers ★★¹⁄₂

Just four inches tall, the Borrowers pride themselves on being quiet, inconspicuous, alert and very good at climbing. Residing beneath the floorboards of the Lender residence, the Clock family survive by 'borrowing' various household items and scraps of food. Then, when the dastardly property developer Ocious P. Potter cheats the Lenders out of their home, the Clocks have to call on all their ingenuity to save the day... While purists blanched at the liberties taken with Mary Norton's novels, the film should stand or fall by its own merits. Set in an intriguing no man's land of time and place (where mobile phones and TV remotes jostle with antiquated appliances), *The Borrowers* starts most promisingly. Yet the gaping holes in the story's logic and the reliance on dog mess and bottom wind for laughs ultimately mar what could have been a magical, heart-warming tale. Still, the special effects are quite amazing. FYI: *The Borrowers* was previously filmed for television, first in 1973, then in 1992.

John Goodman (*Ocious P. Potter*), Jim Broadbent (*Pod Clock*), Mark Williams (*Exterminator Jeff*), Hugh Laurie (*Officer Steady*), Bradley Pierce (*Pete Lender*), Flora Newbigin (*Arrietty Clock*), Tom Felton (*Peagreen Clock*), Raymond Pickard (*Spiller*), Celia Imrie (*Homily Clock*), Aden

the two dudes are repeatedly put on hold as the girls demand ever greater degrees of safe sex. Juggling bad taste with political correctness, the film broadly satirises all types of stereotyping and frequently hits the funny bone with a sledgehammer. While often too eager to spell out a

Gillett (*Joe Lender*), Doon MacKichan (*Victoria Lender*), Ruby Wax, Andrew Duntord, Bob Goody, Patrick Monkton, Alex Winter, David Freeman.

Dir: Peter Hewitt. Pro: Tim Bevan, Eric Fellner and Rachel Talalay. Ex Pro: Walt DeFaria. Co-Pro: Debra Hayward and Liza Chasin. Line Pro: Mary Richards. Screenplay: Gavin Scott and John Kamps. Ph: John Fenner and Trevor Brooker. Pro Des: Gemma Jackson. Ed: David Freeman. M: Harry Gregson-Williams. Costumes: Marie France. Visual effects: Peter Chiang. Special effects: Digby Milner. (PolyGram/ Working Title–PolyGram.) Rel: 5 December 1997. 86 mins. Cert U. UK. 1997.

The Boxer ★★½

Belfast; the present. Imprisoned for 14 years for his part in an IRA job, 'Danny Boy' Flynn has lost none of his passion for boxing – or his love for childhood sweetheart Maggie Hamill. But in the intervening years Maggie has married Danny's best friend and become a mother, only to see her husband put behind bars as well. But now that Danny is finally a free man, their old affections are tentatively rekindled. However, for the wife of an IRA prisoner to 'betray' her husband is a sin that carries a terrible penalty... Masterfully directed, superbly acted and skilfully photographed, *The Boxer* is a shining example of the excellence of cinema. But with an interminable first half and some surprising lapses in continuity (at one point, a cut and bruise on Daniel Day-Lewis's face disappears, only to return in the next scene), *The Boxer* doesn't entirely convince. Only in the last 30 minutes does the story begin to take shape, but by then it's too late. P.S. According to Sheridan, 'the boxer' is a metaphor 'for a guy fighting within the rules'.

Daniel Day-Lewis ('*Danny Boy' Flynn*), Emily Watson (*Maggie Hamill*), Brian Cox (*Joe Hamill*), Ken Stott (*Ike Weir*), Gerard McSorley (*Harry*), Kenneth Cranham (*Matt Maguire*), Ciaran Fitzgerald (*Liam*), Lorraine Pilkington, Maria McDermottroe, Eleanor Methven, Tess Sheridan, David Hayman, Paul Sheridan, John Sheridan, Josie Doherty, Joseph Rea, Peter Sheridan, Britta Smith, Ian McElhinney, Clayon Stewart, and (*uncredited*) Tom Bell.

Dir: Jim Sheridan. Pro: Sheridan and Arthur Lappin. Screenplay: Sheridan and Terry George. Ph: Chris Menges. Pro Des: Brian Morris. Ed: Gerry Hambling. M: Gavin Friday and Maurice Seezer.

Bantamweight drama: Daniel Day-Lewis consoles Emily Watson in Jim Sheridan's masterfully directed, if dramatically underwhelming, *The Boxer* (from UIP)

Costumes: Joan Bergin. Boxing consultant: Barry McGuigan. (Universal/Hell's Kitchen–UIP.) Rel: 20 February 1998. 114 mins. Cert 15. UK/Ireland/USA. 1997.

Breakdown ★★★★★

Driving from Boston, Massachusetts, to their new home in San Diego, California, Jeff and Amy Taylor break down in the middle of the Utah desert. Hitching a lift with the cooperative driver of an 18-wheel juggernaut, Amy goes for help at a diner five miles down the road, leaving Jeff in charge of their Cherokee Jeep. But when Jeff fixes the Jeep himself and goes to pick Amy up, she is nowhere to be found... Building on a very simple premise, *Breakdown* resembles Steven Spielberg's *Duel* in its unrelenting escalation of suspense as a regular guy struggles with the unknown quantities of the open road. Eye-catching locations, persuasive plotting and a credible turn from

White-knuckle ride: Kurt Russell hangs on in Jonathan Mostow's breathless *Breakdown* (from Fox)

Kurt Russell as the Everyman hurled into unbearable circumstances further assert the film's pedigree. In fact, I can't remember when I was last so consistently gripped by a thriller from the opening frames to the final nerve-enervating climax.

Kurt Russell (*Jeff Taylor*), J.T. Walsh (*Red Barr*), Kathleen Quinlan (*Amy Taylor*), M.C. Gainey (*Earl*), Jack Noseworthy (*Billy*), Rex Linn (*Sheriff Boyd*), Ritch Brinkley (*Al*), Moira Harris, Kim Robillard, Thomas Kopache, Jack McGee, Vincent Berry, Steve Waddington.
  Dir: Jonathan Mostow. Pro: Martha De Laurentiis and Dino De Laurentiis. Ex Pro: Jonathan Fernandez and Harry Colomby. Line Pro: Jeffrey Sudzin. Screenplay: Mostow and Sam Montgomery. Ph: Doug Milsome. Pro Des: Victoria Paul. Ed: Derek Brechin and Kevin Stitt. M: Basil Poledouris; numbers performed by Charley Pride, and Robbyn Kirmsse. Costumes: Terry Dresbach. (Spelling Films/Paramount–Fox.) Rel: 1 May 1998. 93 mins. Cert 15. USA. 1997.

Disturbing waters: The alluring Aleksandra Vujcic in Gregor Nicholas's heartfelt *Broken English* (from First Independent)

Breaking Up ★★

Breaking up is hard to do and Steve and Monica just can't seem to get the hang of it. No sooner have they finally ended their tumultuous partnership than they've fallen in love all over again. And so it goes on... A two-character piece written for the theatre is hardly an inviting cinematic prospect and director Robert Greenwald (of *Xanadu* fame, I'm afraid) doesn't help matters by cluttering the flow with stylistic gimmicks (Hi-8 videography, freeze frames, wipe edits and black and white inserts). Which leaves the acting smarts of Russell Crowe and Salma Hayek, not the most gifted performers in the world, but who do, occasionally, ignite the material. Unfortunately, Michael Cristofer's adaptation is decidedly uneven, even if his dialogue hits a number of home runs, reminding us what a mercurial thing love is. [*Ewen Brownrigg*]

Russell Crowe (*Steve*), Salma Hayek (*Monica*), Abraham Alvarez (*minister*).
  Dir: Robert Greenwald. Pro: Greenwald and George Moffly. Ex Pro: Arnon Milchan and David Matalon. Screenplay: Michael Cristofer. Ph: Mauro Fiore. Pro Des: Terrence Foster. Ed: Suzanne Hines.

M: Mark Mothersbaugh; numbers performed by Diesel, John Coltrane, Tiny Tim, Marlene Dietrich, The Dell Vikings, The Five Satins, Shakespear's Sister, World Party, etc. Costumes: Michael Castellano. (Regency Enterprises–Warner.) Rel: 23 January 1998. 89 mins. Cert 15. USA. 1996.

Bring Me the Head of Mavis Davis ★★

Evicted from his home by bailiffs, haunted by his ex-wife for three months' unpaid alimony and intimidated by a disappointed loan shark, record producer Marty Starr has hit rock bottom. His only security is his last tenable client, torch singer Marla Dorland (formerly Mavis Davis), and even her career is on the skids. Then he hits on the brilliant idea of killing her off, thus guaranteeing an instant revival of her back catalogue. This way he can solve all his financial problems and bring Marla the calibre of adulation that she has always craved... A relatively good idea is undermined by a failure to take either one direction or the other. As the hapless producer Rik Mayall is mercifully restrained (in a rather well-judged performance) and his co-stars make a point of not labouring the comedy; but this is neither naturalistic enough for us to believe in the characters nor broad enough to qualify as black farce. Notwithstanding, there are some moments to savour, not least an offbeat turn from Danny Aiello as an Anglophilic Italian American heavy. A good song soundtrack would have reaped dividends.

Rik Mayall (*Marty Starr/Ken Baggs*), Jane Horrocks (*Marla Dorland/Mavis Davis*), Danny Aiello (*Mr Rathbone*), Ronald Pickup (*Percy Stone*), Philip Martin Brown (*Inspector Furse*), Paul Keating (*Paul Rathbone*), Marc Warren (*Clint*), Jaclyn Mendoza (*Cynthia*), Mark Heap (*Duncan*), Daniel Abineri, Steve O'Donnell, Rob Freeman, John Tordoff, Gordon Milne, Heathcote Williams, Jo Farrell, Ross Boatman, Paul Shearer, Stewart Harwood, Joanne Reay.
  Dir: John Henderson. Pro: Stephen Colegrave and Joanne Reay. Ex Pro: John Quested, Guy Collins and David M. Thompson. Co-Pro: Peter Jaques. Screenplay: Craig Strachan, based on an idea by Reay. Ph: Clive Tickner. Pro Des: Michael Carlin. Ed: Paul Endacott. M: Christopher Tyng. Costumes: Helen McCabe. (Goldcrest Films International/

BBC Films/Mission–Feature Film Co.) Rel: 16 January 1998. 100 mins. Cert 15. UK. 1997.

Broken English ★★★★

Three years after relocating to the ethnically diverse suburbs of Auckland, New Zealand, Croatian beauty Nina falls for Eddie, the Maori chef at the restaurant where she works as a waitress. Two cultural outcasts in a harsh, unforgiving world, Nina and Eddie find themselves caught up in a passionate affair, neither suspecting that the biggest obstacle to their happiness would be Nina's own father. It seems that the latter, blinded by his bigotry, has learned nothing from the pointless butchery in his homeland... Focusing an intelligent light on the ongoing problem of racial disharmony, *Broken English* is distinguished by a sure directorial hand and an articulate screenplay that avoids pat, easy answers. Above all, however, it is the glowing central performance of Aleksandra Vujcic, a philosophy student from Croatia (who makes her professional acting debut here), that gives this thoughtful, heartfelt drama its true resonance.

Rade Serbedzija (*Ivan*), Aleksandra Vujcic (*Nina*), Madeline McNamara (*Mira*), Marton Csokas (*Darko*), Elizabeth Mavric (*Vanya*), Julian Arahanga (*Eddie*), Jing Zhao (*Clara*), Li Yang (*Wu*), Michael Langley, Morena Tutugoro, Mona Ross, Temuera Morrison, Barbara Cartwright, Chris Ruka.
   Dir: Gregor Nicholas. Pro: Robin Scholes. Ex Pro: Timothy White. Line Pro: Janet McIver. Screenplay: Nicholas, Johanna Pigott and Jim Salter. Ph: John Toon. Pro Des: Michael Kane. Ed: David Coulson. M: Murray Grindlay and Murray McNab. Costumes: Glenis Foster. (Village Roadshow/Communicado/New Zealand Film Commission/NZ On Air–First Independent.) Rel: 25 July 1997. 92 mins. Cert 18. New Zealand. 1996.

The Butcher Boy ★★★½

Fiercely protective of his neurotic mother and alcoholic father, young Francie Brady grows up in a small Irish town in the shadow of the Cold War. Reared on the violence of comic books and the gung-ho histrionics of *The Lone Ranger*, Francie is given little moral example and well knows

Cold War blues: Fiona Shaw and Andrew Fullerton struggle to rid themselves of Eamonn Owens in Neil Jordan's imaginative, repellent *The Butcher Boy* (from Warner)

that his cheeky charm and the benevolence of others will see him through. And, as disharmony at home increases, so do Francie's alarming flights of fantasy... If one had a burning ambition to translate Patrick McCabe's dark 1992 novel to the screen, then one would be hard put to come up with a more expertly crafted, intrinsically faithful version than this. Brimming with imaginative flourishes, evocatively photographed and crowned by an extraordinarily spirited performance from newcomer Eamonn Owens, the film casts a singular spell. Recalling the disturbing spirit of such cinematic originals as *Lord of the Flies*, *The Tin Drum* and *Hope and Glory*, *The Butcher Boy* is haunting, accomplished and about as efficient as a cutting remark one remembers (with a shudder) from childhood.

Stephen Rea (*Da Brady*), Fiona Shaw (*Mrs Nugent*), Eamonn Owens (*Francie Brady*), Sinead O'Connor (*Our Lady/Colleen*), Alan Boyle (*Joe Purcell*), Peter Gowen (*Leddy*), Aisling O'Sullivan (*Ma Brady*), John Kavanagh (*Dr Boyd*), Niall Buggy (*Father Dom*), Ian Hart (*Uncle Alo*), Brendan Gleeson (*Father Bubbles*), Patrick McCabe

(*Jimmy the Skite*), Milo O'Shea (*Father Sullivan*), Anita Reeves, Gina Moxley, Anne O'Neill, Joe Pilkington, Paraic Breathnach, Brendan Conroy, Sean Hughes, Tony Rohr, Ronan Wilmot, Vinnie McCabe, Gerard McSorley.
   Dir and Ex Pro: Neil Jordan. Pro: Redmond Morris and Stephen Woolley. Screenplay: Jordan and Patrick McCabe. Ph: Adrian Biddle. Pro Des: Anthony Pratt. Ed: Tony Lawson. M: Elliot Goldenthal; Schubert, Rossini; numbers performed by Santo & Johnny, Sinead O'Connor, Dion & The Belmonts, Frank Sinatra, B Bumble & The Stingers, etc. Costumes: Sandy Powell. (Geffen Pictures–Warner.) Rel: 20 February 1998. 110 mins. Cert 15. USA/Ireland. 1997.

The Butterfly Effect – El Efecto Mariposa ★★★★

Camberwell/Madrid/Brighton; the present. A chain of romantic collisions are set in motion when Luis, a Spanish student, comes to England from Madrid to study at the London School of Economics. Like the butterfly effect of the title – the chaos theory which suggests that a butterfly's motion in Beijing can alter the climate in New York – Luis's arrival triggers far-reaching amorous consequences. Not only does he embark on an affair with his aunt, but the latter's husband, a TV actor, beds his co-star, while Luis's own mother falls for Luis's neighbour –

and so on... One of the most delightful surprises of the year, *The Butterfly Effect* is a model of shrewd writing and directorial skill. Furthermore, a most attractive cast invest their parts with affection and consummate comic timing. Quite charming – and very funny. [*Ewen Brownrigg*]

Maria Barranco (*Olivia*), Coque Malla (*Luis*), Rosa Maria Sarda (*Noelia*), James Fleet (*Oswald*), Peter Sullivan (*Duncan*), Cecile Pallas (*Chantal*), Jose Maria Pou, John Faal.
Dir: Fernando Colomo. Pro: Beatriz De La Gandara. Co-Pro: Alexandre Heylen. Assoc Pro: Edmon Roch. Screenplay: Colomo and Joaquin Oristrell. Ph: Jean-Francois Robin. Pro Des: John T. Roberts. Ed: Miguel A. Santamaria. M: Ketama; numbers performed by Ketama, Light House People, Moloko, Tricky, and Jimmy Cliff. Costumes: Vicente Ruiz. (Mainstream/Portman Prods/Oceandeep/TVE Television Espanola/Canal Plus/Eurimages–Blue Dolphin.) Rel: 18 July 1997. 109 mins. Cert 12. Spain/France/UK. 1995.

Career Girls ★★★½

Meeting for the first time in six years, Annie and Hannah – former London flatmates – find themselves plunged into flashback. In the good old bad old days, Annie was an excruciatingly self-conscious psychology student (with a pronounced case of dermatitis), while Hannah was a bitchy,

Burlesque of detail: Katrin Cartlidge in Mike Leigh's uncomfortably funny *Career Girls* (from Film Four)

psychotic control freak. Since then, Hannah has slowed down and Annie has found an inner peace, and the two are surprised to find that their tie of affection has strengthened in the intervening years... While he continues to showcase the formidable talent of his actors, Mike Leigh encourages such over-the-top performances here that he ultimately distances his audience from the reality of his story. In fact, there isn't much story – no *Secrets and Lies* bombshell – which inevitably disappoints after the success of the director's more recent work. What Leigh does do is bring a scalpel to the human condition and frequently, uncompromisingly – sadistically, some might say – cuts to the bone. Even as it barges into the higher reaches of farce, *Career Girls* is much funnier than most of Mike Leigh's oeuvre and is hard to expunge from the memory.

Katrin Cartlidge (*Hannah Mills*), Lynda Steadman (*Annie*), Mark Benton (*Richard 'Ricky' Burton*), Kate Byers (*Claire*), Andy Serkis (*Mr Evans*), Joe Tucker (*Adrian Spinks*), Margo Stanley, Michael Healy.
Dir and Screenplay: Mike Leigh. Pro: Simon Channing-Williams. Ph: Dick Pope. Pro Des: Eve Stewart. Ed: Robin Sales. M: Marianne Jean-Baptiste and Tony Remy; numbers performed by The Cure. (Channel Four/Thin Man Films/Matrix Film–Film Four.) Rel: 19 September 1997. 87 mins. Cert 15. UK. 1997.

Chasing Amy ★★★★

Red Bank, New Jersey; the present. Holden McNeil and Banky Edwards have been inseparable since third

grade and are now the proud creators of the comic-book icons Bluntman & Chronic (described as 'Bill and Ted meet Cheech and Chong' by one fan). At a comic-book convention, Holden falls for the charms of one Alyssa Jones, the effervescent author of *Idiosyncratic Routine*, only to discover that she is a lesbian. However, a friendship develops, albeit one increasingly hampered by Holden's conventional views of male-female bonding... The third instalment of Kevin Smith's New Jersey trilogy (following on from *Clerks* and *Mallrats*), *Chasing Amy* displays the writer-director's characteristic ribaldry and deadpan wit while plumbing new depths of emotional complexity with surprising insight. Splendidly acted by all concerned (Smith's girlfriend Joey Lauren Adams is outstanding), this moving, very funny and eye-opening look at sexual diversity works as the perfect gay antidote to *When Harry Met Sally*. Amazingly, Smith shot the whole thing for a mere $250,000.

Ben Affleck (*Holden McNeil*), Joey Lauren Adams (*Alyssa Jones*), Jason Lee (*Banky Edwards*), Dwight Ewell (*Hooper*), Jason Mewes (*Jay*), Carmen Lee (*Kim*), Kevin Smith (*Silent Bob*), Ethan Suplee, Scott Mosier, Casey Affleck, Guinevere Turner, Brian O'Halloran, Matt Damon, Illeana Douglas.
Dir and Screenplay: Kevin Smith. Pro: Scott Mosier. Ex Pro: John Pierson. Assoc Pro: Robert Hawke. Line Pro: Derrick Tseng. Ph: David Klein. Pro Des: Robert 'Ratface' Holtzman. Ed: Smith and Mosier. M: David Pirner; J.S. Bach; numbers performed by Ernie Isley, Liz Phair, The Hang Ups, The Mighty Mighty Bosstones, Run-DMC, Public Enemy, Faithless, Sponge, Soul Asylum, etc. Costumes: Christopher Del Coro. (Miramax/View Askew–Metrodome.) Rel: 14 November 1997. 113 mins. Cert 18. USA. 1996.

City of Angels ★★½

Los Angeles – aka the City of Angels; the present. Assigned to chaperone the freshly deceased to their new realm, celestial escort Seth finds himself unnaturally drawn to a human doctor, Maggie. Unable to comprehend her feelings of doubt and despair when a patient dies, Seth makes himself visible to her, thus triggering an unusual attraction. Desperate to discover the mystical

sensations of taste, warmth and pain, Seth finds himself increasingly tempted to trade in his immortality... While exercising a powerful mystical grip and displaying a strong visual style, *City of Angels* cannot override the banalities of its inevitable romantic outcome due to a suffocating self-reverence. Unlike such supernatural romances as *Ghost* and *Heaven Can Wait*, the film is practically devoid of humour and, more importantly, self-mockery, allowing the audience to commandeer the last laugh. Still, the film's first half certainly casts a lyrical spell and both Nicolas Cage and Meg Ryan provide charismatic turns – although, ultimately, they cannot transcend the implausibility of the concept. You won't believe.

Nicolas Cage (*Seth Plate*), Meg Ryan (*Maggie*), Andre Braugher (*Cassiel*), Dennis Franz (*Messinger*), Colm Feore (*Jordan*), Robin Bartlett (*Anne*), Joanna Merlin, Sarah Dampf, Rhonda Dotson, Jay Patterson, Dan Desmond, Deirdre O'Connell.

Dir: Brad Silberling. Pro: Dawn Steel and Charles Roven. Ex Pro: Arnon Milchan, Charles Newirth and Robert Cavallo. Screenplay: Dana Stevens, based on Wim Wenders' film *Wings of Desire*. Ph: John Seale. Pro Des: Lilly Kilvert. Ed: Lynzee Klingham. M: Gabriel Yared; Wojciech Kilar; numbers performed by Jimi Hendrix, Eric Clapton, John Lee Hooker, Paula Cole, U2, Louis Prima, Frank Sinatra, Sarah McLachlan, Goo Goo Dolls, Peter Gabriel, and Alanis Morissette. Costumes: Shay Cunliffe. Sound: John Pospisil. (Warner/Monarchy Enterprises/Regency Entertainment–Warner.) Rel: 19 June 1998. 117 mins. Cert 12. USA. 1998.

City of Industry ★★★

Los Angeles/Palm Springs; now. Small-time crook Lee Egan sets up an elaborate jewel heist as his swan song, enlisting the help of an outside driver, his best friend Jorge and his older brother Roy, the latter a hardened thief from the Midwest. Setting his sights on a distribution centre for the Russian diamond trade, Lee explains to his brother that the job is a cinch. However, Roy is not so easily won over, noting, 'If I had a dollar for every time I heard a job was a slam dunk...' As it happens, the robbery goes without a hitch. But what goes down afterwards is another matter... What do

Heterosexual blues: Ben Affleck and Joey Lauren Adams try friendship in Kevin Smith's eye-opening *Chasing Amy* (from Metrodome)

you expect from a Harvey Keitel movie, anyway? You've got brutality, some integrity, a lot of killing and another towering performance from the man himself. More surprising is that this gritty, focused shard of film noir is from English director John Irvin, who last gave us the loopy romantic comedy *A Month By the Lake*. Credit Ken Solarz' blunt, credible and occasionally darkly humorous dialogue and the evocative lighting from Canada's

Thomas Burstyn (as American cinematographers seem to be thin on the ground). Shame about the title, although it's better than *Industrial Estate*.

Harvey Keitel (*Roy Egan*), Stephen Dorff (*Skip Kovich*), Timothy Hutton (*Lee Egan*), Famke Janssen (*Rachel Montana*), Wade Dominguez (*Jorge Montana*), Michael Jai White (*Odell Williams*), Luci Alexis Liu (*Cathi Rose*), Reno Wilson (*Keshaun Brown*), Dana Barron (*Gena*), Francois Chau (*Uncle Luke*), Tamara Clatterbuck (*Sunny*), Elliott

An angel on my shoulder: Nicolas Cage and Meg Ryan break some celestial ground rules in Brad Silberling's straight-faced *City of Angels* (from Warner)

Serious intrigue: Mel Gibson and Julia Roberts face up to the Establishment in Richard Donner's gripping *Conspiracy Theory* (from Warner)

Gould (*Harvey*), Brian Brophy, Flex, Ai Wan.

Dir: John Irvin. Pro: Evzen Kolar and Ken Solarz. Ex Pro: Barr B. Potter. Assoc Pro: Matthew Gayne. Screenplay: Solarz. Ph: Thomas Burstyn. Pro Des: Michael Novotny. Ed: Mark Conte. M: Stephen Endelman; numbers performed by Massive Attack, Death in Vegas, Lush, Tricky, Bomb the Bass, Palm Skin Productions, Red, etc. Costumes: Eduardo Castro. (Largo Entertainment/JVC–PolyGram.) Rel: 4 July 1997. 97 mins. Cert 15. USA. 1996.

Clubbed to Death ★★

When a young woman falls asleep on a late-night bus, she ends up on the outskirts of Paris. There, she finds herself drawn to a buzzing nocturnal rave club and, as she befriends a sultry Arab drug addict, so a new chapter in her life begins... Ignoring such cinematic basics as plot and character development, writer-director Zauberman lets her camera loose on the throbbing tide of ravers, lunging boldly for a sense of in-yer-face immediacy. A telling portrait of club life – if you like that sort of thing. [*Charles Bacon*]

Elodie Bouchez (*Lola Monnet*), Beatrice Dalle (*Saida*), Roschdy Zem (*Emir Areski*), Richard Courcet (*Ismael*), Gerald Thomassin (*Paul*).

Dir: Yolande Zauberman. Pro: Odile Gervais. Ex Pro: Alain Massiot. Screenplay: Zauberman and Noemie Lvovsky. Ph: Denis Lenoir. Pro Des: Olivier Radot. Ed: Francois Gedigier. M: Philippe Cohen-Solal; numbers performed by Gavin Bryars, The Chemical Brothers, Massive Attack, Dirty Jesus, Daft Punk, etc. Costumes: Pierre-Yves Gayraud. (Madar/La Sept Cinema/Meteor Film Prods/Canal Plus, etc.–Artificial Eye.) Rel: 6 February 1998. 88 mins. Cert 18. France/Portugal/The Netherlands. 1996.

Conspiracy Theory ★★★½

Jerry Fletcher is exceptionally screwed up. Even though he's a New York cab driver, he's more talkative and loopy than most. Besides keeping a padlock on the coffee in his fridge (which is also locked), Fletcher believes the Vietnam War was the result of a bet between Howard Hughes and Aristotle Onassis and that Oliver Stone is a disinformation specialist employed by George Bush. Jerry Fletcher is seriously paranoid, but then he might have every reason to be... The scary part of Fletcher's theories is that some of them add up (So why *do* assassins always have three names? And why *has* the Space Shuttle been in orbit during the last six major earthquakes?). While Mel Gibson's obsessive chatterer is hard to take at times (Geoffrey Rush did it better in *Shine*), Richard Donner steers Brian Helgeland's smart script through its paces with style and bravura. Periodically gripping, funny and moving (if seldom credible), *Conspiracy Theory* is pure heroin for conspiracy buffs and star-powered escapism for everybody else. FYI: Julia Roberts (who's very good, by the way) was paid $12 million after Jodie Foster turned the part down.

Mel Gibson (*Jerry Fletcher*), Julia Roberts (*Alice Sutton*), Patrick Stewart (*Dr Jonas/Henry Finch*), Cylk Cozart (*Agent Lowry*), Stephen Kahan (*Wilson*), Terry Alexander, Alex McArthur, Saxon Trainor, Claudia Stedelin, Leonard Jackson, Donal Gibson, Bert Remsen, Kenneth Tigar.

Dir: Richard Donner. Pro: Donner and Joel Silver. Ex Pro: Jim Van Wyck. Co-Pro: Dan Cracchiolo, J. Mills Goodloe and Rick Solomon. Screenplay: Brian Helgeland. Ph: John Schwartzman. Pro Des: Paul Sylbert. Ed: Frank J. Urioste. M: Carter Burwell; 'Can't Take My Eyes Off You' sung by Frankie Valli, Lauryn Hill and Mel Gibson. Costumes: Ha Nguyen. (Warner/Silver Pictures/Shuler Donner/Donner–Warner.) Rel: 29 August 1997. 140 mins. Cert 15. USA. 1997.

Contact ★★★★★

Dubbed the 'high priestess of the desert', radio astronomer Ellie Arroway has been searching for patterns in the chaos of the cosmos since she was a young child. Constantly undermined by her short-sighted superiors, Ellie listens for signs of life from the night sky over New Mexico, convinced that some time, somewhere, on some frequency, she will tune into something extraordinary. Of course, she is unprepared for the political, theological and moral implications should she ever make contact... Trailing in the wake of such preposterous (if entertaining) fantasies as *Independence Day*, *Mars Attacks!* and *Men in Black*, *Contact* takes a plausible, intelligent and courageous look at the possibility of extraterrestrial life in the universe. Based on the 1985 best-selling novel by the late Carl Sagan (1934-96), the film establishes a credible foundation by filling out the backstory of its female protagonist and channelling our own curiosity and wonder through her eyes. Technically accomplished (you'll believe Bill Clinton learned his lines) and intellectually sound, *Contact* fulfils its emotional, scientific and humanitarian agenda with insight and passion.

Jodie Foster (*Ellie Arroway*), Matthew McConaughey (*Palmer Joss*), James Woods (*Michael Kitz*), John Hurt (*S.R. Hadden*), Tom Skerritt (*David Drumlin*), Angela Bassett (*Rachel Constantine*), Jena Malone (*young Ellie*), David Morse (*Ted Arroway*), William Fichtner (*Kent*), Rob Lowe (*Richard Rank*), Jake Busey, Geoffrey Blake, SaMi Chester, Timothy McNeil, William Jordan, Alex Zemeckis, Robin Gammell; and as themselves: Larry King, Geraldo Rivera, Jay Leno, Geraldine A. Ferraro, Ann Druyan, Kathleen Kennedy, Bryant Gumbel, Bernard Shaw, William Jefferson Blythe Clinton IV (*as Bill Clinton*).

Dir: Robert Zemeckis. Pro: Zemeckis and Steve Starkey. Ex Pro: Joan Bradshaw and Lynda Obst. Co-Pro: Carl Sagan and Ann Druyan. Screenplay: Michael Goldenberg. Ph: Don Burgess. Pro Des: Edward Verreaux. Ed: Arthur Schmidt. M: Alan Silvestri; numbers performed by Jimmy Buffett, Harry Nilsson, Norman Greenbaum, The Forester Sisters, etc. Costumes: Joanna Johnston. Visual effects: Ken Ralston. Caterers: For Stars Catering. (South Side Amusement Company / Warner–Warner.) Rel: 26 September 1997. 150 mins. Cert PG. USA. 1997.

Cop Land ★★★½

A sleepy, manicured town lying in the shadow of the Manhattan skyline, Garrison, New Jersey (population: 1,280), is the perfect escape for the constabulary forces of New York's finest. It's also an ideal cover for a bit of slumming in the law enforcement department, activities that go unheeded by the town's sheriff, Freddy Heflin. Denied a place on the force because of his hearing disability, Heflin turns a blind eye (and his deaf ear) to the subtle corruption around him, but there's a limit to what he will tolerate... Waiving his standard $20m fee, Sylvester Stallone not only worked for scale but put on 38 lbs to flesh out his docile sheriff (and, possibly, to show deference to his co-star, Robert De Niro). That he worms his way under the skin of this stunted hero – and wins our sympathy – is not only a tribute to his presence as an actor but to the shrewd command of writer-director James Mangold (Heavy). The latter's colourful dialogue and subtle unveiling of character evokes an underlying tension that grips from the word go.

Sylvester Stallone (*Freddy Heflin*), Harvey Keitel (*Ray Donlan*), Ray Liotta (*Gary 'Figs' Figgis*), Robert De Niro (*Moe Tilden*), Peter Berg (*Joey Randone*), Janeane Garofalo (*Cindy Betts*), Robert Patrick (*Jack Rucker*), Michael Rapaport (*Murray 'Superboy' Babitch*), Annabella Sciorra (*Liz Randone*), Noah Emmerich (*Deputy Bill Geisler*), Cathy Moriarty (*Rose Donlan*), John Spencer, Frank Vincent, Malik Yoba, Arthur J. Nascarella, Edie Falco, Victor L. Williams, Paul Calderon, John Doman, Deborah Harry (*Delores*), Method Man, Paul Herman, Mel Gorham, Robert Castle, Bruce Altman.

Dir and Screenplay: James Mangold. Pro: Cary Woods, Cathy Konrad and Ezra

Terrestrial intelligence: Jodie Foster makes *Contact* (from Warner)

Swerdlow. Ex Pro: Bob Weinstein, Harvey Weinstein and Meryl Poster. Co-Pro: Kerry Orent. Ph: Eric Edwards. Pro Des: Lester Cohen. Ed: Craig McKay. M: Howard Shore; numbers performed by MOD 222, AMG, Smokin' Joe Kubek Band, Bruce Springsteen, Frankie Valli, Boz Scaggs, The Robert Cray Band, Bobby Darin, The Seeds, etc. Costumes: Ellen Lutter. (Miramax / Woods Entertainment / Sundance Institute–Buena Vista.) Rel: 5 December 1997. 104 mins. Cert 15. USA. 1997.

Cremaster 5 ★

The third in Matthew Barney's quintet of 'arty' experiments, *Cremaster 5* features Ursula Andress sporting a pair of large glass bubbles on her head while miming to an aria sung by Adrienne Csengery. Matthew Barney himself plays her

Night falls on New Jersey: Robert De Niro and Sylvester Stallone chew the fat in James Mangold's gripping *Cop Land* (from Buena Vista)

Fun with morphing: Kiefer Sutherland in Alex Proyas's illogical, surreal *Dark City* (from Entertainment)

'Diva', 'Giant' and 'Magician' and submits himself to a number of indignities, usually in the nude. Critics have described this as cinematic Damien Hirst, but it's more like Dali without the excitement. Cineastes and masochists should have fun sifting through the symbolism.

Ursula Andress (*Queen of Chain*), Matthew Barney (*her Diva, her Giant and her Magician*), Joanne Rha, Susan Rha.
Dir and Screenplay: Matthew Barney. Pro: Barney and Barbara Gladstone. Line Pro: Chelsea Romersa. Ph: Michael James O'Brien. Pro Des: Robert Wogan. M: Jonathan Bepler. Costumes: Linda LaBelle and Karen Young. Videography: Peter Strietmann. Sculpture: Paul Pisoni. (Artangel.) Rel: 20 March 1998. 51 mins. Cert 12. USA. 1997.

Dad Savage ★1/2
If you can relish the idea of *Reservoir Dogs* transplanted to the Norfolk Broads with Patrick Stewart as a criminal tulip farmer then you get what you deserve. Highly derivative and a bit of a mess, *Dad Savage* would be a total waste if it weren't for the quality of the performances. [*Ewen Brownrigg*]

Patrick Stewart (*Dad*), Kevin McKidd (*H*), Helen McCrory (*Chrissie*), Joe McFadden (*Bob*), Marc Warren (*Vic*), Jake Wood (*Sav*).
Dir: Betsan Morris Evans. Pro: Gwynneth Lloyd and Robert Jones. Line Pro: Paul Sarony. Screenplay: Steven Williams. Ph: Gavin Finney. Pro Des: Michael Carlin. Ed: Guy Bensley. M: Simon Boswell; numbers performed by The Jam, Patsy Cline, Wilco, Barry Upton & Wild at Heart, Clint Bradley, Nick Drake, etc. Costumes: Rachael Fleming. (Sweet Child–PolyGram.) Rel: 5 June 1998. 104 mins. Cert 18. UK. 1998.

Dancehall Queen ★★
Eking out a meagre existence as a street vendor in Kingston, Jamaica, single parent Marcia relies heavily on the financial support of 'Uncle' Larry. But when Larry seeks to recoup his investment in the form of a tumble with Marcia's 15-year-old daughter, she turns elsewhere for capital. Then, in a bizarre career switch, she transforms herself into a disco diva in order to compete for the prize money in a local 'Dancehall Queen' tournament... Raw, brash and strident, *Dancehall Queen* mixes kitchen sink with kitsch 'n' sync in an old-fashioned romp that attempts to pump fresh adrenalin into the reggae scene. Flawed but fun – and capped by a terrific performance from Audrey Reid. [*Charles Bacon*]

Audrey Reid (*Marcia*), Paul Campbell (*Priest*), Carl Davis ('*Uncle' Larry*), Pauline Stone-Myrie (*Mrs Gordon*), Charine Anderson, Mark Danvers, Patricia Harrison, Anika Grason, Donald Thompson, Henry Brown, Carl Bradshaw, Michael London, Beenie Man, Lady Saw, Anthony B, Chevelle Franklyn.
Dir: Don Letts and Rick Elgood. Pro: Carolyn Pfeiffer and Carl Bradshaw. Ex Pro: Chris Blackwell and Dan Genetti. Screenplay: Letts, Suzanne Fenn and Ed Wallace, from a story by Wallace and Bradshaw. Ph: Louis Mulvey. Pro Des: Elgood. Ed: Fenn. M: Wally Badarou, Maxine Stowe; numbers performed by Chevelle Franklyn & Beenie Man, Chaka Demus & Pliers, Bounty Killer, Lady Shaw, Buccaneer, Grace Jones, Sly & Robbie, Black Uhuru, Third World, Junior Demus, Sugar Minott, etc. (Island Jamaica Films / Hawk's Nest–Island Jamaica Films.) Rel: 26 September 1997. 98 mins. Cert 15. Jamaica. 1997.

Dark City ★★1/2
In an effort to plumb the human psyche, a race of mentally advanced beings on the verge of extinction clandestinely take over the world as we know it (at least, as we knew it in the 1950s). With the ability to stop time and thus banish the detrimental effects of daylight, The Strangers establish an urban, nocturnal playground where they can carry out their distinctive experiments. At the stroke of midnight on the hour every hour, The Strangers mix and match the memories of their human subjects when one John Murdoch wakes up before his erased memories can be replaced... Placing logic to one side (like, what happened to the rest of the world?), *Dark City* attempts to kick around some Important Questions, such as, 'Are we really more than the sum of our memories?' Yet the film's total submersion into a surreal, cloistered nether world detracts from any rational involvement. Thus, it's up to the rampant visual effects and dystopian production design (Terry Gilliam meets *The City of Lost Children*) to engage the interest – along with Kiefer Sutherland's quirky speech pattern.

Rufus Sewell (*John Murdoch*), Kiefer Sutherland (*Dr Daniel Schreber*), Jennifer Connelly (*Emma Murdoch*), William Hurt (*Inspector Bumstead*), Richard O'Brien (*Mr Hand*), Ian Richardson (*Mr Book*), Colin Friels (*Walenski*), Melissa George (*May*), Mitchell Butel, Frank Gallacher, Bruce Spence, John Bluthal, Nicholas Bell, Maureen O'Shaughnessy, Natalie Bollard.
Dir: Alex Proyas. Pro: Proyas and Andrew Mason. Ex Pro: Michael De Luca

and Brian Witten. Screenplay: Proyas, Lem Dobbs and David S. Goyer. Ph: Darius Wolski. Pro Des: George Liddle. Ed: Dov Hoenig. M: Trevor Jones. Costumes: Liz Keogh. Conceptual design: Patrick Tatopolous. (New Line/Mystery Clock–Entertainment.) Rel: 29 May 1998. 100 mins. Cert 15. USA/Australia. 1997.

Darklands ★

South Wales; today. On his 36th birthday, Frazer Truick, a timid reporter with absolutely no private life, investigates the desecration of a local church. Teaming up with an attractive trainee journalist, Frazer begins to suspect a local druid cult for a number of unpleasant activities in the neighbourhood. However, Frazer's editor is unwilling to endorse such far-fetched 'supposition'... Here's one for the record books: a movie practically devoid of characterisation, plausibility, logic, suspense, humour, style or variety, confounded by amateur dialogue, threadbare shock tactics and disastrous miscasting (can any actor as big as Craig Fairbrass have run away from so many characters smaller than himself?). Even the story is nothing but a series of episodes heading for a brick wall. Label this one an object lesson in how not to make a film.

Craig Fairbrass (*Frazer Truick*), Rowena King (*Rachel Morris*), Jon Finch (*David Keller*), Richard Lynch (*Salvy*), Roger Nott (*Dennis Cox*), David Duffy (*Carver*), Nicola Branson (*Becky*), Beth Morris (*Dr Moryan*), William Thomas (*Terry Jarvis*), Hubert Rees, Richard Rees, Grahame Fox, Ieun Rhys, Rhys Evans.
Dir and Screenplay: Julian Richards. Pro: Paul Brooks. Ex Pro: Alan Martin and Peter Edwards. Ph: Zoran Djordjevic. Pro Des: Hayden Pearce. Ed: Mark Talbot-Butler. M: John Murphy and David Hughes; numbers performed by Toffee World. Costumes: Sheena Gunn. Sound: Paul Davies. (Darklands Ltd/Lluniau Lliw Cyf/The Arts Council of Wales– Metrodome.) Rel: 24 October 1997. 90 mins. Cert 18. UK. 1996.

Deceiver

See *Liar*.

Deconstructing Harry ★½

Harry Block, a Manhattan novelist, contracts writer's block and finds his past life and even his fictional characters catching up with him... Once again strapped for a story, Woody Allen rummages through his threadbare cupboard of over-familiar, affluent, middle-class, navel-gazing eccentrics to pad out his 27th film as writer-director in which he, again, plays out his own private neuroses. Potted with facile one-liners, *Deconstructing Harry* reveals that Allen's comic inventiveness has been virtually drained by repetition, leaving his cast of 85 actors little to chew on. Furthermore, the filmmaker has added a cheap smuttiness to his writing that suggests he caught a screening of *Nil By Mouth* and saw the light. Typical line: 'She's dyslexic. She put a tampon up her nose.' FYI: Demi Moore was paid $250,000 for her part as a fanatically Jewish shrink, the highest sum allotted to an Allen co-star.

Caroline Aaron (*Doris*), Woody Allen (*Harry Block*), Kirstie Alley (*Joan*), Bob Balaban (*Richard*), Richard Benjamin (*Ken*), Eric Bogosian (*Burt*), Billy Crystal (*Larry/The Devil*), Judy Davis (*Lucy*), Hazelle Goodman (*Cookie*), Mariel Hemingway (*Beth Kramer*), Amy Irving (*Jane*), Julie Kavner (*Grace*), Eric Lloyd (*Hilly*), Julia Louis-Dreyfus (*Leslie*), Tobey Maguire (*Harvey Stern*), Demi Moore (*Helen*), Elisabeth Shue (*Fay*), Stanley Tucci (*Paul Epstein*), Robin Williams (*Out-of-focus Mel*), Hy Anzell, Philip Bosco, Gene Saks, Annette Arnold, Irving Metzman, Tony Darrow, Jennifer Garner, Paul Giamatti.
Dir and Screenplay: Woody Allen. Pro: Jean Doumanian. Ex Pro: J.E. Beaucaire. Co-Pro: Richard Brick. Co-Ex Pro: Jack Rollins, Charles H. Joffe and Letty Aronson. Ph: Carlo Di Palma. Pro Des: Santo Loquasto. Ed: Susan E. Morse. M: numbers performed by Annie Ross, Django Reinhardt, Stan Getz, Erroll Garner, Woody Allen, Bob Balaban, Hazelle Goodman and Eric Lloyd, Benny Goodman, Stebbins Hall Band, etc. Costumes: Suzy Benzinger. (Magnolia Prods/Sweetland Films–Buena Vista.) Rel: 17 April 1998. 96 mins. Cert 18. USA. 1997.

Deep Crimson – Profundo Carmesi ★★

Sonora, Mexico; 1949. Ashamed of her physical bulk and bad breath, Coral Fabre, a nurse and single mother, dreams of Charles Boyer and sex. Connecting with a 'Spanish' conman, Nicolas Estrella, whom she meets through a lonely hearts' column, Coral refuses to accept his

For the love of killing: Regina Orozco and Daniel Gimenez Cacho in Arturo Ripstein's unnerving *Deep Crimson* **(from Metro Tartan)**

rejection of her and gives up her son and daughter in an effort to win him round. Touched by her sacrifice, Estrella takes Coral in and together they embark on a series of scams in which they rob widows of their inheritance... Like *Henry: Portrait of a Serial Killer*, Arturo Ripstein's unutterably grim document totally deglamorises the process of murder. Tightly framed and poorly lit, the film's construction and photography produces a feeling of inescapable claustrophobia, much like the ugly lives of its pathetic protagonists. On top of this, the fiercely ungratuitous nature of the murders produces a genuine feeling of nausea as the lives of Coral and Nicolas's victims are arbitrarily snuffed out. In spite of Ripstein's conviction that the real-life story of Coral and Nicolas was 'very moving,' the best that can be said for his film is that it strips away the enchantment of murder. Profoundly depressing. P.S. The so-called 'Lonely Hearts' murders were previously explored in the 1970 film *The Honeymoon Killers*.

Regina Orozco (*Coral Fabre*), Daniel Gimenez Cacho (*Nicolas Estrella*), Marisa Paredes (*Irene Gallardo*), Veronica Merchant (*Rebeca Sanpedro*), Patricia Reyes Espindola, Julieta Egurrola, Rosa Furman.

Apocalypse soon: A scene from Mimi Leder's underwhelming *Deep Impact* (from UIP)

Dir: Arturo Ripstein. Pro: Miguel Necoechea and Paolo Barbachano. Co-Pro: Marin Karmitz, Jose Maria Morales and Fernando Sarinana. Screenplay: Paz Alicia Garciadiego. Ph: Guillermo Granillo. Pro Des: Macarena Folache, Marisa Pecanins and Monica Chirinos. Ed: Rafael Castanedo. M: David Mansfield. Costumes: Monica Neumaier. Sound: Gabriel Romo and Carlos Faruolo. (Ivania Films/IMCINE/MK2 Prods/Wanda Films/Canal Plus–Metro Tartan.) Rel: 19 September 1997. 115 mins. Cert 18. Mexico/France/Spain. 1996.

Deep Impact ★★½

Noting an unidentified blip on his telescope's display monitor, scientist Marcus Wolf muses, 'Where are you going in such a hurry, little fella?' A 14-year-old boy argues with his astronomy teacher about the identity of a star he sees through his telescope. A young woman guardedly informs her new, grown-up step-daughter, 'Life goes on.' A rookie TV reporter stumbles on to a top-secret government acronym that stands for 'Extinction Level Event'. Life does go on, but for how much longer? Soon, the whole world bites its lip as a comet larger than Mount Everest heads straight for earth... The

problem with *Deep Impact* is that it tries so hard to be all things to all audiences that it frequently loses its way. Characters recede, narrative trajectories make arbitrary U-turns and the inevitable climax takes an inordinate time in coming. Setting itself up as a big, brassy disaster movie, it is surprisingly low on effects (which, when they come, are *so* yesterday), high on sentiment and poorly lacking in humour. Ultimately, then, this is a popcorn movie with none of the pop and all of the corn.

Robert Duvall (*Spurgeon Tanner*), Tea Leoni (*Jenny Lerner*), Elijah Wood (*Leo Biederman*), Vanessa Redgrave (*Robin Lerner*), Maximilian Schell (*Jason Lerner*), Morgan Freeman (*President Tom Beck*), James Cromwell (*Alan Rittenhouse*), Ron Eldard (*Oren Monash*), Jon Favreau (*Gus Partenza*), Laura Innes (*Beth Stanley*), Mary McCormack (*Andrea Baker*), Leelee Sobieski (*Sarah Hotchner*), Blair Underwood (*Mark Simon*), Rya Kihlstedt (*Chloe*), Alexander Baluev (*Mikhail Tulchinsky*), Charles Martin Smith (*Marcus Wolf*), Richard Schiff, Dougray Scott, Gary Werntz, Bruce Weitz, Betsy Brantley, O'Neal Compton, Joseph Urla, Derek de Lint, Denise Crosby, Kurtwood Smith.
Dir: Mimi Leder. Pro: Richard D. Zanuck and David Brown. Ex Pro: Steven Spielberg, Joan Bradshaw and Walter Parkes. Screenplay: Michael Tolkin and Bruce Joel Rubin. Ph: Dietrich Lohmann. Pro Des: Leslie Dilley. Ed: David Rosenbloom. M: James Horner; Verdi; numbers performed by Randy Travis, Larry Dean & The Shooters, and Tom Jones. Costumes: Ruth Myers. Visual

effects: Industrial Light & Magic. (Dream-Works/Paramount–UIP.) Rel: 15 May 1998. 121 mins. Cert 12. USA. 1998.

Desperate Measures ★★

The nine-year-old son of San Francisco cop Frank Connor is dying from an absurdly rare bone disease. And the sole compatible donor for a bone marrow transplant happens to be a sociopathic killer locked away in maximum security. Somehow, Connor has to appeal to the killer's conscience to save his son's life. But just how far will Connor go to accommodate the wishes of a man with nothing left to lose? Such a scenario certainly offers some promising dramatic possibilities, but under Barbet Schroeder's look-at-me direction, the film all too often tips into absurdity. Garcia does well as a man deaf to the voice of reason as he pursues the killer he must keep alive at all costs, but Keaton makes the fatal error of playing his character's evil up front, like Hannibal Lecter stuck with Roger Moore's eyebrow.

Michael Keaton (*Peter J. McCabe*), Andy Garcia (*Frank Connor*), Brian Cox (*Captain Jeremiah Cassidy*), Marcia Gay Harden (*Dr Samantha Hawkins*), Eric King (*Nate Oliver*), Efraim Figueroa (*Vargus*), Joseph Cross (*Matthew Connor*), Richard Riehle (*Ed Fayne*), Janet Maloney, Tracey Walter, Peter Weireter, Scott Colomby.
Dir: Barbet Schroeder. Pro: Schroeder, Gary Foster, Lee Rich and Susan Hoffman.

Ex Pro: Jeffrey Chernov. Co-Pro: Josie Rosen. Screenplay: David Klass and Neal Jimenez. Ph: Luciano Tovoli. Pro Des: Geoffrey Kirkland. Ed: Lee Percy. M: Trevor Jones. Costumes: Gary Jones. (Mandalay Entertainment/Eaglepoint/ TriStar Pictures–Entertainment.) Rel: 27 February 1998. 100 mins. Cert 15. USA. 1998.

Devil's Advocate ★★★★

Gainesville, Florida/New York; the present. The product of a simple, God-fearing upbringing, Kevin Lomax has emerged into a front-ranking defence attorney who has never lost a case. But just as the ethics of the justice system are beginning to trouble him, he is headhunted by an international law firm and transplanted to New York with all the trappings of the very, very successful. But what is the price Kevin is prepared to pay for such success and what is the real identity of his charismatic boss? A masterful brew of style, verve and imagination, *Devil's Advocate* spins its tale of legal skullduggery with fiendish virtuosity. From the seductive power of Pacino's performance to Bruno Rubeo's handsome, stately production design, this visually alluring adaptation of Andrew Neiderman's novel excels in every department. Even Keanu Reeves, in a very difficult role, is surprisingly good, while the impressive special effects are all the more effective for their minimalism. Diabolical, authoritative and sexy entertainment.

Keanu Reeves (*Kevin Lomax*), Al Pacino (*John Milton*), Charlize Theron (*Mary Ann Lomax*), Jeffrey Jones (*Eddie Barzoon*), Judith Ivey (*Alice Lomax*), Craig T. Nelson (*Alexander Cullen*), Connie Neilsen (*Christabella*), Tamara Tunie (*Jackie Heath*), Ruben Santiago-Hudson (*Leamon Heath*), Debra Monk (*Pam Garrety*), Laura Harrington (*Melissa Black*), Christopher Bauer (*Gettys*), Heather Matarazzo (*Barbara*), Don King (*himself*), Vyto Ruginis, Pamela Gray, George Wyner, Leo Burmester, Bill Moor, Mark Deakins, Alan Manson, Caprice Benedetti, Susan Kellerman, Harsh Nayyar, Vincent Laresca, Jose Fernandes Torres, Monica Keena, Juan Hernandez, E. Katherine Kerr, Michael Lombard, Senator Alfonse D'Amato (*himself*), and (*uncredited*) Delroy Lindo.
   Dir: Taylor Hackford. Pro: Arnon Milchan, Arnold Kopelson and Anne Kopelson. Ex Pro: Hackford, Michael

Tadross, Erwin Stoff, Barry Bernardi and Steve White. Co-Pro: Stephen Brown. Screenplay: Jonathan Lemkin and Tony Gilroy. Ph: Andrzej Bartkowiak. Pro Des: Bruno Rubeo. Ed: Mark Warner. M: James Newton Howard; J.S. Bach; numbers performed by The Rolling Stones, Frank Sinatra, Michael Lang, and Cadillac Moon. Costumes: Judianna Makovsky. Visual effects: Richard Greenberg. Demons design: Rick Baker. (Warner/Regency Enterprises/Kopelson Entertainment– Warner.) Rel: 16 January 1998. 144 mins. Cert 18. USA. 1997.

Devil's Island – Djoflaeyjan ★★★

Dubbed 'Devil's Island', Camp Thule is a settlement for the homeless of Reykjavik, where life is one long series of drinking, brawling and shivering. Based on a collection of

John Grisham with a satanic twist: Al Pacino lets it out in Taylor Hackford's beguiling and handsome *Devil's Advocate* (from Warner)

true stories, *Devil's Island* marks a dramatic U-turn for Fridrik Thor Fridriksson, Iceland's most famous director. Yet while Fridriksson has abandoned the road movie format and spectacular vistas of his *Children of Nature* (1991) and *Cold Fever* (1995), his eccentric sense of humour and affection for his characters are still very much in evidence. [*Ewen Brownrigg*]

Baltasar Kormakur (*Baddi Tomasson*), Gisli Halldorsson (*Tommi Tomasson*), Sigurveig Jonsdottir (*Karolina Tomasson*), Halldora Geirhardsdottir (*Dolli*), Sveinn Geirsson, Magnus Olafsson.
   Dir: Fridrik Thor Fridriksson. Pro: Fridriksson, Peter Rommel, Egil Odegaard and Peter Aalbaek Jensen. Screenplay: Einar Karason. Ph and Line Pro: Ari Kristinsson. Pro Des: Arni Pall Johannsson. Ed: Steingrimur Karlsson and Skule Eriksen. M: Hilmar Orn Hilmarsson; Verdi; numbers performed by Bodda Billo's Band. Costumes: Karl Aspelund. Sound: Kjartan Kjartansson. (Icelandic Film Corporation/Zentropa/European

Script Fund, etc.–Theatrical Experience.) Rel: 16 January 1998. 103 mins. Cert 15. Iceland/Norway/Germany/Denmark. 1996.

Different For Girls ★★★¹/₂

Paul Prentice, a laddish motorbike delivery bloke, bumps into an old schoolfriend who is now transsexual. Unable to fathom his emotional response, Prentice battles with the love-me-gender side of things and creates a scene, ending up in court. As Prentice, Rupert Graves gives a sizzlingly sexy performance to Steven Mackintosh's sensitive portrayal of Karl-turned-Kim. Written by the award-winning play wright and TV dramatist Tony Marchant. [*Marianne Gray*]

Rupert Graves (*Paul Prentice*), Steven Mackintosh (*Kim Foyle*), Miriam Margolyes (*Pamela*), Saskia Reeves (*Jean*), Charlotte Coleman (*Alison*), Neil Dudgeon (*Neil*), Nisha K. Nayar, Lia Williams, Ian Dury, Robert Pugh, Philip Davis, Kevin Allen, Gerard Horan, Edward Tudor-Pole, Adrian Rawlins, Peter Hugo-Daly, Charles De'Ath, Ruth Sheen.
 Dir: Richard Spence. Pro: John Chapman. Ex Pro: George Faber and Laura Gregory. Screenplay: Tony Marchant. Ph: Sean Van Hales. Pro Des: Grenville Horner. Ed: David Gamble. M: Stephen Warbeck; numbers performed by John Otway & Wild Willy Barrett, Kool Moe Dee, Joe Jackson, Buzzcocks, Stiff Little Fingers, Desmond Dekker & The Aces, etc. Costumes: Susannah Buxton. (BBC Films/Maurice Marciano/Great Guns/X Pictures-Blue Dolphin.) Rel: 10 April 1998. 96 mins. Cert 15. UK. 1996.

The Disappearance of Kevin Johnson ★★★

In Los Angeles to produce a documentary on British expats living in Hollywood, a British film crew are intrigued by the disappearance of Kevin Johnson, a bright new player in Tinseltown. And the deeper they dig, the more mysterious and suspect the British entrepreneur becomes... A deliciously po-faced stab at Hollywood excess, Francis Megahy's satire is so real that it's almost indistinguishable from the tacky 'true story' programmes one encounters on late-night TV. Helped by the participation of Pierce Brosnan, James Coburn and Dudley Moore playing themselves, this canny mockumentary is a worthy

successor to such paragons of the genre as *This is Spinal Tap* and *Man of the Year*. [*Charles Bacon*]

Alexander Folk (*police detective*), Bridget Baiss (*Gayle Hamilton*), Carl Sundstrom (*security guard*), Michael Brandon (*Jeff Littman*), Keely Sims (*Leela Kerr*), Hector Elias, John Hillard, Heather Stephens, Rick Peters, Ian Ogilvy, Charlotte Brosnan, Richard Beymer, Stoney Jackson, Scott Coffey, Kari Wuhrer, John Solari.
 Dir and Screenplay: Francis Megahy. Pro: Scott Richard Wolf. Ex Pro: Darren Sakurai. Line Pro: Erica Fox. Ph: John C. Newby. Pro Des: Sandy Grass. Ed: Hudson LeGrand. M: John Coda. Costumes: Marcelle McKay. (Makani Kai/Wobblyscope–The Bedford Communication Group.) Rel: 25 July 1997. 106 mins. Cert 15. USA. 1995.

Double Team ★¹/₂

When leading counter-terrorist expert Jack Quinn bungles an attack on a nefarious crime lord, he's forced to team up with an eccentric arms dealer in order to rescue his pregnant wife... Trapped in yet another brainless, routine actioner, Jean-Claude Van Damme is partially saved here by his colourful co-star (cross-dressing basketball icon Dennis Rodman) and the visual (if exhausting) inventiveness of his director, Hong Kong maestro Tsui Hark. But it's a close thing. Formerly known as *The Colony* and filmed in

Down in the dumps: Paul McGann rescues Susan Lynch in Bharat Nalluri's breathless *Downtime* (from Film Four)

Rome, Nice and Arles. [*Ewen Brownrigg*]

Jean-Claude Van Damme (*Jack Quinn*), Dennis Rodman (*Yaz*), Paul Freeman (*Goldsmythe*), Mickey Rourke (*Stavros*), Natacha Lindinger (*Katherine Quinn*), Valeria Cavalli (*Dr Maria Trifioli*), Jay Benedict, Joelle Devaux-Vullion, Bruno Bilotta, Rob Diem, Hans Meyer.
 Dir: Tsui Hark. Pro: Moshe Diamant. Ex Pro: Don Jakoby and David Rodgers. Co-Pro: Rick Nathanson and Nansun Shi. Screenplay: Jakoby and Paul Mones. Ph: Peter Pau. Pro Des: Marek Dobrowolski. Ed: Bill Pankow. M: Gary Chang. Costumes: Magali Guidasci. Action design: Charles Picerni. (Columbia/Mandalay Entertainment/One Story Pictures–Columbia TriStar.) Rel: 27 March 1998. 93 mins. Cert 18. USA. 1997.

Downtime ★★★

Newcastle; today. Plagued by teenage hooliganism in the near-empty tower block she lives in with her four-year-old son, Chrissy decides to take her own life. Standing on a ledge on the 21st floor, she is approached by a man who spins out fascinating facts: did she know Isaac Newton invented the cat flap? Charming her down from her perch, former police psychologist Rob finds himself strangely attracted to this angry, disturbed woman. Chrissy, however, does not accept charity kindly and rejects his offers of friendship. But soon Rob might be the last hope she has... Far from the cosy domestic war zone of Mike Leigh, a frightening new sickness is eating at the foundations of society: the soiled dignity and boredom of kids. Deprived of any reason to live, these shadows of humanity can and will do anything they damn well like. Part thriller and part social document, *Downtime* confronts very real problems in an entertaining context, which should at least get people to look and think. And, as a thriller, it is breathless stuff.

Paul McGann (*Rob*), Susan Lynch (*Chrissy*), Tom Georgeson (*Jimmy*), David Roper (*Mike*), Denise Bryson (*Jan*), David Horsefield (*Kevin*), Birdy Sweeney (*Pat*), Adam Johnston, Stephen Graham, Dale Meeks, Craig Conway.
 Dir: Bharat Nalluri. Pro: Richard Johns. Ex Pro: Nik Powell and Stephen Woolley. Co-Ex Pro: Marina Gefter. Screenplay: Caspar Berry. Ph: Tony Imi. Pro Des: Chris Townsend. Ed: Les Healey. M: Simon

Boswell. Costumes: Sarah Ryan. (Scala/Channel Four/Arts Council of England/Moving Image/Pandora Cinema/Canal Plus/National Lottery, etc.–Film Four.) Rel: 13 February 1998. 90 mins. Cert 15. UK/France. 1997.

Dream With the Fishes ★★½

The San Francisco Bay Area; the present. A voyeur by nature, Terry has become disgusted by his barren life and decides to end it all. But just as he is about to jump off a bridge, he is spotted by a passing man, Nick, who asks if he can watch. Now unable to jump, Terry reluctantly agrees to give Nick his watch in return for a bottle of sleeping pills. And so begins a most unusual liaison... An intriguing premise (culled from a real-life episode) is vividly explored in this edgy, energetic debut from writer-director Finn Taylor. But in Taylor's effort to distance his film from the conventional mainstream, he alienates his audience with tricky and pretentious photographic techniques (the manipulated contrast levels actually make the film look cheap). Still, the soundtrack is great and the abundant supply of allegory ripe for dinner party discussion.

David Arquette (*Terry*), Kathryn Erbe (*Liz*), J.E. Freeman (*Joe, Nick's father*), Brad Hunt (*Nick*), Patrick McGaw (*Don*), Cathy Moriarty (*Aunt Elise*), Timi Prulhiere, Anita Barone, Allyce Beasley, Peter Gregory, Richmond Arquette, Kristina Robbins, Peaches (*Nick's crematory ashes*).
   Dir and Screenplay: Finn Taylor. Pro: Johnny Wow and Mitchell Stein. Ex Pro: John Sideropoulos and Charles Hsiao. Co-Pro: David Arquette, Laurie A. Miller and Jeffrey Brown. Ph: Barry Stone. Pro Des: Justin McCartney. Ed: Rick Le Compte. M: Tito Larriva; numbers performed by Tindersticks, Ramsey Lewis, Lee Dorsey, The Waterboys, Wilco, The Mavericks, Patti Smith, Squirrel Nut Zippers, Jeremy Enigk, etc. Costumes: Amy Brownson. (Sony/3 Ring Circus–Columbia TriStar.) Rel: 19 June 1998. 96 mins. Cert 18. USA. 1996.

The Edge ★★★½

Escorting his supermodel wife to Alaska on a fashion shoot, the quietly spoken billionaire Charles Morse finds himself wrenched out of his element when he's stranded in the wilderness. Accompanied by his

The edge of the world: Alec Baldwin contemplates the limits of survival in Lee Tamahori's heart-pounding *The Edge* (from Fox)

wife's photographer and assistant, Morse is forced to put his theories of survival into practice as the three men battle cold, hunger and the singular intentions of a merciless Kodiak bear... Rousing, old-fashioned entertainment enhanced by the stunning scenery of Alberta, *The Edge* boasts another towering turn from Anthony Hopkins and an expertly crafted screenplay from David Mamet. Yet it will be the bear attacks that cinemagoers will remember – surely some of the most heart-pounding sequences of beast vs. man ever committed to film. Jerry Goldsmith's eerie score is another plus. Previously known as *Bookworm*, for some reason.

Anthony Hopkins (*Charles Morse*), Alec Baldwin (*Robert Green*), Elle Macpherson (*Mickey Morse*), Harold Perrineau (*Stephen*), L.Q. Jones (*Styles*), Kathleen Wilhoite, David Lindstedt, Gordon Tootoosis, Bart the Bear.
   Dir: Lee Tamahori. Pro: Art Linson. Ex Pro: Lloyd Phillips. Screenplay: David Mamet. Ph: Donald M. McAlpine. Pro Des: Wolf Kroeger. Ed: Neil Travis. M: Jerry Goldsmith. Costumes: Julie Weiss. Title design: Robert Dawson. (Fox.) Rel: 27 February 1998. 117 mins. Cert 15. USA. 1997.

8 Heads in a Duffel Bag ★★

A veteran agent for the Mob, Tommy Spinelli is entrusted with a large duffel bag of heads to deliver as evidence of a 'hit'. He has 48 hours to drop off his cargo in San Diego, California, which, for Tommy, is as routine an assignment as he could ask for. However, at San Diego Airport he picks up the wrong luggage, while his bag falls into the hands of Charlie Pritchett, a nervous medical student about to meet the snooty parents of his girlfriend. So, while Charlie attempts to dispose of the eight heads at an exclusive Mexican hotel, Spinelli dreams up a number of cruel and inventive ways to track Charlie down... Taking the oldest trick in the book – the switched suitcase routine – *8 Heads* turns out to be a mixed bag. Implausible, tasteless and over the top, the film is saved from total humiliation by a priceless turn from Joe Pesci, with fine backup supplied by David Spade and Todd Louiso as Charlie's luckless roommates. Unfortunately, the film's daring sorties into black farce fail to take off as the pace is never allowed to fly. Also, in 'the young Tom Hanks' part, newcomer Andy Comeau has neither the charisma nor a sufficient sense of irony to make this wild and woolly trip worth the fare.

Joe Pesci (*Tommy Spinelli*), Kristy Swanson (*Laurie Bennett*), David Spade (*Ernie*),

A new beginning: Andie MacDowell confronts estranged husband Bill Pullman in Wim Wenders' fascinating *The End of Violence* **(from Artificial Eye)**

George Hamilton (*Dick Bennett*), Dyan Cannon (*Annette Bennett*), Andy Comeau (*Charlie Pritchett*), Todd Louiso (*Steve*), Joe Basile (*Benny*), Ernestine Mercer (*Grandma Fern*), Anthony Mangano, Frank Roman, Howard George, Calvin Levels.

Dir and Screenplay: Tom Schulman. Pro: Brad Krevoy, Steve Stabler and John Bertolli. Ex Pro: Jeffrey D. Ivers. Co-Pro: Tim Foster. Ph: Adam Holender. Pro Des: Paul Peters. Ed: David Holden. M: Andrew Gross; numbers performed by The Contours, Toxic Pets, The Chordettes, etc. Costumes: Sanja Milkovic Hays. (Rank/Orion–Carlton.) Rel: 28 November 1997. 95 mins. Cert 15. USA/UK. 1997.

The End of Violence ★★★½

An observatory poised on a hill above Los Angeles spies on the streets below with powerful intrusion. Its eyes belong to one Ray Bering, an ex-NASA scientist, who glimpses an attack on who he is to discover is a hotshot Hollywood producer of violent movies. The producer then disappears – and his two assailants are found decapitated at the scene of the crime. The purpose of the observatory – which is linked to top-secret satellites and every traffic control camera in the city – is to put an end to violence. But its use is officially unauthorised and Ray Bering has already seen too much... Only someone as intellectually perverse as Wim Wenders could make a non-violent film about violence. Whether cutting away from a saloon brawl or relating vile acts by proxy, Wenders delivers his meditation on the state of brutality in America – and its movies in particular – with a seductive pictorial style and a strong narrative grip. Replete with the director's usual themes of technology and voyeurism, the film introduces a number of fascinating ideas and motifs into a complex structural web that constantly beguiles and fascinates. *The End of Violence* is a rare film in that it succeeds in achieving its aims, even as it is weighed down by Wenders'characteristic *longueurs*.

Bill Pullman (*Mike Max*), Andie MacDowell (*Paige Stockard*), Gabriel Byrne (*Ray Bering*), Traci Lind (*Cat*), Nicole Parker (*Ade*), Daniel Benzali (*Brice Phelps*), Loren Dean (*Doc Block*), K. Todd Freeman (*Six*), Marisol Padilla Sanchez (*Mathilda*), Udo Kier (*Zoltan Koyacs*), Peter Horton (*Brian*), Samuel Fuller (*Louis Bering*), Pruitt Taylor Vince, John Diehl, Richard Cummings, Marshall Bell, Frederic Forrest, Enrique Castillo, Aymara De Liano, Ulysses Cuadra, Victoria Duffy, Black Encyclopedia, Henry Silva, Ulises Cuadra, Karen Ross, Michael Massee, O-Lan Jones.

Dir: Wim Wenders. Pro: Wenders, Deepak Nayar and Nicholas Klein. Ex Pro: Jean-Francois Fonlupt and Ulrich Felsberg. Screenplay: Wenders and Klein. Ph: Pascal Rabaud. Pro Des and Costumes: Patricia Norris. Ed: Peter Przygodda. M: Ry Cooder; numbers performed by Raul Malo, Latin Playboys, Spain, Michael Stipe and Vic Chestnut, Los Lobos, Tom Waits, Howie B, Bono and Sinead O'Connor, Sam Phillips, Roy Orbison, Eels, Ry Cooder, etc. Sound: Elmo Weber. (CiBy 2000/Road Movies/Kintop Pictures–Artificial Eye.) Rel: 9 January 1998. 122 mins. Cert 15. USA/Germany/France. 1997.

Event Horizon ★★

Deep Space; 2047. Thirty-two years after the first permanent colony is established on the moon and fifteen years after commercial mining has commenced on Mars, the crew of the *Lewis and Clark* rescue ship fly out to the boundaries of Jupiter. Their mission: to recover any survivors of the research vessel *Event Horizon* that has mysteriously reappeared after a seven-year disappearing act. But unbeknownst to them, the *Horizon* has passed beyond the gateway of infinity – through a fold in space – and has returned to our universe in a thoroughly altered state. Carrying with it a supernatural force beyond the crew's wildest imagination, the *Event Horizon* has become the evil personification of their deepest seated guilt... While the idea itself is a good one, the premise is reduced to a highly unpleasant shambles by over-active sound design and frantic direction. One sudden bang in a thriller is allowed, but a continuous battery of sonic booms is inexcusable. The effect is like being beaten about the head repeatedly. Furthermore, little attempt has been made to flesh out the characters or to make them in the least bit sympathetic, thus depriving the film of its most indispensable ingredient: suspense.

Laurence Fishburne (*Captain Miller*), Sam Neill (*Dr William Weir*), Kathleen Quinlan (*Peters*), Joely Richardson (*Starck*), Richard T. Jones (*Cooper*), Jack Noseworthy (*Justin*), Jason Isaacs (*D.J.*), Sean Pertwee (*Smith*), Peter Marinker, Holley Chant, Barclay Wright.
   Dir: Paul Anderson. Pro: Lawrence Gordon, Lloyd Levin and Jeremy Bolt. Ex Pro: Nick Gillott. Screenplay: Philip Eisner. Ph: Adrian Biddle. Pro Des: Joseph Bennett. Ed: Martin Hunter. M: Michael Kamen. Costumes: John Mollo. Visual effects: Richard Yuricich. (Paramount/Golar/Impact Pictures–UIP.) Rel: 22 August 1997. 96 mins. Cert 18. USA. 1997.

Excess Baggage ★★
Washington state; the present. When high-tech car thief Vincent Roche steals a BMW from a multi-storey car park, he has no idea what he is taking on. In the boot he discovers a trussed-up, 18-year-old heiress who has engineered her own kidnapping (in order to fleece her father of one million dollars). Now Vincent is the chief suspect in an apocryphal abduction and is saddled with a belligerent, braless hostage with a black belt in karate... It could have been worse. It could not have had Christopher Walken or Benicio Del Toro in it (hand-picked by the film's 19-year-old producer, Alicia Silverstone). It could not have had a terrific song track. And, without the finesse of French cinematographer Jean Yves Escoffier, it could not have looked this good. But it does have

The ultimate guilt trip: Laurence Fishburne prepares for an uneasy expedition down memory lane in Paul Anderson's unpleasant *Event Horizon* (from UIP)

Alicia Silverstone in it, who lacks edge and credibility in equal doses and displays all the sex appeal of a Danish pastry (but with more calories). Marco Brambilla's sluggish direction doesn't help.

Alicia Silverstone (*Emily T. Hope*), Benicio Del Toro (*Vincent Roche*), Christopher Walken ('*Uncle' Ray Perkins*), Jack Thompson (*Alexander Hope*), Nicholas Turturro (*Stick*), Michael Bowen (*Gus*), Sally Kirkland (*Louise Doucette*), Harry Connick Jr (*Greg Kistler*), Robert Wisden, Leland Orser, Carrie Cain Sparko.
   Dir: Marco Brambilla. Pro: Bill Borden, Carolyn Kessler and (*uncredited*) Alicia Silverstone. Co-Pro: B. Casey Grant. Screenplay: Max D. Adams and Dick Clement & Ian La Frenais. Ph: Jean Yves Escoffier. Pro Des: Missy Stewart. Ed: Stephen Rivkin. M: John Lurie; numbers performed by The Dave Matthews Band, Red House Painters, Carmen McRae, Lynyrd Skynyrd, The Wallflowers, etc. Costumes: Beatrix Aruna Pasztor. (Columbia/First Kiss–Columbia TriStar.) Rel: 21 November 1997. 101 mins. Cert 12. USA. 1997.

Face ★★★★½
London's East End; today. Five professional criminals execute the ultimate heist: smashing into a 'counting house' with a makeshift battering ram, the thieves ward off staff with shotguns and are gone in just over four minutes. However, their plunder of £344,780 is a numbing disappointment, leaving them with just £60,000 apiece (after expenses). Then each member's stash is taken overnight, resulting in a dangerous flurry of suspicion and accusation. And the police are closing in... Hard-hitting, uncompromising and grippingly real, *Face* recalls British television at its best, but with a slick cinematic edge underlined by a vibrant, cutting-edge rock soundtrack (see music credits). Intelligently scripted by Ronan Bennett (who once served time at Brixton prison for 'IRA activities') and punchily directed by Antonia Bird (*Priest*), *Face* blends character, atmosphere and story with pounding finesse.

Robert Carlyle (*Ray*), Ray Winstone (*Dave*), Steven Waddington (*Stevie*), Philip Davis (*Julian*), Damon Albarn (*Jason*), Lena Headey (*Connie*), Peter Vaughan (*Sonny*), Sue Johnston (*Alice*), Christine Tremarco (*Sarah*), Andrew Tiernan (*Chris*), Steve

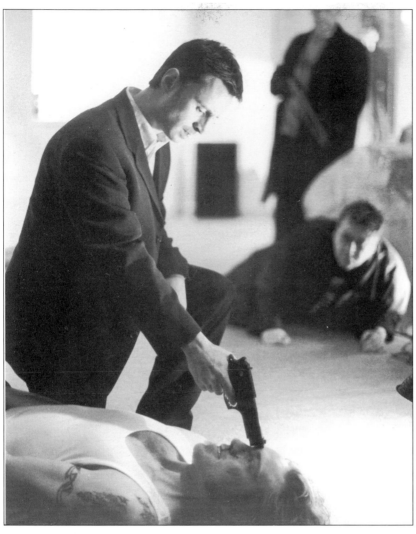

The countenance of crime: Robert Carlyle shows his mettle in Antonia Bird's hard-hitting, uncompromising *Face* (from UIP)

Face value: Nicolas Cage in John Woo's operatically gripping *Face/Off* (from Buena Vista)

Townsend. Ed: St John O'Rorke. M: Andy Roberts, Paul Conboy and Adrian Corker; numbers performed by Paul Weller, Alex Reece, Death in Vegas, The Clash, Billy Bragg, Fluke, Pigforce, New Era, Monkey, Lewis Taylor, A.P.E., Space, Gene, Longpigs, and Puressence. Costumes: Jill Taylor. (BBC Films/Distant Horizon/British Screen–UIP.) Rel: 26 September 1997. 105 mins. Cert 18. UK. 1997.

Sweeney, Gerry Conlon, Hazel Douglas, Arthur Whybrow, Elaine Lordan, Natalie Morse, Kim Taylforth.
  Dir: Antonia Bird. Pro: David M. Thompson and Elinor Day. Ex Pro: Anant Singh. Co-Pro: Paul Tivers. Assoc Pro: Helena Spring. Screenplay: Ronan Bennett. Ph: Fred Tammes. Pro Des: Chris

Face/Off ★★★★½

A biological time bomb is ticking somewhere in the heart of downtown Los Angeles. The man who planted it – Castor Troy – is in a coma and the man who designed it – his brother, Pollux – is refusing to talk. The consequences for LA are horrendous, so FBI agent Sean Archer agrees – reluctantly – to undergo drastic cosmetic surgery, literally taking on the face of the bomber. Thus, he can infiltrate the prison holding Pollux and weed out the bomb's location. Yet while Archer may look like the callous killer – complete with reconstructed physique and voice – he has to *become* him in order to survive the rigours of an internment facility so tough than Amnesty International doesn't even know it exists. Meanwhile, the real Castor Troy wakes from his coma... By establishing the stylistic extremes of his drama before the close of the opening credits, Hong Kong *wunderkind* John Woo creates his own hugely entertaining, operatic logic where virtually anything makes sense. Aided by two dedicated, larger-than-life performances – Travolta and Cage play each other! – *Face/Off* is a throat-grabbing configuration of guts, brains and balls. FYI: Shortly before the film opened in Britain an Australian surgeon announced that it was physically possible to have a full facial transplant, having just sewn back on the ripped-off face of one of his patients.

John Travolta (*Sean Archer/Castor Troy*), Nicolas Cage (*Castor Troy/Sean Archer*), Joan Allen (*Eve Archer*), Gina Gershon (*Sasha Hassler*), Alessandro Nivola (*Pollux Troy*), Dominique Swain (*Jamie Archer*), Nick Cassavetes (*Dietrich Hassler*), Colm Feore (*Dr Malcolm Walsh*), Margaret Cho (*Wanda*), Harve Presnell, John Carroll Lynch, Robert Wisdom, CCH Pounder, Jamie Denton, Matt Ross, Tommy J.

Flanagan, Chris Bauer, Lisa Boyle, Danny Masterson, Megan Paul.

Dir: John Woo. Pro: David Permut, Barrie Osborne, Terence Chang and Christopher Godsick. Ex Pro: Michael Douglas, Steven Reuther and Jonathan D. Krane. Assoc Pro: Jeff Levine. Co-Pro and Screenplay: Mike Werb and Michael Colleary. Ph: Oliver Wood. Pro Des: Neil Spisak. Ed: Christian Wagner. M: John Powell; Handel, Mozart, Chopin; numbers performed by James Brown, Tricky, Doug E. Fresh & The Get Fresh Crew, Olivia Newton-John, and INXS. Costumes: Ellen Mirojnick. Make-up effects: Kevin Yagher. (Paramount/Touchstone Pictures/WCG Entertainment–Buena Vista.) Rel: 7 November 1997. 138 mins. Cert 18. USA. 1997.

Fairy Tale – A True Story ★★★½

Cottingley Glen, Yorkshire/London; 1917. When her eight-year-old niece, Frances, comes to stay, Elsie Wright discovers that she can see the fairies 'at the bottom of the garden' for the first time since her brother died. But when Frances captures the fairies on camera, the girls' days of magic and innocence quickly become a thing of the past as the media moves in... It's quite uncanny how two films based on the same remarkable story should emerge at the same time. Furthermore, while taking entirely different angles, both projects adopt the same approach in that the fairies have the last laugh. Clearly aimed for a younger audience, *Fairy Tale – A True Story* milks the magic of its extraordinary scenario without getting bogged down in special effects or mawkish excess. A moving, enchanting film that should delight children and adults alike. P.S. While the title proclaims this to be a true story, Conan Doyle never actually met the Cottingley tricksters. Q.v. *Photographing Fairies*.

Florence Hoath (*Elsie Wright*), Elizabeth Earl (*Frances Griffiths*), Paul McGann (*Arthur Wright*), Phoebe Nicholls (*Polly Wright*), Harvey Keitel (*Harry Houdini*), Peter O'Toole (*Sir Arthur Conan Doyle*), Bill Nighy (*E.L. Gardner*), Tim McInnerny (*John Ferret*), Bob Peck (*Harry Briggs*), Anthony Calf, Chris Williams, Anton Lesser, Jim Wiggins, Peter Wight, Lynn Farleigh, David Calder, Benjamin Whitrow, John Grillo, Christopher Godwin, Barbara Hicks, Tom Georgeson, Anna Chancellor, Don Henderson, Isabel Rocamora, and (*uncredited*) Mel Gibson.

Smiles of a summer sprite: Florence Hoath and Elizabeth Earl in Charles Sturridge's enchanting *Fairy Tale – A True Story* (from Warner)

Dir: Charles Sturridge. Pro: Wendy Finerman and Bruce Davey. Ex Pro: Paul Tucker. Screenplay: Ernie Contreras, from a story by Contreras, Albert Ash and Tom McLoughlin. Ph: Michael Coulter. Pro Des: Michael Howells. Ed: Peter Coulson. M: Zbigniew Preisner. Costumes: Shirley Russell. Visual effects: Tim Webber. (Icon Prods–Warner.) Rel: 13 February 1998. 98 mins. Cert U. USA. 1997.

Fallen ★★★½

Philadelphia; the present. Shortly before his execution, demonic serial killer Edgar Reese poses a riddle to homicide detective John Hobbes and starts babbling in an ancient language. After his death, Reese's trademark killings continue and Hobbes finds himself pursuing a most unconventional line of enquiry... Taking its stylistic cue from *Seven*, Gregory Hoblit's dark, moody and edgily photographed thriller eases into *Exorcist/Omen* territory with some skill. Annotated with biblical references and the disturbing images of Hieronymus Bosch, *Fallen* stakes out its boundaries with theological authority, keeping silliness at bay with controlled performances and a creditable score from the classical composer Tan Dun. With a dearth of decent supernatural thrillers in recent years, *Fallen* is a welcome addition to the genre.

Denzel Washington (*John Hobbes*), John Goodman (*Jonesy*), Donald Sutherland (*Lt Stanton*), Embeth Davidtz (*Gretta Milano*), James Gandolfini (*Lou*), Elias Koteas (*Edgar Reese*), Gabriel Casseus (*Art*), Michael J. Pagan (*Sam*), Aida Turturro (*Tiffany*), Robert Joy, Frank Medrano, Tara Carnes, Wendy Cutler, Jill Holden.

Dir: Gregory Hoblit. Pro: Charles Roven and Dawn Steel. Ex Pro: Elon Dershowitz, Nicholas Kazan, Robert Cavallo and Ted Kurdyla. Screenplay: Kazan. Ph: Newton Thomas Sigel. Pro Des: Terence Marsh. Ed: Lawrence Jordan. M: Tan Dun; 'Time Is On My Side' sung by The Rolling Stones; other numbers performed by Robert Wait, Beck, and Me'shell Ndegeocello. Costumes: Colleen Atwood. (Turner Pictures/Atlas Entertainment–Warner.) Rel: 13 March 1998. 127 mins. Cert 15. USA. 1998.

Father's Day ★★

Los Angeles/San Francisco/Sacramento/Reno; today. When the 16-year-old son of Colette Andrews runs away from home, she contacts two of her past lovers in a last-ditch attempt to rally help. Thus, she reveals to Jack Lawrence, a successful, happily married attorney, and to Dale Putley, a suicidal avante garde poet, that they have a fifty-fifty chance of being Scott's father. As dissimilar as chalk and Cheshire, Jack and Dale have to iron out their differences to track down the boy that may be their son... While occasionally amusing and never less than pleasing, *Father's Day* just isn't funny enough or ingenious enough to take off. Billy Crystal certainly has his moments, though, and in a quietly tooled, low-key performance he steals the movie from Robin Williams' grotesque, childlike caricature. Based on the 1983 French film *Les Comperes*, which starred Gerard Depardieu and Pierre Richard.

Robin Williams (*Dale Putley*), Billy Crystal (*Jack Lawrence*), Julia Louis-Dreyfus (*Carrie Lawrence*), Nastassja Kinski (*Colette Andrews*), Charlie Hofheimer (*Scott Andrews*), Bruce Greenwood (*Bob Andrews*), Dennis Burkley (*Mr Calvin*), Haylie Johnson (*Nikki*), Jared Harris (*Lee*), Charles Rocket, Patti D'Arbanville, Louis Lombardi, Alan Berger, Jennifer Crystal [*Billy's daughter*], Jason Reitman, Ricky Harris, Paul Herman, Catherine Reitman, Susan Traylor, Harry E. Northup, Frank Medrano, Caroline Reitman, Mel Gibson (*rock groupie*).
 Dir: Ivan Reitman. Pro: Reitman and Joel Silver. Ex Pro: Joe Medjuck, Daniel Goldberg and Francis Veber. Co-Pro: Gordon Webb and Karyn Fields. Screenplay: Lowell Ganz and Babaloo Mandel. Ph: Stephen H. Burum. Pro Des: Thomas Sanders. Ed: Sheldon Kahn and Wendy Greene Bricmont. M: James Newton Howard; numbers performed by

Reel Big Fish, Sugar Ray, Lyle Lovett, The Specials, Merle Haggard, Sly & The Family Stone, The Mighty Mighty Bosstones, and The Muffs. Costumes: Rita Ryack. (Warner/Silver Pictures/Northern Lights Entertainment–Warner.) Rel: 10 October 1997. 99 mins. Cert 12. USA. 1997.

Fetishes ★★★★

This documentary may break taboos by examining the sexual inclinations of the rich clients who seek mistresses and domination at Manhattan's Pandora's Box, but filmmaker Nick Broomfield's approach is exactly right. He himself talks to staff and punters showing as much as they allow, ranging from bondage to adults acting as children in need of discipline. There's no sensationalism, no condemnation: just a gentle concern to investigate, learn and form an attitude from that. Not everyone will want to confront such issues, but the film is insightful, and it is significant that many fetishes seem to have grown out of childhood incidents. *Fetishes* is wide ranging and on occasion unexpectedly amusing, but essentially it is a serious study not afraid to pose the right probing questions. [*Mansel Stimpson*]

With Mistress Natasha, Mistress Catherine, Mistress Delilah, Mistress Raven.
 Dir: Nick Broomfield. Pro: Broomfield and Michelle D'Acosta. Ex Pro: Sheila

Nevins. Co-Pro: Jamie Ader-Brown. Assoc Pro: Nancy Abraham. Line Pro: S.J. Bloom. Ph: Christophe Lanzenberg. Ed: Broomfield and Betty Burkhart. M: Jamie Muhoberac. (Lafayette Film/HBO–Bluelight.) Rel: 5 September 1997. 84 mins. No Cert. UK. 1996.

First Strike

See *Jackie Chan's First Strike*.

Flubber ★

Professor Phillip Brainard is so preoccupied with his search for a new source of energy that he's left his fiancée standing at the altar, not once, but twice. He now has just a few hours left to meet his third – and last – nuptial deadline. But then, if his magical formula for the creation of 'flying rubber' doesn't come off, the fate of Medfield College will be in the balance. And Brainard's fiancée is the president... Ostensibly a remake of Disney's 1961 *The Absent Minded Professor*, *Flubber* is actually an excuse for writer-producer John Hughes to recycle his old formula of sadistic farce welded to sticky sentimentality. Thus, the endearing stereotype of the abstracted scientist is reduced to a caricature of genuine retardation, stretching the bounds of credibility to new levels of irritation. Does for slapstick what *Jingle All the Way* did for Christmas. FYI: Jodi Benson, who supplies the voice of the professor's pet flying saucer, Weebo, was also the voice of Ariel in Disney's *The Little Mermaid*.

Robin Williams (*Professor Phillip Brainard*), Marcia Gay Harden (*Sara Jean Reynolds*),

The Nutty Professor: Robin Williams is flubbergasted in Les Mayfield's irritating *Flubber* (from Buena Vista)

Christopher McDonald (*Wilson Crof*),
Raymond J. Barry (*Chester Hoenicker*),
Clancy Brown (*Smith*), Ted Levine
(*Wesson*), Wil Wheaton (*Bennett Hoenicker*),
Jodi Benson (*voice of Weebo*), Edie McClurg,
Leslie Stefanson, Malcolm Brownson,
Benjamin Brock, Dakin Matthews, Bob
Sarlatte.

Dir: Les Mayfield. Pro: John Hughes
and Ricardo Mestres. Ex Pro: David
Nicksay. Co-Pro: Michael Polaire.
Screenplay: Hughes and Bill Walsh.
Ph: Dean Cundey. Pro Des: Andrew
McAlpine. Ed: Harvey Rosenstock.
M: Danny Elfman. Costumes: April Ferry.
Visual effects: Peter Crosman, Tom Bertino
and Douglas Hans Smith. (Walt Disney/
Great Oaks–Buena Vista.) Rel: 6 February
1998. 93 mins. Cert U. USA. 1997.

Fools Rush In ★★

Alex Whitman is a hard-working,
hard-playing, strait-laced Presbyterian
New Yorker who loves his work.
Isabel Fuentes is a hot-blooded,
carefree, spiritually driven Mexican
Catholic who's devoted to her family.
In Las Vegas to supervise the
construction of a glitzy new nightclub, Alex meets Isabel in the queue
for a loo and they end up in bed for
one night. Three months later, Isabel
turns up on Alex's doorstep with the
news that she is pregnant. She's not
expecting anything from Alex, but
she felt he ought to know. She does,
however, intend to keep the baby...
Easy on the eye and comfortable on
the ear (see music credits), *Fools Rush
In* is the cinematic equivalent of a
light snack at an up-market fast food
establishment (probably Planet
Hollywood). Matthew Perry and
Salma Hayek are an engaging
enough couple for you to want
them to make a go of it, although,
personally, I wouldn't wish Hayek
on anybody, particularly myself.
That fiery temperament and taste in
interior decorating just wouldn't do.
FYI: The actor who plays Matthew
Perry's father is actually Matthew
Perry's father.

Matthew Perry (*Alex Whitman*), Salma
Hayek (*Isabel Fuentes*), Jon Tenney (*Jeff*),
Carlos Gomez (*Chuy*), Tomas Milian
(*Tomas Fuentes*), Jill Clayburgh (*Nan
Whitman*), Siobhan Fallon (*Lanie*), Suzanne
Snyder (*Cathy Stewart*), John Bennett Perry,
Stanley DeSantis, Anne Betancourt,
Angelina Calderon Torres, Andrew Hill
Newman, Michael Badalucco.

Dir: Andy Tennant. Pro: Doug Draizin.
Ex Pro: Michael McDonnell. Co-Pro: Anna

Maria Davis. Screenplay: Katherine
Reback, from a story by Reback and Joan
Taylor. Ph: Robbie Greenberg. Pro Des:
Edward Pisoni. Ed: Roger Bondelli. M:
Alan Silvestri; numbers performed by Burl
Ives, Elvis Presley, The Iguanas, Dean
Martin, Gloria Estefan, Brave Combo,
Mariachi Vargas De Tecalitlan, Peggy Lee,
Luscious Jackson, Chris Isaak, Wayne
Newton, etc. Costumes: Kimberly A.
Tillman. (Columbia Pictures–Columbia
TriStar.) Rel: 31 October 1997. 109 mins.
Cert 12. USA. 1997.

For Roseanna

See *Roseanna's Grave*.

Free Willy 3: The Rescue ★★★

When Max turns ten, he is invited to
accompany his father on a fishing
trip off the coast of the Pacific North-
west. A seasoned fisherman, Max's
father is an icon in the young boy's
eyes – until, that is, Max confronts
the reality of his father's trade.
Meanwhile, Jesse, now 17, takes a
summer job as general dogsbody
with an oceanic research team that
includes his old friend and mentor
Randolph. In the last two years, the
population of the orca – or killer
whale – has decreased by ten per
cent, and Jesse's employers are
determined to find out why. Max
knows why, but how can a ten-year-
old boy betray the man that he has
always idolised? Featuring the glossy
production values associated with
Warner's cetacean franchise (arty
photography, rhapsodic music), *Free
Willy 3* treads dramatic water for
much of its running time, but then
delivers a rousing finale in keeping
with the series' Save the Whales
motif. And, in light of the crisis
facing the fishing industry, its
message could not be more critical
or timely.

Jason James Richter (*Jesse*), August
Schellenberg (*Randolph Johnson*), Annie
Corley (*Drew*), Vincent Berry (*Max Wesley*),
Patrick Kilpatrick (*John Wesley*), Tasha
Simms (*Mary*), Peter Lacroix, Stephen E.
Miller, Ian Tracey.

Dir: Sam Pillsbury. Pro: Jennie Lew
Tugend. Ex Pro: Lauren Shuler Donner,
Richard Donner and Arnon Milchan.
Screenplay: John Mattson, based on
characters created by Keith A. Walker. Ph:
Tobias Schliessler. Pro Des: Brent Thomas.
Ed: Margie Goodspeed. M: Cliff Eidelman;

numbers performed by The Doobie
Brothers, The Skydiggers, The Reverend
Horton Heat, and Little Charlie and The
NightCats. Costumes: Maya Mani.
(Warner/Monarchy Enterprises/Regency
Enterprises–Warner.) Rel: 17 October 1997.
85 mins. Cert U. USA. 1997.

Full Contact – Xia Dao Gao Fei ★★★

Bangkok/Hong Kong; 1992. 'Fear
is no excuse.' So says Jeff, an
indestructible, knife-juggling crook
who's just been betrayed by
everyone but the milkman. However,
being a man of honour, Jeff slings his
enemies just enough rope to excuse
or hang themselves... Pushing the
John Woo envelope, Hong Kong
filmmaker Ringo Lam fills the screen
with fog, close-ups and bullets in
slow motion, not to mention a lot of
very nasty – if fleeting – bursts of
violence. The story is barely
interesting enough to attract a
Hollywood remake (Tarantino
translated Ringo's *City on Fire* into
Reservoir Dogs), but the director's
visual style is in-your-face enough to
guarantee a heroic following.

Chow Yun Fat (*Jeff*), Simon Yam (*Judge*),
Anthony Wong (*Sam*), Ann Bridgewater
(*Mona*), Bonnie Fu (*Virgin*), Nam Yin, Lee
Kin-Sang, Frankie Chin.

Dir and Pro: Ringo Lam. Ex Pro and
Screenplay: Nam Yin. Line Pro: Wellington
W. Fung. Ph: Lau Hung-Chuen, Joe Chan
and Paul Chan. Art: Ray Lam. Ed: Tony
Chow. M: Teddy Robin Kwan. Costumes:
Bruce Yu. (Golden Princess–Made In Hong
Kong.) Rel: 14 November 1997. 97 mins.
Cert 18. Hong Kong. 1992.

The Full Monty ★★★★★

Opening with a priceless old
travelogue called Sheffield – City
On the Move, *The Full Monty*
plunges its tongue firmly into its
cheek. Cutting to the present, the
film reveals a Sheffield that couldn't
be more stationery, with poverty,
unemployment and low morale the
order of the day. Divorced and
jobless, ex-steel welder Gaz is
determined to pony up the £700 he
needs to finance joint custody of his
nine-year-old son. Noting the
hysteria that greets a local gig by the
Chippendales, Gaz reckons that he
could make a tidy bundle if he and
his mates were prepared to go the
whole way – the 'full monty'. But

Naked necessity: Robert Carlyle goes the whole way in Peter Cattaneo's spirited *The Full Monty* (from Fox Searchlight)

how can he persuade his overweight and pigeon-chested friends to 'jiggle about in the buff'? Replete with telling detail and unexpected moments (like Dave fixing the engine of a man who's trying to asphyxiate himself in his car), *The Full Monty* is that funny, truthful breed of British comedy that we should be bloody proud of, right? Yet, in spite of some hysterical sequences, the film also touches on a number of issues seldom explored in the cinema (such as Dave's eating disorder).

Top marks, then, to Simon Beaufoy's witty and insightful script, Peter Cattaneo's breezy direction, Anne Dudley's joyous score and a cast that goes beyond the call of duty.

Robert Carlyle (*Gaz*), Tom Wilkinson (*Gerald*), Mark Addy (*Dave*), Hugo Speer (*Guy*), Paul Barber (*Horse*), Steve Huison (*Lomper*), Emily Woof (*Mandy*), Lesley Sharp (*Jeanie*), William Snape (*Nathan*), Deirdre Costello (*Linda*), Bruce Jones (*Reg*), Paul Butterworth, Dave Hill, Andrew Livingstone, Vinny Dhillon.
   Dir: Peter Cattaneo. Pro: Uberto Pasolini. Co-Pro: Polly Leys and Paul Bucknor. Assoc Pro: Lesley Stewart. Screenplay: Simon Beaufoy. Ph: John De Borman. Pro Des: Max Gottlieb. Ed: Nick Moore and David Freeman. M: Anne Dudley; numbers performed by The British Steel Stockbridge Band, Gary

Glitter, M People, Donna Summer, Hot Chocolate, Serge Gainsbourg and Jane Birkin, Wilson Pickett, Steve Harley and Cockney Rebel, Sister Sledge, Tom Jones, and Irene Cara. Costumes: Jill Taylor. (Fox Searchlight/Redwave Films/Channel Four–Fox.) Rel: 29 August 1997. 91 mins. Cert 15. USA/UK. 1997.

A Further Gesture ★★½

Ronan Bennett's screenplay tells of a disillusioned IRA prisoner escaping from an Irish jail and settling in New York. He then helps the girl he has come to love, a Guatemalan refugee, in the political assassination of a torturer. The film is seen by some as sympathetic to the IRA and by others as the tale of a failed bid to escape from a commitment to violence, which seems to prove my own contention that the script fails to get to grips with what it wants to say. A pity, because Robert Dornhelm's direction is able and the cast impressive, but you can't make real breaks without straw. [*Mansel Stimpson*]

Stephen Rea (*Dowd*), Alfred Molina (*Tulio*), Rosana Pastor (*Monica*), Brendan Gleeson (*Richard*), Pruitt Taylor Vince (*Scott*), Jorge Sanz (*Paco*), Frankie McCafferty, Sean McGinley, Paul Ronan, Maria Doyle Kennedy, Catriona Hinds, Paul Giamatti, Caroline Seymour.
   Dir: Robert Dornhelm. Pro: Chris Curling. Ex Pro: Michiyo Yoshizaki, Rod Stoneman and Ulrich Felsberg. Co-Pro: Bonnie Timmermann and David Collins. Assoc Pro: Laurie Borg. Screenplay: Ronan Bennett, based on an idea by Stephen Rea. Ph: Andrzej Sekula. Pro Des: Kalina Ivanov and Tom McCullagh. Ed: Masahiro Hirakubo. M: John Keane; numbers performed by Black 47, U2, Miles Pena, etc. Costumes: Stephanie Maslansky and Maggie Donnelly. (Channel Four/NDF International/Pony Canyon/Road Movies, etc.–Film Four.) Rel: 12 December 1997. 101 mins. Cert 15. UK/Germany/Japan/Ireland. 1996.

Gallivant ★★

Steering his 85-year-old grandmother and seven-year-old daughter on a trip around the coastline of Britain, experimental filmmaker Andrew Kotting has created a home movie of astonishing tedium and self-indulgence. The concept itself – an odyssey chronicling the landscape and people of this green and pleasant land – is highly promising, particularly as viewed through the eyes of two such extreme beings. Yet Kotting has jazzed the whole thing up with speeded-up film, monochromatic inserts and arbitrary film clips (including a scene from a scratchy old black and white western!), transferring his personal journey into one of cinematic self-indulgence. Yet for all of Kotting's pretentious tinkering in the editing room, the spontaneous charm of the characters he encounters along the way seeps through (the proud proprietor of a public loo in Kyle of Lochalsh is priceless). Ultimately, it's people themselves that make cinema unforgettable.

With: Gladys Morris and Eden Kotting.
Dir: Andrew Kotting. Pro: Ben Woolford. Ex Pro: Ben Gibson and Andy Powell. Ph: N.G. Smith. Ed: Cliff West. M: David Burnand. (Tall Stories/BFI/Channel Four/National Lottery–Electric.) Rel: 19 September 1997. 103 mins. Cert 15. UK. 1996.

The Gambler ★★

St Petersburg; 1866-70. Cornered by the mounting costs of her father's medical bills and the prospect of marriage to a dull government employee, Anna Snitkina, a 20-year-

A novel wager: Michael Gambon as a creatively blossoming Dostoevsky, in Karoly Makk's *The Gambler* (from Film Four)

Set and unmatched: Michael Douglas and acquaintance in David Fincher's relentless and fascinating *The Game* (from PolyGram)

old stenographer, agrees to work for a local writer for the sum of 50 rubles. As it turns out, the writer is one Fyodor Mikhailovich Dostoevsky, who has just 27 days to knock out a 200-page novel or forfeit the rights to all his past and future work. As Dostoevsky cannot guarantee Anna's wages unless he reaches his fantastical deadline, Anna takes a gamble on her future while her sexuality is liberated by the fires of Dostoevsky's imagination... Focusing on an undeniably intriguing episode in the life of an extraordinary writer, *The Gambler* none the less offers precious little material to sustain an entire feature film. Even with scenes from the unfolding novel slotted artfully into the circumstances of their creation, the concept remains dramatically flimsy. In addition, a madly miscast Michael Gambon conveys little of the author's sexual charisma (for a start, Gambon is 11 years older than Dostoevsky was at the time), leaving the 88-year-old, double Oscar-winner Luise Rainer to steal the film (in only her second screen appearance in 54 years).

Michael Gambon (*Fyodor Mikhailovich Dostoevsky*), Jodhi May (*Anna Grigorievna Snitkina*), Polly Walker (*Polina*), Dominic West (*Alexei*), John Wood (*the general*), Angeline Ball (*Blanche*), Luise Rainer (*grandmother*), Johan Leysen (*De Grieux*), Thom Jansen (*Stellovsky*), William Houston (*Pasha Isaev*), Mark Lacey (*Ivan*), Patrick Godfrey, Lucy Davis.
Dir: Karoly Makk. Pro: Marc Vlessing and Charles Cohen. Co-Pro: Rene Seegers. Screenplay: Cohen, Katharine Ogden and Nick Dear. Ph: Jules van den Steenhoven. Pro Des: Ben van Os. Ed: Kevin Whelan. M: Brian Lock; Tchaikovsky. Costumes: Dien van Straalen. Sound: Wim Vonk. (Trendraise Co./Channel Four/UGC DA/Hungry Eye Pictures/KRO Drama, etc.–Film Four.) Rel: 7 November 1997. 97 mins. Cert 15. UK/Netherlands/Hungary. 1997.

The Game ★★★★★

San Francisco; today. An investment banker worth $600 million, Nicholas Van Orton leads an ordered, sterile life of unquestionable power. As ruthless in the boardroom as he is in his own routine, Van Orton uses his position to keep out the ghosts of his past. However, one such spectre – his troubled younger brother, Conrad – presents him with an unusual gift

The science of discrimination: Ethan Hawke (right) regards his alter ego in Andrew Niccol's mind-boggling *Gattaca* (from Columbia TriStar)

token for his 48th birthday. It is a subscription to an enigmatic outfit called Consumer Recreation Services (CRS), a company that tailors elaborate games to suit each client. Although not a man to indulge in petty recreation, Van Orton finds that his curiosity gets the better of him. But as soon as he commits himself to *The Game*, his meticulous world starts to disintegrate as the stakes climb higher and higher... Exerting the same dark mastery he displayed with *Seven*, director David Fincher plays out this gripping psychological thriller with consummate skill. Relentlessly dragging the viewer into its fascinating, labyrinthine plot, the film invents new rules as it gamely enters fresh cinematic waters. Both gripping and original, *The Game* shapes up to be the ultimate blood sport.

Michael Douglas (*Nicholas Van Orton*), Sean Penn (*Conrad Van Orton*), James Rebhorn (*Jim Feingold*), Deborah Kara Unger (*Christine*), Peter Donat (*Sam Sutherland*), Carroll Baker (*Ilsa*), Armin Mueller-Stahl (*Anson Baer*), Anna Katarina (*Elizabeth*), Daniel Schorr (*himself*), Jack Kehoe (*Lt Sullivan*), Linda Manz (*Amy*), Charles Martinet, Scott Hunter McGuire, Elizabeth Dennehy, Caroline Barclay,

Kimberly Russell, James Brooks, Tommy Flanagan, John Cassini, Keena Turner, Jeffrey Michael Young, Mark Boone Junior, Christopher John Fields, John Hammil.
    Dir: David Fincher. Pro: Steve Golin and Cean Chaffin. Ex Pro: Jonathan Mostow. Co-Pro: John Brancato and Michael Ferris. Screenplay: Brancato and Ferris. Ph: Harris Savides. Pro Des: Jeffrey Beecroft. Ed: James Haygood. M: Howard Shore; Debussy; numbers performed by Vise Grip & The Ambassadors, The Red Clay Ramblers, Jefferson Airplane, Matthew Sweet, etc. Costumes: Michael Kaplan. Sound: Ren Klyce. Caterers: The Cast Supper. (PolyGram/Propaganda–PolyGram.) Rel: 10 October 1997. 128 mins. Cert 15. USA. 1997.

Gattaca ★★★½

In the not too distant future, genetic engineering has become such an art form that parents are able to choose which characteristics they would like their children to have: blonde hair, blue eyes, fair skin and so on. In addition, defective genes are a thing of the past, resulting in a new breed of maximum achievers. Vincent Freeman, however, is a 'God-child', an 'in-valid', born from a moment of passion rather than a premeditated act of science. Thus, he is a seething mass of defective genes: short sighted, vertically challenged, at the mercy of his emotions and genetically 'programmed' to die in his early 30s. But Vincent's human resolve to become a member of the elite

personnel at the astronautical Gattaca Corporation – by fair means or foul – may just transcend his 'weaknesses'... Exploring the ramifications surrounding the ethics of genetic tampering, *Gattaca* is awash with mind-boggling concepts. Returning to the antiseptic, dystopian view of the future promoted by such sci-fi dramas as *THX 1138* and *Logan's Run*, the film is guilty of a certain dramatic sterility, but makes up for it in sheer style and intelligence. Formerly known as *The Eighth Day*.

Ethan Hawke (*Vincent Freeman/Jerome Eugene Morrow*), Uma Thurman (*Irene*), Alan Arkin (*Det. Hugo*), Jude Law (*Jerome Eugene Morrow*), Loren Dean (*Anton*), Gore Vidal (*Director Josef*), Ernest Borgnine (*Caesar*), Blair Underwood, Xander Berkeley, Tony Shalhoub, Jayne Brook, Elias Koteas, Elizabeth Dennehy, Mason Gamble, Vincent Nielson, Chad Christ, William Lee Scott, Gabrielle Reece, Ryan Dorin.
    Dir and Screenplay: Andrew Niccol. Pro: Danny DeVito, Michael Shamberg and Stacey Sher. Co-Pro: Gail Lyon. Ph: Slawomir Idziak. Pro Des: Jan Roelfs. Ed: Lisa Zeno Churgin. M: Michael Nyman. Costumes: Colleen Atwood. (Columbia Pictures/Jersey Films–Columbia TriStar.) Rel: 20 March 1998. 106 mins. Cert 15. USA. 1997.

The General ★★★½

Dublin; 1962-1994. Martin Cahill, nicknamed The General, was a hardened criminal who taunted the police, railed against the church, condemned the use and abuse of drugs and repeatedly made his sister-in-law pregnant. He also gave away his spoils to the poor, yet exacted shocking revenge on those who dared to lie to him... Like the title character, *The General* is a big, brawny bear of a film with lashings of charm and even some unexpected flashes of humour. However, unlike its colourful protagonist, it's been printed in black and white (from colour film) so as to summon up a nostalgic ambience and to focus on the 'intensity' of the drama. This is a dubious move, as the conceit actually detracts from the reality of the piece (John Boorman claims we dream in black and white, but I most certainly dream in colour!). Nevertheless, as the brutal, playful Cahill, Brendan Gleeson (*I Went*

Down), is truly in his element, which is more than can be said for Jon Voight, who, as an Irish bobby, is completely out of place. This folly aside, *The General* is actually a splendid piece of storytelling, throwing a compassionate light on a fascinating, paradoxical figure of recent Irish history. Previously known as *I Once Had a Life*.

Brendan Gleeson (*Martin Cahill*), Adrian Dunbar (*Noel Curley*), Sean McGinley (*Gary*), Maria Doyle Kennedy (*Frances*), Angeline Ball (*Tina*), Jon Voight (*Inspector Ned Kenny*), Eanna McLiam (*Jimmy*), Eamon Owens (*young Martin Cahill*), Tom Murphy, Paul Hickey, Tommy O'Neill, John O'Toole, Ciaran Fitzgerald, Colleen O'Neill, Ronan Wilmot, Lynn Cahill, David Wilmot, Barry McGovern, Peter Hugo Daly, Brendan Coyle, Jim Sheridan, Des O'Malley.

   Dir, Pro and Screenplay: John Boorman. Ex Pro: Kieran Corrigan. Ph: Seamus Deasy. Pro Des: Derek Wallace. Ed: Ron Davis. M: Richie Buckley; numbers performed by Van Morrison, and Brendan Gleeson. Costumes: Maeve Paterson. (Nattore/Merlin Films/J&M Entertainment–Warner.) Rel: 29 May 1998. 124 mins. Cert 15. Ireland/UK. 1998.

Military strategy: Brendan Gleeson is threatened by Jon Voight in John Boorman's brawny, humorous *The General* (from Warner)

George of the Jungle ★★★¹⁄₂

On safari in Africa, American heiress Ursula Stanhope is rescued from the clutches of a lion by the intervention of 'George', a linguistically challenged young man sporting nothing but a 'butt flap'. At first concerned about getting back to civilisation, Ursula quickly warms to her companion's unorthodox life-style, while George discovers an untapped 'stirring of special feelings' for his new mate... What is basically a very silly premise updated from the 1967-70 cartoon (itself a spoof of *Tarzan*), *George of the Jungle* is so energetic, playful and inventive that it should thrill children while keeping their parents pleasantly amused. Brendan Fraser perfectly captures the goofy innocence of George (and, after four months of weight training, displays a physique to capture the female audience), while Leslie Mann is an appropriately loopy romantic foil. Furthermore, seldom have special effects been used to such comic effect, whether transforming George's faithful elephant into a frisky mutt or

bringing a degree of painful cognizance to the countenance of a lion. Great family entertainment.

Brendan Fraser (*George Primate*), Leslie Mann (*Ursula Stanhope*), Thomas Haden Church (*Lyle Van de Groot*), Holland Taylor (*Beatrice Stanhope*), Richard Roundtree (*Kwame*), John Cleese (*the voice of Ape*), Greg Cruttwell (*Max*), Abraham Benrubi (*Thor*), Kelly Miller (*Betsy*), John Bennett Perry (*Arthur Stanhope*), Tai (*Shep*), Michael Chinyamurindi, Abdoulaye N'gom, Lydell Cheshier, Sven-Ole Thorsen, Mayor Willie L. Brown Jr. Narrator: Keith Scott.

   Dir: Sam Weisman. Pro: David Hoberman, Jordan Kerner and Jon Avnet. Ex Pro: C. Tad Devlin. Co-Pro: Lou Arkoff. Screenplay: Dana Olsen and Audrey Wells, based upon characters developed by Jay Ward. Ph: Thomas Ackerman. Pro

The jungle kook: Brendan Fraser with Leslie Mann in Sam Weisman's energetic, playful *George of the Jungle* (from Buena Vista)

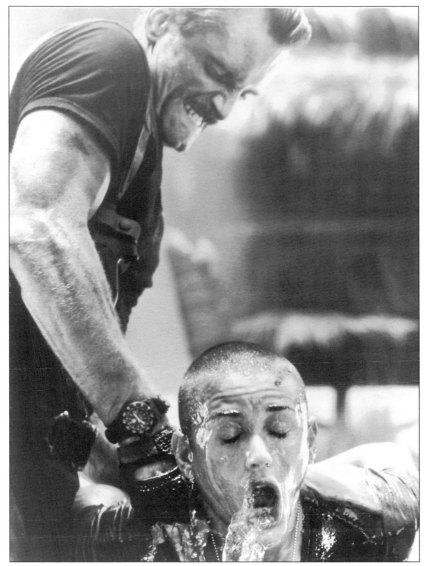

Naval gazing: Viggo Mortensen gives his producer Demi Moore the water treatment in Ridley Scott's muscular *G.I. Jane* (from First Independent)

Des: Stephen Marsh. Ed: Stuart Pappe and Roger Bondelli. M: Marc Shaiman; Beethoven, Haydn; numbers performed by The Presidents of the United States of America, Shaggy, Marvin Gaye, John Cleese, etc. Costumes: Lisa Jensen. Sound: Peter Pav. Visual effects: Tim Landry. Creature effects: Jim Henson's Creature Shop. (Walt Disney / Mandeville Films– Buena Vista.) Rel: 19 December 1997. 93 mins. Cert U. USA. 1997.

Get on the Bus ★★★

On 16 October 1995 a number of black men and boys (a figure put as high as 1.5 million by some estimates) converged on Washington DC from all over the United States. Instigated by the activist Louis Farrakhan as a show of historical solidarity for the black movement, the 'Million Man March' turned out to be a hugely successful – and peaceful – rally for positive change in the African-American community. Shortly afterwards, Spike Lee committed to direct this $2.4 million film inspired by the event, and less than six months later principal photography began. 'Completely funded by 15 African-American men' (including Danny Glover, Will Smith and Wesley Snipes), *Get On the Bus* chronicles the coach journey of 12 strangers from South Central LA to Washington to attend the gathering. Employing his characteristic gimmickry – the use of fast cutting, video playback, black and white inserts, hand-held camera – Spike Lee does manage to overcome such irritations by creating a mood of infectious vivacity. In its attempt to present a microcosm of African-American society, Reggie Rock Blythewood's script is a tad schematic (he's given us a cop, homosexual, actor, thief, social worker, Muslim, film student and so on), but does reap the rewards with some sparkling and provocative dialogue.

Richard Belzer (*Rick*), DeAundre Bonds (*Junior*), Andre Braugher (*Flip*), Thomas Jefferson Byrd (*Evan Thomas Sr*), Gabriel Casseus (*Jamal*), Albert Hall (*Craig*), Hill Harper (*Xavier*), Harry Lennix (*Randall Royale*), Bernie Mac (*Jay*), Wendell Pierce (*Wendell*), Roger Guenveur Smith (*Gary*), Isaiah Washington (*Kyle*), Steve White (*Mike*), Ossie Davis (*Jeremiah*), Charles S. Dutton (*George*), Joie Lee, Kristin Wilson, and (*uncredited*) Randy Quaid.

Dir and Ex Pro: Spike Lee. Pro: Reuben Cannon, Bill Borden and Barry Rosenbush. Screenplay: Reggie Rock Bythewood. Ph: Elliot Davis. Pro Des: Ina Mayhew. Ed: Leander T. Sales. M: Terence Blanchard; numbers performed by Michael Jackson, James Brown, Strictly Difficult, A Tribe Called Quest, The Everly Brothers, Marc Dorsey, Earth Wind & Fire, Stevie Wonder, The Impressions, The Neville Brothers, Curtis Mayfield, etc. Costumes: Sandra Hernandez. (Columbia / 40 Acres &

Bus boy: That fine character actor Ossie Davis displays his considerable talent in Spike Lee's provocative *Get on the Bus* (from Columbia TriStar)

a Mule / A Spike Lee Joint–Columbia TriStar.) Rel: 11 July 1997. 122 mins. Cert 15. USA. 1996.

G.I. Jane ★★★★

In a move to promote female equality in the US navy, a Washington body selects a PR dream to represent their political agenda. Beautiful, intelligent, athletic and career-driven, Jordan O'Neil more than lives up to Washington's expectations as the first woman to enrol in the rigorous navy SEAL training programme. However, the scheme turns out to be just a propaganda exercise and when Jordan starts shaming her male colleagues in 'the most intensive military training known to man', the programme must be scrapped. But nobody knew quite how tough a scapegoat they had taken on... Juggling feminist and political agendas with muscular finesse, *G.I. Jane* quickly transcends its *Rocky* meets *Private Benjamin* scenario and moves into gripping polemical territory. Both an emotional and moral workout, the film raises a number of challenging issues, while never swerving from its aim to engross and entertain. As the tough-as-nails political time bomb, producer and star Demi Moore rises to the formidable demands of her role, obliterating the prospect of any other actress in the role (although, ten years ago, Debra Winger would have been perfect).

Demi Moore (*Lt Jordan O'Neil*), Viggo Mortensen (*Command Master Chief John Urgayle*), Anne Bancroft (*Senator Lillian DeHaven*), Jason Beghe (*Royce*), Scott Wilson (*C.O. Salem*), Lucinda Jenney (*Blondell*), Morris Chestnut (*McCool*), Josh Hopkins, James Caviezel, Angel David, Boyd Kestner, Kevin Gage, David Vadim, Gregg Bello, John Michael Higgins, Stephen Ramsey, Daniel Von Bargen, David Warshofsky, Stephen Mendillo.
   Dir: Ridley Scott. Pro: Scott, Roger Birnbaum, Demi Moore and Suzanne Todd. Ex Pro: Julie Bergman Sender and Chris Zarpas. Co-Pro: Nigel Wooll. Screenplay: Danielle Alexandra and David Twohy. Ph: Hugh Johnson. Pro Des: Arthur Max. Ed: Pietro Scalia. M: Trevor Jones; Mozart; 'O Mio Bambino Caro' by Puccini; numbers performed by The Pretenders, John Lee Hooker, Three Dog Night, Tarnation, Bad Company, and Auntie Christ. Costumes: Marilyn Vance. (Trap-Two-Zero Prods / Hollywood Pictures / Scott Free / Largo Entertainment /

Moving Pictures / First Independent–First Independent.) Rel: 14 November 1997. 125 mins. Cert 15. USA / UK. 1997.

Girls' Night ★★

Rawtenstall, Lancashire, England / Las Vegas; the present. Dawn, 44, works in a dead-end factory job pushing components into circuit boards. Married for 19 years, her one escape from the mundane routine of her life is a night out with the girls playing Bingo. But when her palms start itching, is it a sign of imminent wealth or an omen of something entirely more sinister? Desperately well meaning, *Girls' Night* is a bittersweet, TV-style drama that blocks its own kitchen sink with cliché. Brenda Blethyn and Julie Walters recycle their irritating personae to diminishing returns, making one cringe with embarrassment when good ol' boy Kris Kristofferson picks them up for a date. Predictable and rather forced, *Girls' Night* is like a crystallisation of everything that's worst of England and the US – the drab mediocrity of industrial Lancashire and the shallow vulgarity of Las Vegas.

Brenda Blethyn (*Dawn Wilkinson*), Julie Walters (*Jackie Simpson*), Kris Kristofferson (*Cody*), George Costigan (*Steve Wilkinson*), James Gaddas (*Paul*), Philip Jackson (*Dave Simpson*), Penelope Woodman (*Christine*), Sue Cleaver, Meera Syal, Margo Stanley, Finetime Fontayne, Anthony Lewis, Maxine Peake, Stuart Fox, Howard Crossley, Brent Huff, Nigel Whitmey.
   Dir: Nick Hurran. Pro: Bill Boyes. Ex Pro: Pippa Cross. Screenplay: Kay Mellor. Ph: David Odd. Pro Des: Taff Batley. Ed: John Richards. M: Ed Shearmur; numbers performed by Roy Orbison, and Tammy Wynette. Costumes: Diana Moseley. (Granada Film / Showtime Networks–Granada.) Rel: 26 June 1998. 102 mins. Cert 15. UK / USA. 1997.

The Girl With Brains In Her Feet ★★★½

Leicester, England; 1972. The 13-year-old daughter of a troubled white mother and an absent black father, Jacqueline Jones struggles to find her place in an ambiguous, changing world. A competent art student and an outstanding sprinter, Jackie lives for the day when she can compete in a local running heat. But the temptations of teenage life

Clever clogs: Joanna Ward in Roberto Bangura's honest and terribly moving *The Girl With Brains In Her Feet* (Alliance Releasing)

repeatedly conspire to waylay her ultimate goal... Written partly from autobiographical experience, *The Girl With Brains In Her Feet* displays a ring of truth that transcends its nostalgia-gilded, coming-of-age familiarity. Furthermore, 16-year-old Joanna Ward – in her very first role – radiates a beguiling pluck and innocence welded to a curiosity born from hormonal overdrive. An honest, heartfelt and terribly moving paean to adolescent confusion.

Amanda Mealing (*Vivienne Jones*), Joanna Ward (*Jacqueline Jones aka Jack*), Jodie Smith (*Maxine*), John Thompson (*Mr Loughborough*), Mossie Smith ('*Soft' Aunt Margaret*), Richard Bremmer (*Vic*), Joshua Henderson (*David 'Spanner' Spencer*), Jamie McIntosh, Richard Claxton, Gareth Tudor-Price, Samantha Wheatley, Steve Nallon, Audrey Ardington, Peter Pine, Henderson Williams, Glynis Brooks.
   Dir: Roberto Bangura. Pro: Don Boyd. Co-Pro: Henry Herbert and Stephanie Mills. Assoc Pro: Alison Kerr. Screenplay: Jo Hodges. Ph: Peter Butler. Pro Des: Lynn Bird. Ed: Adam Ross. M: Rob Lane; numbers performed by T-Rex, Slade, The Sweet, Tom Jones, and Symposium. Costumes: John Krausa. (Lexington Films–Alliance Releasing.) Rel: 12 June 1998. 98 mins. Cert 15. UK. 1997.

Where there's a Will: Matt Damon sorts out a little formulae in Gus Van Sant's inspiring *Good Will Hunting* (from Buena Vista)

Going All the Way ★★

Indianapolis, Indiana; 1954. Sonny Burns and Gunner Casselman have just returned from serving their country during the Korean crisis. Gunner fought in Korea, Sonny stuck around in Kansas City. An unlikely duo – Gunner is handsome and confident, Sunny undernourished and neurotic – the guys embark on a summer of sexual endeavour, with varying degrees of success... Adapted by Dan Wakefield from his own cult 1970 novel, *Going All the Way* boasts a number of memorable moments – not least Sonny's interruption of a revival meeting to ask directions to the local whorehouse and his use of a teddy bear as a masturbatory prop – but for all its quirky, squirming insight, the film remains strangely unengaging. As Sonny, Jeremy Davies reprises the nervy, sexually alienated outsider he perfected in *Spanking the Monkey*,

while Ben Affleck (pre *Good Will Hunting*) hands in his performance as the sensitive all-American jock.

Jeremy Davies (*Sonny Burns*), Ben Affleck (*Gunner Casselman*), Amy Locane (*Buddy Porter*), Rose McGowan (*Gale Ann Thayer*), Rachel Weisz (*Marty Pilcher*), John Lordan (*Elwood Burns*), Jill Clayburgh (*Alma Burns*), Lesley Ann Warren (*Nina Casselman*), Bob Swan, Jeff Buelterman, Nick Offerman, Dan Wakefield (*farmer #2*), Shannon Parr.
   Dir: Mark Pellington. Pro: Tom Gorai and Sigurjon Sighvatsson. Ex Pro: Tom Rosenberg, Ted Tannebaum and Michael Mendelsohn. Screenplay: Dan Wakefield. Ph: Bobby Bukowski. Pro Des: There Deprez. Ed: Leo Trombetta. M: tomandandy; numbers performed by Marty Robbins, Harptones, Bobby Smith, Roy Brown, The Orioles, Tony Martin, The Flamingos, Burroughs Family, etc. Costumes: Arianne Phillips. (Lakeshore Entertainment/Gramercy–PolyGram.) Rel: 26 June 1998. 103 mins. Cert 15. USA. 1997.

Good Burger ★

A humble burger joint that prides itself on its old-fashioned, customer-friendly values finds its future threatened by the arrival of the

corporate-owned Mondo Burger... The fast food answer to *Big Night*, this dumb, slight farce is every bit as irredeemable as it sounds. Based on a running sketch from the TV comedy revue *All That*, *Good Burger* displays all the shortcomings of the inflated skit syndrome, from the shallow characterisations to the suspect message of the story. [*Ewen Brownrigg*]

Kenan Thompson (*Dexter Reed*), Kel Mitchell (*Ed*), Abe Vigoda (*Otis*), Sinbad (*Mr Wheat*), Shar Jackson (*Monique*), Dan Schneider (*Mr Bailey*), Jan Schwieterman (*Kurt Bozwell*), Ron Lester, Ginny Schreiber, Josh Server, Shaquille O'Neal (*himself*), George Clinton, Rubert Wuhl.
   Dir: Brian Robbins. Pro: Robbins and Mike Tollin. Ex Pro: Julia Pistor. Co-Pro: Dan Schneider and Diane Batson-Smith. Screenplay: Schneider, Kevin Kopelow and Heath Seifert. Ph: Mac Ahlberg. Pro Des: Steven Jordan. Ed: Anita Brandt-Burgoyne. M: Stewart Copeland; numbers performed by George Clinton, Isaac Hayes, The Presidents of the United States of America, Sister Sledge, Vangelis, Jackson 5, Steve Dorff, Warren G, etc. Costumes: Natasha Landau. (Paramount/Nickelodeon Movies–UIP.) Rel: 13 February 1998. 95 mins. Cert PG. USA. 1997.

Good Will Hunting ★★★★★

Boston; the present. Will Hunting is uncouth, aggressive, arrogant and dangerous. The product of a broken home, he now mops the halls of the Massachusetts Institute of Technology, the best education establishment of its kind in the world. On a whim, he completes a fantastically complex mathematical poser scribbled on the school blackboard. But before his identity can be discovered by the MIT's resident maths professor, he has to serve time for grievous bodily assault. However, if he agrees to see a therapist once a week, he will be given parole... There is a scene in *Good Will Hunting* in which Robin Williams, as the therapist, breaks through Will's cocky facade. Expertly played by Williams, the scene reveals an extraordinary depth of under-standing as Williams explains the difference between empirical and received knowledge. Yet it is Matt Damon, who plays Will, who actually co-wrote the scene with his best friend, Ben Affleck (who plays his best friend). Written while the two actors were still in college, the script reveals a maturity and perspicacity that far more experienced writers can only hope to achieve. The resultant film – consummately acted, intelligently directed and elegantly edited – is a gift to its audience: a thoughtful, funny, credible and terribly moving experience that stops one in one's tracks. In short, the kind of movie that could change someone's life. P.S. When Damon and Affleck sold their script, the latter was sleeping on Damon's sofa. P.P.S. Minnie Driver previously appeared opposite John Cusack in his own co-scripted *Grosse Pointe Blank* and Stanley Tucci in his own co-scripted *Big Night*.

Robin Williams (*Sean McGuire*), Matt Damon (*Will Hunting*), Ben Affleck (*Chuckie*), Stellan Skarsgard (*Professor Gerald Lambeau*), Minnie Driver (*Skylar*), Casey Affleck (*Morgan*), Cole Hauser (*Billy*), Scott Williams Winters (*Clark*), John Mighton, Rachel Majowski, Jennifer Deathe, George Plimpton.
   Dir: Gus Van Sant. Pro: Lawrence Bender. Ex Pro: Su Armstrong, Bob Weinstein, Harvey Weinstein and Jonathan Gordon. Co-Pro: Chris Moore. Co-Ex Pro: Kevin Smith and Scott Mosier. Screenplay: Matt Damon and Ben Affleck. Ph: Jean Yves Escoffier. Pro Des: Melissa Stewart. Ed: Pietro Scalia. M: Danny Elfman; Schubert; numbers performed by Elliott Smith, and Wolfe Tones, Gerry Rafferty, Supergrass, The Dandy Warhols, Del Shannon, Luscious Jackson, Andru Donalds, Jeb Loy Nichols, Minnie Driver, The Waterboys, Al Green, etc. Costumes: Beatrix Aruna Pasztor. (Miramax–Buena Vista.) Rel: 6 March 1998. 126 mins. Cert 15. USA. 1997.

The Grass Harp ★★★★

A small town in Alabama; the 1940s. When his mother dies, 11-year-old Collin Fenwick moves in with his father's maiden cousins, two exceptionally diverse women. It is his imaginative Aunt Dolly he is drawn to, who tells him of the grass harp, nature's instrument which – through the whispering of the wind through the grass – reveals all the stories of people's lives... Mysteriously delayed since its premiere at the Boston festival in September of 1995, this is a most captivating and shrewd adaptation of Truman Capote's highly personal 1951 novel. A to-die-for cast deliver the acting goods with aplomb, while the look of the picture is thankfully free of cliché. A memorable accomplishment. [*Charles Bacon*]

It started with a kiss: Young Finn (Jeremy James Kissner) experiences the power of first love courtesy of Estella (Raquel Beaudene) in Alfonso Cuaron's stylish and quirky *Great Expectations* (from Fox)

Joe Don Baker (*Sheriff Junius Candle*), Nell Carter (*Catherine Creek*), Charles Durning (*Rev. Buster*), Sean Patrick Flanery (*Riley Henderson*), Edward Furlong (*Collin Fenwick*), Piper Laurie (*Dolly Talbo*), Jack Lemmon (*Dr Morris Ritz*), Walter Matthau (*Judge Charlie Cool*), Roddy McDowall (*Amos Legrand*), Sissy Spacek (*Verena Talbo*), Mary Steenburgen (*Sister Ida*), Mia Kirshner (*Maude*), Scott Wilson, Bonnie Bartlett, Doris Roberts, Ray McKinnon, Rebecca Koon, Charles Matthau, Boyd Gaines (*narrator*).
   Dir: Charles Matthau. Pro: Matthau, Jerry Tokofsky, John Davis and Jim Davis. Ex Pro: John Winfield, Solomon LeFlore and Michael Mendelsohn. Co-Pro and Screenplay: Stirling Silliphant and Kirk Ellis. Ph: John A. Alonzo. Pro Des: Paul Sylbert. Ed: Sidney Levin and Tim O'Meara. M: Patrick Williams; numbers performed by Benny Goodman, Bonnie Bartlett and Charles Durning, Jack Lemmon, Tommy Dorsey, Count Basie, Mary Steenburgen, Glenn Miller, and Ella Fitzgerald. Costumes: Albert Wolsky. (Fine Line–Pathe.) Rel: 12 June 1998. 106 mins. Cert PG. USA. 1995.

Great Expectations ★★★½

Brought up by his older sister and her lover, Joe, in the swamp country of Sarasota, Florida, Finn is a solitary child whose future is predetermined by an unsettling encounter with an escaped convict. Not long afterwards, Finn is invited to the ramshackle mansion of Ms Nora Dinsmoor, an eccentric old woman driven mad years ago by the departure of her lover on their wedding day. Committed to

Point Blank: John Cusack struggles with the lover within him, in George Armitage's hilarious *Grosse Pointe Blank* (from Buena Vista)

engineering the humiliation of all men, Ms Dinsmoor intentionally sets Finn up to be broken by his love for her young protégé, the beautiful but scornful Estella... An extremely sensual, stylish and quirky update of Charles Dickens' 1861 novel, Alfonso Cuaron's *Great Expectations* is surprisingly faithful in spirit to the original, in spite of its temporal and geographic adjustments. If one is going to transform a novel to the screen, then this is an object lesson in how to do it: take the bare bones of the plot and then throw away the rest, leaving the imagination to run riot. P.S. The scene in which the ten-year-old Estella slips her tongue into Finn's mouth is likely to become something of a cinematic milestone.

Ethan Hawke (*Finnegan 'Finn' Bell*), Gwyneth Paltrow (*Estella*), Anne Bancroft (*Nora Diggers Dinsmoor*), Robert De Niro (*Arthur Lustig*), Hank Azaria (*Walter Plane*), Chris Cooper (*Uncle Joe Coleman*), Josh Mostel (*Jerry Ragno*), Kim Dickens (*Maggie*), Nell Campbell (*Erica Thral*), Jeremy James Kissner (*Finn, aged ten*), Raquel Beaudene (*Estella, aged ten*), Gabriel Mick, Stephen Spinella, Marla Sucharetza, Isabelle Anderson, Drena De Niro.
Dir: Alfonso Cuaron. Pro: Art Linson.

Ex Pro: Deborah Lee. Co-Pro: John Linson. Screenplay: Mitch Glazer. Ph: Emmanuel Lubezki. Pro Des: Tony Burrough. Ed: Steven Weisberg. M: Patrick Doyle; numbers performed by Buddah Heads, The Grateful Dead, Ray Coniff Jr, Pedro Vargas, The Verve Pipe, Chris Cornell and Alain Johannes, Tori Amos, The Coasters, Scott Weiland, Pulp, Iggy Pop, Cesaria Evora, Mono, etc. Costumes: Judianna Makovsky and Donna Karan. Sound: Richard Beggs. Title design: Gonzalo Garcia Barcha. Artwork: Francesco Clemente. (Fox–Fox.) Rel: 17 April 1998. 111 mins. Cert 15. USA. 1997.

A catalogue of revulsion: Jacob Reynolds dirties the bath in Harmony Korine's disturbing *Gummo* (from Entertainment)

Grosse Pointe Blank ★★★★

Martin Q. Blank, professional hitman, is not happy about his ten-year high school reunion back in Grosse Pointe, Michigan. But even after all these years he harbours an obsessive affection for the sweetheart he stood up on the night of their prom. With a contract to be carried out in the area anyway, Blank turns up out of the blue, but how does he tell his old classmates that he killed the president of Paraguay with a fork? Any film that casts Dan Aykroyd as a cold-blooded killer, Minnie Driver as an American DJ and Alan Arkin as a psychiatrist with a bee in his bonnet about 'battery bunnies', cannot be accused of complacency. Out of commission since his witty, wickedly amoral *Miami Blues* failed to find its audience in 1990, director George Armitage returns on cracking form with this hilarious romantic thriller. Spinning clichés on their head and lacing every scene with equal parts comedy and suspense, *Grosse Pointe Blank* is deft, sharp and original cinema. *Pulp Fiction* with a sweet tooth.

John Cusack (*Martin Q. Blank*), Minnie Driver (*Debi Newberry*), Alan Arkin (*Dr Oatman*), Dan Aykroyd (*Mr Grocer*), Joan Cusack (*Marcella*), Hank Azaria (*Steven Lardner*), K. Todd Freeman (*McCullers*), Mitchell Ryan (*Bert Newberry*), Jeremy Piven (*Paul Spericki*), Benny Urquidez (*Felix*), Ann Cusack (*Amy*), Barbara Harris (*Mary Blank*), Michael Cudlitz, Duffy Taylor, Audrey Kissel, Carlos Jacott, Belita Moreno, Pat O'Neill, Bill Cusack, Brent Armitage.

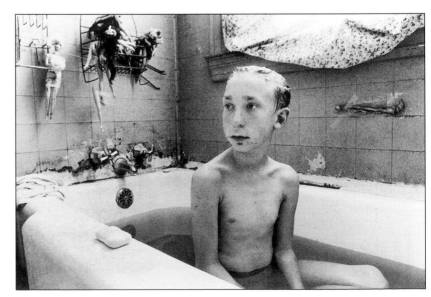

Dir: George Armitage. Pro: Susan Arnold, Donna Arkoff Roth and Roger Birnbaum. Ex Pro: Jonathan Glickman and Lata Ryan. Co-Pro: John Cusack and Steve Pink. Screenplay: Tom Jankiewicz, D.V. DeVincentis, & Pink and Cusack. Ph: Jamie Anderson. Pro Des: Stephen Altman. Ed: Brian Berdan. M: Joe Strummer; Brahms; numbers performed by Johnny Nash, Joe Strummer and Richard Norris, Violent Femmes, The Clash, Guns 'N' Roses, The Jam, The Specials, Echo & The Bunnymen, The Pixies, Motorhead, The Cure, a-ha, Grandmaster Melle Mel, The Bangles, David Bowie and Queen, Siouxsie & The Banshees, Pete Townshend, The English Beat, Nena, The Pogues, etc. Costumes: Eugenie Bafaloukos. (Hollywood Pictures Caravan Pictures/New Crime–Buena Vista.) Rel: 8 August 1997. 107 mins. Cert 15. USA. 1997.

Gummo ★★½

In the tornado-scarred town of Xenia, Ohio, the inhabitants go about their daily business: sniffing glue, drowning cats, urinating off bridges... Variously hailed as 'a work of genius' (*The Observer*) and condemned as 'the worst film of the year', *Gummo* is definitely a startling piece of original cinema, marking the directorial debut of Harmony Korine, the 23-year-old scripter of *Kids*. Snapshots of dysfunctional America (alternately lit by the celebrated cinematographer Jean Yves Escoffier and crudely shot on video), *Gummo* is little more than a catalogue of revulsion. Yet it's not so much the acts of grotesquerie as the pathetic meaninglessness and emptiness of these people's lives that make this one of the most disturbing pictures of America ever committed to celluloid.

Linda Manz (*Solomon's mom*), Max Perlich (*Cole*), Jacob Reynolds (*Solomon*), Chloe Sevigny (*Dot*), Jacob Sewell (*Bunny Boy*), Nick Sutton (*Tummler*), Darby Dougherty (*Darby*), Carisa Bara (*Helen*), Lara Tosh, Harmony Korine, Bryant L. Crenshaw (*gay midget*), Bernadette Resha, Donna Brewster (*albino*).

Dir and Screenplay: Harmony Korine. Pro: Cary Woods. Co-Pro: Robin O'Hara and Scott Macaulay. Ph: Jean Yves Escoffier. Pro Des: Dave Doernberg. Ed: Christopher Tellefsen. M: Randall Poster; numbers performed by Destroy All Monsters, Spazz, Eye Hate God, Mortician, Nifelheim, Bethlehem, Sleep, Buddy Holly, Madonna, Roy Orbison, etc. Costumes: Chloe Sevigny. Sound: Steve Borne.

How does their garden grow? Kerry Fox and Christine Dunsworth in Thom Fitzgerald's dark and funny *The Hanging Garden* (from Alliance Releasing)

(Fine Line/Independent Pictures–Entertainment.) Rel: 17 April 1998. 89 mins. Cert 18. USA. 1997.

Guy ★

Los Angeles; today. A regular guy is stalked by an enigmatic female filmmaker who has randomly chosen him against his will as the subject of a fly-on-the-wall documentary. At first resentful of the intrusion, Guy warms to his starring part in this bizarre game, even at the cost of what he had previously held dear in his life... What may have seemed like a fascinating premise scribbled on the back of an envelope (the whole plot unfolds from the filmmaker's POV) is stretched beyond durability in this poorly developed and facile contemplation on such matters as voyeurism, the invasion of privacy and exhibitionism. The trouble is that the project neither works as pseudo-documentary nor satisfactory fiction as Guy's objections and, later, his complicity, are totally absurd and unbelievable. In short, this is one of the most consistently irritating films I have seen in ages.

Vincent D'Onofrio (*Guy Day*), Hope Davis (*anonymous filmmaker*), Kimber Riddle (*Veronica*), Diane Salinger (*Gail*), Richard Portnow, Michael Massee, John O'Donohue.

Dir: Michael Lindsay-Hogg. Pro: Renee Missel. Ex Pro: Richard Ades and Harris Tulchin. Co Pro: Vincent D'Onofrio. Assoc Pro: Warren Jason. Screenplay: Kirby Dick. Ph: Arturo Smith. Pro Des: Kara Lindstrom. Ed: Dody Dorn. M: Jeff Beal. Costumes: Marissa Borsetto and Amanda Pelisek. Sound: Stefan Korte. (PolyGram/Pandora Film/Filmstiftung, etc.–Poly-Gram.) Rel: 22 May 1998. 94 mins. Cert 18. USA/Germany. 1996.

The Hanging Garden ★★★★½

Sweet William, as he is cruelly christened by his anthomaniacal father (that is, someone obsessed by flowers), was not a happy teenager. Grotesquely overweight and curiously attracted to other boys, William fled from home when the pressure became too much. Ten years later and now lean, handsome and openly gay, he returns for his sister's wedding. He may have changed, but the members of his family are as dysfunctional as ever and are in for some rude awakenings... Throbbing with subtext, *The Hanging Garden* is an intensely personal, densely atmospheric, strange and funny film, like an uncontrollable dream that you periodically wake from to find

Cigarettes, coffee and capital: John C. Reilly and Philip Baker Hall come to an agreement in Paul Thomas Anderson's tantalising, accomplished *Hard Eight* (from Entertainment)

real life staring you back in the face. Written as a testament to the resilience of the human spirit, this is one of the most creative and artistically accomplished features to emerge from Canada in some time, its fusion of colour, music and metaphor blended like a fine whiskey. All things being equal, writer-director Thom Fitzgerald should soon find himself alluded to in the same breath as Atom Egoyan and Denys Arcand.

Chris Leavins (*Sweet William as an adult*), Troy Veinotte (*Sweet William at 15*), Kerry Fox (*Rosemary as an adult*), Sarah Polley (*Rosemary as a teenager*), Seana McKenna (*Iris*), Peter MacNeil (*Whiskey Mac*), Christine Dunsworth (*Violet*), Joel S. Keller (*Fletcher*), Joan Orenstein, Jocelyn Cunningham, Heather Rankin, Ashley MacIsaac, Martha Irving.
　　Dir and Screenplay: Thom Fitzgerald. Pro: Fitzgerald, Louise Garfield and Arnie Gelbart. Assoc Pro: Mark Hammond. Line Pro: Gilles Belanger. Ph: Daniel Jobin. Pro Des: Taavo Soodor. Ed: Susan Shanks. M: John Roby; numbers performed by Ashley MacIsaac, Ani DiFranco, Holly Cole, The Wyrd Sisters, Jane Siberry, The Rankin Family, Aether, Laurel MacDonald, Mary Jane Lammond, Leahy, Lori Yates, etc. Costumes: James A. Worthen. (Triptych Media / Galafilm / Emotion Pictures / Channel 4 / Alliance Communications / Telefilm Canada, etc.–Alliance Releasing.) Rel: 8 May 1998. 91 mins. Cert 15. Canada / UK. 1997.

Happy Together – Cheun Gwong Tsa Sit ★★½

Very much the cult director of 1998 (not least with younger London audiences), Wong Kar-Wai here switches from Hong Kong to Argentina for a story suggested by a novel by Manuel Puig. It's a tale of lovers with contrasted outlooks, and of how one of them tries hard – perhaps too hard – to sustain a relationship until a new opportunity beckons. Wong claims that it is immaterial that the Asian couple abroad (Leslie Cheung and Tony Leung) happen to be gay, but in any case the film only becomes really involving for viewers who can identify with the central situation out of their own experience. There's more style than feeling here, and it's self-conscious style at that. Well acted, this is nevertheless mainly a film for Wong's fans. [*Mansel Stimpson*]

Leslie Cheung (*Ho Po-Wing*), Tony Leung (*Lai Yiu-Fai*), Chang Chen (*Chang*).
　　Dir, Pro and Screenplay: Wong Kar-Wai. Ex Pro: Chan Ye-Cheng. Ph: Christopher Doyle. Pro Des: William Chang Suk-Ping. Ed: William Chang Suk-Ping and Wong Ming-Lam. M: Danny Chung. (Block 2 Pictures / Prenom H. Co Ltd / Seawoo Films / Jet Tone Prods–Artificial Eye.) Rel: 24 April 1998. 97 mins. Cert 15. Hong Kong. 1997.

Hard Eight ★★★★

A dishevelled young man sitting outside a roadside diner is approached by a smartly dressed older gentleman. In exchange for a little conversation, the stranger offers the younger man a cigarette and a coffee. The latter confesses that he needs $6,000 to pay for his mother's funeral, so the stranger lends him $150 and shows him how to capitalise on it in the gambling halls of Reno, Nevada. An unusual relationship develops between the two men, although the younger never seems to question the motives of his benefactor... An intriguing premise is beautifully set up by first-time writer-director Paul Thomas Anderson, who frames his scenes with the mastery of a social realist painter and has cultivated exemplary performances from an outstanding cast. Philip Baker Hall (who played Nixon in Robert Altman's *Secret Honor*) is particularly impressive, giving a performance of unruffled dignity tinged with imperceptible pathos. In an industry that mass-produces baubles and trinkets, *Hard Eight* is a little gem. Original title: *Sydney*.

Philip Baker Hall (*Sydney*), John C. Reilly (*John*), Gwyneth Paltrow (*Clementine*), Samuel L. Jackson (*Jimmy*), F. William Parker, Phillip Seymour Hoffman, Melora Walters.
　　Dir and Screenplay: Paul Thomas Anderson. Pro: Robert Jones and John Lyons. Ex Pro: Keith Samples, Hans Brockmann and Francois Duplat. Co-Pro: Daniel Lupi. Ph: Robert Elswit. Pro Des: Nancy Deren. Ed: Barbara Tulliver. M: Michael Penn and Jon Brion. Costumes: Mark Bridges. Sound: Richard King. (Rysher Entertainment / Green Parrot / Trinity–Entertainment.) Rel: 17 October 1997. 102 mins. Cert 18. USA. 1996.

Hard Rain ★★

When torrential rain and rising flood water force the evacuation of the small town of Huntingburg, Indiana, security guards Tom and Charlie round up the cash from the local banks. However, when their armoured car stalls in the mounting tide, the guards find themselves ambushed by a gang of four men. Keeping his wits about him, Tom wades off into the night dragging the money with him... With its sketched-in characters and contrived plot twists, *Hard Rain* resembles a corny TV movie with a top-heavy budget. Slater, who blew it as an action hero in *Broken Arrow*, slips up again here, this time taking on the additional burden of co-producer. In fact, all the actors are upstaged by the merciless special effects, although Minnie Driver makes the most of what little she's given. Previously known as *The Flood*.

Morgan Freeman (*Jim*), Christian Slater (*Tom*), Randy Quaid (*Sheriff*), Minnie Driver (*Karen*), Ed Asner (*Charlie*), Richard Dysart (*Henry*), Betty White (*Doreen*), Michael Goorjian (*Kenny*), Dann Florek (*Mr Mehlor*), Ricky Harris (*Ray*), Mark Rolston (*Wayne*), Ray Baker, Jay Patterson.
   Dir: Mikael Salomon. Pro: Mark Gordon, Gary Levinsohn and Ian Bryce. Ex Pro: Allison Lyon Segan. Co-Pro: Christian Slater. Screenplay: Graham Yost. Ph: Peter Menzies. Pro Des: J. Michael Riva. Ed: Paul Hirsch. M: Christopher Young. Costumes: Kathleen Detoro. (Mutual Film Co./ PolyGram/Marubeni/BBC/Nordisk Film, etc.–PolyGram.) Rel: 17 April 1998. 96 mins. Cert 15. USA/UK/Japan/Germany/Denmark. 1997.

Head Above Water ★★

Heard the one about the unwanted corpse? Seen *The Trouble With Harry*, *Weekend at Bernie's*, *Over Her Dead Body* or *Sibling Rivalry*? Well, this lumpily paced, farcical addition to the bizarre genre is actually a remake of the 1993 Norwegian film

Rainy day woman: Minnie Driver lends Christian Slater a hand in Mikael Salomon's contrived *Hard Rain* (from PolyGram)

The trouble with Harvey: Harvey Keitel in a serious piece of miscasting in Jim Wilson's *Head Above Water* (from Warner)

Hodet Over Vannet – and suffers in the translation. Harvey Keitel is seriously miscast as a judge who has just married the scatty Cameron Diaz, having encountered her in court on drug and alcohol-related crimes. Trying hard to clean up her act, Diaz house-sits at the couple's holiday abode in Maine while her husband is out on an overnight fishing trip. It is then that she is visited by an ex-lover, the volatile and dashingly handsome Billy Zane,

who begs to sleep over on the sofa. However, just as Keitel returns the following morning, Diaz discovers that Zane is very naked and very dead. In panic, she hides the body in the cellar, activating a series of increasingly improbable misunderstandings... Of course, there's nothing wrong with farce (and even less wrong with Cameron Diaz), but for farce to work it needs a measure of comic momentum. Unfortunately, the pace here is as slack as the corpse's manhood. [*Ewen Brownrigg*]

Harvey Keitel (*George*), Cameron Diaz (*Nathalie*), Craig Sheffer (*Lance*), Billy Zane (*Kent*), Shay Duffin (*cop*).
   Dir: Jim Wilson. Pro: Wilson and John M. Jacobsen. Ex Pro: Guy East and Tristan Whalley. Co-Pro: Helen Pollak. Screenplay: Theresa Marie, based on the screenplay by Geir Eriksen and Eirik Ildahl. Ph: Richard Bowen. Pro Des: Jeffrey Beecroft. Ed: Michael R. Miller. M: Christopher Young. Costumes: Colleen Atwood. (Firmjewel/InterMedia Films/ Fine Line/Tig Prods/Majestic Films– Warner.) Rel: 3 October 1997. 92 mins. Cert 15. USA/UK. 1996.

Hercules ★★

What do you expect from a Disney cartoon? This reinvention of Greek mythology has Hercules carrying out exploits formerly attributed to Perseus and Theseus (namely the trouncing of Medusa and the Minotaur) and bestows him with Pegasus as his equine ally. In addition, the hunk's been given a new mother, Hera, who in the original transcripts was his nemesis (indeed, it was she who drove him

It's a hero thing: *Hercules* pulls the babes in Disney's rape of the cultural heritage of Greece (from Buena Vista)

to kill his own wife and children). Besides the invasion of a new cultural heritage, Disney's 35th full-length animated feature offers little innovation: there's the same old mischievous sidekicks, muscular father-figure, saucer-eyed heroine, hideously frightening monsters, nondescript musical numbers and episodes of unnecessary scare-mongering. Sadly, the magic that once was has been transformed into vulgar formulae, further contaminated by the anodyne demands of the merchandising machine. Having said that, *Hercules* does boast some wit (which James Woods, as Hades, makes the most of), although even this is marked by the over-familiar device of super-imposing modern concepts on to ancient lifestyles.

Voices: Tate Donovan (*Hercules*), Joshua Keaton (*young Hercules, speaking*), Roger Bart (*young Hercules, singing*), Danny DeVito (*'Phil'octetes*), James Woods (*Hades*), Susan Egan (*'Meg'ara*), Rip Torn (*Zeus*), Samantha Eggar (*Hera*), Lillias White (*Calliope*), Cheryl Freeman (*Melpomene*), Lachanze (*Terpsichore*), Roz Ryan (*Thalia*), Vaneese Thomas (*Clio*), Bobcat Goldthwait (*Pain*), Matt Frewer (*Panic*), Hal Holbrook (*Amphitryon*), Barbara Barrie (*Alcmene*), Paul Shaffer (*Hermes*), Amanda Plummer, Carole Shelley, Paddi Edwards, Jim Cummings, Keith David, Kathleen Freeman, Wayne Knight, Phil Proctor, Robert Gant, Charlton Heston (*narrator*).

Dir: John Musker and Ron Clements. Pro: Musker, Clements and Alice Dewey. Assoc Pro: Kendra Haaland. Screenplay: Musker and Clements, Bob Shaw & Donald McEnery, and Irene Mecchi. Pro Des: Gerald Scarfe. Ed: Tom Finan. M: Alan Menken; songs: Menken (music) and David Zippel (lyrics); 'Go The Distance' sung by Michael Bolton. (Walt Disney–Buena Vista.) Rel: 10 October 1997. 93 mins. Cert U. USA. 1997.

Home Alone 3 ★★

Chicago; today. When eight-year-old Alex Pruitt is given a remote-controlled toy car by his neighbour, little does he realise that it contains a top-secret missile-guidance computer chip worth $10 million. But being something of a whiz kid, Alex soon cottons on to the nefarious intentions of four spies who are routinely ransacking the neighbour-hood in search of the chip. 'Home alone' with chickenpox, Alex sets up a serious of ingenious booby traps to foil the goons... Ruthlessly recycling the plot elements of its two pre-decessors (particularly the first), this brazen cash-in escapes total derision due to some inspired buffoonery. But the film's repetitive concentration on comic violence, bland supporting characters and a less-than-sympa-thetic performance from Alex D. Linz (from *One Fine Day*) renders this a tiresome exercise. [*Charles Bacon*]

Alex D. Linz (*Alex Pruitt*), Olek Krupa (*Beaupre*), Rya Kihlstedt (*Alice*), Lenny Von Dohlen (*Jernigan*), David Thornton (*Unger*), Haviland Morris (*Karen Pruitt*), Kevin Kilner (*Jack Pruitt*), Marian Seldes (*Mrs Hess*), Seth Smith, Scarlett Johansson, Christopher Curry, Richard Hamilton.

Dir: Raja Gosnell. Pro: John Hughes and Hilton Green. Ex Pro: Ricardo Mestres. Screenplay: Hughes. Ph: Julio Macat. Pro Des: Henry Bumstead. Ed: Bruce Green, Malcolm Campbell and David Rennie. M: Nick Glennie-Smit; numbers performed by Chuck Berry, Dance Hall Crashers, The Wailers, Shelley Smith, Oingo Boingo, Cartoon Boyfriend, Dean Martin, Jamie Foxx, etc. Costumes: Jodie Tillen. (Fox–Fox.) Rel: 19 December 1997. 102 mins. Cert PG. USA. 1997.

Hotel de Love ★★

Rick Dunne was born two minutes before his twin brother and has remained two steps ahead of him ever since. Now the manager of a tasteless, fantasy-themed honeymoon hotel outside Melbourne, Rick is determined to win back the love of the comely Melissa Morrison, who's visiting the hotel with her new fiancé. But Stephen Dunne is equally resolved to win the hand of the woman that his brother snatched from him all of ten years ago. But what does Melissa want? After a promising opening in which our hero (Simon Bossel as a nervy, Christian Slater-type) clocks the behaviour of couples meeting at Melbourne Airport, *Hotel de Love* slips into Alan Ayckbourn country as various love-battered souls fall in and out of amour at the eponymous lodge. Unfortunately, an unevenness of tone and absence of thespian chemistry – not to mention a lack of real wit – dampens the hilarity. FYI: The premise of the film was inspired by the director's stay at a real honeymoon hotel in Niagara Falls (as featured in *Superman II*).

Aden Young (*Rick Dunne*), Saffron Burrows (*Melissa Morrison*), Simon Bossel (*Stephen Dunne*), Pippa Grandison (*Alison Leigh*), Ray Barrett (*Jack Dunne*), Julia Blake (*Edith Dunne*), Peter O'Brien (*Norman*), Belinda McClory (*Janet*), Alan Hopgood (*Rhone*), Caleb Cluff, Cassandra McGrath, Andrew Bibby, Raelee Hill.

Dir and Screenplay: Craig Rosenberg. Pro: David Parker and Michael Lake. Ex Pro: Peter Heller, Graham Burke, Greg Coote, Richard Pratt and Alex Waislitz. Ph: Stephen Windon. Pro Des: Simon Dobbin. Ed: Mill Murphy. M: Christine

Woodruff; numbers performed by KC and the Sunshine Band, 10CC, Tim Finn, Van Morrison, etc. Costumes: Bruce Finlayson. (Village Roadshow / Pratt Films-Warner.) Rel: 12 June 1998. 97 mins. Cert 15. Australia. 1996.

House of America ★1/2

Stranded in a cultural no-man's-land better known as rural Wales, three siblings struggle to come to terms with their father's departure many years before. With their mother lapsing into bouts of raving eccentricity, Sid and Gwen Lewis invent their own internal world – fermented by Jack Kerouac's *On the Road* – building on the myth of their father's new life in America. But Sid's dream of following in his da's footsteps – taking to the open road on a Harley with Hendrix on his Walkman – is perpetually stifled by the provincial shackles of poverty, unemployment and inertia... While the stark photography of Pierre Aim (*La Haine*) promotes a cinematic sensibility, and more than capable performances keep the conceit alive, the film ultimately fails to shake off the contrived, claustrophobic melodrama of its theatrical origins. *Twin Town* this ain't.

Sian Phillips (*Mam*), Steven Mackintosh (*Sid*), Matthew Rhys (*Boyo*), Lisa Palfrey (*Gwenny*), Pascal Laurent (*Clem*), Richard Harrington, Islwyn Morris, Brian Hibbard, Stephen Spiers, Dave Duffy, Andrew Lennon.
   Dir: Marc Evans. Pro: Sheryl Crown. Ex Pro: David Green. Co-Pro: Hans De Weers. Screenplay: Edward Thomas, based on his play. Ph: Pierre Aim. Pro Des: Mark Tildesley. Ed: Michiel Reichwein. M: John Cale; numbers performed by Tom Jones, Primal Scream, Velvet Underground, Manic Street Preachers, Blur, Teenage Fanclub, Supergrass, Catatonia, Prodigy, Dubstar, Drugstore, and Linoleum. Costumes: Jany Temime. (September Films / Stichting Bergen / British Screen / Arts Council of Wales / National Lottery etc.–First Independent.) Rel: 10 October 1997. 96 mins. Cert 15. UK / Netherlands. 1996.

How To Be a Player ★★

Los Angeles; the present. Dray Jackson is the ultimate player. He has the wheels, the threads, the pad and, above all, he has the appetite. He also has a steady girlfriend, which is

remarkable when you consider that he is simultaneously juggling six mistresses. Dray's sister, though, is cut from a different moral cloth and so sets out to expose her brother on behalf of the sisterhood... While it is never as funny as it thinks it is, *How To Be a Player* is bright and sassy and should be a gift (and warning) to any hormonally functioning male. Indeed, the ensemble of physically talented actresses are a genuine eyeful, making this a must for casting directors of future Afro-American projects. And in his first starring film role, stand-up comic Bill Bellamy displays an engaging combination of good looks and charisma that should guarantee him a promising big-screen career.

Bill Bellamy (*Drayton Jackson*), Natalie Desselle (*Jenny Jackson*), Lark Voorhies (*Lisa*), Mari Morrow (*Katrina*), Pierre (*David*), Jermaine 'Big Hugg' Hopkins (*Kilo*), A.J. Johnson (*Spootie*), Max Julien (*Uncle Fred*), Beverly Johnson (*Robin*), Gilbert Gottfried (*Tony, the doorman*), Bernie Mac (*Buster*), Stach Jae Johnson

Street life: Brendan Sexton III and Isidra Vega in Morgan J. Freeman's authentically affecting *Hurricane Streets* (from First Independent)

(*Sherri*), Elise Neal (*Nadine*), Amber Smith (*Amber*), Devika Parikh (*Barbara*), Bebe Drake (*Mama Jackson*), Gillian Iliana Waters (*Shante*), Marta Boyett (*C.C.*), J. Anthony Brown, Tara Davis, Jazzmin Lewis, Licia Shearer, Edith Grant.
   Dir: Lionel C. Martin. Pro: Marc Burg, Todd Baker, Russell Simmons and Preston Holmes. Ex Pro: Robert Newmyer, Stan Lathan and Jeffrey Silver. Co-Pro: Joanne Milter, Rose Catherine Pinkney and Carrie Morrow. Screenplay: Marc Brown. Pro Des: Bruce Curtis. Ed: William Young. M: Darren Floyd. Costumes: Mimi Melgaard. Sound: Paul Clay. (Island Pictures–Poly-Gram.) Rel: 28 November 1997. 94 mins. Cert 18. USA. 1997.

Hurricane Streets ★★★1/2

East Village, New York City; today. An inveterate petty thief, Marcus Frederick is turning 15 and coming to realise that his dream of returning to New Mexico – his birthplace – might just be a fantasy. With his mother behind bars and his father long dead, Marcus hangs out with other young low-lifes, then meets a spirited 14-year-old Latino girl with problems of her own... Yet another look at contemporary alienated youth, *Hurricane Streets* succeeds where others have failed by investing its characters with compassion and refusing to make superficial judgments. Free of MTV posturing

The big chill: A frosty Sigourney Weaver in Ang Lee's outstanding *The Ice Storm* (from Buena Vista)

or underlit *longueurs*, the film builds its credibility through seemingly spontaneous interaction between the kids and a series of atmospheric shots of the eponymous, omnipresent streets. As the romantic leads, Brendan Sexton III and newcomer Isidra Vega prove remarkably fresh and real and their scenes together uncomfortably believable (were we once so gauche?). Enrique Chediak's lucid camerawork and an unobtrusive score are other major assets. Original US title: *Hurricane*.

Brendan Sexton III (*Marcus Frederick*), Shawn Elliott (*Paco*), L.M. Kit Carson (*Mack*), Lynn Cohen (*Lucy*), Jose Zuniga (*Kramer*), Edie Falco (*Joanne*), David Roland Frank (*Chip*), Antoine McLean (*Harold*), Carlo Alban (*Benny*), Mtume Gant (*Louis*), Damian Corrente (*Justin*), Isidra Vega (*Melena*), David Moscow, Heather Matarazzo, Richard Petrocelli, Adrian Grenier, L.M. Kit Carson.

Dir and Screenplay: Morgan J. Freeman. Pro: Freeman, Galt Niederhoffer and Gill Holland. Ex Pro: L.M. Kit Carson and Cynthia Hargrave. Co-Pro: Nadia Leonelli. Ph: Enrique Chediak. Pro Des: Petra Barchi. Ed: Sabine Hoffman. M: Theodore Shapiro; numbers performed by Bio Ritmo, Vic Chestnutt, Shades of Brooklyn, Supple, Cypress Hill, Sublime, L.M. Kit Carson, Elliott Smith, etc. Costumes: Nancy Brous. (United Artists/ Mayfair Entertainment/giv'an–First Independent.) Rel: 5 June 1998. 89 mins. Cert 15. USA. 1997.

Hurricane

See *Hurricane Streets*.

The Ice Storm ★★★★

New Canaan, Connecticut; November, 1973. It was the year that *The Godfather* won the Oscar for best film, The Carpenters were at the top of the charts and bell-bottoms, corduroy jackets and existentialism were all the rage. It was also the era of Vietnam, Watergate, sexual liberation and moral disenchantment. Reflecting this social unease are Ben and Elena Hood who, in 17 years of marriage, have produced a comfortable lifestyle, two children and a gaping chasm between themselves... A coolly measured time capsule of a serious period of maladjustment, *The Ice Storm* shimmers with metaphor and subtext as it reels in its array of narrative threads and dysfunctional characters. Masterfully orchestrated by the Taiwanese Ang Lee (who previously exhibited his expertise for capturing a foreign time and place with *Sense and Sensibility*), *The Ice Storm* is all of intelligent, insightful, touching, funny and ineffably chilling.

Kevin Kline (*Ben Hood*), Joan Allen (*Elena Hood*), Sigourney Weaver (*Janey Carver*), Henry Czerny (*George Clair*), Adam Hann-Byrd (*Sandy Carver*), Tobey Maguire (*Paul Hood*), Christina Ricci (*Wendy Hood*), Jamey Sheridan (*Jim Carver*), Elijah Wood (*Mikey Carver*), David Krumholtz (*Francis Davenport*), Kate Burton (*Dorothy Franklin*), William Cain (*Ted Shackley*), Michael Cumpsty (*Rev. Philip Edwards*), Katie Holmes (*Libbits Casey*), Maia Danziger, Christine Farrell, Byron Jennings, Larry Pine.

Dir: Ang Lee. Pro: Lee, Ted Hope and James Schamus. Assoc Pro: Alysse Bezahler and Anthony Bregman. Screenplay: Schamus, from the novel by Rick Moody. Ph: Frederick Elmes. Pro Des: Mark Friedberg. Ed: Tim Squyres. M: Mychael Danna; JS Bach; numbers performed by Frank Zappa, Wilson Pickett, Jim Croce, Harry Nilsson, Traffic, Sammi Smith, Free, Elton John, Gerry Mulligan, David Bowie, etc. Costumes: Carol Oditz. (Fox Searchlight/Good Machine–Buena Vista.) Rel: 6 February 1998. 112 mins. Cert 15. USA. 1997.

I Know What You Did Last Summer ★

Following a Fourth of July snogathon on the beach, four disagreeable teenagers leap into their car and inadvertently mow down a pedestrian. Believing the victim to be dead, the kids drag the body to a jetty and dump it in the water, swearing never to talk of the incident again. A year later, Josie, now estranged from her boyfriend, receives an enigmatic note bearing the title of this dumb horror film... Ignoring the golden rule of thrillers – that the audience must sympathise with the characters – *I Know What You Did Last Summer* is a disappointing follow-up to scripter Kevin Williamson's first effort, *Scream*. Desperately lacking in humour, the film is further hamstrung by blah acting, conventional plotting and poorly engineered murder sequences. Only Anne Heche, in the minor role of a backwoods woman, gives the film any resonance.

Jennifer Love Hewitt (*Julie James*), Sarah Michelle Gellar (*Helen Shivers*), Ryan Phillippe (*Barry Cox*), Freddie Prinze Jr (*Ray Bronson*), Johnny Galecki (*Max*), Bridgette Wilson (*Elsa Shivers*), Anne Heche (*Melissa Egan*), Muse Watson (*Benjamin Willis*), Stuart Greer, Deborah Hobart, Rasool J'han, Dan Albright.
   Dir: Jim Gillespie. Pro: Neal H. Moritz, Erik Feig and Stokely Chaffin. Ex Pro: William S. Beasley. Screenplay: Kevin Williamson. Ph: Denis Crossan. Pro Des: Gary Wissner. Ed: Steve Mirkovich. M: John Debney; numbers performed by Type O Negative, Southern Culture On the Skids, Ugly Beauty, Mighty Mighty Bosstones, Toad the Wet Sprocket, Flick, Kula Shaker, Leadbelly, Bing Crosby, Hooverphonic, Isaac Hayes, Green Apple Quick Step, etc. Costumes: Catherine Adair. (Mandalay Entertainment– Entertainment.) Rel: 12 December 1997. 101 mins. Cert 18. USA. 1997.

In & Out ★★★½
Greenleaf, Indiana; the present. Days away from his wedding, drama teacher and Barbra Streisand fan Howard Brackett is accidentally 'outed' on international television when a former student makes an impassioned speech while picking up an Oscar. The sudden focus of a media-feeding frenzy, Brackett is forced to accentuate his masculinity while placating the nerves of his bride, family and colleagues... Unapologetically sentimental and patronising, *In & Out* would be a gross insult if it weren't so damned funny. Furthermore, Kevin Kline captures the nuances of gay body language with consummate skill,

Stories from the closet: Matt Dillon (right) reveals more than he should in Frank Oz's damned funny *In & Out* (from UIP). Tom Selleck and Shalom Harlow look on

even when pushed to the extremes of parody by the heavy-handed direction of Frank Oz. In fact, the cast is uniformly on excellent form (Tom Selleck is a revelation) and the Hollywood in-jokes are priceless. Lest we forget: Steven Segal is elected Oscar nominee for a film called *Snowball in Hell*! FYI: The film is inspired by the occasion when Tom Hanks unintentionally outed his drama teacher when picking up the Academy Award for *Philadelphia*.

Kevin Kline (*Howard Brackett*), Joan Cusack (*Emily Montgomery*), Matt Dillon (*Cameron Drake*), Debbie Reynolds (*Berniece Brackett*), Wilford Brimley (*Frank Brackett*), Bob Newhart (*Tom Halliwell*), Tom Selleck (*Peter Malloy*), Gregory Jbara (*Walter Brackett*), Shalom Harlow (*Sonya*), Shawn Hatosy (*Jack*), Zak Orth (*Mike*), Lauren Ambrose, Alexandra Holden, Lewis J. Stadlen, Deborah Rush, J. Smith-Cameron, Kate McGregor-Stewart, Debra Monk, Ernie Sabella, John Cunningham, Dan Hedaya, Joseph Maher, William Duell, Alice Drummond, Adam LeFevre, MacIntyre Dixon, and (*as themselves*) Glenn Close, Whoopi Goldberg and Jay Leno.
   Dir: Frank Oz. Pro: Scott Rudin. Ex Pro: Adam Schroeder. Co-Pro: G. Mac Brown. Screenplay: Paul Rudnick. Ph: Rob Hahn. Pro Des: Ken Adam. Ed: Dan

Hanley and John Jympson. M: Marc Shaiman; numbers performed by Ethel Merman, Diana Ross, Patsy Cline, Village People (of course), etc. Costumes: Ann Roth. (Paramount/Spelling–UIP.) Rel: 13 February 1998. 90 mins. Cert 12. USA. 1997.

Incognito ★½
Amsterdam/Paris; today. Recognised by underground sources as the world's finest forger, frustrated artist Harry Donovan is plunged into hot water when he's accused of stealing a Rembrandt. The irony is that the masterpiece is his own – a portrait of his own father... An attempt to evoke the fast-paced sophistication of a Hitchcock thriller, *Incognito* is reduced to the level of Euro-trash thanks to a lifeless turn from Jason Patric and plodding direction from John Badham. FYI: Badham took over megaphone duty after the original director, actor Peter Weller, left due to 'creative differences'. [*Ewen Brownrigg*]

Jason Patric (*Harry Donovan*), Irene Jacob (*Marieke van den Brock*), Ian Richardson (*Prosecutor Turley*), Rod Steiger (*Milton A. Donovan*), Thomas Lockyer (*Alistar Davies*), Simon Chandler (*Iain III*), Pip Torrens, Michael Cochrane, Togo Igawa, Joseph Blatchley, Olivier Pierre, Peter Gale, Dudley Sutton, Hugo Bower, John Tordoff, Miriam Karlin.
   Dir: John Badham. Pro: James G. Robinson. Ex Pro: Gary Barber and Bill

Male-icious: Aaron Eckhart and Matt Molloy discuss gender politics in Neil LaBute's corrosive *In the Company of Men* **(from Alliance Releasing)**

Todman Jr. Co-Pro: William P. Cartlidge. Screenplay: Jordan Katz. Ph: Denis Crossan. Pro Des: Jamie Leonard. Ed: Frank Morriss. M: John Ottman. Costumes: Louise Stjernsward. Graffiti artist: Nick Walker. Rembrandts: James Gemmill. (Morgan Creek–Warner.) Rel: 14 November 1997. 107 mins. Cert 15. USA. 1997.

In the Company of Men ★★★

Fort Wayne, Indiana; the present. In an effort to 'restore a little dignity' to their lives, Chad and Howard, two young white executives, decide to pick a woman ('a corn-fed bitch'), romance her and then ditch her – a perfect revenge for the encroaching arrogance of modern woman. They settle on Christine, a pretty, deaf typist in their office, and then slide in for the kill... At a time when guns have become the emotional currency of independent American cinema, *In the Company of Men* brandishes a different weapon: romantic cruelty. Daring to buck the forces of political correctness, the film works more as an intellectual dissertation than as an emotional tract, but Neil LaBute's concise scene setting and sharp dialogue is a commendable exercise in economical, thought-provoking storytelling. Typical joke: Q: 'What's the difference between a golf ball and a G-spot?' A: 'A man will spend twenty minutes looking for a golf ball.' Amazingly, the film was shot in eleven days – for just $25,000.

Aaron Eckhart (*Chad*), Stacy Edwards (*Christine*), Matt Malloy (*Howard*), Michael Martin, Mark Rector, Chris Hayes, Jason Dixie, Emily Cline, Julia Henkel, Laura L. Bartels, Lisa M. Bartels, Michelle Hart.
    Dir and Screenplay: Neil LaBute. Pro: Mark Archer and Stephen Pevner. Ex Pro: Toby Gaff, Mark Hart and Matt Malloy. Line Pro: Lisa M. Bartels. Ph: Tony Hettinger. Pro Des: Julia Henkel. Ed: Joel Plotch. M: Ken Williams and Karel Roessingh. Sound: Tony Moskal and George Moskal. (Stephen Pevner/Atlantic Entertainment/Fair and Square Prods–Alliance Releasing.) Rel: 30 January 1998. 97 mins. Cert 18. USA. 1997.

Inventing the Abbotts ★★

'If the Abbotts didn't exist,' notes Doug Holt, 'my brother would've had to invent them.' Alice, Eleanor and Pamela are the three comely daughters of Lloyd Abbott, a bigwig in the small Midwestern town of Haley, Illinois. The year is 1957 and every lad with a cupful of hormones is falling over himself to get a date with an Abbott. Stuck on the wrong side of the tracks, Doug Holt, 15, and his brother Jacey, 17, stand little chance of a look-in, but then life is full of surprises. Besides, there's a dark secret that links the death of the boys' father with the arrogant, standoffish Lloyd Abbott himself... Continuing America's love affair with growing up in the 1950s, *Inventing the Abbotts* ploughs familiar ground with a sweetness and integrity that is lost on such overworked material. Furthermore, Doug is such an introspective, uncharismatic twerp and his brother a sullen, calculating creep that it's hard to get emotionally involved. Which leaves the distaff cast – led glowingly by Kathy Baker as the boys' wry, long-suffering mother – to carry the film.

Liv Tyler (*Pamela Abbott*), Joaquin Phoenix (*Doug Holt*), Billy Crudup (*Jacey Holt*), Jennifer Connelly (*Eleanor Abbott*), Joanna Going (*Alice Abbott*), Barbara Williams (*Joan Abbott*), Will Patton (*Lloyd Abbott*), Kathy Baker (*Helen Holt*), Alessandro Nivola, Shawn Hatosy, Garrett M. Brown, Michael Sutton, Susan Barnes, Jack Cummins, David Heckendorn.
    Dir: Pat O'Connor. Pro: Ron Howard, Brian Grazer and Janet Meyers. Ex Pro: Karen Kehela and Jack Cummins. Screenplay: Ken Hixon, from the short story by Sue Miller. Ph: Kenneth MacMillan. Pro Des: Gary Frutkoff. Ed: Ray Lovejoy. M: Michael Kamen; numbers performed by The Ray Gelato Giants, David Heckendorn, Leadbelly, The Pastels, etc. Costumes: Aggie Guerard Rodgers. (Fox/Imagine Entertainment–Fox.) Rel: 21 November 1997. 107 mins. Cert 15. USA. 1997.

I Went Down ★★★

Having served eight months in prison for a crime he didn't commit, Git Hynes finds himself in trouble with a local gangster after defending a man who's stolen his girlfriend. To save his hide, he agrees to carry out an errand for the mobster, only to be paired off with a villain one chamber short of a revolver. Still, things could be worse and, sure enough, they get worse... Turning the caper movie on its head, *I Went Down* is a droll, low-key and cheeky diversion that mercifully steers clear of any political grandstanding. Endowed with daft but entirely believable dialogue, the film resembles the deadpan narrative style of Aki Kaurismaki spiced with a strong Irish flavour. Favourite scene: where bound-up captive Peter Caffrey drops the TV remote just as he's tuned into a programme dedicated to the joys of algebra!

Brendan Gleeson (*Bunny Kelly*), Peter McDonald (*Git Hynes*), Peter Caffrey

(*Frank Grogan*), Tony Doyle (*Tom French*), David Wilmot (*Anto*), Antoine Byrne (*Sabrina Bradley*), Michael McElhatton, Joe Gallagher, Carly Baker, Carmel Callan, Denis Conway, Rachel Brady, Anne Kent, Johnny Murphy.

Dir: Paddy Breathnach. Pro: Robert Walpole. Ex Pro: Mark Shivas, David Collins and Rod Stoneman. Screenplay: Conor McPherson. Ph: Cian de Buitlear. Pro Des: Zoe MacLeod. Ed: Emer Reynolds. M: Dario Marinelli; numbers performed by Buddy Guy, The Magnetic Fields, The High Llamas, King Curtis, Junior Wells, Golden Earing, etc. Costumes: Kathy Strachan. (BBC Films/Bord Scannan na hEireann/Irish Film Board–Buena Vista.) Rel: 23 January 1998. 107 mins. Cert 15. Ireland/UK/Spain. 1997.

The Jackal ★★ ½

Moscow/Helsinki/Washington DC/Montreal/London/Chicago; today. When his brother is killed in a confrontation with the FBI, Russian mobster Terek Murad agrees to pay a world-class assassin $70m to make a deadly, spectacular statement in Washington DC. A master of anonymity and disguise, the assassin – dubbed 'The Jackal' – is known only to one man. Unfortunately, that man happens to be an IRA terrorist locked away in an American penitentiary. But with little to go on and with so much at stake, can the FBI afford not to trust the Irishman to help them?

Small beer with a big head: Peter McDonald and Brendan Gleeson contemplate the inevitable in Paddy Breathnach's daft and deadpan *I Went Down* (from Buena Vista)

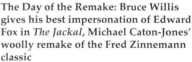

The trouble with making the leading character a villain is that inevitably (albeit reluctantly) one starts to side with him. In spite of the horrendous acts perpetrated by Anthony Hopkins in *The Silence of the Lambs* and John Travolta in *Broken Arrow*,

The Day of the Remake: Bruce Willis gives his best impersonation of Edward Fox in *The Jackal*, Michael Caton-Jones' woolly remake of the Fred Zinnemann classic

one still admired them, enjoyed their company and wished them the best. So it is with Bruce Willis's ingenious, icy killer in this slick, derivative and woolly thriller. The Jackal may kill for money but he's a genuine professional and you have to respect him for that. Richard Gere, on the other hand, solicits little sympathy, in spite of his courageous stab at an Irish accent (no giggling, please).

Bruce Willis (*The Jackal*), Richard Gere (*Declan Mulqueen*), Sidney Poitier (*Carter Preston*), Diane Venora (*Major Valentina Koslova*), Mathilda May (*Isabella Decker*), J.K. Simmons (*Witherspoon*), John Cunningham (*Donald Brown*), Jack Black (*Ian Lamont*), Tess Harper (*The First Lady*), Stephen Spinella (*Douglas*), David Hayman

More of less: Robert De Niro and Bridget Fonda bicker Tarantino-style in Buena Vista's ponderous *Jackie Brown*

(*Terek Murad*), Michael Caton-Jones (*man in video*), Richard Lineback, Leslie Phillips, Sophie Okonedo, Steve Bassett, Laura Viederman, Pamela Poitier, Jonathan Aris, Larry King (*himself*).

Dir: Michael Caton-Jones. Pro: Caton-Jones, James Jacks, Sean Daniel and Kevin Jarre. Ex Pro: Terence Clegg, Hal Lieberman, Gary Levinsohn and Mark Gordon. Screenplay: Chuck Pfarrer, based on the 1973 screenplay by Kenneth Ross. Ph: Karl Walter Lindenlaub. Pro Des: Michael White. Ed: Jim Clark. M: Carter Burwell; Massive Attack; numbers performed by Primal Scream, Fatboy Slim, Bush, Goldie and J. Majik, Massive Attack, The Mike Flowers Pops, Michael Bolton, Agent Provocateur, James Lascelles, etc. Costumes: Albert Wolsky. (Mutual Film Company/Universal Pictures/Alphaville–UIP.) Rel: 9 January 1998. 124 mins. Cert 18. USA. 1997.

Jackie Brown ★★½

A 44-year-old air stewardess working for a third-rate Mexican airline, Jackie Brown finds that her life has just got worse. Caught red-handed with $50,000 in illegal cash and a packet of cocaine, she is unceremoniously dumped into prison. However, Jackie is merely the hook the cops need to reel in the real owner of the money – notorious arms dealer Ordell Robbie. But before anybody gets anything they want, a few deals have to be struck... Invested with the power of *Reservoir Dogs* and *Pulp Fiction*, Quentin Tarantino loosens his belt a bit here, producing a long, self-indulgent blaxploitation homage that wallows in its own self-importance. None the less, the dialogue is still impressive and the performances are terrific from all concerned, with Samuel L. Jackson's dangerous and arrogant Ordell Robbie a particularly unforgettable creation. FYI: A huge fan of 1970s black icon Pam Grier (*Foxy Brown, Sheba Baby*), Tarantino remodelled the role of Elmore Leonard's Jackie Burke especially for her.

Pam Grier (*Jackie Brown*), Samuel L. Jackson (*Ordell Robbie*), Robert Forster (*Max Cherry*), Bridget Fonda (*Melanie*), Michael Keaton (*Ray Nicolette*), Robert De Niro (*Louis Gara*), Michael Bowen (*Mark Dargus*), Chris Tucker (*Beaumont Livingston*), Lisa Gay Hamilton (*Sheronda*), Tommy 'Tiny' Lister Jr (*Winston*), Hattie Winston, Denise Crosby, Aimee Graham, Diana Uribe, Quentin Tarantino (*voice on answering machine*).

Dir and Screenplay: Quentin Tarantino, from the novel Rum Punch by Elmore Leonard. Pro: Lawrence Bender. Ex Pro: Richard N. Gladstein and Leonard, and Bob Weinstein & Harvey Weinstein. Co-Pro: Paul Hellerman. Ph: Guillermo Navarro. Pro Des: David Wasco. Ed: Sally Menke. M: numbers performed by Bobby Womack, Brothers Johnson, The Supremes, Jermaine Jackson, Bill Withers, Johnny Cash, Bloodstone, Pam Grier, Foxy Brown, Randy Crawford, The Delfonics, The Grass Roots, Minnie Riperton, The Vampire Sound Inc., and Elliot Easton's Tiki Gods. Costumes: Mary Claire Hannan. Casting: Jacki Brown. (Miramax Films/A Band Apart–Buena Vista.) Rel: 20 March 1998. 154 mins. Cert 15. USA. 1997.

Jackie Chan's First Strike – Jingcha gushi 4 Zhi Jiandan Renwu ★★★

Hong Kong/the Ukraine/Brisbane, Australia. Recruited by the CIA and a Russian intelligence outfit to keep an eye on a beautiful arms smuggler, 'Jackie', a Hong Kong police officer, finds himself plunged into a tangled international plot. Yet, whether he's scrambling onto an ice floe in the former Soviet Union or scaling a high-rise hotel in Brisbane, Jackie manages to stay alive – just. Dispensing with the superfluous clutter of characterisation, continuity and probability, *Jackie Chan's First Strike* is pared down to the basic constituents of comic escapism. Almost Chaplinesque in his farcical desperation, Chan never misses the opportunity for a joke at his expense: such as when he's forced to strip down to nothing but his furry koala underpants. And, as a stuntman, he is second to none. Whether nimbly defending himself with a table, a broom or even a stepladder, Jackie Chan is to combat what Fred Astaire was to dance.

Jackie Chan (*Jackie*), Jackson Lou (*Tsui*), Chen Chun Wu (*Annie*), Grishajeva Nonna (*Natasha*), Bill Tung, Jouri Petrov, Terry Woo; and the voices of Rosalind Ayres, Neil Dickson, Martin Jarvis, etc.
    Dir and stunt coordinator: Stanley Tong. Pro: Barbie Tung. Ex Pro: Leonard Ho. Screenplay: Stanley Tong, Nick Tramontane, Greg Mellott and Elliot Tong. Ph: Jingle Ma. Pro Des: Oliver Wong. Ed: Peter Cheung and Chi Wai Yau. M: J. Peter Robinson. Animatronic sharks: John Cox's Creature Workshop. (Paragon Films/New Line/Raymond Chow/Golden Harvest–Entertainment.) Rel: 3 October 1997. 84 mins. Cert 12. Hong Kong/USA. 1997.

The James Gang ★★★

When a loan shark burns her Edinburgh house to the ground, Bernadette James drags her four children to London to find their father. There, she makes sure her elusive husband stays by their side by embroiling him in an impromptu robbery of a jewellery store. Now on the run from the police, the James family have no choice but to stay together... Juggling social realism

Family business: Helen McCrory and John Hannah make a runner in Mike Barker's gritty and stylish *The James Gang* (from PolyGram)

with anarchic comedy, *The James Gang* is a British road movie with plenty to say which it does with panache and conviction. Quirky, gritty and stylish, the film moves at an admirable pace and is spiced by a terrific performance from Helen McCrory, England's answer to Judy Davis.

John Hannah (*Spendlove James*), Helen McCrory (*Bernadette James*), Jason Flemyng (*Frank James*), Toni Collette (*Julia Armstrong*), James Nesbitt (*Graham Armstrong*), Darren and David Brownlie (*Spendlove Jr*), Lauren McMurray (*Geraldine James*), Lauren McCracken (*Jessica James*), Elaine Lordan (*Simone*), Brian Pettifer, Tim Woodward, Caroline Berry, Lorraine Kelly, Linda Marlowe.
    Dir: Mike Barker. Pro: Andrew Eaton. Ex Pro: David M. Thompson, Jon Slan and Gareth Jones. Assoc Pro: Sheila Fraser Milne. Screenplay: Stuart Hepburn, based on an idea by Eaton and Paul Lee. Ph: Ben Seresin. Pro Des: Alice Normington. Ed: Guy Bensley. M: Bernard Butler; Morricone; numbers performed by Edwyn Collins, The Cranberries, McAlmont & Butler, John Hannah, Cast, The Fun Lovin'

'Can't sing. Can't act. Can fight a little': Jackie Chan demonstrates his combative skills in Stanley Tong's entertaining *Jackie Chan's First Strike* (from Entertainment)

Sisters under the skin: Michele Burgers and Baby Cele in Les Blair's ground-breaking *Jump the Gun* (from Film Four)

Criminals, The Cowboy Junkies, etc. Costumes: John Krausa. (BBC Films/Paragon Entertainment/Handmade Films/Revolution Films–PolyGram.) Rel: 29 May 1998. 95 mins. Cert 15. UK/Canada. 1997.

John Grisham's The Rainmaker

See *The Rainmaker*.

Joseph Conrad's The Secret Agent ★

Soho, London; 1886. Adolf Verloc, a small-time dealer in pornography, is under the fatal delusion that his wife loves him for who he is and that he is an indispensable cog in Russia's espionage programme. He is also working as an agent for a group of anarchists, a position that is compromised when he is asked by his Russian contact to explode a bomb at the Greenwich Park Observatory, thus casting suspicion on his own associates... This is an astonishingly ill-conceived endeavour that, while clinging slavishly to Conrad's 1907 novel, sacrifices all credibility on the altar of commercialism. The claustrophobic story of a pathetic little man (well played by Hoskins) is hardly helped by the presence of such international stars as Patricia Arquette, Gerard

Depardieu and Robin Williams (the last-named playing a mad bomber). The awkward structure, too, beggars belief, which leaves one cheer for Philip Glass's moody music.

Bob Hoskins (*Adolf Verloc*), Patricia Arquette (*Winnie Verloc*), Gerard Depardieu (*Alexander Ossipon*), Jim Broadbent (*Chief Inspector Heat*), Christian Bale (*Stevie*), Eddie Izzard (*Vladimir*), Elizabeth Spriggs, Peter Vaughan, Julian Wadham, Roger Hammond, George Spelvin, Ralph Nossek, and (*uncredited*) Robin Williams (*The Professor*).
Dir and Screenplay: Christopher Hampton. Pro: Norma Heyman. Ex Pro: Bob Hoskins. Co-Pro: Joyce Herlihy. Ph: Denis Lenoir. Pro Des: Caroline Amies. Ed: George Akers. M: Philip Glass. Costumes: Anushia Nieradzik. (Heyman/Hoskins Prods/Capitol Films–Fox.) Rel: 13 February 1998. 95 mins. Cert 12. UK. 1996.

Journey to the Beginning of the World – Viagem ao Principio do Mundo ★★★★

Two men, one an actor and the other a filmmaker, take a car journey through Portugal which, either through memories aroused or discoveries made, links them with their roots. This latest, poetic film by the veteran Manoel de Oliveira (born 1908) eschews a conventional plot to treat themes of history, inheritance and human experience in a Proustian manner. On its own terms (if you are an admirer of Kiarostami's work and respond favourably to Angelopoulos's

Ulysses' Gaze, there's something here for you), this is a success. Furthermore, it provides the late Marcello Mastroianni with a final role which suits him, that of the elderly film-maker who surely represents de Oliveira himself. [*Mansel Stimpson*]

Marcello Mastroianni (*Manoel*), Jean-Yves Gautier (*Afonso*), Leonor Silveira (*Judite*), Diogo Doria (*Duarte*), Isabel De Castro (*Maria Afonso*), Isabel Ruth, Cecile Sanz de Alba, Jose Pinto.
Dir and Screenplay: Manoel de Oliveira. Pro: Paulo Branco. Line Pro: Antonio Goncalo. Ph: Renato Berta. Pro Des: Maria Jose Branco. Ed: Valerie Loiseleux. M: Emmanuel Nunes. Costumes: Isabel Favila. (Madragoa Filmes/Gemini Filmes/Canal Plus–Artificial Eye.) Rel: 26 June 1998. 95 mins. Cert U. Portugal/France. 1997.

Jump the Gun ★★★

Returning to Johannesburg after a gap of many years, Clint, an oil rig electrician, is surprised by how 'African' it has become – and is aghast by the preponderance of mugging, drugs, transvestitism, guns and refuse on the streets. Arriving in the city on the same day is Gugu, a black singer on the run from a failed marriage. As Clint and Gugu make their separate ways through the rubble of the 'new' South Africa, they are constantly surprised by the changes they see. Clint must learn to adjust to his position as a 'minority', while Gugu must learn to stand on her own two feet as a woman... By daring to bring a sub-Mike Leigh authenticity to the streets of Johannesburg, English director Les Blair has nudged the potential of South African cinema into the open. Utilising genuine street jargon and a low-key ambience, Blair shows the republic as it really is, which should appeal as a novelty item to some and a historical breakthrough to others. However, by lacking the emotional punch of a *Secrets and Lies* or the stylish anarchy of a *Trainspotting*, the film is unlikely to become a huge cult – but it's a very big step, none the less.

Baby Cele (*Gugu*), Lionel Newton (*Clinton*), Rapulana Seiphe-mo (*Thabo*), Thulani Nyembe (*Bazooka aka Zoo*), Michele Burgers (*Minnie*), Danny Keogh (*J.J.*), Marcel van Heerden (*Johnnie Fouche*), Joe Nina, Nomsa Nene, Grace Mahlaba.

Dir: Les Blair. Pro: Indra de Lanerolle. Co-Pro: Jeremy Nathan. Ex Pro: Sarah Curtis. Ph: Seamus McGarvey. Pro Des: David Barkham. Ed: Oral N. Ottey. M: Joe Nina. Costumes: Ruy Filipe. (Channel Four/Parallax/Xencat Pictures–Film Four.) Rel: 22 August 1997. 124 mins. Cert 15. UK/South Africa. 1996.

Junk Mail – Budbringeren ★★★

Oslo, Norway; today. A postman by trade, Roy Amundsen leads a life of shocking anonymity, an existence pockmarked by urban noise, karaoke and tinned spaghetti. Then, following one moment of absent-mindedness, Roy is handed the key to a journey of voyeurism, obsession and, perhaps, redemption... Wandering into the bleakly comic domain of fellow Scandinavian Aki Kaurismaki, first-time director Pal Sletaune paints a sardonic picture of dysfunctional beings inhabiting a dysfunctional world. Roy himself is a fascinating creation, a faceless, amoral sadsack who repeatedly (and inadvertently) pulls off heroic acts. Conversely, when he attempts to do good, he fouls up. Droll, unsettling and spellbinding. Oslo will never seem the same again.

Robert Skjaerstad (*Roy Amundsen*), Andrine Saether (*Line Groberg*), Per Egil Aske (*Georg Rheinhardsen*), Eil Anne Linnestad (*Betsy*), Henriette Steenstrup (*Gina*), Trond Hevik, Adne Olav Sekkelsten.

Dir: Pal Sletaune. Pro: Dag Nordahl and Peter Boe. Co-Pro: Tom Remlov and Anders Berggren. Screenplay: Sletaune and Jonny Halberg. Ph: Kjell Vassdal. Pro Des: Karl Juliusson. Ed: Pal Gengenbach. M: Joachim Holbek. Costumes: Bente Winther-Larsen. (Moviemakers AS/ Norwegian Film Institute/Danish Film Institute/Atlas Film, etc.–Metro Tartan.) Rel: 10 April 1998. 81 mins. Cert 15. Norway/Denmark. 1996.

Keep the Aspidistra Flying ★★

London; 1934. A king among advertising copywriters, Gordon Comstock is promoted to 'head of creativity' at The New Albion Publicity Co. – and promptly hands in his notice. You see, Comstock wants to be a 'poet and free man' but is a little optimistic about his universal appeal. In no time at all, he is reduced to living in a gloomy

Second-class delivery: Andrine Saether and Robert Skjaerstad in Pal Sletaune's droll and unsettling *Junk Mail* (from Metro Tartan)

bedsit and working for a poky book shop. Only the patient love of his occasional girlfriend, Rosemary, keeps him from losing it entirely, but even she cannot convince Comstock to discard a worthy life of poverty for comfortable middle-class values... Better known for his hard-nosed political allegories *1984* and *Animal Farm*, George Orwell also wrote a couple of humorous novels, *Keep the Aspidistra Flying* (1936) and *Coming Up for Air* (1939), both focusing on the comic plight of the common man. The former was based on his own travails as a struggling writer and the director Robert Bierman (*Vampire's Kiss*) has gone to great pains to highlight the comedy in the piece. Unfortunately, the character of Comstock is presented as such an egotistical prat that it's hard to sympathise with, or even laugh at, his self-inflicted misery. A straighter, darker approach would have made him far more endearing – and the humour more honest.

Richard E. Grant (*Gordon Comstock*), Helena Bonham Carter (*Rosemary*), Julian Wadham (*Ravelston*), Jim Carter (*Erskine*), Harriet Walter (*Julia Comstock*), Lesley Vickerage (*Hermione*), Barbara Leigh Hunt (*Mrs Wisbeach*), Liz Smith (*Mrs Meakin*), John Clegg (*Mr McKechnie*), Bill Wallis, Lill Roughley, Malcolm Sinclair, Ben Miles,

Richard Dixon, Eve Ferret, Roger Frost, Joan Blackham, Roy Evans.

Dir: Robert Bierman. Pro: Peter Shaw. Ex Pro: Bierman and John Wolstenholme. Assoc Pro: Joyce Herlihy. Screenplay: Alan Plater. Ph: Giles Nuttgens. Pro Des: Sarah Greenwood. Ed: Bill Wright. M: Mike Batt. Costumes: James Keast. (Overseas Filmgroup/Arts Council of England/Bonaparte Films/UBA/Sentinel Films–First Independent.) Rel: 28 November 1997. 101 mins. Cert 12. UK. 1997.

Keys to Tulsa ★★

Tulsa, Oklahoma; the present. The son of a wealthy serial divorcee, film critic Richter Boudreau is sinking into trouble way too deep. Led astray by his libido, he is not only falling for a volatile junkie/stripper but is unable to resist the physical charms of his partner's wife. In addition, he is failing to meet his deadlines at the office and is reluctantly being drawn into a blackmail plot pitched against the son of a local bigwig... In spite of its abundant layers and subtextual tension, Leslie Greif's *Keys to Tulsa* is the sort of smart, smug movie in which the characters invariably swear, smoke a lot and snort coke (in various combinations) or otherwise are just plain obnoxious. More-over, the initial comic momentum is quickly swallowed up by a thickening plot that seems superimposed merely to keep the characters engaged. Still, there's plenty of steamy local atmosphere and a slew of quirky performances, notably from Deborah Kara Unger, Joanna Going and James Spader (the latter in an uncharacteristic turn as an unstable low-life). P.S. Cameron Diaz delivers a divine cameo as Richter's blind date from hell ('I don't listen to dead singers,' she drawls. 'Gives me the creeps').

Eric Stoltz (*Richter Boudreau*), Cameron Diaz (*Trudy*), Randy Graff (*Louise Brinkman*), Mary Tyler Moore (*Cynthia Whitlow Boudreau Simpson Rawling*), James Coburn (*Harmon Shaw*), Deborah Kara Unger (*Vicky Ann Michaels Stover*), Michael Rooker (*Keith Michaels*), Peter Strauss (*Chip Carlson*), Joanna Going (*Cherry/Eleanor*), James Spader (*Ronnie Stover*), Josh Ridgway (*Billy*), Dennis Letts, Marco Perella, George Greif, Doran Ingrham, Randy Means.
  Dir: Leslie Greif. Pro: Greif and Harley Peyton. Ex Pro: Michael Birnbaum and Peter Isacksen. Line Pro: Elliot Rosenblatt. Screenplay: Peyton. Ph: Robert Fraisse. Pro Des: Derek R. Hill. Ed: Eric L. Beason, Louis F. Cioffi and Michael R. Miller. M: Stephen Endelman; numbers performed by Sammy Davis Jr, Chris Duarte Group,

Oklahoma crude: Joanna Going goes through her routine in Leslie Greif's atmospheric *Keys to Tulsa* (from PolyGram)

Full Keel Music, Bob Boykin and FirePower, etc. Costumes: Marie France. (ITC/PolyGram–PolyGram.) Rel: 22 August 1997. 113 mins. Cert 18. USA. 1996.

Killer Tongue – La Lengua Asesina ★

Having just left the sanctuary of a petrol-pumping convent, bank robber Candy inadvertently slurps up a bit of meteorite in her soup. Taken over by an alien life force, she develops a serpentine, sex-crazed speaking tongue with a deadly appetite for human flesh. Meanwhile, Candy's four poodles have been transformed into a quartet of bitchy drag queens... This sounds a lot better than it is. Aiming for high camp and some kind of cult status, heavy-handed direction and an underdeveloped script pull the whole thing down to the level of an amateur *Carry On*. [*Ewen Brownrigg*]

Melinda Clarke (*Candy*), Jason Durr (*Johnny*), Mapi Galan (*Rita*), Robert Englund (*Chief Screw*), Doug Bradley (*Wig*), Edward Tudor Pole (*Flash*), Mabel Karr, Jonathan Rhys Myers, Miss Kimberley, Nigel Whitmey, Tusse Silberg.
  Dir and Screenplay: Alberto Sciamma. Pro: Christopher Figg and Andres Vicente Gomez. Ex Pro: Volkert Struycken, Michael Cowan and Jason Piette. Ph: Denis Crossan. Pro Des: Jose Luis Del Barco. Ed: Jeremy Gibbs. M: Fangoria. Costumes: John Krausa. Tongue effects: Image Animation. (Lolafilms/Sogetel/The Spice Factory/Canal Plus/European Script Fund, etc.–Entertainment.) Rel: 3 April 1998. 98 mins. Cert 18. Spain/UK. 1996.

Kissed ★★★

As a girl, Sandra Larson would rub dead birds across her naked neck and thighs. As a young woman, she works for the local funeral home and tends to the physical, spiritual and sexual needs of the corpses. For Sandra, believing that the dead can still feel, is unable to resist the 'absolute addiction' of the dead's shining stillness... Dipping politely and gracefully into what must be the last taboo in mainstream cinema, first-time feature director Lynne Stopkewich explores an explosive theme with remarkable restraint. If anything, Stopkewich's stiffs are accorded a sensual reverence, in keeping with the protagonist's loving respect for them. A poetic,

fascinating and mildly mischievous divertissement.

Molly Parker (*Sandra Larson*), Peter Outerbridge (*Matt*), Jay Brazeau (*Mr Wallis*), Natasha Morley (*the young Sandra*), Jessie Winter Mudie, James Timmons, Joe Maffei, John Pozer (*classy carcass*), Raul Inglis (*lucky stiff*).
  Dir: Lynne Stopkewich. Pro: Stopkewich and Dean English. Ex Pro: John Pozer. Assoc Pro: Jessica Fraser. Screenplay: Stopkewich and Angus Fraser, from the short story *We So Seldom Look On Love* by Barbara Gowdy. Ph: Gregory Middleton. Pro Des: Eric McNab. Ed: Stopkewich, Pozer and Peter Roeck. M: Don MacDonald; numbers performed by Lava Hay, Kristy Lee Thirsk, Taste of Joy, Ginger, Mystery Machine, Sarah McLachlan, etc. Costumes: Barb Nixon. Sound: Marti Richa and Susan Taylor. (Boneyard Film/British Columbia Film/The Canada Council/Telefilm Canada, etc.–Metro Tartan.) Rel: 9 January 1998. 78 mins. Cert 18. Canada. 1996.

Kiss Me Guido ★½

New York; the present. When Frankie Zito answers a flat-share ad in *The Village Voice*, he mistakes the initials GWM for 'guy with money' – not 'gay, white male'. However, Frankie's desire to escape his stifling roots and to follow his dream to become an actor forces him to share close quarters with his family's worse nightmare... A neat concept is botched by poor acting and an attempt to have its cake and swallow it. Both sentimental in its conclusion and offensive in its stereotyping, *Kiss Me Guido* is old-fashioned, clumsy and unconvincing. [*Charles Bacon*]

Nick Scotti (*Frankie Zito*), Anthony Barrile (*Warren*), Anthony DeSando (*Pino*), Craig Chester (*Terry*), Domenick Lombardozzi (*Joey Chips*), Molly Price, Christopher Lawford, David Deblinger, Jennifer Esposito, Anthony Vitale, Guinevere Turner.
  Dir and Screenplay: Tony Vitale. Pro: Ira Deutchman and Christine Vachon. Ex Pro: Jane Barclay, Tom Carouso, Sharon Harel and Christopher Lawford. Line Pro: Katie Roumel. Ph: Claudia Raschke. Pro Des: Jeffrey Rathaus. Ed: Alexander Hall. Music Supervisor: Randall Poster; numbers performed by Miquel Brown, Machine, Edwin Starr, The Trammps, The Gap Band, Gloria Gaynor, Nick Scotti, etc. Costumes: Victoria Farrell. (Paramount/Capitol Films and Kardana/Swinsky Films/Redeemable Features–UIP.) Rel: 19 December 1997. 89 mins. Cert 15. USA/UK. 1997.

Kiss the Girls ★★

Casanova, as he calls himself, likes
to look at girls. Not just any girls,
mind you, but extremely attractive,
talented and strong-willed girls. He
collects them in his North Carolina
hideaway and only kills them if
they break the rules... Treading
determinedly in the footsteps of
Seven, *Kiss the Girls* is strong on
style but very weak on credibility.
Vital steps in the narrative are left
unattended to, while characters
that we are told are exceptionally
intelligent repeatedly insist on doing
very stupid things. Surprising,
too, that a film so straitjacketed
by convention should have been
brought to us by the director of the
sublimely quirky *Things To Do in
Denver When You're Dead*.

Morgan Freeman (*Alex Cross*), Ashley Judd
(*Kate Mctiernan*), Cary Elwes (*Nick Ruskin*),
Tony Goldwyn (*Will Rudolph*), Jay O.
Sanders (*Kyle Craig*), Alex McArthur
(*David Sikes*), Bill Nunn (*John Sampson*),
Brian Cox (*Chief Hatfield*), Richard T. Jones
(*Seth Samuel*), William Converse-Roberts
(*Dr Wick Sachs*), Gina Ravera (*Naomi
Cross*), Roma Maffia, Jeremy Piven, Helen
Martin, Heidi Schanz, Billy Blanks,
Deborah Strang, and (*uncredited*) Tracey
Walter.
  Dir: Gary Fleder. Pro: David Brown and
Joe Wizan. Ex Pro: C.O. Erickson.
Screenplay: David Klass, from the novel
by James Patterson. Ph: Aaron Schneider.
Pro Des: Nelson Coates. Ed: William
Steinkamp and Harvey Rosenstock.
M: Mark Isham; J.S. Bach; numbers
performed by John Lee Hooker, Hurricane,
James Brown, Little Richard, etc.

**Deadly serious: Molly Parker embraces
a stiff one in Lynne Stopkewich's tender,
eye-opening *Kissed* (Metro Tartan)**

**Born to be king: the young Dalai Lama in
Martin Scorsese's poetic *Kundun* (from
Buena Vista)**

Costumes: Abigail Murray. (Paramount/
Rysher Entertainment–UIP.) Rel: 6 March
1998. 116 mins. Cert 18. USA. 1997.

Kitchen ★

In adapting Banana Yoshimoto's
novel *Kitchen* and transferring it to
Hong Kong, Yim Ho, distinguished
director of *The Day the Sun Turned
Cold*, misguidedly seeks to imitate
the manner of Wong Kar-Wai.
Although it touches on the theme of
overcoming grief, this is mainly a
story of chequered love, in which for
no obvious reason the girl is given a
mother who was her father before a
sex change. The film moves uneasily
between contrasting moods while
embracing such tiresome devices as
filters, slow motion and confusing
intercut flashbacks. When seeking to
be poetic, it's banal. Not even an able
cast – Jordan Chan and Yasuko
Tomita as the lovers, Law Kar-Ying
as the transsexual – can save this film
from pretentiousness. [*Mansel
Stimpson*]

Jordan Chan (*Louie*), Yasuko Tomita
(*Aggie*), Law Kar-Ying (*Emma*), Karen Mok
(*Jenny*), Lau Siu-Ming, Lo Koon-Lan.
  Dir and Screenplay: Yim Ho. Pro: Yim
Ho and Akira Morishige. Ex Pro:
Raymond Chow and Yokichi Osato. Ph:
Poon Hang-Sang. Pro Des: James Leung
and Jason Mok. Ed: Poon Hang-Yiu. M:
Otomo Yoshihide and Uchihashi
Kazuhisa. (Golden Harvest/Amuse Inc.–
Alliance Releasing.) Rel: 26 December
1997. 111 mins. Cert 15. Hong Kong/
Japan. 1997.

Kundun ★★★

Tibet; 1937-1959. Just two years old,
Tenzin Gyatso, the youngest child of
a peasant family, is 'discovered' to be
the 14th reincarnation of the Buddha
of Compassion. Thus, his spiritual
education begins and so he is
scrupulously schooled in the ancient
arts of Tibetan philosophy, leading
to his enthronement as the spiritual

Knocking the road to Dreamland: Russell Crowe and Guy Pearce disguise their Australian accents in Curtis Hanson's quintessentially American film noir, *L.A. Confidential* (from Warner)

and political leader of his people... Inevitably inviting comparisons to *Seven Years in Tibet*, *Kundun* fails to capture the sense of place of the earlier film but more than compensates with its authentic detail and sheer sense of poetry. A triumph of cinema craftsmanship, the film is a magnificent feast of colour, music and ceremony, a celebration of Tibet that overawes the senses even as it deadens the bottom. FYI: No single performer in the cast is a professional actor, but authentic Tibetan exiles from India, Canada and the US.

Tenzin Thuthob Tsarong (*adult Dalai Lama*), Gyurme Tethong (*Dalai Lama, aged 12*), Tulku Jamyang Kunga Tenzin (*Dalai Lama, aged five*), Tenzin Yeshi Paichang (*Dalai Lama, aged two*), Tencho Gyalpo (*mother*), Tsewang Migyur Khangsar (*father*), Tsering Lhamo (*Tsering Dolma*), Geshi Yeshi Gyatso (*Lama of Sera*), Sonam Phuntsok (*Reting Rinpoche*), Tsewang

Jigme Tsarong (*Taktra Rinpoche*), Jampa Lungtok (*Nechung Oracle*), Henry Yuk (*General Tan*), Robert Lin (*Chairman Mao*).
Dir: Martin Scorsese. Pro: Barbara De Fina. Ex Pro: Laura Fattori. Co-Pro and Screenplay: Melissa Mathison. Ph: Roger Deakins. Pro Des and Costumes: Dante Ferretti. Ed: Thelma Schoonmaker. M: Philip Glass. Technical advisor: the Dalai Lama. (Touchstone Pictures/Capra/De Fina–Buena Vista.) Rel: 3 April 1998. 134 mins. Cert 12. USA. 1997.

L.A. Confidential ★★★★½
Los Angeles; the early 1950s. The publicity may paint L.A. as the 'City of Angels', but there's trouble in paradise. Yet while corruption and random brutality is escalating within the ranks of America's finest, there is one cop – Ed Exley – who is not afraid of the contempt doled out by the officers he snitches on. But then a massacre at a diner threatens to suck Exley, his nemesis Bud White, the criminal underworld, a local millionaire, the drug trade and the porn industry into an unstoppable vortex of violence and revelation... Extremely stylish and ingeniously plotted, *L.A. Confidential* takes a time-

worn scenario and pumps it with a dynamism and intelligence that takes the breath away. Presenting a catalogue of exceptionally well-delineated characters and spilling out artful twists along the way, this masterly adaptation of James Ellroy's novel is an object lesson in how to transform a complex narrative into compelling drama.

Kevin Spacey (*Jack Vincennes*), Russell Crowe (*Bud White*), Guy Pearce (*Ed Exley*), James Cromwell (*Dudley Smith*), David Strathairn (*Pierce Patchett*), Kim Basinger (*Lynn Bracken*), Danny DeVito (*Sid Hudgens*), Ron Rifkin (*Ellis Loew*), Graham Beckel (*Richard Stensland*), Amber Smith (*Susan Lefferts*), Marisol Padilla Sanchez (*Inez Soto*), Brenda Bakke (*Lana Turner*), Matt McCoy, Paul Guilfoyle, Paolo Seganti, Allan Graf, Darrell Sandeen, Simon Baker Denny, Shawnee Free Jones, John Mahon, Jack Conley, Gene Wolande, Michael Chieffo, Gwenda Deacon, Jim Metzler, Robert Barry Fleming, Jeremiah Birkett, Salim Grant, Karreem Washington.
Dir: Curtis Hanson. Pro: Hanson, Arnon Milchan and Michael Nathanson. Ex Pro: David L. Wolper and Dan Kolsrud. Co-Pro: Brian Helgeland. Screenplay: Helgeland and Hanson. Ph: Dante Spinotti. Pro Des: Jeannine Oppewall. Ed: Peter Honess. M: Jerry Goldsmith;

numbers performed by Johnny Mercer, Lee Wiley, Bing Crosby, Dean Martin, Chet Baker, Betty Hutton, Gerry Mulligan Quartet, Jackie Gleason, etc. Costumes: Ruth Myers. Sound: Terry Rodman and Roland Thai. (Monarchy Enterprises/ Regency Entertainment–Warner.) Rel: 31 October 1997. 138 mins. Cert 18. USA. 1997.

Last Summer in the Hamptons ★★★★½

Three generations of a celebrated theatrical family gather for one last summer at the family retreat in East Hampton, Long Island. There, the incarnation of the new comic-strip sensation Mary Marvel finds herself artistically and intellectually out of her depth, while her own fame and beauty touches everyone around her (however hard they may deny it)... With apologies to Chekhov, Joyce and Jean Renoir, Henry Jaglom's most ambitious film to date is a satire of *The Cherry Orchard* (and its ilk), a gift to his actress wife Victoria Foyt (who co-scripted) and a valentine to the late, great Viveca Lindfors in her last role. Employing his traditional technique of mixing real life with fiction, Jaglom has created an invigorating, very funny tapestry of theatrical life in which Lindfors presides as the philosophical matriarch. Highlights include a sexually charged tumble between Foyt and Andre Gregory (pretending to be leopards), and Lindfors sitting up at night watching herself in an old black and white movie with Ronald Reagan. FYI: The celebrated playwright Jon Robin Baitz (*The Substance of Fire*) plays the gay celebrated playwright Jake Axelrod.

Victoria Foyt (*Oona Hart*), Viveca Lindfors (*Helena Mora*), Jon Robin Baitz (*Jake Axelrod*), Savannah Boucher (*Suzanne*), Roscoe Lee Browne (*Freddy*), Andre Gregory (*Ivan Axelrod*), Nick Gregory, son of Andre Gregory (*George*), Melissa Leo (*Trish Axelrod*), Roddy McDowall (*Thomas*), Martha Plimpton (*Chloe Garfield*), Ron Rifkin (*Eli Garfield*), Diane Salinger (*Marian Mora Garfield*), Brooke Smith (*Lois Garfield*), Kristoffer Tabori, son of Viveca Lindfors (*Nick Mora*), Holland Taylor (*Davis Mora Axelrod*), Henry Jaglom (*Max Berger*), Arnold Leo, Michael Emil, Sabrina Marie Jaglom.
Dir, Ex Pro and Ed: Henry Jaglom. Pro: Judith Wolinsky. Screenplay: Jaglom and Victoria Foyt. Ph: Hanania Baer. Scenic design: Bruce Postman and Jeff Monte. M:

Stage struck: Scenarist Victoria Foyt and playwright Jon Robin Baitz speak their own lines in Henry Jaglom's invigorating *Last Summer in the Hamptons* (from Revere Releasing)

Rick Baitz. (Jagtoria/Rainbow Film Company–Revere Releasing.) Rel: 14 November 1997. 108 mins. Cert 15. USA. 1995.

The Last Time I Committed Suicide ★★★½

Based on a part of Beat poet Neal Cassady's life (played admirably by Thomas Jane) in the early 1950s, this covers the brief interlude when he'd settled in Middle America and fallen in love with a depressive beauty (Forlani). En route to a job interview he bumps into old drinking buddy Harry (Reeves), an old flame (Mol) and of course all shifts back to square one. This is a hot cool movie that showcases the best of the current wave of new talent. [Marianne Gray]

Thomas Jane (*Neal Cassady*), Keanu Reeves (*Harry*), Claire Forlani (*Joan*), Adrien Brody (*Ben*), Marg Helgenberger (*Lizzy*), Gretchen Mol (*Mary 'Cherry' Greenway*)

Lucinda Jenney (*Rosie Trickle*), John Doe (*Lewis*), Jim Haynie, Christine Rose, Pat McNamara, Alexandra Holden, Tom Bower, Meadow Sisto, Edward Bates.
Dir and Screenplay: Stephen Kay. Pro: Edward Bates and Louise Rosner. Ex Pro: Peter Abrams, Robert L. Levy, J.P. Guerin, Peter Locke, Donald Kushner and Lawrence Mortorff. Ph: Bobby Bukowski. Pro Des: Amy Ancona. Ed: Dorian Harris. M: Tyler Bates; numbers performed by Miles Davis, Charlie Parker and Dizzy Gillespie, Ella Fitzgerald, The Andrews Sisters, Thelonious Monk, Cassandra Wilson, Pet, etc. Costumes: Denise Wingate. (Alpine Releasing/Kushner-Locke Co./Tapestry Films/Bates Entertainment–Feature Film Co.) Rel: 19 June 1998. 93 mins. Cert 15. USA. 1996.

Lawn Dogs ★★★★

Transplanted to the sterile housing estate of Camelot Gardens, outside Louisville, Kentucky, ten-year-old Devon Stockard plays the adoring daughter to her upwardly mobile parents, but secretly acts out an agenda of rebellion. Drawn to fellow misfit Trent Burns, the social outcast who tends the local lawns, Devon instigates a precarious friendship that fuels their mutual individuality

The grass is meaner: Sam Rockwell and Mischa Barton discover a common thread in John Duigan's arresting *Lawn Dogs* (from Carlton)

– but is fraught with danger... What is so satisfying about this unsettling black satire (scripted by the Kentucky-born playwright and poet Naomi Wallace) is its multiple layers of ambiguity. Nobody is who they seem, with even the most sympathetic characters performing dark deeds under cover of their own privacy. For the seemingly compassionate security guard is actually a snooping bigot and Devon's own mother a reckless adulteress. Intriguing, too, is the arresting style employed by the director, John Duigan (*Flirting*), who casts the 'normal' landscape of suburbia into surrealism while investing Trent's bizarre back-woods retreat with the film's few moments of naturalism. Compelling, surprising and provocative cinema, *Lawn Dogs* is well served by Sam Rockwell's deceptively simplistic maverick and by Mischa Barton's canny portrayal of infantile confusion.

Sam Rockwell (*Trent Burns*), Christopher McDonald (*Morton Stockard*), Kathleen Quinlan (*Clare Stockard*), Bruce McGill (*Nash*), Mischa Barton (*Devon Stockard*), Eric Mabius (*Sean*), David Barry Gray (*Brett*), Angie Harmon (*Pam Gregory*), Beth Grant (*Beth*), Tom Aldredge (Jake), Miles Meehan.
  Dir: John Duigan. Pro: Duncan Kenworthy. Ex Pro: Ron Daniels. Co-Pro: David Rubin. Line Pro: Amy Kaufman. Screenplay: Naomi Wallace. Ph: Elliot Davis. Pro Des: John Myhre. Ed: Humphrey Dixon. M: Trevor Jones; numbers performed by Jubilee, Sister Sledge, Alannah Myles, Bruce Spring-steen, Dwight Yoakam, Hues Corporation, J.J. Cale, Bob Dylan, etc. Costumes: John Dunn. Title design: Chris Allies. (Rank/Toledo Pictures–Carlton.) Rel: 21 November 1997. 101 mins. Cert 15. UK. 1997.

The Leading Man ★★★½

London; today. 'The British are suspicious of happy endings,' notes leading English playwright Felix Webb. 'We distrust happiness.' Webb himself has the perfect existence: international renown, a beautiful wife, three gorgeous children and a comfortable pile by the river. Of course, he works hard for his quality of life, but when he takes up with a lovely young actress and casts her in his new play, *The Hit Man*, he exerts undue pressure on his marriage. Then, the American star of the play offers a surprising solution – with strings attached... Developed in Australia, this quintessential English scenario – something Pinter or Hare would feel perfectly at home with – is given a smart, slick polish. Jon Bon Jovi is perfect casting as the unctuous Lothario and is well matched by Lambert Wilson as the tortured, Stoppardian writer and by the eternally wonderful Thandie Newton as the level-headed girl in the middle. A tad schematic at times, *The Leading Man* is nonetheless a skilful realisation of an intriguing premise. FYI: The screenplay was written by the director's sister.

Jon Bon Jovi (*Robin Grange*), Anna Galiena (*Elena Webb*), Lambert Wilson (*Felix Webb*), Thandie Newton (*Hilary Rule*), Barry Humphries (*Humphrey Beal*), Patricia Hodge (*Delvene Cianelli*), Diana Quick, David Warner, Harriet Walter, Tam Dean Burn, Clare Cox, Victoria Smurfitt, Sheridan Morley, Lizzie Spender, Nicole Kidman (*herself*).
  Dir: John Duigan. Pro: Bertil Ohlsson and Paul Raphael. Ex Pro: Julia Palau and Michael Ryan. Line Pro: Peter McAleese. Screenplay: Virginia Duigan. Ph: Jean

Francois Robin. Pro Des: Caroline Hanania. Ed: Humphrey Dixon. M: Edward Shearmur; Debussy, Dvorak; numbers performed by Talking Heads, Dubstar, Peter Sarstedt, Cecil, Gerry and The Pacemakers, Beausoleil, Peter Skellern, Gary Barlow, and Milla Jovovich. Costumes: Rachel Fleming and Gianni Versace. (J&M Entertainment–Guild.) Rel: 26 September 1997. 100 mins. Cert 15. UK. 1996.

Liar ★★

When the bisected body of a prostitute is discovered in two areas of South Carolina, a rich playboy is brought in for questioning. The police don't have much – just the man's telephone number on the corpse – so they hope a polygraph test will shed some light on their investigation. But their suspect is far more intelligent than they and quickly manipulates the situation to his own advantage... The 27-year-old twin brothers Jonas and Joshua Pate (*The Grave*) have come up with several intriguing ideas here but fail to convert them into gripping cinema. Self-consciously arty and intellectually glib, the film coldly casts its characters into their respective niches of IQ (complete with on-screen captions), but is too knowing and schematic for its own good. At its best, *Liar* is well-filmed theatre. Previously known as *Deceiver*.

Tim Roth (*John Walter Wayland, IQ: 151*), Chris Penn (*Phil W. Braxton, IQ: 102*), Michael Rooker (*Kennesaw, IQ: 122*), Renee Zellweger (*Elizabeth Loftus*), Ellen Burstyn (*Mook*), Rosanna Arquette (*Mrs Kennesaw*), Michael Parks (*Dr Banyard*), Mark Damon (*Mr Wayland*), Bob Hungerford (*Jebby*), Don Winston, J.C. Quinn, Jody Wilhelm, Paul Smith.

Dir and Screenplay: Jonas and Joshua Pate. Pro: Peter Glatzer. Ex Pro: Mark Damon. Co-Pro: Don Winston. Ph: Bill Butler. Pro Des: John Kretschmer. Ed: Dan Lebental. M: Harry Gregson-Williams; numbers performed by Buddy Holly, Sun Ra, The Robins, Steven Burns, Joe Sample, Paul Robb, etc. Costumes: Dana Allyson Greenberg. (MDP Worldwide–First Independent.) Rel: 15 May 1998. 102 mins. Cert 18. USA. 1997.

A Life Less Ordinary ★★★

When celestial matchmakers O'Reilly and Jackson suffer 'a bad run', they are given an ultimatum by Chief Gabriel. Should they fail to unite the

Stage craft: Lambert Wilson and Anna Galiena in John Duigan's intriguing *The Leading Man* (from Guild)

destinies of Robert and Celine – their next romantic assignment – their stay in heaven will be terminated. But how on earth can a beautiful American heiress fall for a Scottish janitor who's just lost his job, girlfriend and car? Tough one. Any other romantic fantasy this good would probably have elicited ecstatic

praise, but as this is the third film from the *Shallow Grave/Trainspotting* team it is a marginal disappointment. As a comic thriller it is surprisingly short on laughs and suspense, although it is never less than stylish and does boast a strong sense of

Heaven must wait: Ewan McGregor clumsily kidnaps Cameron Diaz in Danny Boyle's underwhelming *A Life Less Ordinary* (from PolyGram)

Flesh wounds: Liberto Rabal and Angela Molina indulge each other in Pedro Almodovar's immensely entertaining *Live Flesh* **(from Pathe)**

'whatever will happen next?' Yet even as it aims for quirky novelty, its elements recall a number of other movies (*A Matter of Life and Death, It Happened One Night* – even *Excess Baggage,* for crying out loud), while the rapport between Ewan McGregor and Cameron Diaz fails to overcome its improbability.

Ewan McGregor (*Robert*), Cameron Diaz (*Celine Naville*), Holly Hunter (*O'Reilly*), Delroy Lindo (*Jackson*), Ian Holm (*Mr Naville*), Ian McNeice (*Mayhew*), Stanley Tucci (*Elliot*), Dan Hedaya (*Chief Gabriel*), Tony Shalhoub (*Al*), K.K. Dodds (*Lily*), Maury Chaykin (*Tod*), Christopher Gorham (*Walt*), Judith Ivey, David Stifel, Frank Kanig, Mel Winkler, Timothy Olyphant.
   Dir: Danny Boyle. Pro: Andrew Macdonald. Line Pro: Margaret Hilliard. Screenplay: John Hodge. Ph: Brian Tufano. Pro Des: Kave Quinn. Ed: Masahiro Hirakubo. M: David Arnold; numbers performed by Beck, REM, Ash, Underworld, Luscious Jackson, Alabama 3, Sneaker Pimps, Folk Implosion, Prodigy, The Cardigans, Diana Ross, Elastica, The Shirelles, Orbital, Gladys Knight, Oasis, etc. Costumes: Rachael Fleming, Gucci and Gianni Versace. Animation: Mike Mort. (PolyGram/Figment/Channel Four–PolyGram.) Rel: 24 October 1997. 103 mins. Cert 15. UK. 1997.

Live Flesh – Carne Tremula ★★★★

Born on a Madrid bus at the height of Franco's oppressive dictatorship, Victor Plaza has grown into a young man of uncommon directness and innocence. When he loses his virginity to a beautiful young woman in a nightclub loo, he is mystified when the latter rebuffs him a week later. Then, when she pulls a gun on him, two cops drop by and a single gunshot alters the inexorable trajectory of all their lives … Pedro Almodovar and Ruth Rendell may sound like an odd match, but the former's vibrant style married to the latter's narrative discipline proves to be an irresistible combination. Moving the story's London and Essex setting to Madrid in the 1990s, Almodovar (who also scripted) has brought a humorous, picturesque vigour to Rendell's dark tale of coincidence and betrayal that sharpens the story's absurdity to immensely entertaining ends. And Francesca Neri, as the drug addict turned loyal wife, is a star in the making. Great soundtrack, too.

Javier Bardem (*David*), Francesca Neri (*Elena*), Liberto Rabal (*Victor Plaza*), Angela Molina (*Clara*), Jose Sancho (*Sancho*), Pilar Bardem (*Dona Centro*), Penelope Cruz (*Isabelle*), Alejando Angulo, Mariola Fuentes.
   Dir: Pedro Almodovar. Ex Pro: Agustin Almodovar. Screenplay: Pedro Almodovar, Ray Loriga and Jorge Guerricaechevarria, based on the novel by Ruth Rendell. Ph: Affonso Beato. Pro Des: Esther Garcia. Ed: Jose Salcedo. M: Alberto Ingesias. Costumes: Jose Ma De Cossio. (El Deseo, SA/CiBy 2000/France 3/European Script Fund–Pathe.) Rel: 15 May 1998. 101 mins. Cert 18. Spain/France. 1997.

Lolita ★★★★

New England/New Orleans/Texas; 1947. Traumatised by the death of his first love at 14, Humbert Humbert has never been able to shake off his desire for the ideal of the pubescent girl he was never allowed to possess. Now a middle-aged professor of French literature, he moves to New England to teach and falls for the charms of Dolores Haze, a leggy, gawky, playful and promiscuous 14 year old he calls 'Lolita'. He then marries Dolores's mother to be closer to her… As a dramatisation of Vladimir Nabokov's 1955 novel, Adrian Lyne's daring venture certainly captures the poetic power of the author's form. As a film, it is an intelligent and graceful study of obsession and exercises a hypnotic power of its own. Explicit or gratuitous it is not. Indeed, its most potent passages are artfully implied, such as the scene in which, dressed just in Humbert's pyjama shirt, Lolita is reading the funny pages from a newspaper. She is on Humbert's lap, he on a rocking chair, and only gradually do we realise that he is actually inside her. Lyne is obviously reaching into inflammable territory here, but he does so with insight and compassion and without sensationalism. FYI: *Lolita* was first filmed by Stanley Kubrick in 1962 from a screenplay by Nabokov (which the latter disowned after the director's substantial changes).

Child play: Jeremy Irons and Dominique Swain in Adrian Lyne's daring and poetic *Lolita* (from Pathe)

Jeremy Irons (*Humbert Humbert*), Melanie Griffith (*Charlotte Haze*), Frank Langella (*Clare Quigley*), Dominique Swain (*Dolores Haze – 'Lolita'*), Emma Griffiths-Malin (*Annabel Leigh*), Suzanne Shepherd, Keith Reddin, Erin J. Dean, Pat P. Perkins, Michael Goodwin, Angela Paton, Ben Silverstone, Ronald Pickup, Michael Culkin, Annabelle Apsion, Dawn Mauer (*Ms Swain's body double*).
    Dir: Adrian Lyne. Pro: Mario Kassar and Joel B. Michaels. Screenplay: Stephen Schiff. Ph: Howard Atherton. Pro Des: Jon Hutman. Ed: Julie Monroe and David Brenner. M: Ennio Morricone; Johann Strauss, Mussorgsky/Rimsky-Korsakov, Grieg; numbers performed by Lena Horne, Ella Fitzgerald, Artie Shaw, Vera Lynn, Count Basie, Fats Waller, The Andrews Sisters, Louis Prima, etc. Costumes: Judianna Makovsky and Jenny Beavan. (Mario Kassar/Pathe–Pathe.) Rel: 8 May 1998. 137 mins. Cert 18. France/USA. 1997.

Lost Highway ★½

Fred Madison, a successful tenor saxophonist living in LA, should have known something was up. At a party he meets a man who claims that he's simultaneously back at Fred's place – and to prove it he hands Fred a mobile to ring him there. Then there are the anonymous video tapes. The first shows the exterior of the Madisons' house. The second reveals the Madisons asleep in their bed. And the third shows Fred in the process of dismembering his wife. Then, sentenced to death for his wife's murder, Fred turns into Balthazar Getty... The helpful publicity notes clarify that *Lost Highway* 'is not only about the human psyche, it actually takes place inside it'. David Lynch himself describes it as a '21st century noir horror film'. But is it art? Or entertainment? Or just creative masturbation? Superbly crafted, *Lost Highway* promises much in its first half hour but fails to live up to it. It then swerves off the highway and meanders down a dirt road rutted with pot holes. A real cheat – although some diehard cultists will no doubt embrace it.

Bill Pullman (*Fred Madison*), Patricia Arquette (*Renee Madison/Alice Wakefield*)), Balthazar Getty (*Pete Raymond Dayton*), Robert Blake (*Mystery Man*), Natasha Gregson Wagner (*Sheila*), Robert Loggia (*Mr Eddy/Dick Laurent*), Gary Busey (*Bill Dayton*), Richard Pryor (*Arnie*), Michael Massee (*Andy*), Lucy Butler (*Candace Dayton*), John Roselius, Lou Eppolito, Henry Rollins, Michael Shamus Wiles, Mink Stole, Leonard Termo, David Byrd, Carl Sundstrom, John Solari, Giovanni Ribisi, Scott Coffey, Greg Travis, Jack Nance, Lisa Boyle, Marilyn Manson.
    Dir and Sound: David Lynch. Pro: Deepak Nayar, Tom Sternberg and Mary Sweeney. Screenplay: Lynch and Barry Gifford. Ph: Peter Deming. Pro Des and Costumes: Patricia Norris. Ed: Mary Sweeney. M: Angelo Badalamenti and Barry Adamson; numbers performed by David Bowie, This Mortal Coil, Barry Adamson, Smashing Pumpkins, Nine Inch Nails, Lou Reed, Marilyn Manson, Rammstein, etc. (CiBy 2000/Asymmetrical–PolyGram.) Rel: 22 August 1997. 134 mins. Cert 18. USA. 1996.

The Lost World: Jurassic Park ★★★★★

Four years after the catastrophic termination of his dream to open a dinosaur zoo, Scottish billionaire John Hammond reveals to chaos theorist Ian Malcolm that, all along, there has been a second island, Isla

Don't go into the shed! Vanessa Lee Chester, Jeff Goldblum and Julianne Moore run for cover in Steven Spielberg's thrilling *The Lost World: Jurassic Park* **(from UIP)**

Sorna, which was used as 'a factory floor'. In the interim, a hurricane has wrecked the island and the genetically reconstructed prehistoric creatures have broken free of their enclosures to roam where they will. Malcolm wants nothing to do with it – until, that is, he discovers that his palaeontologist girlfriend is already there... Four years after the success of his last film, *Schindler's List*, Steven Spielberg returns to more familiar territory with this thrilling, intelligent and astonishingly realistic monster epic (watch those velociraptors slip and slide!). Even the techniques that Spielberg once championed and have since become hackneyed through overuse by other directors (such as 'the Spielberg zoom') have been ditched here in favour of new effects. But some old tricks never lose their bite: the scene in which Goldblum, Moore and Chester are trapped in a shed by a

trio of velociraptors should go down in history as the finest example of its kind. For the first time since *Jaws*, this critic literally jumped out of his seat. Pure cinema. One false note, though: how could Goldblum's daughter have stowed away on his trailer without him noticing her initial disappearance?

Jeff Goldblum (*Ian Malcolm*), Julianne Moore (*Sarah Harding*), Pete Postlethwaite (*Roland Tembo*), Arliss Howard (*Peter Ludlow*), Richard Attenborough (*John Hammond*), Vince Vaughn (*Nick Van Owen*), Vanessa Lee Chester (*Kelly Curtis*), Peter Stormare (*Dieter Stark*), Richard Schiff (*Eddie Carr*), Joseph Mazzello (*Tim Murphy*), Ariana Richards (*Alexis Murphy*), Harvey Jason, Thomas F. Duffy, Thomas Rosales, Cyd Strittmatter, Robin Sachs, Ian Abercrombie, David Koepp, Bernard Shaw (*himself*).
   Dir: Steven Spielberg. Pro: Gerald R. Molen and Colin Wilson. Ex Pro: Kathleen Kennedy. Screenplay: David Koepp, based on the novel by Michael Crichton. Ph: Janusz Kaminski. Pro Des: Rick Carter. Ed: Michael Kahn. M: John Williams. Live action dinosaurs: Stan Winston. Technical advisor/palaeontology consultant: Jack Horner. (Universal/Amblin Entertainment–UIP.) Rel: 18 July 1997. 129 mins. Cert PG. USA. 1997.

Love etc ★★★

Best friends for 20 years, Benoit and Pierre have managed to stay remarkably unalike. Then, while Pierre is on one of his many jaunts abroad, Benoit answers a personals ad and falls for the discreet charm of Marie, a 25-year-old art restorer. When Pierre returns he finds that he, too, is enormously attracted to Marie... There's a lot of still water in Marion Vernoux's second feature, but there are a handful of scenes that really take off. The film's major confrontation, in which Benoit turns up Leonard Cohen on the hi-fi to fuel his building anger, is exquisitely Parisian, while the sequence in the karaoke bar skilfully underlines Benoit's growing unease. In fact, *Love etc* makes good use of its musical context: Charlotte Gainsbourg, who performs the opening song with hesitant sincerity, sounds uncannily like her mother, Jane Birkin.

Charlotte Gainsbourg (*Marie*), Yvan Attal (*Benoit*), Charles Bering (*Pierre*), Thibault De Montalembert (*Bernard*), Elodie Navarre (*Elenore*), Marie Adam, Charlotte Maury Sentier, Yvan Martin, Daniel Duval, Dominique Raymond.

Dir: Marion Vernoux. Pro: Patrick Godeau. Ex Pro: Francoise Galfre. Screenplay: Vernoux and Dodine Herry, based on the novel *Talking It Over* by Julian Barnes. Ph: Eric Gautier. Pro Des: Francois Emmanuelli. Ed: Jennifer Auge. M: Alexandre Desplat; Puccini; numbers performed by Charlotte Gainsbourg, Leonard Cohen, etc. Costumes: Pierre-Yves Gayraud. (Aliceleo/France 3 Cinema/Canal Plus, etc.–Pathe.) Rel: 20 March 1998. 104 mins. Cert 15. France. 1996.

Love! Valour! Compassion! ★★★½

Eight gay friends gather at the lakeside residence of choreographer Gregory Mitchell over three memorable weekends – Memorial Day, Fourth of July and Labour Day. During that time they drink, smoke, swim, argue, play games and tiptoe round the fact that Buzz has Aids. They also grow stronger... A *Big Chill* for the Aids generation, Terrence McNally's Tony-winning play is successfully opened out (helped by frequent, picturesque skinny dips)

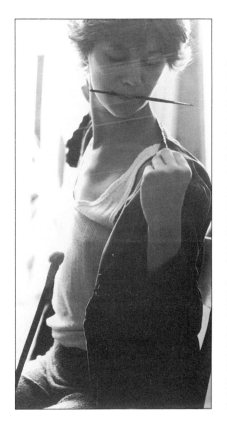

Je t'aime, et ainsi de suite: Charlotte Gainsbourg in Marion Vernoux' perfectly French *Love etc* (from Pathe)

Entertaining with truth: Stephen Bogardus and Jason Alexander in Joe Mantello's witty and thought-provoking *Love! Valour! Compassion!* (from Entertainment)

and is superbly realised by an outstanding cast who, with the sole exception of Jason Alexander, recreate their original stage roles. If, at times, sentimentality threatens to engulf the proceedings, there is more than enough love, valour and compassion – and wit – to compensate.

Randy Becker (*Ramon Fornos*), Stephen Bogardus (*Gregory Mitchell*), John Glover (*John Jeckyll/James Jeckyll*), John Benjamin Hickey (*Arthur Pape*), Justin Kirk (*Bobby Brahms*), Stephen Spinella (*Perry Sellars*), Jason Alexander (*Buzz Hauser*).
Dir: Joe Mantello. Pro: Doug Chapin and Barry Krost. Ex Pro: Ruth Vitale, Jonathan Weisgal and Amy Labowitz. Line Pro: Diane Conn. Screenplay: Terrence McNally. Ph: Alik Sakharov. Pro Des: Francois Seguin. Ed: Colleen Sharp. M: Harold Wheeler; numbers performed by Mungo Jerry, and Ella Fitzgerald. Costumes: Jess Goldstein. (New Line Prods/Fine Line Features–Entertainment.) Rel: 25 July 1997. 114 mins. Cert 15. USA. 1997.

Lucie Aubrac ★★★★

Lyon, France; 1943. A big cog in the French Resistance, Raymond Samuel carries out his acts of subterfuge against the occupying German forces with businesslike efficiency. He is also a devoted husband to his wife Lucie and a loving father to their son, Booboo. When he is betrayed by an informer and captured by the Gestapo, Lucie embarks on a tireless quest to free him so that they can fulfil their pact to be together on the anniversary of their first love-making... A powerful and authentic evocation of war-time France, Lucie Aubrac joins Louis Malle's *Lacombe Lucien* and *Au Revoir, Les Enfants* as one of the most vivid portraits of the Occupation in all of French cinema. Because Claude Berri directs so well – with broad, confident strokes and no distracting trickery – the characters gain a credibility that makes their plight all the more unbearable. The magnificent photography of old Lyon and the surrounding countryside is another definite plus.

Carole Bouquet (*Lucie Aubrac/Lucie Bernard*), Daniel Auteuil (*Francois Vallet/Raymond Samuel/Claude Ermelin*),

High resistance: Daniel Auteuil and Carole Bouquet in Claude Berri's powerfully moving _Lucie Aubrac_ (from Pathe)

Jean-Roger Milo (_Maurice_), Eric Boucher (_Serge_), Patrice Chereau (_Max_), Heino Ferch (_Klaus Barbie_), Jean Martin (_Paul Lardanchet_), Bernard Verley, Marie Pillet, Olga Grumberg.
   Dir: Claude Berri. Pro: Patrick Bordier. Ex Pro: Pierre Grunstein. Screenplay: Berri and Arlette Langmann, from the book _Outwitting the Gestapo_ by Lucie Aubrac. Ph: Vincenzo Marana. Pro Des: Olivier Radot. Ed: Herve De Luze. M: Philippe Sarde. Costumes: Sylvie Gautrelet. (Renn Prods/TF1 Films/Canal Plus, etc.–Pathe.) Rel: 23 January 1998. 115 mins. Cert 12. France. 1997.

Glass act: Leonardo DiCaprio learns the social graces from John Malkovich in Randall Wallace's heavy-handed _The Man in the Iron Mask_ (from UIP)

The Man in the Iron Mask ★★½

Paris/Versailles; 1662. When the arrogant and spiteful young Louis XIV asks Aramis to track down and kill the leader of the Jesuit insurgents, Aramis knows that the king must go. And so he cooks up an audacious plan, but can he persuade his old friends Athos, Porthos and D'Artagnan to help him carry it out? When one starts to scrutinise the props and costumes with undue interest, you know that a film is in trouble. The fact remains that the casting of an Irishman, Englishman, American and Frenchman as D'Artagnan and The Three Musketeers bodes ill and no amount of splendid locations and rousing music can change the fact. The story itself (inspired by Alexandre Dumas's novel) is stretched to encompass new improbabilities, further hampering the credit of what should be a jolly good romp. Director Randall Wallace may have written _Braveheart_, but then Mel Gibson did at least attempt a Scottish accent.

Leonardo DiCaprio (_King Louis XIV/ Philippe_), Jeremy Irons (_Aramis_), John Malkovich (_Athos_), Gerard Depardieu (_Porthos_), Gabriel Byrne (_D'Artagnan_), Anne Parillaud (_Queen Anne_), Judith Godreche (_Christine_), Edward Atterton (_Lt Andre_), Peter Sarsgaard (_Raoul_), Hugh Laurie, David Lowe, Brigitte Boucher, Francois Montagut, Andrew Wallace, Leonor Varela, Laura Fraser, Brigitte Auber.
   Dir and Screenplay: Randall Wallace. Pro: Wallace and Russell Smith. Ex Pro: Alan Ladd Jr. Co-Pro: Paul Hitchcock and Rene Dupont. Ph: Peter Suschitzky. Pro Des: Anthony Pratt. Ed: William Hoy. M: Nick Glennie-Smith. Costumes: James Acheson. Sword fights: William Hobbs. (United Artists–UIP.) Rel: 20 March 1998. 132 mins. Cert 12. USA. 1998.

The Man Who Knew Too Little ★★★

When Des Moines video salesman and birthday boy Wallace Ritchie pops over to London to surprise his brother, he turns up at the worst possible time. To salvage the situation, James Ritchie arranges an impromptu birthday present for his sibling by signing him up for an evening with the 'Theatre of Life'. The gift is a dramatised adventure in which the 'participant' takes the part of a character in a pre-scripted scenario acted out by professional performers at a variety of different venues. Unfortunately, Wallace walks into a real life-and-death situation and nothing will convince him that it isn't all a big joke … A surprisingly old-fashioned espionage comedy, *The Man Who Knew Too Little* recalls the London-based spy capers of the 1960s, even down to the mischievous opening credits and cymbal-brushed score. It is appropriate then that Bill Murray, as the sublimely obnoxious American tourist, should employ such outmoded words as 'bloke' and 'bobby' (for policeman) in order to blend in with the natives. Murray is certainly in his element (as he can only be when he's out of it), and is all the funnier for the supporting cast's straight playing. A special mention, then, to Isabel Hernandez, whose deceptively blank performance as Peter Gallagher's uncomprehending Spanish maid must not go unnoted. Formerly known as *Watch That Man*.

Bill Murray (*Wallace Ritchie*), Peter Gallagher (*James Ritchie*), Joanne Whalley (*Lori*), Richard Wilson (*Daggenhurst*), Alfred Molina (*Boris*), John Standing (*Embleton*), Simon Chandler (*Hawkins*), Anna Chancellor (*Barbara Ritchie*), Nicholas Woodeson (*Sergei*), Isabel Hernandez (*Consuela*), Geraldine James, Cliff Parisi, John Thomson, Janet Henfrey,

Terry O'Neill, Donald Pickering, Venetia Barrett, Terence Harvey, Cate Fowler, Richard Dixon, Sarah Crowden, Barnaby Kay, Sheila Reid, Dexter Fletcher, Bob Holmes, Paul Shearer, Roger Morlidge, Ashley Gunstock, Malcolm Storry, Eddie Marsan, Tat Whalley, Sarah Greene, Mike Smith, J.E. Freeman, Maxwell Caulfield.

Dir: Jon Amiel. Pro: Arnon Milchan, Michael Nathanson and Mark Tarlov. Ex Pro: Elisabeth Robinson and Joe Caracciolo Jr. Screenplay: Robert Farrar and Howard Franklin, based on the novel *Watch That Man* by Robert Farrar. Ph: Robert Stevens. Pro Des: Jim Clay. Ed: Pamela Power. M: Christopher Young; numbers performed by The Three Suns, Tommy Kinsman, The Brand New Heavies, etc. Costumes: Janty Yates. Titles: Graham McCallum. (Regency Enterprises / Polar Prods–Warner.) Rel: 15 May 1998. 94 mins. Cert 12. USA. 1997.

Marius et Jeannette ★★★½

L'Estaque, Marseilles; today. Romance turns up in the most unexpected places. Jeannette has two children and has lost two men. Marius is single and lives on his own. Jeannette sings, Marius whistles. Jeannette drinks, Marius smokes. But are Marius and Jeannette really that different – and what will it take for Marius to find 'enough music in his heart to make his life dance'? A warm, low-key and honest love story rich in atmosphere, Robert Guediguian's film is refreshing in that it deals with real, lived-in people surmounting recognisable, everyday hurdles. In addition, the exotic, cosmopolitan setting of

The Accidental Spy: Bill Murray as *The Man Who Knew Too Little* **(from Warner)**

Marseilles is a real plus, as are the supporting players who all come equipped with their own romantic agendas.

Ariane Ascaride (*Jeannette*), Gerard Meylan (*Marius*), Pascale Roberts (*Caroline*), Jacques Boudet (*Justin*), Frederique Bonnal (*Monique*), Jean-Pierre Darroussin (*Dede*), Laetitia Pesenti (*Magali*), Miloud Nacer (*Malek*), Pierre Banderet (*M. Ebrard*).

Dir: Robert Guediguian. Pro: Gilles Sandoz. Screenplay: Guediguian and Jean-Louis Milesi. Ph: Bernard Cavalie. Pro Des: Karim Hamzaoui. Ed: Bernard Sasia. M: various classical pieces. (La Sept Cinema / Agat Films & Cie / Canal Plus–Porter Frith.) Rel: 5 December 1997. 102 mins. Cert 15. France. 1997.

Martha – Meet Frank, Daniel and Laurence ★★★½

Because of a good deal on a flight from Minneapolis, Martha opts to start the rest of her life in London. At the airport she meets Daniel, an English music executive who promptly falls in love with her. Paying $5000 to have her clandestinely moved to his own plane, Daniel spins out his best seductive strategy. But then he

Waylaid for each other: Ariane Ascaride and Gerard Meylan in Robert Guediguian's refreshing *Marius et Jeannette* **(from Porter Frith)**

cross between Julia Roberts and Lauren Holly) nor Joseph Fiennes (John Shea rearranged by Christopher Lambert) disappoint.

Monica Potter (*Martha*), Rufus Sewell (*Frank*), Tom Hollander (*Daniel*), Joseph Fiennes (*Laurence*), Ray Winstone (*Pedersen*), Jan Pearson, Steven O'Connell, Rebecca Craig.
    Dir: Nick Hamm. Pro: Grainne Marmion. Assoc Pro: Lesley Stewart. Screenplay: Peter Morgan. Ph: David Johnson. Pro Des: Max Gottlieb. Ed: Michael Bradsell. M: Ed Shearmur; numbers performed by Serious Jones, Texas, Echo & The Bunnymen, Dusty Springfield, etc. Costumes: Anna Sheppard. (Channel Four/Banshee–Film Four.) Rel: 8 May 1998. 88 mins. Cert 15. UK. 1998.

Four's a catastrophe: Monica Potter samples another version of the British male (Rufus Sewell) in Nick Hamm's fresh and vibrant *Martha – Meet Frank, Daniel and Laurence* (from Film Four)

A rose by any other name: Georges Du Fresne with psychologist Marie Bunel in Alain Berliner's irresistible *Ma Vie en Rose* (from Bluelight)

hadn't bargained on the effect Martha would have on his two best friends, Frank and Laurence... Relying heavily on coincidence for its dramatic moves, *Martha...* makes up for such contrivances with a number of neat twists. In addition, the employment of fresh, talented faces adds a welcome touch and neither Monica Potter (a piquant

Ma Vie en Rose ★★★★

Ludovic Fabre is seven years old and he wants to be a girl. Immune to the pleasures of football and toy guns, Ludovic is never happier than when applying his mother's lipstick or entering the dream world of his favourite doll, Pam. However, the boy's unorthodox predilections cause a storm in the suburban teacup of his family's ordered, manicured world. But who will change first? Ludovic? Or those who proclaim to love him for who he is? Thanks to a dream performance from the diminutive, 12-year-old Georges Du Fresne, this charming, piquant parable proves hard to resist. Recalling the welcome idiosyncrasies of such European fare as *My Life as a Dog* and *Toto the Hero*, the film wields its satirical edge with the finesse of a surgeon. FYI: Interestingly, Tim Burton's *Edward Scissorhands* was a major inspiration.

Michèle Laroque (*Hanna Fabre*), Jean-Philippe Ecoffey (*Pierre Fabre*), Hélène Vincent (*Elisabeth*), Georges Du Fresne (*Ludovic Fabre*), Daniel Hanssens (*Albert*), Laurence Bibot (*Lisette*), Julien Riviere (*Jérome*), Cristina Barget (*Zoé Fabre*), Anne Coesens (*schoolteacher*), Jean-Francois Gallotte, Caroline Baehr, Grégory Diallo, Erik Cazals De Fabel, Raphaelle Santini, Marie Bunel, Delphine Cadet, Vincent Grass, Alexandra Genoves (*Pam*).
    Dir: Alain Berliner. Pro: Carole Scotta. Co-Pro: Berliner, John McGrath and Jacqueline Pierreux. Screenplay: Berliner and Chris Vander Stappen. Ph: Yves Cape. Pro Des: Veronique Melery. Ed: Sandrine Deegen. M: Dominique Dalcan. Costumes: Karen Muller Serreau. (Haut et Court/ WFE/Freeway Films/CAB/La Sept

Cinema/Canal Plus, etc.–Bluelight.)
Rel: 24 October 1997. 89 mins. Cert 12.
France/Belgium/UK/Switzerland. 1997.

Ma Vie Sexuelle – How I Got Into an Argument ★★★¹/₂

In his second feature, writer-director Arnaud Desplechin daringly devotes three hours to his study of the attitudes and relationships of contemporary Parisians in their twenties. Intellectual in tone and carrying echoes of Godard, Rivette and Eustache, it's a film as French in character as the work of Eric Rohmer. The playing of Desplechin's largely unknown cast, his witty script and the depth of characterisation all help, even though this challenging film sometimes leaves you wishing that, as with a book, you could go back to check that you've understood the work's complexities. Occasionally daunting, often rewarding, the film also features an excitingly adroit use of music of varying kinds. [*Mansel Stimpson*]

Mathieu Amairic (*Paul*), Emmanuelle Devos (*Esther*), Emmanuel Salinger (*Nathan*), Marianne Denicourt (*Sylvia*), Thibault de Montalembert (*Bob*), Chiara Mastroianni (*Patricia*), Denis Podalydes (*Jean-Jacques*), Jeanne Balibar (*Valerie*), Fabrice Desplechin, Helene Lapiower, Michel Vuillermoz, Roland Amstutz.

Dir: Arnaud Desplechin. Pro: Pascal Caucheteux. Screenplay: Desplechin and Emmanuel Bourdieu. Ph: Eric Gautier, Stephane Fontaine and Dominique Perrier-Royer. Pro Des: Antoine Platteau. Ed: Francois Gedigier. M: Krishna Levy; numbers performed by Cameo, Darkman, Bill Evans, and Ella Fitzgerald. Costumes: Claire Gerard-Hirne and Delphine Hayat. (Why Not Productions/La Sept Cinema/France 2 Cinema/Canal Plus, etc.–Guild.) Rel: 8 August 1997. 180 mins. Cert 15. France. 1996.

Maximum Risk ★¹/₂

Nice/Paris/New York; today. When French cop Alain Moreau encounters Mikhail Suverov for the first time, he notices that he is a deadringer for himself. He also notices that he is dead, a condition that Alain might soon emulate if he doesn't get to the bottom of why his twin brother – who was adopted at birth by Russian parents – was being chased all over Nice by the Russian Mafia. Adopting his sibling's identity, Alain swings by Little Odessa in New York only to

Who you gonna call? A sprinkling of alien immigrants show Tommy Lee Jones that they can make a damn fine cup of coffee, in Barry Sonnenfeld's monster hit *Men in Black* (from Columbia TriStar)

discover that everybody he meets can't tell the difference between a Russian and a French accent. Even Mikhail's girlfriend thinks that Alain is Mikhail, in spite of his newly enhanced martial arts skills... Exhibiting a woodenness that's even bland by his standards, Jean-Claude Van Damme alternately sleepwalks and kicks his way through this humourless shuffle. Villains turn up looking like villains (complete with jutting jaws and sneers), comic opportunities are misplaced and the plot chugs along on automatic pilot, steamrolling over an obstacle course of illogicality. The best that can be said for *Maximum Risk* is that it displays a handsome sheen and that Canada's Natasha Henstridge looks as good as ever with her shirt off.

Jean-Claude Van Damme (*Alain Moreau/Mikhail Suverov*), Natasha Henstridge (*Alex*), Jean-Hugues Anglade (*Sebastien*), Zach Grenier (*Ivan*), Paul Ben-Victor (*Pellman*), Frank Senger (*Loomis*), David Hemblen (*Kirov*), Stephane Audran (*Chantal Moreau*), Stefanos Miltsakakis, Frank Van Keeken, Dan Moran, Donald Burda, Henry Gomez.

Dir: Ringo Lam. Pro: Moshe Diamant. Ex Pro: Roger Birnbaum. Screenplay: Larry Ferguson. Ph: Alexander Gruszynski. Pro Des: Steven Spence. Ed: Bill Pankow. M: Robert Folk. Costumes: Joseph Porro. (Columbia–Columbia TriStar.) Rel: 7 November 1997. 100 mins. Cert 18. USA. 1996.

Men in Black ★★★★

Unbeknownst to humanity at large, there are 15,000 'intergalactic refugees' hiding out on earth, and not all of them are New York cab drivers. It's up to the men in black – the best-kept secret in the universe – to preserve the aliens' anonymity and to make sure that the few renegades among them keep their place. Armed with a nifty memory eraser, Agent K recruits a new partner, the hot-headed Agent J, to help him prevent the escape of a particularly ruthless extraterrestrial bug disguised as a redneck farmer... Unlike most adaptations of comic strip material, *Men in Black* maintains a perfectly straight face while unleashing some of the most impressive special effects ever undertaken by Industrial Light & Magic. Vacuum-packed with more gags, action, ideas and effects than a decade of *Batmans*, this lean, tight shot of escapism is an object lesson in sci-fi cool. And what a great ending! Favourite line: coroner Laurel Weaver, tired of the smart-alec conduct of a co-worker: 'I hate the living.'

Tommy Lee Jones (*Agent K*), Will Smith (*Agent J, formerly James Darrel Edwards*), Linda Fiorentino (*Dr Laurel Weaver*), Vincent D'Onofrio (*Edgar*), Rip Torn (*Zed*), Tony Shalhoub (*Jeebs*), Siobhan Fallon (*Beatrice*), Mike Nussbaum (*Gentle Rosenberg*), Carel Struycken (*Arquillian*), Richard Hamilton (*D*), Jon Gries, Sergio Calderon, Fredric Lane, Kent Faulcon, Willie C. Carpenter.
 Dir: Barry Sonnenfeld. Pro: Walter F. Parkes and Laurie MacDonald. Ex Pro: Steven Spielberg. Co-Pro: Graham Place. Screenplay: Ed Solomon, based on the Malibu Comic by Lowell Cunningham. Ph: Don Peterman. Pro Des: Bo Welch. Ed: Jim Miller. M: Danny Elfman; numbers performed by Will Smith and Elvis Presley. Costumes: Mary E. Vogt. Sound: Chuck Michael and Van Ling. Visual effects: Eric Brevig. Alien make-up effects: Rick Baker. Bug wrangler: Mark Jackson. (Columbia/Amblin Entertainment–Columbia TriStar.) Rel: 1 August 1997. 98 mins. Cert PG. USA. 1997.

Middleton's Changeling ★★

Alicante, Spain; somewhere between the 17th and 20th century. Espying the darkly alluring Beatrice Joanna at worship, the noble Alsemero swears his undying love – only to discover that she is already betrothed to the noble Alonso. Enraptured by the stranger's shapely doublet and hose, Beatrice Joanna enters into a perfidious covenant with her father's deformed servant, De Flores, leading to an unstoppable vortex of deceit, betrayal and tragedy... Preserving the original dialogue of Thomas Middleton and William Rowley's 1622 Jacobean tragedy, this brave and visually accomplished curio forces a contemporary note into the proceedings (blending black limousines with horse-drawn carriages) to mixed results. Lacking the visual dynamism of Baz Luhrmann's *Romeo + Juliet*, the film's mix-and-match period detail (Beatrice Joanna wears sneakers beneath her brocade gown) dilutes the drama with unintentional snickers. Favourite line (delivered by Beatrice Joanna to the ignoble De Flores): 'You stagnant toad pool... you're wasting my fucking time.'

Amanda Ray-King (*Beatrice Joanna*), Colm Ò Maonlai (*Alsemero*), Ian Dury (*De Flores*), Richard Mayes (*Vermandero*), Leo Wringer (*Jasperino*), Moya Brady (*Isabella*), Guy Williams (*Alonso*), Julia Tarnoky (*Diaphanta*), John Cooper-Clarke (*poet*), Vivian Stanshall (*himself*), Billy Connolly, Joe Dixon, Duncan Duff, James Maker, Frank Scantori.
 Dir, Pro, Screenplay and Ed: Marcus Thompson. Ex Pro: Peter Greer and Maria Figueroa. Assoc Pro: Peter King, Carole King and Richard Cotton. Ph: Richard K.J. Butland. Pro Des: Rob Swinburn. M: Brian Gray; 'The Changeling' theme by Gary Moore. Costumes: Elizabeth Emanuel. (United Independent Pictures.) Rel: 6 March 1998. 96 mins. Cert 18. UK. 1997.

Midnight in the Garden of Good and Evil ★★★

Savannah, Georgia; the present. Asked to cover a Christmas party thrown by the prominent restoration specialist Jim Williams, New York journalist John Kelso finds himself utterly beguiled by the eccentric millionaire. But when, hours later, Williams is arrested for the murder of his male lover, Kelso's story takes on a whole different hue... Once again Clint Eastwood shows what a consummate craftsman he is with this intelligent, beautifully paced drama. Here, he never betrays the machinery of his technique, but just lets the music, editing and camera moves subtly serve the story. He has also elicited peerless performances from his colourful cast, with priceless turns from Irma P. Hall as a cackling voodoo priestess and The Lady Chablis as himself. Unfortunately, the depth and width of John Berendt's best-selling novel (supposedly based on fact) does weigh on the film's running time, which will play on the patience of some viewers. Favourite line: 'It's like *Gone With the Wind* on mescaline' (John Cusack summing up the bizarre, affluent world of his host).

Kevin Spacey (*Jim Williams*), John Cusack (*John Kelso*), Jude Law (*Billy Hanson*), Jack Thompson (*Sonny Seiler*), Paul Hipp (*Joe Odom*), Alison Eastwood (*Mandy Nicholls*), Irma P. Hall (*Minerva*), The Lady Chablis (*Chablis Deveau*), Kim Hunter (*Betty Harty*), Geoffrey Lewis (*Luther Driggers*), Leon Rippy (*Det. Boone*), Bob Gunton (*Finley Largent*), Sonny Seiler (*Judge White*), Dorothy Loudon, Anne Haney, Richard Herd, Patricia Herd, Patrika Darbo, Emma

Kelly, Shannon Eubanks, Jo Ann Pflug, Michael Rosenbaum, Dan Biggers, Georgia Allen, Ann Cusack, Jerry Spence.
 Dir: Clint Eastwood. Pro: Eastwood and Arnold Stiefel. Ex Pro: Anita Zuckerman. Co-Pro: Tom Rooker. Screenplay: John Lee Hancock. Ph: Jack N. Green. Pro Des: Henry Bumstead. Ed: Joel Cox. M: Lennie Niehaus; numbers performed by k.d. lang, Rosemary Clooney, Paula Cole, Alison Eastwood, Joe Williams, Kevin Mahogany, Tony Bennett, etc. (Warner/Malpaso/Silver Pictures–Warner.) Rel: 17 April 1998. 155 mins. Cert 15. USA. 1997.

Mimic ★½

New York; the near future. When bug expert and geneticist Susan Tyler designs an artificial insect to quash a deadly epidemic, her gamble with nature backfires terribly. A mutant strain of cockroach quickly establishes itself in the nether regions of Gotham, where it grows to an inordinate size and mimics the very appearance of man ... Definitely a case of too many cooks, this, even with chefs of the calibre of John Sayles, Steven Soderbergh and Matthew Robbins contributing to the screenplay. A mishmash of recycled ideas clash in this over-directed, muddled scenario that thinks sudden loud effects, underlit tunnels and plenty of gelatin is a recipe for sophisticated terror. However, underdeveloped characters, implausible dialogue and a woeful lack of humour take the fun away.

Miro Sorvino (*Dr Susan Tyler*), Jeremy Northam (*Dr Peter Mann*), Josh Brolin (*Josh Maslow*), Giancarlo Giannini (*Manny*), Alexander Goodwin (*Chuy*), Alix Koromzay (*Remy*), F. Murray Abraham (*Dr Gates*), Charles S. Dutton (*Leonard*), James Costa, Javon Barnwell, Norman Reedus.
 Dir: Guillermo Del Toro. Pro: Bob Weinstein, B.J. Rack and Ole Bornedal. Ex Pro: Michael Phillips. Co-Pro: Cary Granat, Richard Potter and Andrew Rona. Co-Pro: Scott Shiffman and Michael Zoumas. Screenplay: Del Toro and Matthew Robbins, and (*uncredited*) John Sayles, Steven Soderbergh and Matthew Greenberg, based on the short story by Donald A. Wolheim. Ph: Dan Laustsen. Pro Des: Carol Spier. Ed: Patrick Lussier. M: Marco Beltrami. Costumes: Marie-Sylvie Deveau. Sound: Randy Thom and Steve Boeddeker. Visual effects: Brian M. Jennings and Jeffrey Okun. Creature design: Rob Bottin and Tyruben Ellingson. Termite wrangler: Steven

Kutcher. (Miramax/Dimension Films–Buena Vista.) Rel: 26 June 1998. 106 mins. Cert 15. USA. 1997.

Money Talks ★¹⁄₂

Los Angeles; today. A fast-mouthed ticket scalp wrongly accused of a bloody jailbreak teams up with a strait-laced TV reporter preparing for his wedding day. They're an unlikely duo, but with the police and a gang of merciless diamond thieves on their tail, they've got to come to terms with each other... A loud, chaotic and derivative buddy movie, *Money Talks* imitates the Eddie Murphy oeuvre to death. But then hasn't Eddie Murphy already done that? Anyway, apparently some people find stand-up comic Chris Tucker really funny. [*Charles Bacon*]

Chris Tucker (*Franklin Maurice Hatchett*), Charlie Sheen (*James Russell*), Paul Sorvino (*Guy Cipriani*), Heather Locklear (*Grace Cipriani*), Elise Neal (*Paula Hatchett*), Gerard Ismael (*Raymond Villard*), Paul Gleason (*Det. Bobby Pickett*), Damian Chapa, Michael Wright, Veronica Cartwright, David Warner, Daniel Roebuck, Larry Hankin, Faizon Love, Dexter Tucker, Norris Tucker, Rance Howard.
    Dir: Brett Ratner. Pro: Walter Coblenz and Tracy Kramer. Ex Pro: Chris Tucker. Screenplay: Joel Cohen and Alec Sokolow. Ph: Russell Carpenter and Robert Primes. Pro Des: Robb Wilson King. Ed: Mark Helfrich. M: Lalo Schifrin; numbers performed by Barry White, Rose Royce, Al Green, Vic Damone, Lisa Stansfield, Curtis Mayfield, Dean Martin, Stevie Wonder, Rick James, and Sly and The Family Stone. Costumes: Sharen Davis. (New Line Cinema–Entertainment.) Rel: 24 April 1998. 95 mins. Cert 15. USA. 1997.

Mortal Kombat 2 Annihilation ★

No sooner have the photogenic gladiators Liu Kang, Sonya Blade, Johnny Cage and Princess Kitana defeated the awesome Shang Tsung, than the Emperor of Outworld declares war on the world as we know it. Worse still, this giant irritation with the face of Death is abandoning the sacred rules of Mortal Kombat so that he can, literally, make hell on earth... An unbelievably incompetent sequel to the 1995 hit (itself based on the video game), *Annihilation* fails on virtually every level. Yet while some fans

Gone With the Wind on mescaline: John Cusack and Kevin Spacey live it up in Clint Eastwood's intelligent adaptation of *Midnight in the Garden of Good and Evil* (from Warner)

of the genre may forgive the film's leaden spirit and retarded dialogue, they will not excuse the unimaginative, routine fight sequences. [*Ewen Brownrigg*]

Robin Shou (*Liu Kang*), Talisa Soto (*Princess Kitana*), Brian Thompson (*Shao-Kahn*), Lynn Red Williams (*Commander 'Jax' Briggs*), Sandra Hess (*Sonya Blade*), James Remar (*Lord Rayden*), Litefoot (*Nightwolf*), Irina Pantaeva (*Jade*), Chris Conrad (*Johnny Cage*), Reiner Schoene, Musetta Vander, Marjean Holden, Deron McBee, Dana Lynn Hee, Keith Hirabayashi, J.J. Perry, Carolyn Seymour.
    Dir: John R. Leonetti. Pro: Lawrence Kasanoff. Screenplay: Brent V. Friedman and Bruce Zabel. Ex Pro: Alison Savitch, Carla Fry and Brian Witten. Co-Pro: Kevin Reidy. Ph: Matthew F. Leonetti. Pro Des: Charles Wood. Ed: Peck Prior. M: George S. Clinton; numbers performed by The Immortals, Lunatic Calm, Alien Factory, The Future Sound of London, Urban Voodoo, KMFDM, Megadeth, etc. Costumes: Jennifer L. Parsons. Sound: David Farmer. Visual effects: Savitch and Chuck Comisky. (New Line Cinema/Threshold Entertainment–Entertainment.) Rel: 13 February 1998. 94 mins. Cert 15. USA. 1997.

Most Wanted ★★

When Marine sniper James Dunn refuses to shoot a ten-year-old courier in the Gulf War, his superior officer attacks him. In the ensuing struggle a gun goes off, the officer is killed and Dunn is sentenced to death. Five years later, 30 days before his execution, Dunn is offered a last-ditch alternative to oblivion: to join an elite, covert operation to assassinate a corrupt industrialist selling biotechnology on the black market. When the hit backfires and The First Lady is killed instead, Dunn is set up as scapegoat... A rather simplistic premise is stretched beyond the bounds of credibility in this attempt to log on to some timely paranoia. However, slick production values and notable stunts go some way in tempering the paper-thin characterisations and leaps in probability. Besides, it's always fun to watch Jon Voight over-act (cf. *Anaconda*).

Keenen Ivory Wayans (*Sgt James Anthony Dunn*), Jon Voight (*Lt Col. Grant Casey/General Adam Woodward*), Jill Hennessy (*Victoria Constanini*), Paul Sorvino (*Ken Rackmill*), Robert Culp (*Donald Bickhart*), Wolfgang Bodison (*Capt. Steve Braddock*), Eric Roberts (*Assistant Deputy Director Spencer*), Simon Baker Denny (*Stephen Barnes*), Michael Milhoan, Lee deBroux, David Groh, John Diehl, Eddie Velez,

Donna Cherry (*The First Lady*), Tucker Smallwood, Amanda Kravat.

Dir: David Glenn Hogan. Pro: Eric L. Gold. Ex Pro: Keenen Ivory Wayans and Tony Mark. Screenplay: Wayans. Ph: Marc Reshovsky. Pro Des: Jean-Philippe Carp. Ed: Michael J. Duthie and Mark Helfrich. M: Paul Buckmaster. Costumes: Ileane Meltzer. (New Line Cinema/Ivory Way–Entertainment.) Rel: 3 April 1998. 99 mins. Cert 15. USA. 1997.

Mother and Son – Mat i Syn ★★★★

In the last hours of her life, a dying woman is accompanied by her son on an excursion into the surrounding countryside – and into the memories of their past together... An intensely personal, poetic exploration of the bond that binds parent to child, *Mother and Son* is a staggering achievement that calls as much for patience from the viewer as it does an open heart. As the mother and son, Gudrun Geyer and Alexei Ananishnov are extraordinary, all the more so as neither are professional actors (she is head of the International Documentary Film Festival in Munich, he the manager of Pepsi Cola in St Petersburg). Yet it is the photography that truly distinguishes Sokurov's film, a palette of light and colour that

transforms the bleak landscape into an almost abstract representation of a Turner exhibition. FYI: For his visual reference, Sokurov actually took Caspar David Friedrich's *The Monk at the Sea* – for its 'freedom of the composition and its simultaneous rigour'. [*Charles Bacon*]

Gudrun Geyer (*mother*), Alexei Ananishnov (*son*).

Dir: Alexandr Sokurov. Pro: Thomas Kufus. Ex Pro: Katrin Schlosser, Martin Hagemann and Aleksandr Golutva. Screenplay: Yuri Arabov. Ph: Aleksei Fyodorov. Pro Des: Vera Zelinskaya and Esther Ritterbusch. Ed: Leda Semyonova. M: Mikhail Glinka, Otmar Nussio and Giuseppe Verdi. (Goskino Rossii/Zero Film, etc.–Blue Light.) Rel: 27 March 1998. 73 mins. Cert U. Russia. 1997.

MouseHunt ★★★

When mismatched brothers Ernie and Lars Smuntz inherit a dilapidated old house from their late father, little do they realise its worth. However, as soon as they cotton on to its value (a minimum $10m) they discover that the building is already inhabited – by

Taking the Mickey: The rodent that roared — in Gore Verbinski's farcical *MouseHunt* (from UIP)

a mouse. And not just any old mouse, but a wily, highly intelligent rodent with an uncanny knowledge of physics and human psychological weakness... While succumbing to the farcical excesses of such similar fare as *Home Alone*, *Casper* and *The Borrowers*, *Mouse Hunt* is at least distinguished by some sparkling dialogue and an unparalleled performance from the mouse. Furthermore, Nathan Lane and Lee Evans provide better value than your average goons, and the visual effects are really outstanding. There's also a delicious cameo from Christopher Walken and some unexpectedly dark seams of humour that will delight older audiences. FYI: The visual effects are supervised by Charles Gibson, who won an Oscar for his work on *Babe*.

Nathan Lane (*Ernie Smuntz*), Lee Evans (*Lars Smuntz*), Maury Chaykin (*Alexander Falko*), Christopher Walken (*Caesar*), Vicki Lewis (*April Smuntz*), Michael Jeter (*Quincy Thorpe*), William Hickey (*Rudolf Smuntz*), Debra Christofferson (*Ingrid*), Camilla Soeberg (*Hilde*), Ernie Sabella (*Maury*), Eric Christmas, Ian Abercrombie, Annabelle Gurwitch, Eric Poppick, Cliff Emmich, Peter Gregory.

Dir: Gore Verbinski. Pro: Alan Riche, Tony Ludwig and Bruce Cohen. Screenplay: Adam Rifkin. Ph: Phedon Papamichael. Pro Des: Linda DeScenna. Ed: Craig Wood. M: Alan Silvestri; Johann Strauss. Costumes: Jill Ohanneson. Mouse and cat design: Stan Winston. (Dream-Works–UIP.) Rel: 3 April 1998. 98 mins. Cert PG. USA. 1997.

Mr Magoo ★

Refusing to accept that he's desperately in need of contact lenses, a myopic millionaire finds himself the reluctant beneficiary of a priceless stolen gem, the Star of Kuristan. Thus, he becomes the focus of an international manhunt as the FBI, CIA, a pair of bumbling cat burglars, a world-class criminal and a Brazilian mobster close in for the kill... Occasionally a film comes along which is so bad that it defies belief. Bereft of the comic ingenuity that Hong Kong director Stanley Tong brought to his action-comedies with Jackie Chan, *Mr Magoo* is a pathetically inept attempt to bring the UPA cartoon to feature-length life. The only laugh turns up just

Highland fling: Billy Connolly and Judi Dench in John Madden's gilt-edged *Mrs Brown* (from Buena Vista)

prior to the closing credits, when an apologetic disclaimer assures us that the film is not intended as 'an accurate portrayal of blindness or poor eyesight' and that 'all people with disabilities deserve a fair chance to live'. How magnanimous.

Leslie Nielsen (*Mr Magoo*), Kelly Lynch (*Luanne*), Matt Keeslar (*Waldo*), Nick Chinlund (*Bob Morgan*), Stephen Tobolowsky (*Agent Chuck Stupak*), Ernie Hudson (*Agent Gus Anders*), Jennifer Garner (*Stacey Sampanahoditra*), Malcolm McDowell (*Austin Cloquet*), Miguel Ferrer (*Ortega Peru*), L. Harvey Gold, Art Irizawa, John Tierney.
 Dir: Stanley Tong. Pro: Ben Myron. Ex Pro: Henry G. Saperstein, Andre Morgan and Robert L. Rosen. Co-Pro: Justis Greene. Screenplay: Pat Proft and Tom Sherohman. Ph: Jingle Ma. Pro Des: John Willett. Ed: Stuarte Pappe, David Rawlins and Michael R. Miller. M: Michael Tavera; Mozart, Verdi; numbers performed by Johnny Nash, and Village People. Costumes: Tom Bronson. (Walt Disney Pictures–Buena Vista.) Rel: 1 May 1998. 87 mins. Cert PG. USA. 1997.

Mrs Brown ★★★★★

The Isle of White/Scotland/London; 1864-1883. Following the death of her husband, Prince Albert, Queen Victoria becomes 'devoted to ferocious introspection' and retreats into 'unfettered morbidity'. With the future of the monarchy at stake, the royal household is desperate for their queen to snap out of her stupor and take the empire by the horns once again. But Victoria is not a woman to be lectured and lets nobody forget their place. Not, that is, until the arrival of Prince Albert's Scottish 'outdoor' servant, John Brown, whose honest outspokenness and indifference to etiquette at first incenses Her Majesty and then stirs an unfamiliar affection... Beautifully written and economically played, *Mrs Brown* is British filmmaking at its best. From Judi Dench's superbly nuanced performance as the austere monarch to the inspired casting of Billy Connolly as the bullying, brash yet tender John Brown (not to mention a wily turn from Antony Sher as Disraeli), the film doesn't put a foot wrong.

Judi Dench (*Queen Victoria*), Billy Connolly (*John Brown*), Antony Sher (*Benjamin*

Disraeli), Geoffrey Palmer (*Henry Ponsonby*), Richard Pasco (*Dr Jenner*), David Westhead (*Bertie, Prince of Wales*), Gerard Butler (*Archie Brown*), Oliver Ford Davies (*Dean Wellesley*), Elaine Collins, Jimmy Chisholm, Jason Morell, Claire Nicolson, Finty Williams, Sarah Stewart, Delia Lindsay.
 Dir: John Madden. Pro: Sarah Curtis. Ex Pro: Douglas Rae, Andrea Calderwood, Nigel Warren-Green and Rebecca Eaton. Screenplay: Jeremy Brock, based on an idea by George Rosie. Ph: Richard Greatrex. Pro Des: Martin Childs. Ed: Robin Sales. M: Stephen Warbeck. Costumes: Deirdre Clancy. (BBC Scotland/Ecosse Films/BBC Films/WGBH/Boston/Irish Screen/Mobil Masterpiece Theatre–Buena Vista.) Rel: 5 September 1997. 103 mins. Cert PG. UK/USA/Ireland. 1997.

Mrs Dalloway ★★★½

London; 13 June 1923. Clarissa Dalloway is preparing for one of her society parties, an event she is looking forward to and dreading in equal parts. Yet, having obsessed over every trifling detail, she finds her mood transformed with the arrival from India of an old boyfriend and by the palpable presence in the vicinity of a shell-shocked soldier... A meticulous,

Fancy free: Natascha McElhone as the young Clarissa Dalloway – with Lena Headey – in Marleen Gorris's meticulous and eloquent *Mrs Dalloway* (from Artificial Eye)

eloquent realisation of Virginia Woolf's 1925 novel, *Mrs Dalloway* is a rare example of the positive fusion of literature and cinema. Of course, it helps that the novel's form was influenced by the infant medium, while scenarist Eileen Atkins has done well to commandeer much of

Woolf's elegant prose as Clarissa's voice-over. But without the sensitive, intuitive direction of Marleen Gorris (*Antonia's Line*) and the performances of a peerless cast, such advantages could well have been squandered. Only Vanessa Redgrave, as the trivial, emotionally delicate Mrs Dalloway, seems miscast, even as she

bestows the author's words with the measure they deserve. FYI: Clarissa Dalloway appeared as a supporting character in Virginia Woolf's very first novel, *The Voyage Out* (1915).

Vanessa Redgrave (*Mrs Clarissa Dalloway*), Natascha McElhone (*the young Clarissa Dalloway*), Rupert Graves (*Septimus Warren Smith*), Michael Kitchen (*Peter Walsh*), Alan Cox (*young Peter Walsh*), Lena Headey (*young Sally Seton*), Amelia Bullmore (*Rezia Warren Smith*), Sarah Badel (*Lady Rosseter, formerly Sally Seton*), Oliver Ford Davies (*Hugh Whitbread*), Katie Carr (*Elizabeth Dalloway*), John Standing (*Richard Dalloway*), Robert Hardy (*Sir William Bradshaw*), Margaret Tyzack (*Lady Bruton*), Robert Portal (*young Richard Dalloway*), Phyllis Calvert (*Aunt Helena*), Selina Cadell, Hal Cruttenden, John Franklyn-Robbins, Richenda Carey, Amanda Drew, Janet Henfrey, Derek Smee, Denis Lill, Neville Phillips, Peter Cellier, Tony Steedman, Faith Brook.
  Dir: Marleen Gorris. Pro: Stephen Bayly and Lisa Katselas Pare. Ex Pro: Chris J. Ball, William Tyrer, Simon Curtis and Bill Shepherd. Screenplay: Eileen Atkins. Ph: Sue Gibson. Pro Des: David Richens. Ed: Michiel Reichwein. M: Ilona Sekacz; Verdi. Costumes: Judy Pepperdine. (First Look Pictures/Bergen Film/Newmarket Capital Group/BBC Films/The Dutch Film Fund, etc.–Artificial Eye.) Rel: 6 March 1998. 97 mins. Cert PG. USA/UK/The Netherlands. 1997.

Black man in the White House: Wesley Snipes with Diane Lane and Daniel Benzali in Dwight Little's *Murder at 1600* (from Warner)

Murder at 1600 ★★★

When the body of a beautiful secretary is found knifed to death in a bathroom at 1600 Pennsylvania Avenue – the address of the White House – homicide detective Harlan Regis is called in to investigate. However, the laws that apply to police work elsewhere in the capital do not apply in the White House, and Regis finds himself tied up in red tape. But where there's a will, there's a way to wipe away the whitewash... While *Murder at 1600* may be as formulaic as the next conspiracy thriller, it at least has the good grace to offer reasonably complex characters in an interesting setting. Wesley Snipes does the best he can with his stock cop, while an impressive supporting cast manage to stir their stuffed suits to life. The film is also handsomely mounted by production designer Nelson Coates (*Things To Do in Denver...*) and intelligently paced by editor Billy Weber.

Lather of the bride: Julia Roberts gives Cameron Diaz more than she bargained for in P.J. Hogan's inventive, irresistible *My Best Friend's Wedding* (from Columbia TriStar)

Wesley Snipes (*Harlan Regis*), Diane Lane (*Nina Chance*), Alan Alda (*Alvin Jordan*), Daniel Benzali (*Nick Spikings*), Ronny Cox (*President Jack Neil*), Dennis Miller (*Det. Stengel*), Diane Baker (*Kitty Neil*), Tate Donovan (*Kyle Neil*), Harris Yulin (*General Clark Tully*), Mary Moore (*Carla Town*), Tom Wright, Nicholas Pryor, Charles Rocket, Nigel Bennett, Tamara Gorski, Tony Nappo, David Gardner.

Dir: Dwight Little. Pro: Arnold Kopelson and Arnon Milchan. Ex Pro: Anne Kopelson, Michael Nathanson and Stephen Brown. Co-Pro: Ralph S. Singleton. Screenplay: Wayne Beach and David Hodgin. Ph: Steven Bernstein Pro Des: Nelson Coates. Ed: Billy Weber. M: Christopher Young. Costumes: Denise Cronenberg. (Warner/Monarchy Enterprises/Regency Enterprises–Warner.) Rel: 11 July 1997. 106 mins. Cert 15. USA. 1997.

My Best Friend's Wedding ★★★★

Julianne Potter is a successful New York restaurant critic, an independent, driven and pointedly unsentimental professional who has cried three times in her life and never said 'I love you' to anyone. But, nine years ago, she made a pact with her best friend, Michael, that she would marry him if neither found their ideal partner by the age of 28. Now fast approaching 28, Julianne discovers the impossible: Michael is marrying a beautiful Chicago heiress in four days' time... A perfect marriage of script, performance and direction, *My Best Friend's Wedding* is a feel-good concoction with plenty of edge and a good dose of reality. Thanks to the credible, inventive direction of Australia's P.J. Hogan (*Muriel's Wedding*), the film steers clear of sentimental overkill and is constantly surprising, moving and very, very funny. As the desperate and devious Julianne, Julia Roberts has never been more watchable, but is matched tooth and nail by an irrepressible supporting cast. As Julianne's gay editor and confidante, Rupert Everett is exceptionally effective: the scene in which he fabricates a romantic past with her, breaking into a rendition of Dionne Warwick's 'I Say A Little Prayer' in a crowded restaurant is a classic. This, surely, will go down in cinema history as one of the great restaurant scenes, alongside Monty Python's *The Meaning of Life* and *When Harry Met Sally*...

Julia Roberts (*Julianne Potter*), Dermot Mulroney (*Michael O'Neal*), Cameron Diaz (*Kimmy Wallace*), Rupert Everett (*George Downes*), Philip Bosco (*Walter Wallace*), M. Emmet Walsh (*Joe O'Neal*), Rachel Griffiths (*Samantha Newhouse*), Carrie Preston (*Amanda Newhouse*), Susan Sullivan (*Isabelle Wallace*), Chris Masterson (*Scott O'Neal*), Paul Giamatti (*Richard*), Raci Alexander, Jennifer Garrett, Kelly Sheerin, Bree Turner, Lucina Paquet, Charlotte Zucker, Burton Zucker, Harry Shearer.

Dir: P.J. Hogan. Pro: Jerry Zucker and Ronald Bass. Ex Pro: Gil Netter and Patricia Whitcher. Screenplay: Bass. Ph: Laszlo Kovacs. Pro Des: Richard Sylbert. Ed: Garth Craven and Lisa Fruchtman. M: James Newton Howard; Rachmaninoff; numbers performed by Ani DiFranco, Jann Arden, Lloyd Price, Jimmy Soul, Diana King, Tony Bennett, Jackie DeShannon, and Amanda Marshall. Costumes: Jeffrey Kurland. Choreography: Toni Basil. (TriStar Pictures/Jerry Zucker/Predawn–Columbia TriStar.) Rel: 19 September 1997. 105 mins. Cert 12. USA. 1997.

My Mother's Courage – Mutter's Courage ★★

Returning to her house in Budapest one day in July of 1944, Elsa Tabori – a Hungarian Jew – is stopped by two elderly gentlemen and informed that she is to be deported. Attempting to look on the bright side, Elsa apologises to the men for the

Culture crash: Om Puri, Rachel Griffiths and Stellan Skarsgard in Udayan Prasad's unbearably poignant *My Son the Fanatic* **(from Feature Film Co.)**

inconvenience, suspecting that, as she has done nothing wrong, every thing will turn out all right. Elsa is in fact on her way to 'the Jewish Bakery', now better known as Auschwitz... By employing the 80-year-old Hungarian playwright George Tabori to narrate his own mother's story on screen, *My Mother's Courage* at least adds a personal touch to familiar territory. However, Elsa's tale is not that remarkable, its dramatic limitations forcing Pauline Collins to scramble through her bag of reaction shots while the Nazis for the most part are portrayed as snorting caricatures.

Pauline Collins (*Elsa Tabori*), Ulrich Tukur (*SS officer*), Natalie Morse (*Maria*), Heribert Sasse (*Kelemen*), Gunter Bothur, Buddy Elias, Peter Radtke, Tatjana Vilhelmova, George Tabori (*himself*).
Dir, Pro and Screenplay: Michael Verhoeven, based on the novel by George Tabori. Ex Pro: James Mitchell. Line Pro: Christine Rothe. Assoc Pro: Ann Wingate. Ph: Michael Epp and Theo Bierkens. Pro Des: Wolfgang Hundhammer. Ed: David Freeman. M: Julian Nott and Simon Verhoeven; Liszt, Haydn, Mozart. Costumes: Rosemarie Hettman. (Sentana Film/Little Bird/BBC Films, etc.–Clarence Pictures.) Rel: 7 November 1997. 90 mins. Cert 12. Germany/UK/Austria. 1995.

My Son the Fanatic ★★★½

Parvez has found his place in life. He's been driving his taxi through the streets of Bradford for 25 years now and is thrilled at the prospect of his only son's imminent marriage to the daughter of the local police chief. But when the boy dumps his fiancée in favour of a sudden zest for fundamentalist Islam, Parvez's fragile world starts to fall apart at the seams... At times almost unbearably poignant, Udayan Prasad's second theatrical feature (following the eye-opening *Brothers in Trouble*) reveals in bold strokes the painful dichotomy of what it means to be Pakistani and living in England. As usual, Om Puri turns in a commanding performance as the pathetic, bitter taxi driver trapped by convention, while the Melbourne-raised Rachel Griffiths, as the Yorkshire prostitute Parvez befriends, stokes her reputation as an antipodean Meryl Streep. Hanif Kureishi, the leading spokes-man for Anglo-Pakistani relations, scripted from his own *New Yorker* short story.

Om Puri (*Parvez*), Rachel Griffiths (*Bettina*), Stellan Skarsgard (*Schitz*), Akbar Kurtha (*Farid*), Gopi Desai (*Minoo*), Harish Patel (*Fizzy*), Sarah Jane Potts (*Madelaine*), Bhasker Patel (*Maulvi*), Judi Jones, Geoffrey Bateman, Moya Brady, Andy Devine, Rowena King.
Dir: Udayan Prasad. Pro: Chris Curling. Ex Pro: George Faber. Line Pro: Anita Overland. Screenplay: Hanif Kureishi. Ph: Alan Almond. Pro Des: Grenville Horner. Ed: David Gamble. M: Stephen Warbeck; numbers performed by Dreadzone, Zakir Hussain, Dinah Washington, Brook Benton, Louis Armstrong, Tricky, Jimmy Witherspoon, Barrington Levy, etc. Costumes: Mary-Jane Reyner. (Zephyr Films/BBC Films/UGC DA International/ The Arts Council of England–Feature Film Co.) Rel: 1 May 1998. 87 mins. Cert 15. UK. 1997.

The Myth of Fingerprints ★★½

Maine; today. Lena and Hal prepare to welcome their four grown-up children for the Thanksgiving weekend. It has been three years since the whole family has been together, and now there is the addition of Mia's boyfriend and Jake's new girlfriend. But this is an uncomfortable lot, and inevitably old wounds are opened as the family struggles to come to terms with its differences. As blood is thicker than water, so it can congeal – and curdle – all the quicker... Borrowing its title from the Paul Simon song (from the *Graceland* LP), *The Myth of Fingerprints* is an assured, wry and often insightful contemplation of family politics. Yet for all its intellectual complexity and subtle nuances, it never really allows us into the hearts of its protagonists – nor reveals the motive for their behaviour. In fact, it's rather like eavesdropping on someone else's conversation – intriguing, but highly unsatisfying.

Blythe Danner (*Lena*), James LeGros (*Cezanne/Leonard Morrison*), Julianne Moore (*Mia*), Roy Scheider (*Hal*), Noah Wyle (*Warren*), Arija Bareikis (*Daphne*), Hope Davis (*Margaret*), Laurel Holloman (*Leigh*), Brian Kerwin (*Elliott*), Michael Vartan (*Jake*), Chris Bauer, Christopher Duva.
Dir and Screenplay: Bart Freundlich. Pro: Mary Jane Skalski, Tim Perell and Freundlich. Ex Pro: James Schamus and Ted Hope. Line Pro: Victoria McGarry. Assoc Pro: Howard Bernstein, Anthony Bregman and Noah Wyle. Ph: Stephen Kazmierski. Pro Des: Susan Bolles. Ed: Kate Williams and Ken J. Sackheim. M: David Bridie and John Phillips; numbers performed by The Rozz Nash Sextet, My Friend the Chocolate Cake, Rufus Wainwright, etc. Costumes: Lucy W. Corrigan. (Good Machine/Eureka Pictures–Feature Film Company.) Rel: 28 November 1997. 90 mins. Cert 15. USA. 1996.

Night Falls on Manhattan ★★★

New York; the present. When a notorious drugs baron murders three cops and critically wounds a fourth, the son of the latter is invited to prosecute the killer in court. Although a legal greenhorn, assistant DA Sean Casey would appear to be locking an open-and-shut case. But then he hadn't bargained on the corruption that sparked the incident in the first place... Sidney Lumet, who brought us *Serpico*, *Prince of the City* and *Q & A*, fuels his fascination with bent cops with his own intelligently fashioned account of Robert Daley's novel *Tainted Evidence*. And, again, he has secured exemplary performances from a first-rate cast. A glowing exponent of the 'stillness' school of acting, Andy Garcia, as Casey, glides confidently into the wake of the young Pacino, while James Gandolfini and Ron Leibman are also outstanding. Only Ian Holm, cast wildly against type as an Irish-American cop, sounds a false note. P.S. Richard Dreyfuss, as Garcia's legal rival, is made up to look like an exact facsimile of Lumet regular Jack Warden – is that an in-joke or what? P.P.S. It's comforting to know that after such turkeys as *Close to Eden* and *Guilty as Sin*, Lumet hasn't lost his touch after all.

Domestic fury: Ray Winstone as the monstrous Ray in Gary Oldman's harrowing, ear-bending *Nil By Mouth* (from Fox)

Andy Garcia (*Sean Casey*), Richard Dreyfuss (*Sam Vigoda*), Lena Olin (*Peggy Lindstrom*), Ian Holm (*Liam Casey*), James Gandolfini (*Joey Allegretto*), Colm Feore (*Elihu Harrison*), Ron Leibman (*District Attorney Morgenstern*), Shiek Mahmud-Bey (*Jordan Washington*), Dominic Chianese (*Judge Impelliteri*), Jude Ciccolella (*Lt Wilson*), Paul Guilfoyle, Robert Sean Miller, Marcia J. Kurtz, John Randolph Jones, Chuck Pfeiffer, Richard Bright, Jim Moody, Frank Vincent.
Dir and Screenplay: Sidney Lumet. Pro: Thom Mount and Josh Kramer. Co-Pro: John H. Starke. Ph: David Watkin. Pro Des: Philip Rosenberg. Ed: Sam O'Steen. M: Mark Isham. Costumes: Joseph G. Aulisi. (Spelling Films–First Independent.) Rel: 5 September 1997. 113 mins. Cert 15. USA. 1996.

Nil By Mouth ★★★★

The Bonamy Estate, Deptford, South London; today. Trapped in a culture that promotes drinking, drugs and spontaneous outbursts of violence, Ray and Val live lives of dull desperation. An alcoholic, Ray pays his way via various illegal activities and for recreation frequents the pub, strip joints and gambling arcades. A victim of his own loveless upbringing, Ray just lives the life that's been handed him, but the circle of brutality is getting out of hand. Val puts up with her lot because she knows no better. However, there's a limit to what she will

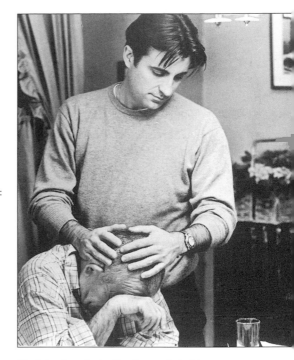

Dark justice: Andy Garcia comforts his father Ian Holm in Sidney Lumet's accomplished *Night Falls on Manhattan* (from First Independent)

endure – or is there? Closing his directorial debut with the words 'In memory of my father', Gary Oldman administers an ironic slap. Adopting the cinematic texture of Ken Loach and infusing it with the broad character delineation of Mike Leigh (with a dash of Tarantino dialogue), Oldman directs from the heart and gut and delivers a harrowing shard of autobiographically driven *cinema verite*. Yet even as *Nil By Mouth* serves as an eye-opening, ear-bending catharsis, it is not without irony, humour or tenderness. FYI: Unable to secure the second half of his £3 million budget, Oldman invested £1.5m of his own money to get the film made.

Kathy Burke (*Val*), Charlie Creed-Miles (*Billy*), Edna Dore (*Kath*), Laila Morse (*Janet*), Ray Winstone (*Ray*), Chrissie Cotterill (*Paula*), Jamie Foreman (*Mark*), Jon Morrison (*Angus*), Steve Sweeney (*Danny*), Leah Fitzgerald (*Michelle*), Terry Rowley, Sam Miller, Neil Maskell, John Blundell, Ronny Fox, Frances Ashman.
Dir and Screenplay: Gary Oldman. Pro: Oldman, Luc Besson and Douglas Urbanski. Co-Pro: Hilary Heath. Assoc Pro: Marc Frydman. Ph: Ron Fortunato. Pro Des: Hugo Luczyc-Wyhowski. Ed:

November 1997. 98 mins. Cert 15. USA. 1997.

Black and white in colour: Tim Robbins and Martin Lawrence take control of the situation in Steve Oedekerk's amusing *Nothing to Lose* (from Buena Vista)

Brad Fuller. M: Eric Clapton; numbers performed by Tony Christie, Crazy Tad, NLH, Frances, Adam Faith, Kathleen Oldman, and The Andrews Sisters. Costumes: Barbara Kidd. (SE8 Group–Fox.) Rel: 10 October 1997. 128 mins. Cert 18. UK/USA. 1997.

Nothing to Lose ★★★½

When successful advertising executive Nick Beam catches his wife in bed with his boss, his perfect world collapses around his ears. So much so, that when an armed robber breaks into his car and shoves a gun in his face, Beam's despair turns into anger and he takes the unsuspecting mugger hostage. After all, he has nothing to lose... Yet another black/Caucasian buddy comedy-thriller, *Nothing to Lose* transcends the clichés of its genre with verve and ingenuity. From the priceless opening in which Tim Robbins' sombre discourse to the camera turns out to be a denunciation aimed at his wife, which, in turn, happens to be a pre-coital game, *Nothing to Lose* keeps the surprises coming and sustains the comic momentum. Although essentially a vehicle for the stand-up comic Martin Lawrence, the film works because Robbins plays his straight man straight, while Lawrence's colourful wild card is more than just a racial stereotype. Even the mandatory goons for once exude genuine menace and the secondary characters are invariably amusing in their own right (who can forget the dancing security guard, played by the film's writer-director?), while the numerous loose ends are all neatly attended to.

Martin Lawrence (*Terrance Paul Davison*), Tim Robbins (*Nick Beam*), John C. McGinley (*Davis 'Rig' Lanlow*), Giancarlo Esposito (*Charlie Dunt*), Kelly Preston (*Ann Beam*), Michael McKean (*Phillip Barrow*), Rebecca Gayheart (*Danielle*), Susan Barnes (*Delores*), Irma P. Hall (*Bertha*), Steve Oedekerk (*Baxter, security guard*), Samaria Graham, Marcus Paulk, Penny Bae Bridges, Clark Reiner, Patrick Cranshaw, Dave Lea, Lance August, Joe Minjares.
Dir and Screenplay: Steve Oedekerk. Pro: Martin Bregman, Dan Jinks and Michael Bregman. Ex Pro: Louis A. Stroller. Ph: Donald E. Thorin. Pro Des: Maria Caso. Ed: Malcolm Campbell. M: Robert Folk; numbers performed by Tony Toni Tone, Ice Cube, Naughty By Nature, Morphine, Keb Mo, The Presidents of the United States of America, Mark Lennon, Lyle Lovett, All-4-One, Sonia Dada, Buddy Guy, Lil' Kim, Kool & The Gang, Des'ree, Coolio, etc. Costumes: Elsa Campbell. (Touchstone Pictures–Buena Vista.) Rel: 21

Nowhere ★½

Los Angeles; today. A Keanu Reeves mope-alike 'pumps his handle' in the shower. A chick observes that 'dogs eating people is cool'. A dude is stripped, tied up and spanked by his girlfriend. A dickweed called Handjob has his brains beaten out with a tin of tomatoes. An extraterrestrial vaporises a trio of gossiping Valley girls... It's a 'scuz bucket world' and writer-director Gregg Araki seems to relish (and labour) the point in this final instalment of his 'Teen Apocalypse' trilogy (following on from *Totally F***ed Up* and *The Doom Generation*). Employing the totally cool lingo of *Clueless* and shoving his camera into zit-caressing close-ups, Araki doesn't so much probe the zeitgeist of the Generation X as stick his finger down its throat to make it throw up. Some of the dialogue is amusing for its shock value, but the film's relent-lessly subversive nature and absence of a narrative structure quickly erodes the patience. Totally wasted.

James Duval (*Dark*), Rachel True (*Mel*), Kathleen Robertson (*Lucifer*), Sarah Lassez (*Egg aka Polly*), Scott Caan (*Ducky*), Nathan Bexton (*Montgomery*), Thyme Lewis (*Elvis*), Jaason Simmons (*Doug*), Christina Applegate, Joshua Mayweather, Jordan Ladd, Guillermo Diaz, Ryan Phillippe, Heather Graham, Mena Suvari, Jeremy Jordan, Alan Boyce, Chiara Mastroianni, Debi Mazar, John Enos, Nicky Katt, Brian Buzzini, Denise Richards, Beverly D'Angelo, John Ritter, Christopher Knight, Eve Plumb, David Leisure, Gibby Haynes, Charlotte Rae, Traci Lords, Shannen Doherty, Rose McGowan, Lauren Tewes, Peter Alexander, Trash.
Dir, Screenplay and Ed: Gregg Araki. Pro: Araki and Andrea Sperling. Ex Pro: Nicole Arbib, Pascal Caucheteux, Gregoire Sorlat and Ilene Staple. Ph: Arturo Smith. Pro Des: Patti Podesta. M: Peter M. Coquillard; numbers performed by Slowdive, Hole, Catherine Wheel, Massive Attack, Cocteau Twins, James, The Chemical Brothers, Lush, Sonic Youth, Curve, Future Sound of London, Blur, The Verve, Filter, Nine Inch Nails, Mojave 3, Ruby, The Jesus and Mary Chain, Seefeel, Portishead, Marilyn Manson, Radiohead, Elastica, My Life with the Thrill Kill Kult, The The, etc, etc. Costumes: Sara Slotnick. (Why Not Prods/Kill/Desperate Pictures/Blurco–Pathe.) Rel: 5 June 1998. 81 mins. Cert 18. USA/France. 1997.

The Object of My Affection ★★½

New York; the present. Nina Borowski is a social worker living in a small Brooklyn apartment. George Hanson is a first-grade teacher who rents her spare room. They are the perfect couple, as candid, loving and supportive as two people can be. And the fact that George is gay shouldn't make a blind bit of difference … It's tempting to brand this politically self-conscious comedy a flip side of *Chasing Amy*, scrubbed clean of grit, intelligence and irony and then subjected to an insulin transfusion. And while that verdict may be fun, it's not entirely true. Director Hytner has coaxed some winning performances from his cast and has forged a number of memorable scenes. Paul Rudd, a sort of amalgam of Ben Affleck and Martin Donovan, is a real find, and Nigel Hawthorne brings genuine class to his few scenes. But the weighty hand of contrivance is never far from view and the film's most intensely emotional scenes fail to take off.

Jennifer Aniston (*Nina Borowski*), Paul Rudd (*George Hanson*), Alan Alda (*Sidney Miller*), Nigel Hawthorne (*Rodney Fraser*), John Pankow (*Vince McBride*), Tim Daly (*Dr Robert Joley*), Allison Janney (*Constance Miller*), Steve Zahn (*Frank Hanson*), Amo Gulinello (*Paul James*), Kevin Carroll (*Louis Crowley*), Kali Rocha (*Melissa Marx*), Marilyn Dobrin (*Mrs Sarni*), Liam Aiken, Bradley White, Joan Copeland, Bruce Altman, Samia Shoaib, Peter Maloney, Sarah Knowlton, Alfred Uhry, Christopher Durang.
Dir: Nicholas Hytner. Pro: Laurence Mark. Co-Pro: Diana Pokorny. Screenplay: Wendy Wasserstein, based on the novel by Stephen McCauley. Ph: Oliver Stapleton. Pro Des: Jane Musky. Ed: Tariq Anwar. M: George Fenton; Wagner; numbers performed by Sting, and Gene Kelly. Costumes: John Dunn. (Fox–Fox.) Rel: 26 June 1998. 111 mins. Cert 15. USA. 1998.

187 ★★

In a world in which pupils are legally protected as 'clients' and yet show no respect for decency, property or even human life, a teacher is an endangered species. Having refused to give one of his students a pass grade, the dedicated and religious science master Trevor Garfield finds one of his books daubed with the number 187. The California state penal code for murder, 187 has been adopted by young gangs as a forewarning of death and, sure enough, Garfield is set upon by his degraded pupil with a makeshift knife. Laid off for 15 months, Garfield attempts to resume his teaching career in a new school, in Los Angeles – but, if anything, he discovers that things have got even worse... Morally ambivalent and over-stylised, *187* is a frightening, uncompromising addition to the teacher vs student genre that has run the gamut from *Blackboard Jungle* to *Dangerous Minds*. Although ennobled by a charismatic turn from Samuel L. Jackson, the film too often resembles a music video in the hands of director Kevin Reynolds (*Robin Hood: Prince of Thieves*, *Waterworld*), who seems ill at ease with his material. Still, the screenplay by real-life teacher Scott Yagemann steers away from many of the familiar clichés of the genre and leaves its own stamp of disturbing authenticity.

Samuel L. Jackson (*Trevor Garfield*), John Heard (*Dave Childress*), Kelly Rowan (*Ellen Henry*), Clifton Gonzalez Gonzalez (*Cesar*), Tony Plana (*Garcia*), Karina Arroyave (*Rita*), Lobo Sebastian (*Benny Chacon*), Jonah Rooney (*Stevie Middleton*), Richard Riehle (*Walter*), Jack Kehler, Method Man, Donal Gibson, Leonard L. Thomas, Esther Scott.
Dir: Kevin Reynolds. Pro: Bruce Davey and Stephen McEveety. Screenplay: Scott Yagemann. Ph: Ericson Core. Pro Des: Stephen Storer. Ed: Stephen Semel. M: Chris Douridas; numbers performed by Galliano, Massive Attack, Prodigy, Miles Davis, Everything But the Girl, D*Note, God Within, Brian Eno, David Darling, etc. Costumes: Darryle Johnson. (Icon Entertainment–Warner.) Rel: 12 September 1997. 119 mins. Cert 15. USA. 1997.

One Fine Day ★★★

New York City; the present. Following a bad night, architect and single parent Melanie Parker finds herself stuck with her five-year-old son when Jack Taylor, the father of another child, makes the kids miss their day trip. So, in an increasingly hectic series of compromises, Melanie and Jack switch baby-sitting duty as they juggle the demands of their professional lives... While posing as a romantic comedy, *One Fine Day* presents such a catalogue of disasters that it's hard to summon a laugh. One can guffaw at the plight of an idiot who gets his come-uppance, but Melanie and Jack are real people desperately trying to keep their act together. Notwithstanding, Michelle Pfeiffer and George Clooney bring enormous charisma and comic expertise to their roles of the tormented parents, enough so that we can identify with their perilous day. Clooney in particular reveals effortless star

No laughing matter: George Clooney and Michelle Pfeiffer (with Mae Whitman and Alex D. Linz) go through hell and back in Michael Hoffman's slick, poignant *One Fine Day* (from Fox)

The unforgiving minute: Nastassja Kinski and Wesley Snipes in Mike Figgis's atmospheric *One Night Stand* (from Entertainment)

wattage, as comfortable with children in this as he was with guns and vampires in *From Dusk Till Dawn*. Slick, engrossing and frequently quite poignant.

Michelle Pfeiffer (*Melanie Parker*), George Clooney (*Jack Taylor*), Mae Whitman (*Maggie Taylor*), Alex D. Linz (*Sammy Parker*), Charles Durning (*Lew*), Ellen Greene (*Elaine Lieberman*), Sheila Kelley (*Kristen*), George Martin (*Smith Leland*), Michael Massee (*Eddie*), Amanda Peet (*Celia*), Holland Taylor (*Rita*), Rachel York (*Liza*), Jon Robin Baitz, Joe Grifasi, Pete Hamill, Anna Maria Horsford, Gregory Jbara, Barry Kivel, Robert Klein, Bitty Schram, Marianne Muellerleile, Michael Badalucco.
    Dir: Michael Hoffman. Pro: Lynda Obst. Ex Pro: Kate Guinzburg and Michelle Pfeiffer. Co-Pro: Mary McLaglen. Screenplay: Terrel Seltzer and Ellen Simon. Ph: Oliver Stapleton. Pro Des: David Gropman. Ed: Garth Craven. M: James Newton Howard; Puccini; numbers performed by Natalie Merchant, The Ad Libs, The Shirelles, Shawn Colvin, Keb'

Mo', Tony Bennett, Harry Connick Jr, Tina Arena, Van Morrison, The Chiffons, Ella Fitzgerald, Kenny Loggins, Prong, etc. Costumes: Susie DeSanto. (Fox 2000/Via Rosa–Fox.) Rel: 4 July 1997. 109 mins. Cert PG. USA. 1996.

One Night Stand ★★½

Max Carlyle is an extremely successful commercials director with a sexy, intelligent Asian-American wife, two kids and a dog. In New York on business, he misses his flight back to LA and is invited to a violin recital by Karen, a woman he meets at his hotel. Afterwards, they narrowly escape a vicious mugging and Jack consoles Karen back at her room. One thing inevitably leads to another and Jack finds himself dramatically transformed by his chance meeting... While *One Night Stand* offers many pleasures, there is no getting away from the fact that the underlying premise is exceedingly thin. It was as if Joe Eszterhas dreamed up this neat little idea, scribbled it on a napkin and didn't know where to go next. However, in the capable hands of

Mike Figgis (*Leaving Las Vegas*) the story has been filled out with considerable nuance, both psychological and cinematic. Sumptuously photographed and lovingly detailed, the film is a superb example of style supplementing subject and as such it is seductive cinema. Yet it is the domestic frisson accomplished in the early scenes between Wesley Snipes and Ming-Na Wen that sounds the strongest note, far more than the soapy contrivance of Eszterhas's 'concept'.

Wesley Snipes (*Max Carlyle*), Nastassja Kinski (*Karen*), Kyle MacLachlan (*Vernon*), Ming-Na Wen (*Mimi Carlyle*), Robert Downey Jr (*Charlie*), Glenn Plummer (*George*), Amanda Donohoe (*Margaux*), Thomas Haden Church (*Don*), Marcus Paulk, Zoe Nathenson, Vincent Ward, John Ratzenberger, Susan Barnes, Julian Sands, Donovan Leitch, Mike Figgis (*John, hotel clerk*), Ione Skye, Xander Berkeley, Greta Gaines, Bill Raymond, Saffron Burrows.
    Dir: Mike Figgis. Pro: Figgis, Annie Stewart and Ben Myron. Ex Pro: Robert Engelman. Co-Ex Pro: Michael DeLuca and Richard Saperstein. Screenplay: Figgis and (*uncredited*) Joe Eszterhas. Ph: Declan Quinn. Pro Des: Waldemar Kalinowski. Ed: John Smith. M: Figgis; Beethoven, J.S. Bach; numbers performed by Mark Whitfield, The Tottenville High School Marching Band, Nina Simone, Blondie, Greta Gaines & Donovan Leitch, Padlock, etc. Costumes: Laura Goldsmith and Enid Harris. Paintings: Annmari Olsson. (New Linc/Red Mullet–Entertainment.) Rel: 28 November 1997. 103 mins. Cert 18. USA. 1997.

Oscar and Lucinda ★★★

Oscar and Lucinda are unlikely kindred spirits and have been kept apart by more than circumstance and breeding. Lucinda is an heiress from the Australian Outback and is obsessed by glass. Oscar is the humble son of a Devon preacher and is dedicated to God. However, in their way they are both misfits and share a passion for gambling. Then Oscar proposes an audacious plan that, should it succeed, would glorify both their fixations... Impeccably crafted and luminously acted, *Oscar and Lucinda* is an elephantine romantic drama that doesn't really hit its stride until the second hour. However, Ralph Fiennes, with awkward shuffle and ingenuous gaze, brings Oscar to extraordinary life, while Cate Blanchett is a constant joy as his radiant, impish soul mate. In addition, the film is blessed with some beautifully written dialogue and a premise that is quite unforgettable in its originality. Based on the 1988 Booker Prize-winning novel by Peter Carey.

Ralph Fiennes (*Oscar Hopkins*), Cate Blanchett (*Lucinda Leplastrier*), Ciaran Hinds (*Rev. Dennis Hasset*), Tom Wilkinson (*Hugh Stratton*), Richard Roxburgh (*Mr Jeffris*), Clive Russell (*Theophilus Hopkins*), Bille Brown (*Percy Smith*), Josephine Byrnes (*Miriam Chadwick*), Barnaby Kay (*Wardley-Fish*), Barry Otto, Linda Bassett, Polly Cheshire, Gillian Jones, Robert Menzies, Adam Hayes, James Tingby, Matyelok Gibbs, Peter Whitford, Lynette Curran, Norman Kaye, Chris Haywood, Geoffrey Rush (*narrator*).

 Dir: Gillian Armstrong. Pro: Robin Dalton and Timothy White. Assoc Pro: Mark Turnbull. Screenplay: Laura Jones. Ph: Geoffrey Simpson; and Russell Boyd. Pro Des: Luciana Arrighi. Ed: Nicholas Beauman. M: Thomas Newman; Bruckner, JS Bach, Beethoven. Costumes: Janet Patterson. (Fox/Australian Film Finance Corporation/Dalton Films, etc.–Fox.) Rel: 3 April 1998. 132 mins. Cert 15. USA/Australia. 1997.

Reconcilable differences: Cate Blanchett and Ralph Fiennes find love and affection in Gillian Armstrong's luminous *Oscar and Lucinda* (from Fox)

Palmetto ★★★

Palmetto, Florida; today. The trouble with Harry is that he just can't resist 'the pink and the green' – the pink of female flesh and the green of freshly laundered bank notes. Fresh out of prison after serving two years of a trumped-up charge, newspaper reporter Harry Barber is offered the chance to make a quick $50,000 by providing the voice of an ersatz kidnapper over the phone. The joy is that there is no kidnapping; the scam is set up by the abductee and her beautiful stepmother, both of whom have an eye for Harry Barber... The trouble with *Palmetto* is that its hero is such a doofus it's hard to sympathise with him. Harry is so amoral and slipshod in covering his tracks, he deserves what he gets. Still, the story – based on James Hadley Chase's *Just Another Sucker* is a good one, and is astutely and atmospherically told.

Woody Harrelson (*Harry Barber*), Elisabeth Shue (*Rhea Malroux*), Gina Gershon (*Nina*), Rolf Hoppe (*Felix Malroux*), Michael Rapaport (*Donnelly*), Chloe Sevigny (*Odette*

Malroux), Tom Wright (*John Renick*), Marc Macaulay, Peter Paul Deleo, Richard Booker.

 Dir: Volker Schlondorff. Pro: Matthias Wendlandt. Ex Pro: Al Corley, Bart Rosenblatt and Eugene Musso. Screenplay: E. Max Frye. Ph: Thomas Kloss. Pro Des: Claire Jenora Bowin. Ed: Peter Przygodda. M: Klaus Doldinger; numbers performed by The Abyssinians, J.J. Cale, The

Chieftains, Tito Guizar, Gregory Isaacs, OMC, David Byrne, etc. Costumes: Terry Dresbach. (Castle Rock/Rialto Film–Warner). Rel: 26 June 1998. 113 mins. Cert 15. USA. 1998.

Palookaville ★★★

New Jersey, today. Sid has received an eviction notice and has had his phone disconnected, Jerry cannot

Small deal in New Jersey: William Forsythe, Vincent Gallo and Adam Trese in Alan Taylor's droll *Palookaville* (from Metrodome)

POW blues: Glenn Close coaxes fellow internees Johanna Ter Steege, Kitty Clingnet, Tessa Humphries and Alwine Seinen in Bruce Beresford's over-ambitious *Paradise Road* (from Fox)

afford to buy a stroller for his kid (let alone such luxuries as a washing machine, carpets or milk for the cereal) and Russ is still living with his mother. For three guys in their thirties, there's got to be more to life than this. So Sid, Jerry and Russ attempt to break into a local jewellery shop – and end up in the bakery next door, collecting a king's ransom of $135. Next step: to stick up an armoured car... Deadpan, endearing and deliciously oddball, *Palookaville* is a crime film of rare charm, punctuated by moments of price-less absurdity (such as when, for inspiration, the trio watch the 1950 melodrama *Armored Car Robbery* on TV and are joined by Russ's mother, sister and brother-in-law). FYI: The movie was inspired by the 1958 Italian caper *Big Deal on Madonna Street*, which was previously remade in 1984 as *Crackers* starring Donald Sutherland and Sean Penn.

William Forsythe (*Sid Dunleavy*), Vincent Gallo (*Russ*), Adam Trese (*Jerry*), Frances McDormand (*June*), Gareth Williams (*Ed*), Lisa Gay Hamilton (*Betty*), Bridgit Ryan (*Enid*), Kim Dickens (*Laurie*), Suzanne Shepherd (*Mother*), Nicole Burdette (*Chris*), Robert Lupone, Walter Bryant, William Duell, Paul Austin, Sam Coppola, Jerome Lepage.
Dir: Alan Taylor. Pro: Uberto Pasolini. Ex Pro: Lindsay Law. Screenplay: David Epstein. Ph: John Thomas. Pro Des: Anne Stuhler. Ed: David Leonard. M: Rachel Portman. Costumes: Katherine Jane Bryant. (Public Television Playhouse/Playhouse International/Samuel Goldwyn/Redwave Films–Metrodome.) Rel: 25 July 1997. 92 mins. Cert 15. USA. 1995.

Paradise Road ★★★

10 February 1942–24 August 1945; Singapore-Sumatra. Shortly after the Japanese invaded Singapore in 1942, they threw out the rule book and rounded up British, Australian and Dutch women and dumped them into spartan camps in Sumatra. Forced to jettison their differences, a group of disparate internees struggle to hold on to their sanity and dignity in the face of mounting odds, aided by an English woman's determination to form a superlative

choral ensemble... A magnificent array of exceptional actresses flocked to this incredible story assembled from the diaries of POW survivors, channelled here into a forceful portrait of female courage and diversity by writer-director Bruce Beresford. Yet while much of the violence inflicted on these women is at times hard to stomach, the film's ambitious reach fails to consolidate the emotions. Notwithstanding, this is a bracing slice of personal history that grips the attention until the drama loses steam in its final quarter. While the female cast uniformly give of their best, Pauline Collins and Cate Blanchett are particularly impressive.

Glenn Close (*Adrienne Pargiter*), Frances McDormand (*Dr Verstak*), Pauline Collins (*Margaret 'Daisy' Drummond*), Cate Blanchett (*Susan Macarthy*), Jennifer Ehle (*Rosemary Leighton-Jones*), Johanna Ter Steege (*Sister Wilhelminia*), Julianna Margulies (*Topsy Merritt*), Elizabeth Spriggs (*Mrs Roberts*), Wendy Hughes (*Mrs Dickson*), Pamela Rabe (*Mrs Tipper*), Tessa Humphries (*Celia Roberts*), Clyde Kusatsu (*The Snake*), Sab Shimono (*Colonel Hiroyo*), Stan Egi (*Captain Tanaka*), David Chung (*interpreter*), Paul Bishop (*Dennis*), Penne Hackforth-Jones, Pauline Chan, Anita Hegh, Susie Porter, Lia Scallon, Julie

Anthony, Aden Young, Stephen O'Rourke, Vincent Ball, Nicholas Hammond, Noel Ferrier, Robert Grubb, Steven Grives, Arthur Dignam.

Dir and Screenplay: Bruce Beresford, from a story by David Giles and Martin Meader and the diaries of Betty Jeffrey. Pro: Sue Milliken and Greg Coote. Ex Pro: Andrew Yap and Graham Burke. Co-Ex Pro: Giles, Meader and Graeme Rattigan. Ph: Peter James. Pro Des: Herbert Pinter. Ed: Tim Wellburn. M: Ross Edwards. Costumes: Terry Ryan. Title design: Belinda Bennetts. (Fox/YTC Motion Pictures/Village Roadshow/Australian Film Commission, etc.–Fox.) Rel: 5 December 1997. 121 mins. Cert 15. USA/Australia. 1997.

Paws ★★½

Glebe, Sydney; the present. Pooling their formidable knowledge of computers, a Jack Russell terrier and a 14-year-old boy concoct a mobile voice unit enabling the dog to speak in the manner of Billy Connolly. Thus endowed, the terrier informs his new human friend that the evil mistress of his late master will stop at nothing to obtain a floppy disc containing the where abouts of a A$ million fortune... Featuring all the raw charm of an Australian TV special, *Paws* makes up in energy what it lacks in style. Aided by a surprisingly focused performance from Forrest (in his first role), the film bounds along cheerfully enough, although Sandy Gore's villainess is no Cruella DeVil.

Billy Connolly (*voice of PC*), Nathan Cavaleri (*Zac Feldman*), Emilie Francois (*Samantha Arkwright*), Joe Petruzzi (*Stephen Feldman*), Caroline Gillmer (*Susie Arkwright*), Rachael Blake (*Amy Feldman*), Sandy Gore (*Anja*), Norman Kaye (*Alex*), Freyja Meere (*Binky Feldman*), Forrest (*PC*), Alyssa-Jane Cook (*Trish*), Ben Connolly (*Billy*), Rebel Penfold Russell (*Carla*).

Dir: Karl Zwicky. Pro: Andrena Finlay and Vicki Watson. Ex Pro: Rebel Penfold Russell. Screenplay: Harry Cripps. Ph: Geoff Burton. Ed: Nicholas Holmes. M: Mario Millo. Costumes: David Rowe. Caterers: Feeding Frenz. (The Australian Film Finance Corp/Latent Image–Poly-Gram.) Rel: 13 February 1998. 83 mins. Cert PG. Australia/UK. 1997.

The Peacemaker ★½

On its way to a disarmament zone in the Urals, a cargo of nuclear warheads is hijacked by Bosnian terrorists. In an effort to screen their tracks, the renegades detonate one 75 kiloton bomb and wipe the smile off Eastern Europe. Sensing a potentially explosive situation, the White House Nuclear Smuggling Group gives nuclear scientist Dr Julia Kelly the green light to mobilise code red. In tandem with military intelligence officer Thomas Devoe, Kelly embarks on a breathless, high-tech operation to locate the missing bomb... Opening with an interminable *Boy's Own* prologue, this post-Cold War thriller struggles to gain momentum in the face of escalating odds. Hampered by an incomprehensible plot cluttered with extraneous detail, the film darts all over the place in an effort to feign animation. Under the circumstances, George Clooney and Nicole Kidman are given little opportunity to generate any emotional sparks. First-time feature director Mimi Leder does her best to keep the action moving, but is frustrated by a script that puts technical detail before human involvement.

George Clooney (*Thomas Devoe*), Nicole Kidman (*Julia Kelly*), Armin Mueller-Stahl (*Dimitri Vertikoff*), Marcel Iures (*Dusan*

Road rage: Nicole Kidman and George Clooney in Mimi Leder's incomprehensible *The Peacemaker* (from UIP)

Gavrich), Alexander Baluev (*General Alexsander Kodoroff*), Michael Boatman (*CPN Beach*), Rene Medvesek, Gary Werntz, Randall Batinkoff, Jim Haynie, Joan Copeland, Carlos Gomez, Jay Acovone.

Dir: Mimi Leder. Pro: Walter Parkes and Branko Lustig. Ex Pro: Michael Grillo and Laurie MacDonald. Co-Ex Pro: John Wells. Screenplay: Michael Schiffer. Ph: Dietrich Lohmann. Pro Des: Leslie Dilley. Ed: David Rosenbloom. M: Hans Zimmer; Chopin, Mozart. Costumes: Shelley Komarov and Calvin Klein. (Dream-Works–UIP.) Rel: 24 October 1997. 124 mins. Cert 15. USA. 1997.

Persons Unknown ★★★

Long Beach, California; the present. When alcoholic, disgraced ex-cop Jim Holland is seduced by an attractive blonde on rollerblades, he decides to investigate. It transpires that she's involved with some decidedly shady types and shortly afterwards robs a storeroom of a whole lotta drug money. Watching from the shadows, Holland moves in later and swipes the booty for himself... Thanks to some sharp dialogue and edgy photography, *Persons Unknown* keeps one absorbed in spite of its slippery logic. Would someone as anally retentive as Holland (his own words) really fall for a promiscuous junkie after five minutes? And how come he only

Constant nymphs: Frances Barber in Nick Willing's strangely haunting *Photographing Fairies* (from Entertainment)

noticed her needle-bruised arm days *after* their sexual encounter? Still, the film's tough skin stretched over a fragile heart makes a nice change to a familiar landscape. P.S. Director George Hickenlooper previously helmed *Hearts of Darkness*, the award-winning documentary about the making of *Apocalypse Now*.

Joe Mantegna (*Jim Holland*), Kelly Lynch (*Amanda Chenoweth Janelle*), Naomi Watts (*Molly L. Chenoweth*), J.T. Walsh (*Cake*), Xander Berkeley (*Tosh*), Jon Favreau (*Terry*), Michael Nicolosi (*Alvarez, aka 'Blitzen'*), Channon Roe (*Lewis*), George Hickenlooper (*'cigar cop'*), Christian Meoli, Antoni Corone, Jim Ortega, Brent J. Williams.
   Dir: George Hickenlooper. Pro: David Lancaster. Ex Pro: Jon Kramer and David Newlon. Assoc Pro: Amy Krell. Screenplay: Craig Smith. Ph: Richard Crudo. Pro Des: Jerry Fleming. Ed: Suzanne Pettit. M: Ed Tomney. Costumes: Alexandra Welker. (Promark Entertain-

ment/Spectator Films/Videal–Metro Tartan.) Rel: 12 December 1997. 99 mins. Cert 18. USA. 1996.

Photographing Fairies ★★★★

No, this is not a film about Robert Mapplethorpe, but a straight-faced contemplation of the spiritual obsession that gripped English society following the Great War – in particular its belief in fairies. Inspired by a true event in which, in 1917, two young girls from Yorkshire (Elsie Wright and Frances Griffiths) captured pixies on film, *Photographing Fairies* imagines what it must have been like to have one's fundamental beliefs turned around by such a preposterous notion. While the photographs (then authenticated by Kodak and championed by Sir Arthur Conan Doyle) were later exposed as a hoax, the film's protagonists didn't know that at the time. Elegantly adapted from the novel by Steve Szilagyi, the film's main conceit is a masterful one: we cannot see fairies because we move in an alternative time frame to theirs.

However, aided by the narcotic effect of a rare wild flower, mourning photographer Charles Castle enters an altered state which allows him to 'slow down' and catch sight of the speeding nymphs. Quite arresting in its unusualness, the film demands attention for exploring such dubious terrain with so much style, conviction and sobriety.

Toby Stephens (*Charles Castle*), Emily Woof (*Linda*), Frances Barber (*Beatrice Templeton*), Philip Davis (*Roy*), Ben Kingsley (*Reverend Templeton*), Hannah Bould (*Clara Templeton*), Miriam Grant (*Ana Templeton*), Rachel Shelley (*Anne-Marie*), Edward Hardwicke (*Sir Arthur Conan Doyle*), Clive Merrison, Stephen Churchett, Mary Healey, Donald Douglas, Neville Phillips.
   Dir: Nick Willing. Pro: Michele Camarda. Ex Pro: Mike Newell and Alan Greenspan. Co-Pro: Fonda Snyder and Lawrence Weinberg. Screenplay: Willing and Chris Harrald. Ph: John de Borman. Pro Des: Laurence Dorman. Ed: Sean Barton. M: Simon Boswell. Costumes: Hazel Pethig. Fairies: Ron Mueck. (The Starry Night Film Company/PolyGram/British Screen/BBC/The Arts Council of England/Dogstar Films/National Lottery–PolyGram.) Rel: 19 September 1997. 106 mins. Cert 15. UK. 1997.

Picture Perfect ★★

New York; today. Kate Mosley is an advertising executive who cannot seem to break her cycle of dud dates. Setting her sights on a ten-page layout in *Vanity Fair*, she finds herself passed over for promotion because of her single status and inappropriate 'college student' lifestyle. So her colleague and best friend Darcy fabricates a fiancé for her – inspired by an innocently compromising photograph – immediately leading to an upswing in Kate's career. But when the oblivious beau is transformed into an overnight celebrity, Kate is forced to devise a romantic arrangement... Devoid of style and snappy one-liners, *Picture Perfect* limps along for the first hour as it attempts to beef up its premise into a full-blown movie. The tragedy is that the 'concept' would have made a nice subplot in a more ambitious film, but is stretched to breaking point in this slick, shallow sitcom. Only in the final act do things pick up, with Jennifer Aniston rallying some of her potential as a big-screen presence, but then everything is thrown away in a hastily contrived ending.

Jennifer Aniston (*Kate Mosley*), Jay Mohr (*Nick*), Kevin Bacon (*Sam Mayfair*), Olympia Dukakis (*Rita Mosley*), Illeana Douglas (*Darcy O'Neal*), Kevin Dunn (*Alan Mercer*), Anne Twomey (*Sela*), John Rothman (*Jim Davenport*), Faith Prince, Margaret Gibson, Paul Cassell, Peter McRobbie, Sean Patrick Thomas, Amelia Campbell.
  Dir: Glenn Gordon Caron. Pro: Erwin Stoff. Ex Pro: William Teitler and Molly Madden. Screenplay: Arleen Sorkin & Paul Slansky and Caron. Ph: Paul Sarossy. Pro Des: Larry Fulton. Ed: Robert Reitano. M: Carter Burwell; numbers performed by Jane Kelly Williams, Kirsty MacColl, K.C. & The Sunshine Band, Dion, Captain and Tennille, From Good Homes, Donna Summer, Cathy Dennis, Texas, Swing Out Sister, Aimee Mann, Marie-Claire Alain, etc. Costumes: Jane Robinson. (Fox/3 Arts–Fox.) Rel: 9 January 1998. 101 mins. Cert PG. USA. 1997.

Ponette ★★½

When her mother is killed in a car crash, four-year-old Ponette is forced to confront some pretty harsh realities. Plied with conflicting views of death by her father, aunt and young cousins, Ponette invents her

Cold snap: Jennifer Aniston and Jay Mohr in Glenn Gordon Caron's limp, contrived *Picture Perfect* (from Fox)

own scenario, convinced that her mother will return to save the day... Only the French could build an entire film around a four-year-old girl grieving for her dead mother and then forget to provide a story. It has to be said, though, that director Jacques Doillon has elicited a remarkable performance from Victoire Thivisol, but that is still no excuse for a feature-length film. As a short, it would have been magic. Voted Best Foreign Language Film by The New York Critics' Circle.

Marie Trintignant (*Marie*), Xavier Beauvois (*the father*), Claire Nebout (*the aunt*), Victoire Thivisol (*Ponette*), Aurelie Verillon, Matiaz Bureau Caton, Delphine Schiltz, Leopoldine Serre.
  Dir and Screenplay: Jacques Doillon. Pro: Alain Sarde. Ex Pro: Christine Gozlan. Ph: Caroline Champetier. Pro Des: Henri Berthon. Ed: Jacqueline Fano. M: Philippe Sarde. Costumes: Astrid Traissac. (Les Films Alain Sarde/Rhone-Alps Cinema/ Canal Plus–Metro Tartan.) Rel: 26 June 1998. 97 mins. Cert PG. France. 1996.

Portrait Chinois ★★

Paris; the present. Over a period of two years, nine friends immersed in either fashion or film argue, laugh and fall in and out of love with each other. Strangely, it is their

dissemblance and inability to reveal their true feelings to one another that seems to bind them together... A tad over-ambitious for its own good, this pleasant trifle is hard to follow at times but is compensated by an array of engaging performances (notably from Helena Bonham Carter and Miki Manojlovic). Free-wheeling and brimming with nice visual touches, Martine Dugowson's second feature (following *Mina Tannenbaum*) is aggravating, enchanting and eminently forgettable. FYI: Translated literally, *Portrait Chinois* means *Chinese Portraits* which, in English, would read as *Pictures in Greek* (as in 'It's Greek to me').

Helena Bonham Carter (*Ada*), Romane Bohringer (*Lise Andrea*), Marie Trintignant (*Nina*), Elsa Zylberstein (*Emma*), Yvan Attal (*Yves Maurier*), Sergio Castellito (*Guido*), Jean-Philippe Ecoffey (*Paul*), Miki Manojlovic (*Alphonse*), Jean-Claude Brialy (*Rene Sandre*), Sophie Simon (*Agnes*), Emmanuelle Escourrou (*Stephanie*), Mathilde Seigner, Artus de Penguern, Katia Mechera, Rebecca Hampton.
  Dir: Martine Dugowson. Pro: Georges Benayoun. Assoc Pro: Yves Marmion and Cameron McCracken. Screenplay: Dugowson and Peter Chase. Ph: Antoine Roch. Pro Des: Pierre Guffroy. Ed: Martine Barraque and Noelle Boisson. M: Chase; numbers performed by Elsa Zylberstein, Johnny Hallyday, Leonard Cohen, etc. Costumes: Pierre Matard. (IMA Films/ UGC Images/France 2 Cinema/Polar Prods/Canal Plus/Channel Four, etc.– Film Four.) Rel: 25 July 1997. 111 mins. Cert 15. France/UK. 1996.

Return to sender: Kevin Costner in his own catastrophic *The Postman* **(from Warner)**

The Postman ★

How Costner has managed to produce and direct yet another post-apocalyptic opus defies reason (as if *Waterworld* wasn't enough). More promising was the simple story of *The Postman*, based on the award-winning science fiction novel by David Brin. Costner plays a travelling actor who survives the wilderness by delivering out-of-date post – and hope! – to fortress towns throughout the war-razed American north-west of 2013. Simple, maybe, but Costner makes it into 177 minutes of fascist-dodging, mule-killing, spoon-threatening nonsense which constantly refers to his previous successes *Robin Hood: Prince of Thieves* and *Dances With Wolves*. The jokes are bad, the dialogue worse: 'You give out hope like it was candy in your pocket,' cries a desperate young wife (a crummy role well played by Brit Olivia Williams). Add saccharin sentiments, bloated subplots and overblown action and you've got the bum-number of 1997. US critics called it 'goofy'. Let's call it *Dirtworld*. [*Karen Krizanovich*]

Kevin Costner (*The Postman*), Will Patton (*Bethlehem*), Larenz Tate (*Ford*), Olivia Williams (*Abby*), James Russo (*Idaho*), Tom Petty (*Bridge City Mayor*), Daniel Von Bargen (*Sheriff Briscoe*), Scott Bairstow, Giovanni Ribisi, Roberta Maxwell, Joe Santos, Peggy Lipton, Todd Allen, Rex Linn, Anne Costner, Ellen Geer, Lily Costner, Andy Garrison, George Wyner, Joe Costner.
Dir: Kevin Costner. Pro: Costner, Jim Wilson and Steve Tisch. Screenplay: Eric Roth and Brian Helgeland, based on the book by David Brin. Ph: Stephen Windon. Pro Des: Ida Random. Ed: Peter Boyle. M: James Newton Howard; 'You Didn't Have To Be So Nice,' sung by Costner and Amy Grant; other numbers performed by Jono Manson, and John Coinman. Costumes: John Bloomfield. (Warner/Tig–Warner.) Rel: 20 February 1998. 177 mins. Cert 15. USA. 1997.

Preaching to the Perverted ★★

Following the tabloid exposé of The House of Thwax, an outrageous S&M establishment, moral crusader Henry Harding, MP, dispatches young Peter Emery to infiltrate the ranks of the depraved in order to gain incriminating evidence. However, Peter, a virgin and former employee of the Holy Hardware computer company, is ill-equipped to blend in with such unusual types and repeatedly bungles his eye-opening forays into London's sexual underground... By introducing predictable stereotypes and a decided nudge-nudge wink-wink nature to its material, the film labours its comical attack. But with little, if any, wit to go round, this approach merely debases what could have been a fascinating insight into a world rarely explored with integrity by the cinema. Still, there's enough t&a to keep the raincoat brigade diverted, although many of the more bizarre acts of fetishism are so fleetingly revealed that it's hard to know what's up (or isn't, as it happens).

Guinevere Turner (*Tanya Cheex*), Christien Anholt (*Peter Emery*), Tom Bell (*Henry Harding, MP*), Julie Graham (*Eugenie*), Georgina Hale (*Miss Wilderspin*), Julian Wadham (*M'Learned Friend*), Ricky Tomlinson (*Fibbin' Gibbins*), Roger Lloyd Pack (*Mr Cutts Watson*), Sue Johnston, Don Henderson, Imogen Bain, Edward Jewesbury, Angela Easterling, Keith Allen, Enzo, Sarah George, Andy Coath, Tutu, Trixie Demar.
Dir:, Pro and Screenplay: Stuart Urban. Ex Pro: Danny Unger. Co-Pro: Keith Hayley. Ph: Sam McCurdy. Pro Des: James Hendy. Ed: Julian Rodd. M: Maya and Magnus Fiennes; numbers performed by Fluke, The Aloof, Rejuvination, etc. Costumes: Nicky Rapley and Chas Hines. Ms Turner's nipple double: Charlotte Brennan. Ms Turner's tongue double: Trixie Demar. Ms Graham's bottom double: Sarah George. Fetish casting: Tutu. (Cyclops Vision/European Script Fund–Entertainment.) Rel: 4 July 1997. 100 mins. Cert 18. UK. 1997.

Pretty Village, Pretty Flame – Lepa Sela Lepo Gore ★★★½

Trapped in an abandoned tunnel in the mountains, a platoon of Serbian soldiers recall their past and confront their worst fears as, one by one, they are picked off by enemy fire... Borrowing a pinch of the robust surrealism of Emir Kusturica's award-winning *Underground*, Srdjan Dragojevic's *Pretty Village, Pretty Flame* is another vivid, lively look at the appalling destruction and waste of human life that marked the Bosnian conflict. Based on a true incident that took place during the first winter of the war in 1992, the film offers a palette of earthy, colourful characters as likely to do good as evil whether they be Serb, Croat or Muslim. Leaping between several time frames, the film offers a number of memorable images: soldiers machine gunning sheep and setting fire to flower boxes ('Please look after my geraniums,' Nazim's wife had pleaded) and an American war correspondent sharing a plastic bottle of urine with a gaggle of parched Serbs. P.S. The film is dedicated to 'the film industry of a country that no longer exists'.

Dragan Bjelogrlic (*Milan*), Nikola Kojo
(*Velja Kozic*), Velimir-Bata Zivojinovic
(*Gvozden – 'Travolta'*), Dragan Maksimovic
(*Petar*), Zoran Cvijanovic (*Brzi*), Nikola
Pejakovic (*Halil*), Dragan Petrovic (*Laza*),
Milorad Mandic ('*Fork'*), Lisa Moncure
(*Liza Linel*), Dragan Zaric (*Nazim*).
   Dir: Srdjan Dragojevic. Pro: Goran
Bjelogrlic, Dragan Bjelogrlic and Nikola
Kojo. Ex Pro: Milko Josifov. Screenplay:
Dragojevic, Vanja Bulic and Nikola
Pejakovic. Ph: Dusan Joksimovic. Pro Des:
Mile Jeremic. Ed: Petar Markovic. M:
Aleksander Sasa Habic. Costumes: Tajana
Strugar Dragojevic. (Cobra Film/RTV
Serbia–Guild Pathe.) Rel: 16 January 1998.
129 mins. Cert 18. Serbia. 1996.

Prince Valiant ★★
Long, long, long ago the Vikings
nipped over to England, popped into
Camelot during jousting season and
nicked King Arthur's legendary
sword, Excalibur. Incensed by this
turn of events, the king sends
Gawain to recover the weapon, not
realising that his knight is still
unconscious from a nasty knock on
the head. However, Gawain's squire
dons his master's armour and takes
on the assignment, a most valiant
move under the circumstances...
Adapted from Harold R. Foster's
1937 comic strip, *Prince Valiant*
adopts an appropriately irreverent
tone, while employing a few
effective visual flourishes and some
splendid Welsh locations. Yet in spite
of its breathless pacing – or perhaps
because of it – the film quickly
becomes tiresome, which no amount
of silliness or picturesque armour can
alleviate. Imagine Monty Python
collaborating with Paul Verhoeven
on *Excalibur*.

Stephen Moyer (*Prince Valiant*),
Katherine Heigl (*Princess Ilene*), Thomas
Kretschmann (*Thagnar*), Edward Fox (*King
Arthur*), Udo Kier (*Sligon*), Joanna Lumley
(*Morgan Le Fey*), Ron Perlman (*Boltar*),
Warwick Davis (*Pechet*), Anthony Hickox
(*Sir Gawain*), Benjamin Pullen, Marcus
Schenkenberg, Chesney Hawkes, Zach
Galligan, Walter Gotel, Gavan O'Herlihy,
Hamish Campbell-Robertson.
   Dir: Anthony Hickox. Pro: Carsten
Lorenz. Ex Pro: Bernd Eichinger and Jim
Gorman. Co-Ex Pro: Robert Kulzer.
Screenplay: Michael Frost Beckner, Hickox
and Lorenz. Ph: Roger Lanser. Pro Des:
Crispian Sallis. Ed: Martin Hunter. M:
David Bergeaud. Costumes: Lindy
Hemming. Make-up effects: Bob Keen.
Title design: Michael Otto. (Constantin/
Lakeshore Entertainment/Hearst

**Carry On Flogging: A scene from Stuart
Urban's naughty** *Preaching to the
Perverted* **(from Entertainment)**

Entertainment/Legacy Film/Celtridge–
Entertainment.) Rel: 19 December 1997.
91 mins. Cert PG. Germany/UK/Ireland/
USA. 1997.

Prisoner of the Mountains –
Kavkazskii Plennik ★★★★
Opening here after *Pretty Village,
Pretty Flame*, the most powerful and
disturbing of anti-war movies, this
Russian film, set in the Caucasus in
recent times but adapted from
Tolstoy, is inevitably overshadowed.
It's also true that with the director's
son, Sergei Bodrov Jr, playing the
lead role, and with occasional
moments not fully persuasive, this
tale of two soldiers held as hostages

in a Chechen village lacks the impact
of Bodrov's 1989 masterpiece,
Freedom is Paradise. But that is to
quibble. The folly of war and the
tragedy of those, both soldiers
and civilians, caught up in it are
passionately felt. Audiences who find
Pretty Village, Pretty Flame unbearable
will be moved by this deeply sincere
and unsentimental award winner.
[*Mansel Stimpson*]

Oleg Menshikov (*Sacha*), Sergei Bodrov Jr
(*Vania*), Djemel Sikharulidze (*Abdul-
Murat*), Susanna Mekhralieva (*Dina*),
Alexei Zharkov, Valentina Fedotova.
   Dir: Sergei Bodrov. Pro: Bodrov and
Boris Giller. Ex Pro: Giller. Screenplay:
Bodrov, Giller and Arif Aliev. Ph: Pavel
Lebeshev. Pro Des: Valerii Kostrin. Ed:
Olga Grinshpun, Vera Kruglova and
Alain Baril. M: Leonid Desiatnikov.
Costumes: Vera Romanova. (Karavan
Joint Stock/BG Prods–Metro Tartan.)
Rel: 20 February 1998. 99 mins. Cert 15.
Russia/Kazakhstan. 1996.

Attorney at war: Mary Kay Place is grilled by Jon Voight in Francis Ford Coppola's meaty *The Rainmaker* (from UIP)

Pusher ★★

Cruising the streets of the Vesterbro district of Copenhagen, drug dealers Frank and Tonny swap tales of sexual derring-do and fantasise about wild feats of perversion. A cocaine addict himself, Frank owes his supplier 50,000 kroner and treats his prostitute girlfriend with contempt. Then, when a drug deal goes wrong, Frank realises that his days are severely numbered. Unrelentingly grim, *Pusher* is yet another fly-on-the-wall document set in the nether regions of society. It's hard to imagine any reason to see it, other than to check out the latent talent of 26-year-old Danish film-maker Nicolas Winding Refn. FYI: The inspiration for the film was apparently sparked by Ken Loach's *Raining Stones*.

Kim Bodnia (*Frank*), Zlatko Buric (*Milo*), Mads Mikkelsen (*Tonny*), Laura Drasbaek (*Vic*), Slavko Labovic (*Radovan*), Peter Anderson, Vanja Bajicic, Lisbeth Rasmussen, Gordon Kennedy.

Dir: Nicolas Winding Refn. Pro: Henrik Danstrup. Ex Pro: Peter Aalbaek Jensen and Teddy Gerberg. Screenplay: Refn and Jens Dahl. Ph: Morten Soborg. Pro Des: Kim Lovetand Julebaek. Ed: Anne Osterud. M: Peter Peter; numbers performed by The Prisoner, Bleeder, Koxbox, etc. Costumes: Loa Miller. Sound: Peter Schultz. (Balboa Enterprises/Danish Film Institute–Metrodrome.) Rel: 10 October 1997. 110 mins. Cert 18. Denmark. 1996.

The Quest ★

After a little set-to in a New York bar, an old man in a terrible wig tells the bartender his life story. It transpires he used to be a Fagin figure to a gang of street urchins, jumped on board a gun-running pirate ship (to evade police) and ended up in the Far East. There he befriended Roger Moore (as 'Dobbs, Lord Dobbs'), who inveigles him into representing the US in an international combat tournament. And so on. A genuine contender for Worst Film of the Year, Jean-Claude Van Damme's directorial debut is not of the *Dances With Wolves* variety. Weighed down by clumsy exposition, appalling dialogue and wide-eyed reaction shots, the film would have been forgivable had the fights themselves been exciting. As it is, this poor retread of *Mortal Kombat* and Van Damme's own *Bloodsport* is downright dull and embarrassing. P.S. Just one indication of the film's absurdity is its total ignorance of geography: each contestant in the tournament is meant to represent a different country, but includes one delegate from Scotland (in a kilt, no less) and another from Africa!

Jean-Claude Van Damme (*Chris Dubois*), Roger Moore (*Lord Dobbs*), James Remar (*Maxie*), Janet Gunn (*Carrie Newton*), Jack McGee (*Harry Smith*), Aki Aleong (*Khao*), Abdel Qissi (*Khan*), Louis Mandylor, Chang Ching Peng Chaplin, Ryan Cutrona, Jen Sung Outerbridge, Peter Wong, Kitao, Michael Ian Lambert, Gordon Masten, Manon Marcoux.

Dir: Jean-Claude Van Damme. Pro: Moshe Diamant. Ex Pro: Peter Macdonald. Line Pro: Jason Clark. Screenplay: Steven Klein and Paul Mones, from a story by Van Damme and Frank Dux. Ph: David Gribble. Pro Des: Steve Spence. Ed: John F. Link and William J. Meshover. M: Randy Edelman. Costumes: Joseph Porro. (Universal/MDP Worldwide–UIP.) Rel: 4 July 1997. 95 mins. Cert 18. 1996. USA.

The Rainmaker ★★★★¹/₂

Memphis, Tennessee; today. In a city overcrowded with attorneys, law school graduate Rudy Baylor is forced to accept a non-salaried job for a sleazy outfit with underworld connections. Determined to make a difference, Baylor battles corruption to serve the needs of his clients, whatever the cost to his own pocket. But is his naive idealism any match for the ruthless, unprincipled facility of his opponents? For David read the young, inexperienced lawyer drawing on his unshakeable belief in the sacredness of the American justice system. For Goliath read the all-powerful, morally bankrupt infrastructure that preys on those it proclaims to serve. Of course, it's a scenario that John Grisham has employed to good use in *The Firm, The Pelican Brief, A Time to Kill* and *The Chamber,* but here – thanks to Francis Ford Coppola's fine-tuning – the characters take over from the conspiracy theories to cook up a meaty drama that grabs the throat and ignites one's moral indignation. A terrific cast delivers the goods (and then some) in the most dramatically satisfying adaptation of a Grisham page-turner yet. FYI: To trigger an appropriate look of surprise from Jon Voight in one scene, Matt Damon turned to him – off-camera – with his testicles hanging out of his trousers!

Matt Damon (*Rudy Baylor*), Claire Danes (*Kelly Riker*), Jon Voight (*Leo F. Drummond*), Mary Kay Place (*Dot Black*), Mickey Rourke (*Bruiser Stone*), Danny DeVito (*Deck Shifflet*), Danny Glover (*Judge Tyrone Kipler*), Virginia Madsen (*Jackie Lemanczyk*), Roy Scheider (*Wilfred Keeley*), Teresa Wright (*Miss Birdie*), Dean Stockwell (*Judge Harvey Hale*), Andrew Shue (*Cliff Riker*), Johnny Whitworth (*Donny Ray Black*), Red West (*Buddy Black*), Michael Girardin (*Everett Lufkin*), Wayne Emmons, Adrian Roberts, Randy Travis, Sonny Shroyer, Pamela Tice Chapman, Daniel O'Callaghan.

Dir: Francis Ford Coppola. Pro: Michael Douglas, Steven Reuther and Fred Fuchs. Co-Pro: Georgia Kacandes. Screenplay: Coppola; narration written by Michael Herr. Ph: John Toll. Pro Des: Howard Cummings. Ed: Barry Malkin. M: Elmer Bernstein; numbers performed by Big Joe Turner, B.B. King, Muddy Waters, and Slim Harpo. Costumes: Aggie Guerard Rodgers. (Constellation Films/American Zoetrope–UIP.) Rel: 24 April 1998. 135 mins. Cert 15. USA/Germany. 1997.

A Blonde Alley: Elizabeth Berkley and Matthew Modine in Tom DiCillo's sprightly *The Real Blonde* (from Metrodome)

The Real Blonde ★★★

Manhattan; the present. Joe is an out-of-work actor and part-time waiter who aspires to a serious career on the stage. Mary is his live-in girlfriend of six years who dreams of a better life. And Bob is Joe's friend looking for the real thing: a genuine blonde. They're all searching for what they believe to be their ideal, but how realistic is their quest? In the superficial worlds of show business and fashion, idealism is only skin deep... A sprightly, quirky comedy, *The Real Blonde* is not up to the standard of DiCillo's earlier films (*Johnny Suede, Living in Oblivion*) but, as it walks the crooked line between parody and the uncomfortable truth, it definitely has its moments. It's also DiCillo's most ambitious feature to date, boasting a cast of starry cameos and old regulars, the latter gaining the most mileage from their short-hand with the director (Catherine Keener, who has appeared in all of DiCillo's films, is certainly the most convincing). Classic moments: when Joe's criticism of *The Piano* sparks a restaurant-wide debate, and when Bob's inability to achieve an erection cruelly brings about his 'comeuppance'.

Matthew Modine (*Joe*), Catherine Keener (*Mary*), Daryl Hannah (*Kelly*), Maxwell Caulfield (*Bob*), Elizabeth Berkley (*Tina*), Marlo Thomas (*Blair*), Bridgette Wilson (*Sahara*), Buck Henry (*Dr Leuter*), Christopher Lloyd (*Ernest*), Kathleen Turner (*DeeDee*), Denis Leary (*Doug*), Steve Buscemi (*Nick, music video director*), Dave Chappelle, Jim Fyfe, Tony Hendra, Daniel Von Bargen, Beatrice Winde, David Thornton, Schecter Lee, Tom DiCillo, Alexandra Wentworth, Vincent Laresca, Colin Mochrie.

Dir and Screenplay: Tom DiCillo. Pro: Marcus Viscidi and Tom Rosenberg. Ex Pro: Sigurjon Sighvatsson. Line Pro: Meredith Zamsky. Ph: Frank Prinzi. Pro Des: Christopher Nowak. Ed: Camilla Toniolo. M: Mozart and various; numbers performed by Ching Tsai, Yello, Madonna, Space, Tricky, Fluke, Jeff Beal and Joan Beal, etc. Costumes: Jennifer Von Mayrhauser. Title design: Michael Ventresco and Jennifer Cossetto. (Lakeshore Entertainment/Paramount–Metrodome.) Rel: 22 May 1998. 105 mins. Cert 15. USA. 1997.

War requiem: a scene from Gillies
MacKinnon's handsome, contemplative
Regeneration (from Artificial Eye)

Red Corner ★★½

In Beijing to negotiate the first
Chinese-American satellite TV
venture, American businessman Jack
Moore finds himself drawn to an
enigmatic fashion model. Then,
following a night of passion and
champagne, he wakes up to find
himself accused of the model's
murder. Stripped, hosed down and
locked in a dark cell, Moore quickly
realises that the legal system in China
doesn't allow for much benefit of the
doubt... Handsome production
design, colourful locations and a
contentious subject matter go some
way to alleviate the mediocrity of
this slick thriller which, in spite of
some chilling observations, seems to
be numb from the waist down. Still,
there's a terrific performance from
Bai Ling as Moore's conscientious
attorney and a lush, exotic score from
Thomas Newman. FYI: *Red Corner*
is the first Hollywood film to use
genuine Beijing locations, captured
surreptitiously on a 35mm Leica
camera.

Richard Gere (*Jack Moore*), Bai Ling (*Shen
Yuelin*), Bradley Whitford (*Bob Ghery*),
Robert Stanton (*Ed Pratt*), Tsai Chin
(*Chairman Xu*), James Hong (*Lin Shou*),
Tzi Ma (*Li Cheng*), Peter Donat, Ulrich
Matschoss, Richard Venture, Jessey Meng,
Roger Yuan, Li Chi Yu, Henry O.
   Dir: Jon Avnet. Pro: Avnet, Jordan
Kerner, Charles B. Mulveghill and Rosalie
Swedlin. Ex Pro: Wolfgang Petersen and
Gail Katz. Co-Pro: Martin Huberty and
Lisa Lindstron. Screenplay: Robert King.
Ph: Karl Walter Lindenlaub. Pro Des:
Richard Sylbert. Ed: Peter E. Berger. M:
Thomas Newman; numbers performed by
Village People, Marvin Gaye, Michael
Jackson, Madonna, and Bryan Adams.
Costumes: Albert Wolsky. (MGM–UIP.)
Rel: 5 June 1998. 122 mins. Cert 15. USA.
1997.

Regeneration ★★★½

Craiglockart Castle, Scotland; 1917.
Both a celebrated poet and war hero,
Siegfried Sassoon is shipped off to a
psychiatric clinic when he makes a
public pronouncement that what
began as a war of liberation has
become a war of aggression.
Meanwhile, the clinic's chief
psychiatrist, Dr William Rivers, is
beginning to absorb the trauma of
his own shell-shocked patients...
Crisp photography and commendably
restrained performances set the tone
for this handsome, contemplative
adaptation of Pat Barker's opening
chapter in her World War I trilogy
(also comprising *The Eye in the Door*
and the Booker Prize-winning *The
Ghost Road*). The scenes of trench
warfare themselves are authentically
realised, although too fleetingly
visited to convey the full horror,
while the music does tend to drone
on at times for no apparent reason.
The scenes between Sassoon and the
burgeoning poet Wilfred Owen,
however, are particularly affecting.

Jonathan Pryce (*Dr William Rivers*), James
Wilby (*Siegfried Sassoon*), Jonny Lee Miller
(*Billy Prior*), Stuart Bunce (*Wilfred Owen*),
Tanya Allen (*Sarah*), David Hayman (*Dr
Bryce*), Dougray Scott (*Robert Graves*), John
Neville (*Dr Yealland*), Paul Young, Alastair
Galbraith, Eileen Nicholas, Julian
Fellowes, David Robb, Kevin McKidd,
Rupert Proctor, Jeremy Child.
   Dir: Gillies MacKinnon. Pro: Allan Scott
and Peter R. Simpson. Ex Pro: Saskia
Sutton and Mark Shivas. Co-Ex Pro: Eddie
Dick and Kathy Avrich Johnson. Line Pro:
Eric Coulter. Screenplay: Scott. Ph: Glen

MacPherson. Pro Des: Andy Harris. Ed: Pia Di Ciaula. M: Mychael Danna. Costumes: Kate Carin. (Rafford Films/Norstar/BBC/Scottish Arts Council Lottery Fund/Telefilm Canada, etc.–Artificial Eye.) Rel: 21 November 1997. 114 mins. Cert 15. UK/Canada. 1997.

Remember Me? ★

Surrey, England; today. Trapped in a crumbling marriage, Ian and Lorna find that their worries are thrown into a new perspective with the arrival of Jamie, an old flame of Lorna's. The latter is in deep financial trouble and has his Rolls repossessed outside the house during an impromptu and disastrous dinner party. Then there's the question of a couple of hitmen and the unexpected appearance of Jamie's vengeful wife... A door-slamming farce in the tradition of Brian Rix and Ray Cooney, Remember Me? boasts all the elements of high comedy except for the indispensable one of pace. Directed with the velocity of a zimmer frame race, the film languishes in theatrical stasis and outmoded concepts of what is funny. [Ewen Brownrigg]

Robert Lindsay (Jamie), Rik Mayall (Ian), Imelda Staunton (Lorna), Brenda Blethyn (Shirley), James Frain (Donald), Haydn Gwynne (Jamie's wife), Natalie Walter (Georgina), Emily Bruni (Jessica), Tim Matthews (Mark), Razaaq Adotui, Barbara Hicks, Bridget Turner.
   Dir: Nick Hurran. Pro: Alan Shallcross and Alan Wright. Screenplay: Michael Frayn. Ph: David Odd. Pro Des: Christopher Bradshaw. Ed: John Wilson. M: Michael Kamen and Ed Shearmur; 'Over My Shoulder' performed by Mike and the Mechanics. Costumes: Charlotte Walter. (Channel Four/Talisman–Film Four.) Rel: 18 July 1997. 77 mins. Cert PG. UK. 1996.

The Replacement Killers ★

Los Angeles; the present. When Chinese immigrant and ace assassin John Lee is unable to carry out a hit on the seven-year-old son of a cop, he is forced to protect his own wife and daughter from the ruthless retribution of his employer. But first he must somehow get back to Shanghai to find them, which is easier said than done... This is the sort of film in which 1,000 rounds of high-velocity ammunition are fired at a getaway car, but nobody thinks of shooting the tyres. Then there are the gangs of professional killers who, flying through the air, die with that bemused expression on their faces that says, 'How could I have forgotten to wear my bulletproof vest the one day...' Affecting a John Woo air, The Replacement Killers is just too stupid, artless and humourless to even lick the ground Woo walks on. FYI: For the climactic scene in which Chow Yun-Fat empties 546 rounds of ammunition on his enemies (utilising six guns), the actor's hands became so swollen and blistered that medics were on standby to administer bandages in between takes.

Chow Yun-Fat (John Lee), Mira Sorvino (Meg Coburn), Michael Rooker (Stan 'Zeedo' Zedkov), Jurgen Prochnow (Michael Kogan), Frank Medrano (Rawlins), Kenneth Tsang (Terence Wei), Clifton Gonzalez Gonzalez (Loco), Carlos Gomez, Danny Trejo, Til Schweiger, Patrick Kilpatrick, Randall Duk Kim, Leo Lee, Andrew J. Marton, Albert Wong, Chris Doyle.
   Dir: Antoine Fuqua. Pro: Brad Grey and Bernie Brillstein. Ex Pro: John Woo, Terence Chang, Christopher Godsick and Matthew Baer. Co-Pro: Michael McDonnell. Screenplay: Ken Sanzel. Ph: Peter Lyons Collister. Pro Des: Naomi Shohan. Ed: Jay Cassidy. M: Harry Gregson-Williams. Costumes: Ariane Phillips. (Columbia Pictures/WCG Entertainment–Columbia TriStar.) Rel: 5 June 1998. 87 mins. Cert 18. USA. 1998.

Resurrection Man ★½

Belfast, Northern Ireland; 1975. A Loyalist by habit, Victor Kelly gets his kicks by picking up random targets from the street and slowly, lovingly carving them into minced beef. Then his victim has two options: to bleed to death or to die from the pain. If Belfast didn't have enough of its own Troubles, they've now got this psychotic animal on their hands... Strutting into the wake of a number of brutal IRA-inspired thrillers, this slick number injects a powerful dose of sadism into its routine of pub, kitchen and bedroom scenes, with plenty of downbeat, unpleasant characters and some ghastly seventies fashion sense. It's hard to imagine why anybody would want to watch this, let alone make it. Filmed on location in Manchester, Liverpool and Warrington.

Stuart Townsend (Victor Kelly), Geraldine O'Rawe (Heather Graham), James Nesbitt (Ryan), John Hannah (Darkie Larche), Brenda Fricker (Dorcas Kelly), James Ellis (Ivor Coppinger), Sean McGinley (Sammy McIure), Derek Thompson (Herbie Ferguson), Zara Turner (Dr Elizabeth Ryan), George Shane (James Kelly), B.J. Hogg (Hacksaw McGrath), Alan Devlin, Gerard McCartney, Michael Liebmann, Sean Rafferty, Sean Caffrey, Billy Clarke.
   Dir: Marc Evans. Pro: Andrew Eaton. Ex Pro: Stewart Till and Michael Winterbottom. Assoc Pro: Gina Carter. Screenplay: Eoin McNamee, from his novel. Ph: Pierre Aim. Pro Des: Mark Tildesley. Ed: John Wilson. M: David Holmes, Gary Burns and Keith Tenniswood; Verdi; numbers performed by Jackie Wilson, Mud, Jackie Gleason, The Walker Brothers, The Rubettes, Freddie Fender, etc. Costumes: Nic Ede. (PolyGram/Revolution Films–PolyGram.) Rel: 30 January 1998. 101 mins. Cert 18. UK. 1997.

Romy and Michele's High School Reunion ★★★

Michele is desperate to win back the favour of her best friend since, like, for ever: 'You're as cute as me,' she argues. 'You really are. In some cultures, even cuter.' Romy and Michele are on their way to their ten-year high school reunion and are desperate to make an impression. Outsiders at school, they haven't progressed much in life and are afraid to remain the laughing stock of Sagebrush High. It's enough to split a friendship, not to mention a few hairs... Overhearing a conversation between two women in the loo of a trendy LA nightclub, writer Robin Schiff was roused to devise a whole play around these airheads. The result, Ladies' Room, premiered in 1988 and now serves as the inspiration for this broad satire of Beverly Hills insignificance. The scary thing is that dialogue this inane and funny can be heard in any disco washroom on any Saturday night. But as delivered by Lisa Kudrow and Mira Sorvino, the lines take on a resonance that is truly comical, deliciously tempered by Janeane Garofalo's no-nonsense bitch. These actresses knock the strained shrillness of Midler, Hawn and Keaton into a cocked perm – it's just a shame that David Mirkin's direction never rises above the standard of a TV sitcom.

Facing the music: Lisa Kudrow, Janeane Garofalo and Mira Sorvino in David Mirkin's inane and funny *Romy and Michele's High School Reunion* (from Buena Vista)

Mira Sorvino (*Romy White*), Lisa Kudrow (*Michele Weinberger*), Janeane Garofalo (*Heather Mooney*), Alan Cumming (*Sandy Frink*), Julia Campbell (*Christie*), Mia Cottet (*Cheryl*), Vincent Ventresca (*Billy Christiansen*), Camryn Manheim (*Toby*), Justin Theroux (*Cowboy Clarence*), Jacob Vargas (*Ramon*), Kristin Bauer, Elaine Hendrix, Kathy Long, Deezer D.

Dir: David Mirkin. Pro: Laurence Mark. Ex Pro: Barry Kemp and Robin Schiff. Co-Pro: Richard Luke Rothschild. Screenplay: Schiff. Ph: Reynaldo Villalobos. Pro Des: Mayne Berke. Ed: David Finfer. M: Steve Bartek; Bach, Beethoven, Johann Strauss; numbers performed by No Doubt, The Village People, Thomas Dolby, Wang Chung, Robert Palmer, Devo, Cyndi Lauper, Kenny Loggins, Culture Club, The Pretenders, The Go-Go's, Bananarama, Howard Jones, Tears For Fears, Belinda Carlisle, etc. Costumes: Mona May. (Touchstone Pictures/Bungalow 78–Buena Vista.) Rel: 22 August 1997. 91 mins. Cert 12. USA. 1997.

Roseanna's Grave ★★

Sermoneta, Latium, Italy; today. Consumed by a mysterious malady, Roseanna Beatto makes one last demand of her husband Marcello: that she be buried in the ancient family plot. However, due to a recent spate of deaths there is now only three places left in the whole of the town's churchyard. And so Marcello takes it upon himself to prevent any further fatalities in his parish, acting as doctor, suicide counsellor and even traffic cop. Because he loves her that much... A strange mixture of black comedy, marital romance and outright farce, *Roseanna's Grave* attempts to capture the innocent charm of an *Il Postino* with the heavy-handed contrivance of a foreign co-production. In spite of

Pet cemetery: Jean Reno and Roberto Della Casa in Paul Weiland's lacklustre *Roseanna's Grave* (from PolyGram)

the lovely locations, rich hues of Henry Braham's photography and a stand-out performance from Mercedes Ruehl as the dying, all-too-lively Roseanna, the film misses its magic. Above all, under the lack-lustre direction of Paul Weiland (*City Slickers II: The Legend of Curly's Gold*, no less), the film lacks flair and grace, not to mention credibility. US title: *For Roseanna.*

Jean Reno (*Marcello Beatto*), Mercedes Ruehl (*Roseanna Beatto*), Polly Walker (*Cecilia*), Mark Frankel (*Antonio*), Luigi Diberti (*Capestro*), Giuseppe Cederna (*Father Bramilla*), Roberto Della Casa (*Bruno Rossi*), Giovanni Pallavicino (*Enzo*), Renato Scarpa (*Dr Sergio Benvenuto*), Trevor Peacock (*Iaccoponi*), George Rossi (*Sgt Baggio*), Fay Ripley (*Francesca*), Jorge Krimer, Romano Ghini, Peter Gunn.

Dir: Paul Weiland. Pro: Paul Trijbits, Alison Owen and Dario Poloni. Ex Pro: Miles Donnelly. Line Pro: Chris Thompson. Screenplay: Saul Turteltaub. Ph: Henry Braham. Pro Des: Rod McLean. Ed: Martin Walsh. M: Trevor Jones; 'Lunda Da Lei' from Verdi's 'La Traviata' sung by Luciano Pavarotti. Costumes: Annie Hardinge. (Spelling Films/PolyGram/ Hungry Eye Trijbits/Worrell/Remote– PolyGram.) Rel: 8 August 1997. 98 mins. Cert 12. USA/UK. 1996.

Rumble in the Bronx – Hongfan Qu ★★★

In New York to attend his uncle's wedding, Hong Kong cop Keung discovers that a Chinese supermart is under siege from a ruthless gang of motorcycle thugs. Offering to

Death and birth in Serbia: Dennis Quaid and Natasa Ninkovic in Pedrag 'Gaga' Antonijevic's searing and poetic *Saviour* (from First Independent)

stay on to sort these characters out, Keung quickly finds himself enmeshed in darker forces, locking horns with the Mafia itself... Crudely plotted, shoddily crafted and completely illogical, *Rumble in the Bronx* cannot be accused of artistic pretension. But as a showcase for the extraordinary balletic skills of Hong Kong's biggest celluloid export, the film is nothing short of awe-inspiring. Chan not only performs his own mind-boggling stunts, but exhibits an invigorating sense of self-deprecatory humour that has his admirers comparing him to Chaplin and Keaton. [*Charles Bacon*]

Jackie Chan (*Keung*), Anita Mui (*Elaine*), Francoise Yip (*Nancy*), Bill Tung (*Uncle Bill*), Marc Akerstream (*Tony*), Garvin Cross, Morgan Lam, Richard O'Sullivan.
  Dir: Stanley Tong. Pro: Barbie Tung. Ex Pro: Leonard Ho. Co-Pro: Roberta Chow. Screenplay: Edward Tang and Ma Fibe. Ph: Ma Jingle. Pro Des: Oliver Wong. Ed: Peter Cheung. M: J. Peter Robinson. (Paragon Films/New Line/Raymond Chow/Golden Harvest–Buena Vista.) Rel: 4 July 1997. 89 mins. Cert 15. Hong Kong. 1996.

Salut Cousin! ★★★★
Barbes, Paris; the present. An Algerian innocent, Alilo arrives in Paris for the first time to pick up a suitcase of clothes for his employer. Hooking up with his cousin Mokrane, an aspiring rap singer, Alilo is given a crash course in the sophisticated ways of the city. But Mokrane's engineered cynicism and Alilo's wide-eyed guilelessness quickly prove to be unsavoury bedfellows... A colourful, credible and touching film, *Salut Cousin!* sheds a fresh light on Paris as seen through the eyes of its Algerian immigrants, a city at once glamorised for its historical romanticism and denigrated for its Western corruption. Furthermore, this canny, accomplished comedy manages to enjoy its quirky, displaced characters without actually patronising them. A little miracle.

Gad Elmaleh (*Alilo*), Mess Hattou (*Mokrane 'Mok' Bensalem*), Megaly Berdy (*Fatoumata*), Ann Gisel Glass (*Laurence*), Xavier Maly (*Claude*), Jean Benguigui, Dalila Renault, Fatiha Cheriguene, Malek Kateb, Mohamed Ourdache.
  Dir: Merzak Allouache. Pro: Jacques Bidou. Screenplay: Allouache and Caroline Thivel. Ph: Pierre Aim. Pro Des: Olivier Raoux. Ed: Denise De Casablanca. M: Safy Boutella. Costumes: Anne Schotte. (JBA Productions/La Sept Cinema/Artemis Prods/Canal Plus, etc.–Arrow.) Rel: 22 May 1998. 86 mins. Cert 15. France/Belgium/Algeria/Luxemburg. 1996.

Saviour ★★★★
An old peasant woman offers a Serbian soldier an apple. It is not enough: so he takes her ring as well, cutting off her finger to retrieve it. It is OK, though, she is just a Muslim bitch and deserves to bleed to death. American mercenary Joshua Rose looks on with eyebrow-knotted disapproval. But who is he to talk? He just shot a boy for target practice. If *Saviour* was not inspired by a true story (embellished with real-life incidents witnessed by its director) the violence it displays would be reprehensible. Yet its gore is nowhere near as explicit as that shown in contemporary horror films. But it is violence involving real people.

Dennis Quaid, as the mandatory outsider, is a soldier desensitised to war by the murder of his photogenic wife and son. Then, when he saves a baby from certain death and is forced to care for it, his humanity begins to return. Almost daring in its relentless, unapologetic roll-call of brutality, *Saviour* begs no easy answers. At times almost unwatchable, the film is redeemed in part by the poetic cinematography of Ian Wilson (*The Crying Game, Emma*) and by some stunning location work. FYI: *Saviour* is the first American production filmed in Serbia since the Bosnian conflict.

Dennis Quaid (*Joshua Rose/Guy*) Nastassja Kinski (*Maria Rose*), Stellan Skarsgard (*Peter*), Natasa Ninkovic (*Vera*), Catlin Foster (*Christian Rose*), Sergej Trifunovic (*Goran*), Miodrag Krstovic (*Vera's father*), Nebojsa Glogovac (*Vera's brother*), John Maclaren, Dusan Janicijevic, Vesna Trivalic.
   Dir: Pedrag 'Gaga' Antonijevic. Pro: Oliver Stone and Janet Tang. Ex Pro: Cindy Cowan. Assoc Pro: Molly M. Mayeux and Scott Moore. Screenplay: Robert Orr. Ph: Ian Wilson. Pro Des: Vladislav Lasic. Ed: Gabriella Cristiani and Ian Crafford. M: David Robbins. Costumes: Boris Caksiran. (Initial Entertainment Group–First Independent.) Rel: 19 June 1998. 103 mins. Cert 18. USA. 1997.

Screaming for more: David Arquette and Courteney Cox experience *déjà vu* in Wes Craven's ingenious *Scream 2* (from Buena Vista)

The Scarlet Tunic ★½

England; 1802. Having promised her hand to the middle-aged business-man Humphrey Gould, the daughter of a prosperous landowner finds her heart stolen by a dashing German officer... Yet another dramatically underwhelming endeavour from the parsimonious school of filmmaking which casts its investors as extras (cf. *Chasing the Deer*). Here, the acting is particularly uneven, the camera-work uninspired and the direction bum-numbingly plodding. Most of the budget seems to have been spent on the costumes. [*Ewen Brownrigg*]

Jean-Marc Barr (*Sgt Matthaus Singer*), Emma Fielding (*Frances Elizabeth Groves*), Simon Callow (*Captain John Fairfax*), Jack Shepherd (*Dr Edward Groves*), John Sessions (*Humphrey Gould*), Lynda Bellingham (*Emily Marlowe*), Thomas Lockyer, Andrew Tiernan, Gareth Hale, Lisa Faulkner, Tom McCabe.
   Dir: Stuart St Paul. Pro: Daniel Figuero and Zygi Kamasa. Ex Pro: William P. Cartlidge. Co-Ex Pro: Tom McCabe. Screenplay: St Paul, Mark Jenkins and Colin Clements, from the short story *The Melancholy Hussar* by Thomas Hardy. Ph: Malcolm McLean. Pro Des: Richard Elton. Ed: Don Fairservice. M: John Scott. Costumes: Gary Lane. (Scarlet Films / The Bigger Picture / Scorpio Prods–Indy UK.) Rel: 12 June 1998. 92 mins. Cert 12. UK. 1997.

Scream 2 ★★★

Windsor College, small-town Ohio; the present. Just two years after the Woodsboro killings, a book and movie chronicling the grisly events have surfaced. As Heather Graham ('playing' Drew Barrymore) re-enacts the opening scene from *Scream* in the movie-within-the-movie (*Stab*), an audience of horror fans watches in bloodthirsty anticipation. Supplied with promotional ghost masks, the congregation unwittingly provides a perfect cover for the first brutal act in a new cycle of murders. Fuelled by the Woodsboro revival, a copycat psycho is on the loose and the real-life survivors of the first bloodbath are about to experience a nasty dose of *déjà vu*... Waving its sequel status like a banner, *Scream 2* exploits its numerical rank with a self-reverential vengeance. One character argues that, 'All sequels are by nature inferior', while another points out that *The Godfather Part II* was better than the original. This spin-off is certainly no worse than its predecessor, benefiting from wily dialogue, ingenious plotting and a welter of in-jokes and pop-cultural references. Horror fans will have a field day, although the uninitiated could view it as just another slick slasher-fest.

David Arquette (*Dwight 'Dewey' Riley*), Neve Campbell (*Sidney Prescott*), Courteney Cox (*Gale Weathers*), Sarah Michelle Gellar (*Casey 'Cici' Cooper*), Jamie Kennedy (*Randy Meeks*), Jerry O'Connell (*Derek*), Jada Pinkett (*Maureen Evans*), Liev Schreiber (*Cotton Weary*), Elise Neal (*Hallie*), Timothy Olyphant (*Mickey*), Duane Martin (*Joel*), Lewis Arquette (*Chief Louis Hartley*), Omar Epps (*Phil Stevens*), Heather Graham (*Casey Becker on screen*), Kevin Williamson (*Cotton's interviewer*), Laurie Metcalf (*Debbie Salt*), Rebecca Gayheart, Portia De Rossi, Craig Shoemaker, Nina Pertronzio, Marisol Nichols, Nancy O'Dell, Tori Spelling, Luke Wilson, Corey Parker, Wes Craven (*man at hospital*).
   Dir: Wes Craven. Pro: Cathy Konrad and Marianne Maddalena. Ex Pro: Bob Weinstein & Harvey Weinstein, Kevin Williamson. Co-Pro: Daniel Lupi. Co-Ex Pro: Cary Granat, Richard Potter and Andrew Rona. Screenplay: Williamson. Ph: Peter Deming. Ed: Patrick Lussier. Pro Des: Bob Ziembicki. M: Marco Beltrami; 'Brothers' and 'Secure' composed by Hans Zimmer (borrowed from his score to *Broken Arrow*); 'Cassandra Aria' by Danny Elfman; numbers performed by Dave Matthews Band, Jessica Craven and Mike Mancini, Nick Cave and The Bad Seeds, eels, Everclear, Foo Fighters, Collective Soul, Tonic, Sugar Ray, etc. Costumes:

Kathleen Detoro. (Miramax/Dimension Films/Konrad Pictures/Craven/Maddalena Pictures–Buena Vista.) Rel: 1 May 1998. 120 mins. Cert 18. USA. 1997.

The Secret Agent
See *Joseph Conrad's The Secret Agent*.

Seven Years in Tibet ★★
Austria/India/Tibet; 1939-1951. Seeking self-glorification in his quest to conquer the summit of Nanga Parbat, the Austrian mountaineer Heinrich Harrer abandons his pregnant wife, only to find himself incarcerated in a British POW camp. Only years later, isolated in the wilds of the Himalayas, does Harrer discover self-redemption... The relatively true story of Heinrich Harrer is a remarkable one and one that lends itself to the big screen. However, the endless mountainous trek from Austria to Lhasa is rendered so flat that by the time Harrer exhibits any signs of sympathy as a character, the patience has been worn fatally thin. Even the spectacular views of the Himalayas are denied the cinematic sweep that David Lean or Ridley Scott could have rustled up, while Brad Pitt's soporific voice-over induces instant catatonia. Nevertheless, there are some delightful touches, albeit arriving too late in the day: the Dalai Lama's enchantment with all things Western ('Do you like movies?'), David Thewlis teaching Lhakpa Tsamchoe to skate and the rescue of worms from the construction of the first cinema in Lhasa. Filmed in Argentina, Canada, Austria and the Himalayas.

Brad Pitt (*Heinrich Harrer*), David Thewlis (*Peter Aufschnaiter*), B.D. Wong (*Ngawang Jigme*), Mako (*Kungo Tsarong*), Danny Denzongpa (*Regent*), Victor Wong (*Chinese 'Amban'*), Ingeborga Dapkunaite (*Ingrid Harrer*), Jamyang Jamtsho Wangchuk (*14-year-old Dalai Lama*), Lhakpa Tsamchoe (*Pema Lhaki*), Jetsun Pema, the Dalai Lama's real-life sister (*Great Mother*), Ama Ashe Dongtse (*Tashi*), Sonam Wangchuk (*eight-year-old Dalai Lama*), Dorjee Tsering, Ric Young, Duncan Fraser, Benedick Blythe.
  Dir: Jean-Jacques Annaud. Pro: Annaud, John H. Williams and Iain Smith. Ex Pro: Richard Goodwin, Michael Besman and David Nichols. Screenplay: Becky

Johnston, from the book by Heinrich Harrer. Ph: Robert Fraisse. Pro Des: At Hoang. Ed: Noelle Boisson. M: John Williams; Debussy; cello solos: Yo-Yo Ma. Costumes: Enrico Sabbatini. (Mandalay Entertainment/Reperage/Vanguard Films/Applecross–Entertainment.) Rel: 21 November 1997. 136 mins. Cert PG. USA/UK. 1997.

Shadow Play
See *Portrait Chinois*.

Shall We Dance? ★★★★½
Tokyo/Blackpool; the present. Shohei Sugiyama is a 42-year-old accountant with a wife, daughter and a newly acquired house. But something is missing in Sugiyama's life and so, unbeknownst to friends,

Strictly secret: Koji Yakusho practises his moves in the office in Masayuki Suo's very, very funny *Shall We Dance?* (from Buena Vista)

colleagues and family, he takes up lessons in ballroom dancing. While deeply embarrassed by his new passion (a pastime fit for losers and letches), Sugiyama cannot disguise his excitement, immediately setting off alarm bells in his neglected wife's head... As much a statement on contemporary Japan and the condition of marriage there as it is a hymn to the joys of dance, Masayuki Suo's bittersweet comedy has become the top-grossing Japanese picture ever released overseas. Touching, enlightening and very,

Bitchcraft: Kathleen Turner exercises her powers of persuasion in Michael Ritchie's imaginative and sprightly *A Simple Wish* (from UIP)

very funny, the film knocks spots off *Strictly Ballroom*, both for its refusal to kowtow to Hollywood formula and for its allegiance to its characters' motives. Furthermore, its reverence for the magical town of Blackpool should do wonders for the resort's tarnished reputation at home.

Koji Yakusho (*Shohei Sugiyama*), Tamiyo Kusakari (*Mai Kishikawa*), Naoto Takenaka (*Tomio Aoki/Danny Aoki*), Eriko Watanabe (*Toyoko Takahashi*), Yu Tokui (*Tokichi Hattori*), Hiromasa Taguchi (*Masahiro Tanaka*), Reiko Kusamura (*Tamaka Tamura*), Hideko Hara (*Masako Sugiyama*), Ayano Nakamura (*Chikage Sugiyama*), Akira Emoto, Syuichiro Moriyama, Masahiro Motoki, Misa Shimizu, Hiroshi Miyasaka.
    Dir and Screenplay: Masayuki Suo. Pro: Yasuyoshi Tokuma. Ex Pro: Hiroyuki Kato, Seiji Urushido, Shigeru Ohno and Kazuhiro Igarashi. Line Pro: Tetsuya Ikeda. Ph: Naoki Kayano. Pro Des: Kyoko Heya. Ed: Jun'ichi Kikuchi. M: Yoshikazu Suo; 'Shall We Dance?' sung by Taeko Ohnuki. Costumes: Kazushi Yamaguchi,

Hiroko Yamaguchi and Masahiro Yanagida. (Altamura Pictures/NTV Network/Nippon Shuppan–Buena Vista.) Rel: 8 May 1998. 119 mins. Cert PG. Japan. 1995.

Shooting Fish ★★½

London; the present. Wards of St Mary's Orphanage of the Tortured Souls, London, and The Friendly Home For Boys, New York, respectively, Jez and Dylan have always shared a dream of owning their own stately home. And what with Jez's technical wizardry and Dylan's social prowess, they make a perfect double act, selling everything from bogus voice-receptive computers to mobile strip lighting. But no sooner do they hire a secretarial accomplice than their past starts catching up with them... Not the triumph its own publicity would suggest, *Shooting Fish* nevertheless has some ingenuity and plenty of charm. In the role of the lads' female cohort, Kate Beckinsale sparkles as usual, while Dan Futterman and Stuart Townsend at least look like they're having fun.

N.B. 'Shooting fish' is American slang for fraud and deception.

Dan Futterman (*Dylan*), Stuart Townsend (*Jez*), Kate Beckinsale (*Georgie*), Nickolas Grace (*Mr Statton-Luce*), Dominic Mafham (*Roger*), Claire Cox (*Floss*), Nicholas Woodeson (*Mr Collyns*), Ralph Ineson, Phyllis Logan, Nicola Duffett, Darren Renouf, Peter Capaldi, Tom Chadbon, John Clegg, Geoffrey Whitehead, Jane Lapotaire, Rowena Cooper, Annette Crosbie, Kim Vithana, Catherine Russell.
    Dir: Stefan Schwartz. Pro: Richard Holmes and Glynis Murray. Ex Pro: Gary Smith. Co-Pro: Neil Peplow. Co-Ex Pro: Graham Hampson Silk and Chris Craib. Assoc Pro: Lesley McNeil. Screenplay: Schwartz and Holmes. Ph: Henry Braham. Pro Des: Max Gottlieb. Ed: Alan Strachan. M: Stanislas Syrewiz; numbers performed by Space, Strangelove, The Supernaturals, Silver Sun, Jackie DeShannon, David McAlmont, Dionne Warwick, Supereal, The Wannadies, Symposium, The Bluetones, Dubstar, Passion Star, The Divine Comedy, and Huge Big Thing. Costumes: Stewart Meachem. (The Gruber Brothers/Winchester Films/Arts Council of England/Tomboy Films/National Lottery–Entertainment.) Rel: 17 October 1997. 112 mins. Cert 12. UK. 1997.

Sick – The Life and Death of Bob Flanagan, Supermasochist ★★★½

Both famous and infamous (this is the much praised documentary which includes close shots of the late Bob Flanagan hammering a nail through his penis), *Sick*'s title alone is enough to alert those who wouldn't wish to see it. But it's a sympathetic portrait of a victim of cystic fibrosis who challenged his pain by turning it into S&M sex with his devoted partner Sheree Rose. He put all of this into performance art, writing and, finally, this film, replete with black humour and no self-pity. A broader view might have added more to our understanding, but, within its limitations, the film succeeds and would have pleased Flanagan. The filmmaker, Kirby Dick, was a friend. [*Mansel Stimpson*]

Interviewers: Kathe Burkhart, Kirby Dick, Rita Valencia.
    Dir and Pro: Kirby Dick. Co-Pro: Sheree Rose. Ph: Dick, Rose, Jonathan Dayton and Geza Sinkiovicks. Ed: Dick and Dody Dorn. M: Blake Leyh; numbers performed by Nine Inch Nails, Bob Flanagan, and Leyh, Tom Kidding and The Nothings.

(The Peter Norton Family Foundation– BFI.) Rel: 13 February 1998. 90 mins. No cert. USA. 1997.

A Simple Wish ★★★

New York; today. Seven-year-old Anabel Greening has a simple enough wish: she doesn't want to go to Nebraska. But if her widowed father fails his audition for the lead in the new Broadway musical *Two Cities*, he, she and her brother Charlie will be forced to up sticks and move out of the Big Apple. Just then Anabel's fairy godmother – Murray – materialises, although 'he' proves to be something of a novice at the game. In fact, he forgets that he's meant to be at the North American Fairy Godmothers' Association annual meeting. Yet it is at that very conference that all of the godmothers' magic wands are abducted by the excommunicated power-hungry fairy Claudia. Which just leaves Murray's magic wand to save the day... A sprightly contemporary fairy tale, *A Simple Wish* is slick, imaginative and amusing – and refreshingly free of nightmarish bombast. In addition, the film succeeds in areas that others might ignore. The special effects are inventive and effective (Ruby Dee is, literally, reduced to a one-dimensional mannequin), the casting welcomely offbeat (Martin Short as fairy godmother, Kathleen Turner as witch), while *Two Cities* looks and sounds every bit as good as a bona fide Broadway triumph.

Martin Short (*Murray*), Mara Wilson (*Anabel Greening*), Robert Pastorelli (*Oliver Greening*), Amanda Plummer (*Boots*), Kathleen Turner (*Claudia*), Francis Capra (*Charlie Greening*), Ruby Dee (*Hortense*), Teri Garr (*Rena*), Alan Campbell (*Tony Sable*), Jonathan Hadary (*Lord Richard*), Deborah Odell (*Jeri*), Lanny Flaherty, Clare Coulter, Neil Foster, Jaime Tirelli, Jack McGee, Lillian Ritchie, Miriam Ritchie, H.D. Trayer, Bunty Webb, Peter Samuels (Oliver Greening's singing voice).
Dir: Michael Ritchie. Pro: Sid, Bill and Jon Sheinberg. Co-Pro: Michael S. Glick and Jeff Rothberg. Screenplay: Rothberg. Ph: Ralf Bode. Pro Des: Stephen Hendrickson. Ed: William Scharf. M: Bruce Broughton. Songs: Music by Lucy Simon; lyrics by Michael Ritchie. Costumes: Luke Reichle. Visual effects: Tim Healey. (Universal/The Bubble Factory–UIP.) Rel: 17 October 1997. 89 mins. Cert U. USA. 1997.

The Slab Boys ★

For those not acquainted with carpet factory jargon, slab boys are the lowly employees who mix the paint on slabs for designers to choose their colours from. It's a demeaning existence and can only rake in £1 a week, but then it is 1957. The factory's also in Paisley, Scotland, so there's not a whole lot to get excited about – besides, that is, a fellow employee's facial rash and the prospect of the staff dance. Based on his semi-autobiographical plays *The Slab Boys* and *Cuttin' a Rug*, this marks the directorial debut of the painter/set designer/playwright John Byrne, who displays an inventive and vigorous narrative style. Yet, while necessity may be the mother of invention, why was it necessary to keep the whole thing confined to a makeshift studio warehouse in Glasgow? Oppressively claustrophobic, the film fails to escape the shackles of its theatrical origins, in spite of spirited playing from a largely inexperienced cast. Punctuated by period pop songs and frequent flashes of unpleasantness, the thing recalls a provincial Dennis Potter burlesque with impenetrable accents. It's hard to imagine who this could possible appeal to besides 50- to 60-year-old former slab boys from the Glasgow area.

A dangerous corner: Gwyneth Paltrow and John Hannah go underground in Peter Howitt's audacious, charming *Sliding Doors* (from UIP)

Robin Laing (*Paul McCann*), Duncan Ross (*Alan Downie*), Russell Barr (*George 'Spanky' Farrell*), Bill Gardiner (*Hector McKenzie*), Louise Berry (*Lucille Bentley*), Anna Massey (*Elsie Walkinshaw*), Tom Watson (*Bill Curry*), Moray Hunter (*Jack Hogg*), Julie Wilson Nimmo (*Bernadette Rooney*), David O'Hara (*Terry Skinnedar*).
Dir, Screenplay and Costumes: John Byrne. Pro: Simon Relph and Lauren Lowenthal. Ex Pro: Ann Skinner. Ph: Seamus McGarvey. Pro Des: Luana Hanson. Ed: John MacDonnell. M: Jack Bruce; numbers performed by Little Richard, Proclaimers, Eddi Reader, Julie Wilson Nimmo, Lulu, Pat Kane, Edwyn Collins, Tom Watson, The Largie Boys Big Band, Louise Berry and Russell Barr, etc. Sound: Stuart Wilson. (Channel Four/ Skreba Slab Boys/The Scottish Arts Council/National Lottery–Film Four.) Rel: 29 August 1997. 98 mins. Cert 15. UK. 1997.

Sliding Doors ★★★½

London; the present. When Helen, a PR executive, loses her job, her life – and the film – divides into two. In one story/life she catches her train, returns home early and finds her live-in boyfriend in bed with another woman. Yet the day from hell actually turns out to be a propitious turning point. In the other turn of events, she misses her train, gets mugged while hailing a taxi and returns home to find her boyfriend alone. Her life goes on – and so does the travesty of her existence... Borrowing a page from J.B. Priestly's book, first-time writer-

director Peter Howitt takes an audacious narrative conceit and stays with it until the film's final, highly satisfying conclusion. The results are decidedly mixed, but *Sliding Doors* is to be given a gold watch for trying, even when it forces the viewer to work for his entertainment. The two story strands do get a little confusing at times (particularly in the first half hour), but John Hannah's unabashed charm and the script's frequent wit keeps one with it. And Gwyneth Paltrow, affecting a perfect London accent, is nothing short of exquisite, her unending neck and short hair recalling Audrey Hepburn at her prime.

Gwyneth Paltrow (*Helen*), John Hannah (*James*), John Lynch (*Gerry*), Jeanne Tripplehorn (*Lydia*), Zara Turner (*Anna*), Douglas McFerran (*Russell*), Paul Brightwell (*Clive*), Nina Young, Virginia McKenna, Kevin McNally, Peter Howitt, Joanna Roth, Evelyn Duah.
  Dir and Screenplay: Peter Howitt. Pro: Sydney Pollack, William Horberg and Philippa Braithwaite. Ex Pro: Guy East and Nigel Sinclair. Co-Pro: David Wisnievitz. Assoc Pro: Sandy Poustie. Line Pro: Helen Booth. Ph: Remi Adefarasin. Pro Des: Maria Djurkovic. Ed: John Smith. M: David Hirschfelder; numbers performed by Blair, Elton John, Aimee Mann, Those Magnificent Men, Aqua, Dodgy, Jamiroquai, Brand New Heavies, Abra Moore, Space Monkeys, Olive, Patty Larkin, Dido, etc. Costumes: Jill Taylor. (Paramount/Miramax/Intermedia Films/Mirage–UIP.) Rel: 1 May 1998. 99 mins. Cert 15. UK/USA. 1997.

Smilla's Feeling For Snow ★★¹/₂

Uprooted from her native Greenland to Copenhagen at the age of six, Smilla Jaspersen has never been able to fit in. More interested in mathematics and the complexities of ice and snow than people, Smilla only ever allowed one person into her heart – Isaiah, the six-year-old Inuit boy who lives next door. When the latter slips to his death off the snow-covered roof of their apartment block, Smilla suspects foul play. Isaiah had always been afraid of heights and his footprints in the snow suggest to her that he had been chased. But the more Smilla searches for the truth, the more her path is blocked by bureaucratic red tape... Adapted from Peter Hoeg's award-

winning bestseller (*Miss Smilla's Feeling For Snow*), Bille August's ambitious film benefits from a fascinating central character (crisply realised by Julia Ormond) and by the striking cinematography of Jorgen Persson. But the deeper the film slips into far-fetched intrigue, the more shallow and improbable the characters become. In short, what starts promisingly like a glacial *English Patient* eventually melts into an improbable companion piece to Alistair MacLean's *Bear Island*. US title: *Smilla's Sense of Snow*.

Julia Ormond (*Smilla Jaspersen*), Gabriel Byrne (*The Mechanic*), Richard Harris (*Tork*), Robert Loggia (*Moritz Johnson*), Vanessa Redgrave (*Elsa Lubing*), Jim Broadbent (*Lagermann*), Peter Capaldi (*Birgo Lander*), Emma Croft (*Benja*), Tom Wilkinson (*Professor Loyen*), Bob Peck (*Ravn*), Jurgen Vogel (*Nils Jakkelsen*), Agga Olen (*Juliane*), Clipper Miano (*Isaiah*), Mario Adorf, Matthew Marsh, Charlotte Bradley, Ann Queensberry, David Hayman.
  Dir: Bille August. Pro: Bernd Eichinger and Martin Moszkowicz. Assoc Pro: Roseanne Korenberg. Screenplay: Ann Biderman. Ph: Jorgen Persson. Pro Des: Anna Asp. Ed: Janus Billeskov Jansen. M: Harry Gregson Williams and Hans Zimmer. Costumes: Barbara Baum and Marit Allen. Sound: Friedrich M. Dosch. (Constantin Film/Smilla Film/Greenland Film/Bavaria Film/Danish Film Institute, etc.–Fox.) Rel: 31 October 1997. 121 mins. Cert 15. Germany/Denmark/Sweden. 1996.

Snow White: A Tale of Terror ★

The Black Forest, Germany; 1493-1509. Once upon a time a narcissistic bitch took exception to her stepdaughter's youthful beauty... Struck by its chilling nature and contemporary resonance, producer Tom Engelman has sought to put the grim back into the Grimm brothers' fairy tale. He was also keen to emphasise the historical accuracy of the piece, so great pains were taken to find the right costumes, furnishings and locations to help create this revisionist take on the classic story of a dysfunctional family. A nice premise, but who's idea was it to saddle the largely British cast with American accents and have the heroine pluck an apple off an oak tree? With virtually every

basic ground rule of cinematic logic ignored and Snow White herself resembling a product of an American modelling college, this insult to injury wears its made-for-TV blandness on its sleeve. Filmed in Valdec in the Czech Republic.

Sigourney Weaver (*Claudia Hoffman*), Sam Neill (*Frederick Hoffman*), Gil Bellows (*Will*), Taryn Davis (*Little Lilli*), Monica Keena (*Lilli Hoffman*), Anthony Brophy (*Rolf*), Frances Cuka (*Nannau*), Miroslav Taborsky (*Gustav*), Dale Wyatt (*Ilsa, the maidservant*), Joanna Roth (*Liliana*), Brian Glover, David Conrad, Christopher Bauer, John Edward Allen, Andrew Tiernan, Bryan Pringle.
  Dir: Michael Cohn. Pro: Tom Engelman. Ex Pro: Ted Field, Robert W. Cort and Scott Kroopf. Co-Pro: Tim Van Rellim. Screenplay: Tom Szollosi and Deborah Serra. Ph: Mike Southon. Pro Des: Gemma Jackson. Ed: Ian Crafford. M: John Ottman. Costumes: Marit Allen. (PolyGram/Interscope Communications–PolyGram.) Rel: 31 October 1997. 100 mins. Cert 15. UK/USA. 1996.

Someone Else's America – L'Amérique des Autres ★★★★

In a crowded corner of Brooklyn, a Spanish bar owner, Alonso, and an illegal Montenegran immigrant, Bayo, struggle to scrape together a living. With their hearts still buried in their respective homelands, Alonso and Bayo hang on to their American Dream, albeit one diluted by the Chinese restaurant next door and Alonso's love for a Syrian girl. Meanwhile, Bayo's mother and three children land in Mexico in the hope of a reunion... A warm and human comedy-drama, *Someone Else's America* superimposes magic surrealism on to an urban American context with enormous ingenuity and charm. Recreating Brooklyn on the backlot of Studio Hamburg in Germany, the film retains its American flavour with frequent establishing shots of the Manhattan skyline and a lively soundtrack of police sirens and street noise. But it is the creation of Alonso and Bayo's unique cross-cultural world that captivates the imagination, embodied by the wedding sequence that marries Chinese, Spanish and Serbo-Croatian traditions. And, best of all, in spite of its resolutely feel-good factor, the film remains uncompromisingly un-Hollywood.

Tom Conti (*Alonso*), Miki Manojlović (*Bayo*), Maria Casarès (*Alonso's mother*), Zorka Manojlović (*Bayo's mother*), Sergej Trifunović (*Luka*), Jose Ramon Rosario (*Panchito*), Lanny Flaherty, Michalis Yannatos, Michael Willis, Chia-Ching Niu.

Dir: Goran Paskaljevic. Pro: Antoine De Clermont-Tonnerre, David Rose and Helga Bahr. Screenplay: Gordan Mihić. Ph: Yorgos Arvanitis. Pro Des: Miljen Kljakovic 'Kreka'. Art: Wolf Seesselberg. Ed: William Diver. M: Andrew Dickson. Costumes: Charlotte Holdich. (Mact Prods/Intrinsica Films/Pandora Cinema/Canal Plus/European Co-Production Fund/Channel Four, etc.–Film Four.) Rel: 11 July 1997. 96 mins. Cert 15. France/UK/Germany. 1995.

Something to Believe In ★★

Las Vegas/Paris/Trevino/Naples; today. When Maggie, a struggling actress, discovers that she has a fatal case of lymphoma, she decides to capitalise on her faith. Investing the lion's share of her savings on the tables in Vegas, she wins enough money to pay for her fare to Italy, where a weeping Madonna is said to be curing the sick. Meanwhile, handsome, impoverished pianist Mike Lewis is driving to Naples to compete in a piano competition that could turn his career around. He doesn't think much of religion, but when he bumps into Maggie he finds something else to believe in... An astonishingly old-fashioned romance, *Something to Believe In* boldly ventures into beautiful disease-of-the-week domain with neither the wit nor savvy to surmount the inherent hurdles of the genre. While heartfelt and sincere, the movie is the sort that crosses language barriers with astounding ease and generally behaves as if it were made 30 years ago. Still, any film with lashings of piano music, Italian countryside and Maria Pitillo can't be all bad.

William McNamara (*Mike Lewis*), Maria Pitillo (*Maggie*), Tom Conti (*Monsignor Calogero*), Maria Schneider (*Maria Faccino*), Ian Bannen (*Don Pozzi*), Robert Wagner (*Brad*), Fiona Hutchinson (*Elaine*), Kari Whitman (*Justine*), Jill St John, Roddy McDowall, William Hootkins, Scott Lavin, Donna Schifrin, Lalo Schifrin, Neil Dixon, Shawn Klugman, Craig Vincent, Paolo Triestino, Franco Fantasia, Paolo Gasparini, Bruno Armando.

Dir and Pro: John Hough. Ex Pro: Lew Grade and Mario Cotone. Assoc Pro: Marcia Stanton, Claude Nedjar and Howard Alston. Screenplay: Hough and John Goldsmith. Ph: Tony Pierce Roberts. Pro Des: Nello Giorgetti. Ed: Peter Tanner. M: Lalo Schifrin; 'Something To Believe In' by Schifrin and Tim Rice sung by Placido Domingo. Costumes: Evelyn Thompson. (The Grade Company/The Kirch Group–Warner.) Rel: 8 May 1998. 113 mins. Cert PG. UK/Germany. 1997.

Soul Food ★★★

The weekly dinners of traditional soul food dished up by Mother Joe are what keep her family together. So, when Mama Joe is hospitalised

Fiddling the American Dream: Tom Conti in Goran Paskaljevic's warm and magical *Someone Else's America* (from Film Four)

and lapses into a coma, her three headstrong daughters find their lives rapidly coming apart at the seams... Inspired by the Sunday gatherings of his own childhood in the Midwest, writer-director George Stillman Jr

Eat Drink Bro' Sister: Vanessa L. Williams, Nia Long and Vivica A. Fox encounter man trouble in George Tillman Jr's affectionate, colourful *Soul Food* (from Fox)

has fashioned an affectionate, colourful film, rich in character and narrative strands. One could argue that his protagonists are all a step or two removed from the unsightly tedium of real life (with the exception of Mekhi Phifer's ex-con), but his cast of beautiful actors give good impressions of themselves, with Vanessa L. Williams (the singer and disgraced Miss America) particularly impressive in the selfless role of the frigid, materialistic eldest daughter. FYI: Traditional soul food comprises such staples as black-eyed peas, butter beans, cornbread, sweet potato pie and red-eye gravy.

Vanessa L. Williams (*Teri*), Vivica A. Fox (*Maxine*), Nia Long (*Bird*), Michael Beach (*Miles*), Mekhi Phifer (*Lem*), Brandon Hammond (*Ahmad*), Jeffrey D. Sams (*Kenny*), Gina Ravera (*Faith*), Irma P. Hall (*Mother Joe*), Carl Wright (*Rev. Williams*), Mel Jackson (*Simuel St James*), Morgan Mechelle Smith, John M. Watson Sr, M.T. Alexander, Sylvester Phifer, Malik Yoba, Kenneth 'Babyface' Edmonds, Kevon Edmonds, Melvin Edmonds.
   Dir and Screenplay: George Tillman Jr. Pro: Tracey E. Edmonds and Robert Teitel. Ex Pro: Kenneth 'Babyface' Edmonds. Ph: Paul Elliott. Pro Des: Maxine Shepard. Ed: John Carter. M: Wendy Melvoin and Lisa Coleman; numbers performed by Boyz II Men, Milestone, Dru Hill, En Vogue, Tony Toni Tone, Puff Daddy and Lil' Kim, Earth Wind &

Call me Al: Michael Jai White exhibits his new look in Mark A.Z. Dippe's fevered, depraved *Spawn* (from Entertainment)

Fire, Kurtis Blow, Kenneth 'Babyface' Edmonds, A Few Good Men, Laurnea, etc. Costumes: Salvador Perez. (Fox 2000 Pictures/Edmonds Entertainment–Fox.) Rel: 12 June 1998. 114 mins. Cert 15. USA. 1997.

Spawn ★★

Trained to be the US government's ultimate weapon of subterfuge, Al Simmons begins to suffer pangs of guilt when his missions repeatedly wipe out innocent lives. When he realises that his direct superior is planning a biochemical Armageddon, Al is summarily burnt to a crisp in an apocalyptic conflagration. Torn from the wife and daughter that he worships, the hideously burned agent is given back his life in return for leading Satan's army against the forces of heaven and earth. What's a soul to do? Utilising all the expertise and ingenuity of Industrial Light & Magic, this screen incarnation of Image Comics' superhero vaults to new reaches of the imagination to implement the diabolical excesses of hell. Combining a fevered imagination and a dark, depraved humour, *Spawn* goes where no film has dared (or could afford) to go before. A must for those who cherish the sound of Prodigy and admire the wit of Beavis and Butthead. P.S. John Leguizamo must go down in history for having played both the ugliest and most beautiful men on screen: the flatulent, grotesquely overweight midget 'Clown' here (Satan's henchman), and the sexy, feminine drag queen Chi Chi Rodriquez in *To Wong Foo*...

John Leguizamo (*Clown*), Michael Jai White (*Al Simmons/Spawn*), Martin Sheen (*Jason Wynn*), Theresa Randle (*Wanda Simmons*), Nicol Williamson (*Cogliostro*), D.B. Sweeney (*Terry Fitzgerald*), Melinda Clarke (*Jessica Priest*), Miko Hughes (*Zack*), Sydni Beaudoin (*Cyan*), Michael Papajohn, Frank Welker (*voice of the Devil Malebolgia*), Robia LaMorte, Chris Coppola, Jack Coleman, Laura Stepp, Todd McFarlane (*alley bum*).
   Dir: Mark A.Z. Dippe. Pro: Clint Goldman. Ex Pro: Todd McFarlane and Alan C. Blomquist. Co-Ex Pro: Brian Witten and Adrianna A.J. Cohen. Screenplay: Alan McElroy, from a story by McElroy and Dippe, based on the comic book by McFarlane. Ph: Guillermo Navarro. Pro Des: Philip Harrison. Ed:

Michael N. Knue. M: Graeme Revell; numbers performed by Orbital, Incubus, Marilyn Manson, silverchair and Vitro, Stabbing Westward and Wink, Prodigy, Filter and The Crystal Method, 808 State vs. Mansun, Slayer and Atari Teenage Riot, Metallica, etc. Costumes: Dan Lester. Visual effects: Steve 'Spaz' Williams. Animation: Dennis Turner. (New Line Cinema–Entertainment.) Rel: 19 September 1997. 96 mins. Cert 12. USA. 1997.

Speed 2: Cruise Control ★★

Having parted ways with daredevil cop Jack Traven, Annie Porter is now in a solid relationship with a more down-to-earth law enforcer, Alex Shaw. However, when she discovers that Alex is actually a member of a crack SWAT team, she wants out – until he engineers a reconciliation with a pair of tickets for a Caribbean cruise on the 'world's most luxurious' liner. Of course, Alex hadn't bargained on a crazy terrorist wiring the ship to explode... Where *Speed* took one great concept and polished it to a lean, mean shine, this unwieldy sequel grabs a number of second-hand opportunities and bulks them up with an exorbitant budget (some rumours suggested the final tab spiralled to $160m). In spite of her reported $15.3m payday, the film's main attraction – Sandra Bullock – is far too seldom on screen, leaving the action to the men. As Keanu Reeves' replacement, Jason Patric proves to be an uncharismatic action hero, like a mannequin on automatic pilot, while Willem Dafoe's psycho is of the textbook variety. As for the stunts, there are just so many that it's hard to keep track of what exactly is going on. But as this is ultimately a safe, formulaic ride, you know that everything will turn out all right and that the stars, the deaf girl and the dog will be unharmed. N.B. No oceans were polluted in the making of this film.

Sandra Bullock (*Annie Porter*), Jason Patric (*Alex Shaw*), Willem Dafoe (*John Geiger*), Temuera Morrison (*Juliano*), Brian McCardie (*Merced*), Christine Firkins (*Drew*), Michael G. Hagerty (*Harvey*), Jeremy Hotz (*Ashton*), Royale Watkins (*Dante*), Tim Conway (*Mr Kenter*), Colleen Camp, Lois Chiles, Francis Guinan, Tamia, Enrique Murciano Jr, Susan Barnes, Bo Svenson, Glenn Plummer, Allison Dean.
   Dir: Jan De Bont. Pro: De Bont, Steve Perry and Michael Peyser. Ex Pro: Mark

Gordon. Screenplay: Randall McCormick and Jeff Nathanson, from a story by De Bont and McCormick. Ph: Jack N. Green. Pro Des: Joseph Nemec III and Bill Kenney. Ed: Alan Cody. M: Mark Mancina; Puccini; numbers performed by Shaggy, Common Sense, Tamia, TK, Maxi Priest, UB40, Mark Morrison, Jimmy Cliff, etc. Costumes: Louise Frogley. Visual effects: Industrial Light & Magic; supervisor: Bert Terreri. (Fox/Blue Tulip–Fox.) Rel: 15 August 1997. 125 mins. Cert PG. USA. 1997.

Sphere ★★½

A spacecraft half a mile long is discovered at the bottom of the Pacific Ocean. The odd thing is that 300 years' worth of coral is encrusted on the hull, yet a hum can be detected from within. So, amid the strictest secrecy, a psychologist, biochemist, astrophysicist and the mandatory skeptical mathematician are rounded up to investigate – 1000 ft beneath the surface... After a terrific start, this slick, derivative techno-thriller stumbles into deep water as its premise increasingly fails to hold, er, water. Even such exemplary actors as Hoffman, Stone and Jackson are unable to bring any credibility to their stock characters, leaving the bells and whistles of the special effects department to deliver the shocks (which they do very nicely, thank you). Still, *Sphere* is better than *Event Horizon*, whose plot it echoes with uncanny precision. But then *The Abyss*, *Alien*, *Contact* and *Species* also spring to mind all too regularly. You will not believe.

Dustin Hoffman (*Dr Norman Goodman*), Sharon Stone (*Dr Beth Halperin*), Samuel L. Jackson (*Harry Adams*), Peter Coyote (*Harold C. Barnes*), Liev Schreiber (*Dr Ted Fielding*), Queen Latifah (*Fletcher*), Marga Gomez (*Jane Edmunds*), Huey Lewis (*helicopter pilot*), Bernard Hocke, James Pickens Jr.
   Dir: Barry Levinson. Pro: Levinson, Michael Crichton and Andrew Wald. Ex Pro: Peter Giuliano. Screenplay: Stephen Hauser and Paul Attanasio, from the novel by Crichton. Ph: Adam Greenberg. Pro Des: Norman Reynolds. Ed: Stu Linder. M: Elliot Goldenthal; Mozart; numbers performed by Arthur Lyman, The Ink Spots with Ella Fitzgerald, Harry James and His Orchestra, etc. Sound: Richard Beggs. Visual effects: Jeffrey A. Okun. (Baltimore Pictures/Constant c/Punch Productions–Warner.) Rel: 27 March 1998. 134 mins. Cert 12. USA. 1998.

With all the velocity of a runaway glacier: Jason Patric samples some heroism in Jan De Bont's unwieldy *Speed 2: Cruise Control* (from Fox)

Spiceworld The Movie ★

The five members of an all-girl band prepare for their first live gig as an inept documentary crew attempts to penetrate their professional patina and a tabloid photographer hounds them for a compromising photograph. But all the girls really, really, really want is to have some fun... Exposed beneath the unblinking gaze of the celluloid magnifying glass, The Spice Girls prove to be even less than we had feared, displaying little wit, talent or even showbiz savvy. The film itself – a series of limp, loosely connected sketches – resolutely refuses to offer any insight into the group's psychological make-up, and lacks the visual daring and imagination of, say, *A Hard Day's Night* or *Head*. The scene in which Michael Barrymore puts the girls through their military paces reaches a new low in cinematic crassness. FYI: Gary Glitter's cameo in the film was cut out at the last minute when the singer was arrested for possession of child pornography.

Emma Bunton (*Baby Spice*), Geri Halliwell (*Ginger Spice*), Victoria Adams (*Posh Spice*), Melanie Brown (*Scary Spice*), Melanie Chisholm (*Sporty Spice*), Richard E. Grant (*Clifford*), Alan Cumming (*Piers Cuthbertson-Smyth*), George Wendt (*Martin Barnfield*), Claire Rushbrook (*Deborah*), Mark McKinney (*Graydon*), Richard O'Brien (*Damien*), Roger Moore (*The Chief*), Meatloaf (*Dennis*), Naoko Mori (*Nicola*), Barry Humphries (*Kevin McMaxford*), David Fahm, Steven O'Donnell, Jason Flemyng, Elvis Costello, Michael Barrymore, Stephen Fry, Kevin Allen, Jennifer Saunders, Bob Geldof, Jools Holland, Bill Paterson, Dominic West, Hugh Laurie, Richard Briers, Jonathan Ross, Kevin McNally, Bob Hoskins, Neil Fox, Elton John, Simon Chandler, Craig Kelly, Neil Mullarky, Simon Shepherd, and Peter Sissons (*himself*).
   Dir: Bob Spiers. Pro: Uri Fruchtman and Barnaby Thompson. Ex Pro: Simon Fuller. Co-Pro: Peter McAlese. Screenplay: Kim Fuller. Ph: Clive Tickner. Pro Des: Grenville Horner. Ed: Andrea MacArthur. M: Paul Newcastle. Costumes: Kate Carin. (PolyGram/Icon Entertainment/Fragile Films–PolyGram.) Rel: 26 December 1997. 93 mins. Cert PG. UK. 1997.

Star Kid ★★½

Neglected by his father, derided by his sister and bullied at school, 12-year-old Spencer Griffith only has his comic-book hero MidKnight Warrior to keep him from going completely loco. Then he's befriended by a seven-foot-tall extraterrestrial robot, an advanced fighting machine that Spencer can actually climb into and operate from within... An amusing piece of sci-fi tosh designed to entertain boys of a certain age, this harmless cross between *RoboCop* and *My Bodyguard* offers plenty of action,

A bug in the system: Casper Van Dien under attack in Paul Verhoeven's slam-bang *Starship Troopers* (from Buena Vista)

serviceable special effects and a light-hearted spirit that is strangely affecting. Kids should love it.

Joseph Mazzello (*Spencer Griffith*), Richard Gilliland (*Roland Griffith*), Corinne Bohrer (*Janet Holloway*), Alex Daniels (*Cyborsuit*), Joey Simmrin (*Turbo Bruntley*), Ashlee Levitch (*Stacey Griffith*), Danny Masterson (*Kevin*), Lauren Eckstrom (*Lauren*), Jack McGee (*Hank Bruntley*).
    Dir and Screenplay: Manny Coto. Pro: Jennie Lew Tugend. Ex Pro: Mark Amin. Ph: Ronn Schmidt. Pro Des: C.J. Strawn. Ed: Bob Ducsay. M: Nicholas Pike; numbers performed by Edgar Winter, Medicine Wheel, Snail, etc. Costumes: Ileane Meltzer. Visual effects: Thomas C. Rainone. Make-up effects: Thomas R. Burman and Bari Dreiband-Burman. Broadwarrior ships: Screaming Mad George. (Trimark Pictures–Entertainment.) Rel: 22 May 1998. 101 mins. Cert PG. USA. 1997.

Starship Troopers ★★★½
Millions of years ahead of us in their evolutionary cycle, a race of extraterrestrial insects are getting to be a damned nuisance. Endowed with enormous claws and the nimble attack action of scorpions, the bugs prove to be deadly opponents. Furthermore, their rate of reproduction is phenomenal, not to mention their knack for launching interplanetary asteroids. When war is officially declared between earth and the planet Klendathu, the raw recruits of the Federation army must put their personal differences to one side and get ready to kick some alien butt... If you fancy a cross between *Men in Black* and *Independence Day* (with a dash of TV's *Space Academy*) from the director of *RoboCop*, then *Starship Troopers* is your cup of sodapop – with a shot of the hard stuff. On its own terms, however, it hits its marks with slam-bang efficiency, even when it sheepishly follows certain conventions of the genre (for instance, the miraculous recovery of key characters after being impaled by giant talons). The effects though are everything and are nothing short of awe-inspiring (and very gruesome). But with a budget of $100m – and no star wallets to satisfy – they would have to be. Filmed in Wyoming and South Dakota.

Casper Van Dien (*Johnny Rico*), Dina Meyer (*Dizzy Flores*), Denise Richards (*Carmen Ibanez*), Jake Busey (*Ace Levy*), Neil Patrick Harris (*Carl Jenkins*), Patrick Muldoon (*Zander Barcalow*), Michael Ironside (*Jean Rasczak*), Clancy Brown (*Sergeant Zim*), Marshall Bell (*General Owen*), Seth Gilliam (*Sugar Watkins*), Eric Bruskotter (*Breckinridge*), Rue McClanahan, Matt Levin, Blake Lindsley, Brenda Strong, John Cunningham, Dale A. Dye.
    Dir: Paul Verhoeven. Pro: Alan Marshall and Jon Davison. Co-Pro and Screenplay: Ed Neumeier, from the book by Robert A. Heinlein. Ph: Jost Vacano. Pro Des: Allan Cameron. Ed: Mark Goldblatt and Caroline Ross. M: Basil Poledouris; numbers performed by Zoe Poledouris, Alisha's Attic, Mazzy Star, and The Bomboras. Costumes: Ellen Mirojnick. Sound: Stephen Hunter Flick. Special effects: John Richardson. Visual effects: Scott Squires. Creature effects: Phil Tippett. Prosthetic make-up: Kevin Yagher. Spaceship effects: Scott E. Anderson. (TriStar Pictures/Touchstone Pictures–Buena Vista.) Rel: 2 January 1998. 129 mins. Cert 15. USA. 1997.

Stella Does Tricks ★★
The life and various humiliations of a teenage prostitute working the streets of London... Gritty, grimy and appropriately sordid, *Stella Does Tricks* hardly offers anything new to contemplate, even if it is based on the genuine experiences of prostitutes from London, Manchester and Glasgow. It is all pretty believable, though, and James Bolam is inspired casting as Stella's grotesque pimp.

Kelly Macdonald (*Stella McGuire*), James Bolam (*Mr Peters*), Hans Matheson (*Eddie*), Ewan Stewart (*Francis McGuire*), Andy Serkis (*Fitz*), Joyce Henderson (*Auntie Aileen*), Suzanne Madock (*Carol*), Emma Faulkner (*Belle*), Nick Stringer,

Andrej Borkowski, Richard Syms.
Dir: Coky Giedroyc. Pro: Adam Barker.
Ex Pro: Ben Gibson. Co-Pro: Angus
Lamont. Co-Ex Pro: Madeleine French and
Eddie Dick. Screenplay: Alison Kennedy.
Ph: Barry Ackroyd. Pro Des: Lynne
Whiteread. Ed: Budge Tremlett. M: Nick
Bicat; 'This Is Mine' performed by P.J.
Harvey. Costumes: Annie Symons.
(BFI/Channel Four/Scottish Arts Council
Lottery Fund/Compulsive Films/Side-
walk–BFI.) Rel: 30 January 1998. 98 mins.
Cert 18. UK. 1996.

Stephen King's Thinner ★

Fairview, Maine; the present. In
an attempt to convince her obese
husband that there's more to life
than food, Heidi Halleck indulges in
a bit of the old oral as he drives them
home after an evening out. Thus
distracted, the 300 lb Billy Halleck
knocks down and kills an old gypsy
woman crossing the road. The
victim's father, the even older Tadzu
Lempke, then makes Billy's dream
come true: a supernatural diet in
which he can consume 1,200 calories
a day and still lose weight! And lose
weight, and lose weight... Stephen
King really knows what makes us
squirm: unapologetic and mean-
spirited xenophobia, an overweight
man obsessively stuffing his face,
people hurting the ones they love...
All great stuff. The problem with
adapting the novels of King is that
most of his ideas are just narrative
gimmicks and lose their emotional
power when magnified on the big
screen. Here, under the direction of
Tom Holland (*Fright Night*, *Child's
Play*) his 1985 best-seller is trivialised
by bad acting and shoddy character
development, which just leaves a bad
taste in the mouth.

Robert John Burke (*Billy Halleck*), Michael
Constantine (*Tadzu Lempke*), Lucinda
Jenney (*Heidi Halleck*), Kari Wuhrer
(*Gina Lempke*), John Horton (*Judge Cary
Rossington*), Sam Freed (*Dr Mike Houston*),
Daniel Von Bargen (*Chief Duncan Hopley*),
Joe Mantegna (*Richie Ginelli*), Elizabeth
Franz (*Leda Rossington*), Joy Lenz (*Linda
Halleck*), Terrence Kava (*Gabe Lempke*),
Stephen King (*Dr Bangor*), Josh Holland
(*Frank Spurton*), Walter Bobbie, Howard
Erskine, Jeff Ware, Antonette
Schwartzberg, Peter Maloney, Sean
Hewitt.
Dir: Tom Holland. Pro: Richard P.
Rubinstein and Mitchell Galin. Ex Pro:
Stephen F. Kesten. Screenplay: Holland
and Michael McDowell, based on the book

Alien nation: Giovanni Ribisi and
Nicky Katt ruminate on life and stuff
in Richard Linklater's powerful,
unblinking *subUrbia* (from Carlton)

by Richard Bachman (King). Ph: Kees Van
Oostrum. Pro Des: Laurence Bennett. Ed:
Marc Laub. M: Daniel Licht. Costumes:
Ha Nguyen. Make-up: Greg Cannom.
(Spelling Films–Warner.) Rel: 11 July 1997.
92 mins. Cert 18. USA. 1996.

Stiff Upper Lips ★

A very broad spoof of the Laura
Ashley school of filmmaking, *Stiff
Upper Lips* adopts the *Hot Shots!*
brand of parody by reproducing
famous scenes from various films.
Thus, we open on the college hurdle
race from *Chariots of Fire* and are
subsequently provided with a
guided tour of *The Remains of the Day*,
Oliver!, *A Room With a View*, *Death in
Venice*, *A Passage to India* and so on.
Liberally sprinkled with in-jokes
(such as characters named after the
film directors James Ivory and Hugh
Hudson) and hackneyed musical
pointers (Mahler's 'Adagietto' from
his fifth symphony, Puccini's 'O Mio
Babbino Caro'), the film mistakenly
believes that reproduction is the
height of wit. Few of the gags hit
their mark, while the tiresome
mugging from the cast only
exacerbate matters. Still, the location
work is glorious, making this the

best-looking, least funny British
comedy – ever. Filmed in Italy, India
and on the Isle of Man.

Peter Ustinov (*Horace*), Prunella Scales
(*Aunt Agnes Ivory*), Georgina Cates (*Emily*),
Samuel West (*Edward*), Brian Glover (*Eric*),
Frank Finlay (*Hudson Junior*), Robert Portal
(*Cedric Trilling*), Richard Braine (*Mr
Tweeb*), Sean Pertwee (*George*), Nicholas
Selby, John Boswall, Anna Livia Ryan,
Geoffrey Palmer, David Ashton, Mac
McDonald, Kate Harper, Shri Vallabh
Vyas, John Winter.
Dir: Gary Sinyor. Pro: Sinyor and
Jeremy Bolt. Ex Pro: Nigel Savage. Co-Pro:
Keith Richardson and Bobby Bedi. Co-Ex
Pro: Andrew Cohen, Babs Thomas and
Stephen Margolis. Line Pro: Simon Hardy
and Simon Scotland. Screenplay: Sinyor
and Paul Simpkin. Ph: Simon Archer. Pro
Des: Mike Grant. Ed: Peter Hollywood. M:
David A. Hughes and John Murphy;
Rossini, Rachmaninov, Mascagni, Puccini,
Mahler, Vivaldi, Handel. Costumes:
Stephanie Collie. (Cavalier Features/
Impact Pictures/Yorkshire Films/
Kaleidoscope India PVT/The Isle of Man
Film Commission–Metrodome.) Rel: 12
June 1998. 90 mins. Cert 15. UK. 1996.

subUrbia ★★★★

A group of 20-year-old suburbanites
gather outside an all-night food
mart. They are waiting to greet their
friend 'Pony,' who is returning for
the first time since making a name
for himself in the rock business.
Setting the scene with cheerless
vistas of American suburbia

Ice cold with Atom: Sir Ian Holm bruises the process of grief in Atom Egoyan's complex, absorbing *The Sweet Hereafter* (from Electric)

(accompanied by Gene Pitney singing 'Town Without Pity'), Richard Linklater's bleak, incisive adaptation of Eric Bogosian's play swiftly cuts to the bone. As with his previous films *Slacker, Dazed and Confused* and *Before Sunrise*, Linklater exhibits an uncanny knack for soliciting honest, convincing performances from his largely unknown cast. And, again, his characters hang out, smoke, swig beer and talk themselves into corners they can't crawl out of. All the more unsettling for its credibility, *subUrbia* boasts some powerful moments in this unblinking stare at 20-something alienation – and hits home all the harder because of its refusal to kow tow to Hollywood convention. What happens in this night of unresolved differences doesn't just happen once in a blue moon, but every night. And there lies the film's power.

Jayce Bartok (*Pony*), Amie Carey (*Sooze*), Nicky Katt (*Tim*), Ajay Naidu (*Nazeer*), Parker Posey (*Erica*), Giovanni Ribisi (*Jeff*), Samia Shoaib (*Pakeesa*), Dina Spybey (*Bee-Bee*), Steve Zahn (*Buff*), Kitt Brophy, Keith Preusse, Bill Wise.
Dir: Richard Linklater. Pro: Anne Walker-McBay. Ex Pro: John Sloss. Line Pro: Ginger Sledge. Screenplay: Eric Bogosian. Ph: Lee Daniel. Pro Des:

Catherine Hardwicke. Ed: Sandra Adair. M: Sonic Youth; numbers performed by Gene Pitney, Meat Puppets, Ministry, Girls Against Boys, Elastica, Beck, Superchunk, Jayce Bartok, Sonic Youth, The Flaming Lips, Boss Hog, Butthole Surfers, etc. Costumes: Melanie Armstrong. (Castle Rock/Detour–Carlton.) Rel: 17 October 1997. 120 mins. Cert 18. USA. 1996.

The Sweet Hereafter ★★★

Taking its title from a Negro spiritual – 'in the sweet hereafter, we'll all live together' – Atom Egoyan's film examines the grief that engulfs a small British Columbia community when 14 children are killed in a bus crash. A lawyer, haunted by the loss of his own daughter to drugs, turns up to channel the citizens' anger into a lucrative class-action suit. Skilfully manipulating the parents' emotions, the outsider fails to recognise that he is actually tearing the town apart... Taking the strands of narrative from Russell Banks' spiroid novel and threading them into a cinematically palatable structure, writer-director Egoyan (*The Adjuster, Exotica*) has fashioned a complex scenario, occupying a number of parallel time frames. Aided by Paul Sarossy's stark, haunting cinematography and Mychael Danna's hypnotic, pervasive music, this makes *The Sweet Hereafter* a continually absorbing experience. Yet while the active subtext is never less than intellectually tantalising, the

emotional pay-off does leave the viewer with a frustrating vacuum.

Ian Holm (*Mitchell Stephens*), Maury Chaykin (*Wendell Walker*), Peter Donaldson (*Schwartz*), Bruce Greenwood (*Billy Ansell*), David Hemblen (*Abbott Driscoll*), Brooke Johnson (*Mary Burnell*), Arsinee Khanjian (*Wanda Otto*), Tom McCamus (*Sam Burnell*), Stephanie Morgenstern (*Alison*), Earl Pastko (*Hartley Otto*), Sarah Polley (*Nicole Burnell*), Gabrielle Rose (*Dolores Driscoll*), Alberta Watson (*Risa Walker*), Caerthan Banks, daughter of the novel's author (*Zoe Stephens*), Russell Banks (*Dr Robeson*).
Dir and Screenplay: Atom Egoyan. Pro: Egoyan and Camelia Frieberg. Ex Pro: Robert Lantos and Andras Hamori. Assoc Pro: David Webb. Line Pro: Sandra Cunningham. Ph: Paul Sarossy. Pro Des: Phillip Barker. Ed: Susan Shipton. M: Mychael Danna; numbers performed by The Sam Dent Band, Sarah Polley, and The Tragically Hip. Costumes: Beth Pasternak. Sound: Steven Munro. (Speaking Parts/Alliance Communications/Ego Film Arts/Telefilm Canada, etc.–Electric.) Rel: 26 September 1997. 112 mins. Cert 15. Canada. 1997.

Swept By the Sea
See *Amy Foster*.

Swingers ★★★

Hollywood; today. Relocating to Los Angeles from New York, Mike is an insecure stand-up comic and some-time actor who cannot get his ex-girlfriend off his mind. Desperate for work and a new 'honey', he cruises the clubs of Hollywood with his four best friends and drives them nuts with his hard-luck banter. How pathetic can a guy get? Shot for a minuscule $250,000 on real locations around Los Angeles, *Swingers* is based on an autobiographical screenplay by Jon Favreau, who has written wonderful parts for himself (*Mike*) and his real-life friends (who play themselves). Refreshingly honest in its portrayal of male insecurity and bonding, *Swingers* opens a giant window on the lives of guys hanging out together. Far from talking about sport and the size of women's breasts, these ironically styled 'swingers' chat about love while sweetly attempting to buttress their own fragile egos. Albeit a little loose on plot, the film makes up for any *longueurs* with lashings of atmosphere and jokey references to other movies (particularly *Reservoir Dogs* and *GoodFellas*).

Cast: Jon Favreau (*Mike*), Vince Vaughn (*Trent*), Ron Livingston (*Rob*), Patrick Van Horn (*Sue*), Alex Desert (*Charles*), Heather Graham (*Lorraine*), Deena Martin (*Christy*), Katherine Kendall, Brooke Langton, Blake Lindsley, Stephanie Littleson, Vernon Vaughn, Joan Favreau, Maddie Corman, Rio Hackford, Nicole Shay Lagoggia (*Michelle's voice on phone*).

Dir and Ph: Doug Liman. Pro: Victor Simpkins. Ex Pro: Cary Woods. Co-Pro and Screenplay: Jon Favreau. Line Pro: Nicole Shay Lagoggia. Pro Des: Brad Halvorson. Ed: Stephen Mirrione. M: Justin Reinhardt; numbers performed by Dean Martin, George Jones, Love Jones, Count Basie and Tony Bennett, Heart, Roger Miller, Average White Band, The Commodores, Big Bad Voodoo Daddy, Bobby Darin, etc. Costumes: Genevieve Tyrrell. (Miramax/Alfred Shay–Guild.) Rel: 11 July 1997. 96 mins. Cert 15. USA. 1996.

Sydney
See *Hard Eight*.

The Tango Lesson ★★★
This semi-autobiographical film finds Sally Potter herself playing a filmmaker named Sally who, taking tango lessons with a professional in Paris, falls in love with him. But, although she can fulfil his dream of appearing in a film, her dance partnership with him develops into a conflict of egos. Dancewise, the film is wonderful, capturing the moods of the tango with subtlety and mastery, but it's boringly slow to get started and unconvincing in its closing scenes. Also, the main material, which cries out for colour, is shot in black and white. A rare mixture, then: when it's feeble it's really irritating, but when it works it's great. [*Mansel Stimpson*]

Sally Potter (*Sally*), Pablo Veron (*Pablo*), Carolina Iotti, Gustavo Naveira, Carlos Copello, Fabian Salas, Peter Eyre, Heathcote Williams.

Dir and Screenplay: Sally Potter. Pro: Christopher Sheppard. Co-Pro: Oscar Kramer, Christian Keller Sarmiento and Simona Benzakein. Ph: Robby Muller. Pro Des: Carlos Conti. Ed: Herve Schneid. M: Potter and Fred Frith. Costumes: Paul Minter. Choreography: Pablo Veron. (Adventure Pictures/OKCK Films/PIE/Pandora Film/The Arts

Council of England/National Lottery, etc.–Artificial Eye.) Rel: 28 November 1997. 102 mins. Cert PG. UK/France/Argentina/Japan/Germany. 1997.

A Taste of Cherry – Ta'ame-gilass ★★
In an interview with *Newsweek*, the Romanian philosopher E.M. Cioran remarked, 'Without the possibility of suicide, I would have killed myself long ago.' It was this statement that prompted the Iranian filmmaker Abbas Kiarostami (*Through the Olive Trees*) to embark on his ninth feature, the story of a disillusioned man searching for someone to bury him after his suicide. Visually bleak and remorselessly repetitive (endless shots of a Range Rover driving round arid waste ground), *A Taste of Cherry* offers no easy answers. Its contemplations may be creditable, but stretched to 99 minutes, the film's message is less life-affirming than sleep-inducing. Amazingly, it won the *Palme d'Or* at the 1997 Cannes festival.

Homayon Ershadi (*Mr Badii*), Ahdolhossein Bagheri (*the museum guard*), Afshin Bakhtiari (*the worker*), Safar Ali Moradi (*the soldier*), Mir Hossein Noori, Ahmad Ansari, Hamid Massomi.

Dir, Ex Pro, Screenplay and Ed: Abbas Kiarostami. Ph: Homayon Payvar. Pro Des: Hassan Yekta Panah. (Abbas Kiarostami–Artificial Eye.) Rel: 5 June 1998. 99 mins. Cert PG. Iran. 1997.

Telling Lies in America ★¹/₂
A 17-year-old Hungarian immigrant, Karchy Jones escapes the harsh realities of 1961 Cleveland through the local airwaves. The Platters, Jackie Wilson and Jerry Lee Lewis are in the charts and Karchy dreams of becoming the next Billy Magic, master DJ and the King of Cool. Thanks to his effortless ability to spin lies, Karchy gets to befriend Magic and even ends up working as his gofer. But lies can only get one so far... Abandoning his customary shock tactics, scenarist Joe Eszterhas returns to his home town for this semi-autobiographical wallow in nostalgia. However, no end of familiar pop songs can pump life into what is ultimately a limp, unconvincing rites-of-passage saga. Lacklustre direction and a

staggeringly dull performance from Brad Renfro speed the coffin's nail.

Kevin Bacon (*Duane, 'Billy Magic'*), Brad Renfro (*Karchy Jonas*), Maximilian Schell (*Dr Istvan Jonas*), Calista Flockhart (*Diney Majeski*), Paul Dooley (*Father Norton*), Jonathan Rhys Myers (*Kevin Boyle*), Luke Wilson (*Henry*), Damen Fletcher (*Amos*), Jerry Swindall, K.K. Dodds, James Kisicki, Tuesday Knight.

Dir: Guy Ferland. Pro: Ben Myron and Fran Rubel Kuzui. Ex Pro: Naomi Eszterhas, Brian Swardstrom and Mickey Liddell. Co-Ex Pro: Kaz Kuzui. Screenplay: Joe Eszterhas. Ph: Reynaldo Villalobos. Pro Des: Jim Gelarden. Ed: Jim Savitt. M: Nicholas Pike; numbers performed by Hank Ballard and The Midnighters, Jackie Wilson, The Platters, Jerry Lee Lewis, The Coasters, The Fendermen, Ike & Tina Turner, Dion, Damen Fletcher, etc. Costumes: Laura Cunningham. (Banner Entertainment/Ben Myron Prods/Kuzui Enterprises– First Independent.) Rel: 3 April 1998. 101 minutes. Cert 15. USA. 1997.

Temptress Moon – Fengyue ★★
Suzhou/Shanghai; 1911-1921. On the last night of Dynastic rule in China, the hallowed halls of the Pang family notice little change. This is old China and thousands of years of tradition die hard. Notwithstanding, when the Pang master dies ten years later, he is replaced by his daughter, Ruyi (as his eldest son has been rendered brain-dead by the effects of opium). Then the old order is disrupted by the return of Zhongliang, Ruyi's cousin, who is determined to wreak revenge for having been treated like a servant in his youth. But Ruyi exercises a strong sexual hold over Zhongliang, as does Xiuyi, his very own sister... Adopting the opulent pictorial style of *Raise the Red Lantern* and introducing the theme of a young woman thrust into power as depicted in *Red Firecracker, Green Firecracker*, Chen Kaige's *Temptress Moon* is actually intended as an allegory for the emotional tumult of contemporary China. Unfortunately, the tumult for the audience is as much a narrative one as it is emotional as the film's ambitious scope loses much in the translation and in its truncated form here. FYI: Halfway through the film's shoot, the leading actress (Wang Ching-ying) was fired, leading to a

five-month delay before Gong Li took over the role of Ruyi.

Leslie Cheung (*Yu Zhongliang*), Gong Li (*Pang Ruyi*), Kevin Lin (*Pang Duanwu*), He Saifei (*Yu Xiuyu, Zhongliang's sister*), Lin Lianqun (*Pang An*), Xie Tian (*Boss*), Zhou Yemang (*Pang Zhengda*), Zhang Shi, Ge Xiangting, David Wu, Zhou Jie.
Dir: Chen Kaige. Pro: Tong Cunlin and Hsu Feng. Ex Pro: Sunday Sun. Screenplay: Shu Kei, from a story by Chen Kaige and Wang Anyi. Ph: Christopher Doyle. Pro Des: Huang Qiagui. Ed: Pei Xiaonan. M: Zhao Jiping. Costumes: William Chang Sukping and Chen Changmin. (Tomson/Shanghai Film Studios–Artificial Eye.) Rel: 10 October 1997. 116 mins. Cert 15. Hong Kong/China. 1996.

This is the Sea ★★½

Northern Ireland; 1995. Recently baptised in the age-old tradition of the Plymouth Brethren, Hazel Stokes is an innocent raised in an environment of bucolic simplicity, physical hardship and an over-abundance of prayer meetings. Then she meets Malachy McAliskey, a handsome, charismatic Catholic from Belfast whose brother works for the IRA. Coming from such different backgrounds, Hazel and Malachy are naive to believe that their friendship can transcend such odds... Drawing a telling contrast between the rural values of outmoded Puritanism and the fast lane of modern Belfast, *This is the Sea* promises more than it actually delivers. Spectacular views of the 'Glens' and an over-zealous rock score ladle on the icing, but there is little nutrition in the emotional subtext. Notwithstanding, Samantha Morton makes a most beguiling heroine, a wilful innocent caught in the crossfire of cultural politics, while Richard Harris is subtly enigmatic as the wolf in bear's clothing.

Richard Harris (*Old Man Jacobs*), Gabriel Byrne (*Rohan*), John Lynch (*Padhar McAliskey*), Dearbhla Molloy (*Ma Stokes*), Samantha Morton (*Hazel Stokes*), Ross McDade (*Malachy McAliskey*), Ian McElhinney (*Da Stokes*), Marc O'Shea (*Jef Stokes*), Stella McCusker (*Ma McAliskey*), Mary McGuckian (*Cathy*), Des McAleer (*Inspector Wilson*), Jim Sheridan (*station master*), Rick Leaf, Caolan Byrne, James Nesbitt, Brian Kennedy, Lorcan Byrne.
Dir and Screenplay: Mary McGuckian. Pro: Michael Garland. Ph: Des Whelan. Pro Des: Clare Kenny. Ed: Kant Pan. M:

Mike Scott, The Waterboys and Brian Kennedy. Costumes: John Rocha. (Pembridge Pictures/The Irish Film Board/Electric Pictures/PolyGram–Electric/PolyGram.) Rel: 13 February 1998. 104 mins. Cert 15. Ireland. 1997.

This World, Then the Fireworks ★★

Chicago/California; 1926/1956. Leaving his overweight wife and son behind him, conman Marty Lakewood skips town when the cops close in. Returning to the house of his youth, Marty hooks up with his equally amoral sister, Carol, who now makes a living as a prostitute. United by the childhood tragedy that put their father behind bars and their mother into a psychological tailspin, the siblings set about lining their pockets and sating their ardent libidos... Taking his cue from such film noir classics as *Touch of Evil*, *In a Lonely Place* and *Detour*, director Michael Oblowitz anchors Jim Thompson's short story in the stylised components of the genre. Thus, from the Saul Bass-inspired opening credit sequence and tilted camera angles to Billy Zane's soporific voice-over, the film is nothing so much as an exercise in style. Still, the sheer unpleasantness of the material should fend off sleep for a while. FYI: Thompson wrote his short story in 1955, but it wasn't published until six years after his death, in 1983.

Billy Zane (*Marty Lakewood*), Gina Gershon (*Carol Lakewood-Wharton*), Sheryl Lee (*Lois Archer*), Rue McClanahan (*Mom Lakewood*), Seymour Cassel (*Det. Harris*), Will Patton (*Lt Morgan*), William Hootkins (*Jake Krutz*), Richard Edson, Robert Pentz, Marianna Alacchi, Orson Oblowitz, Willie Cobbs.
Dir: Michael Oblowitz. Pro: Chris Hanley, Brad Wyman and Larry Gross. Ex Pro: Barr B. Potter and Billy Zane. Co-Pro: Al Dickerson. Screenplay: Gross. Ph: Tom Priestley Jr. Pro Des: Maia Javan. Ed: Emma E. Hickox. M: Pete Rugolo; numbers performed by Shaky Jake, Peggy Lee, and Chet Baker. Costumes: Dan Moore. Sound: Skip Lievsay. Title design: Dan Perri. (Largo Entertainment/A Muse, Balzac's Shirt, Wyman Prod–First Independent.) Rel: 5 December 1997. 100 mins. Cert 18. USA. 1996.

A Thousand Acres ★★

Iowa; today. When prominent land-owner Larry Cook decides to divide

his 1000 acres between his three daughters (to avoid inheritance tax), he is offended when his youngest offspring, Caroline, displays some reservations, activating a chain reaction of deep-seated resentment and devastating revelation... Developed in collaboration with Michelle Pfeiffer and Jessica Lange's respective production companies, *A Thousand Acres* affords both actresses the opportunity to flex their artistic potential. And while Lange tends to fall back on her expanding repertoire of mannerisms, Pfeiffer possibly provides the best work of her career as the spiky, knowing Rose. However, the material itself, beautifully composed by cinematographer Tak Fujimoto, lacks dramatic form and plays like several disease-of-the-week movies shoehorned into one evening. Take your pick: there's cancer, alcoholism, child abuse, wife battery, senile dementia, adultery and – a favourite, this – incest. Meanwhile, Jocelyn Moorhouse (*Proof*, *How To Make an American Quilt*) directs with the creative ingenuity of a bricklayer. Based on the Pulitzer Prize-winning novel by Jane Smiley, itself inspired by *King Lear*.

Michelle Pfeiffer (*Rose Cook Lewis*), Jessica Lange (*Ginny Cook Smith*), Jennifer Jason Leigh (*Caroline Cook*), Colin Firth (*Jess Clark*), Keith Carradine (*Ty Smith*), Kevin Anderson (*Peter Lewis*), Pat Hingle (*Harold Clark*), Jason Robards (*Larry Cook*), John Carroll Lynch, Anne Pitoniak, Vyto Ruginis, Michelle Williams, Elizabeth Moss, Ray Toler, Kenneth Tigar, Ray Baker, Beth Grant.
Dir: Jocelyn Moorhouse. Pro: Marc Abraham, Steve Golin, Lynn Arost, Kate Guinzburg and Sigurjon Sighvatsson. Ex Pro: Armyan Bernstein and Thomas A. Bliss. Co-Pro: Diana Pokorny. Screenplay: Laura Jones. Ph: Tak Fujimoto. Pro Des: Dan Davis. Ed: Maryann Brandon. M: Richard Hartley; numbers performed by Ron Keel, God's Children, The Ramblers, William Topley, and Pastiche. Costumes: Ruth Myers. (PolyGram/Beacon Pictures/Propaganda Films/Via Rosa Prods/Prairie Films–PolyGram.) Rel: 12 June 1998. 105 mins. Cert 12. USA. 1997.

Tierra ★★

Once again the Spanish writer/director Julio Medem proves that he has a wonderfully cinematic eye. But the story of Angel, who could be

That sinking feeling: James Cameron's mammoth *Titanic* hits troubled waters (from Fox)

someone from another world or simply schizophrenic, provides an obscure metaphysical drama which, in seeming to champion respect for cosmic forces as opposed to traditional religious beliefs, recalls the late Andrei Tarkovsky at his most baffling. Possibly the fact that Angel becomes sexually involved with two contrasted women, effectively incarnated by Emma Suarez and Silke Klein, helped to make this a hit in Spain, but the film's appeal is a specialised one, and even then audiences will be split in their responses. [*Mansel Stimpson*]

Carmelo Gomez (*Angel Bengoelxeo*), Emma Suarez (*Angela*), Karra Elejalde (*Patricio*), Silke Klein (*Mari*), Nancho Novo (*Alberto*), Txema Blasco (*Tomas*), Ane Sanchez, Juan Jose Suarez, Ricardo Amador.
  Dir and Screenplay: Julio Medem. Ex Pro: Fernando Garcillan. Assoc Pro: Manuel Lombardero. Ph: Javier Aguirresarobe. Pro Des: Satur Idarreta. Ed: Ivan Aledo. M: Alberto Iglesias. Costumes: Estibaliz Markiegi. (Sogetel/Lola Films/Canal Plus–Metro Tartan.) Rel: 8 August 1997. 125 mins. Cert 18. Spain. 1995.

Titanic ★★★★

1912/1997; the North Atlantic. Nicknamed 'the ship of dreams', RMS *Titanic* was the largest moving object ever created by the hand of man, a veritable floating palace believed to be unsinkable due to its sixteen watertight compartments. When, in a game of poker, itinerant artist Jack Dawson wins a third-class ticket for the *Titanic*'s maiden voyage, little does he realise that he is about to meet the woman of his dreams. However, Rose DeWitt Bukater is already engaged to the dashing – albeit narrow-minded – Cal Hockley, heir to untold millions and beneficiary of a pathological contempt for the working classes. When Jack saves Rose from an untimely watery death, he salvages more than her life – for the time being... A sweeping romance of *Romeo and Juliet* intensity, *Titanic* is the realisation of an epic vision conceived by James Cameron, director of *The Terminator*, *Aliens* and *The Abyss*. A mammoth undertaking, the film is both an emotional and technical sensation as it weaves a number of complex elements into its narrative quilt, tailoring history,

politics, satire, humour, romance and horror into an epic entertainment. If only Cameron had curtailed some of his more melodramatic flourishes – and the one-dimensional villainy of Billy Zane and David Warner – he could have created a definitive masterpiece. FYI: In order to attain the realism that his historical epic demanded, Cameron built his own studio – equipped with a six-acre outdoor tank – at a cost of $40 million. In all, the price of his film – co-financed by Twentieth Century Fox and Paramount – came to an unprecedented $200m.

Leonardo DiCaprio (*Jack Dawson*), Kate Winslet (*Rose DeWitt Bukater*), Billy Zane (*Cal Hockley*), Kathy Bates (*Margaret 'Molly' Brown*), Frances Fisher (*Ruth DeWitt Bukater*), Bernard Hill (*Captain E.J. Smith*), Jonathan Hyde (*Bruce Ismay*), Danny Nucci (*Fabrizio De Rossi*), David Warner (*Spicer Lovejoy*), Bill Paxton (*Brock Lovett*), Gloria Stuart (*old Rose*), Victor Garber (*Thomas Andrews*), Suzy Amis (*Lizzy Calvert*), Lewis Abernathy, Nicholas Cascone, Dr Anatoly M. Sagalevitch, Jason Barry, Ewan Stewart, Mark Lindsay Chapman, Eric Braeden, Bernard Fox, Michael Ensign, Jenette Goldstein, Camilla Overbye Roos, Linda Kerns, Martin Jarvis, Rosalind Ayres, Craig Kelly, James Lancaster, Tricia O'Neil.

Tomorrow's bad news today: Michelle Yeoh teams up with 007 (Pierce Brosnan) in Roger Spottiswoode's chillingly satirical *Tomorrow Never Dies* (from UIP)

Dir and Screenplay: James Cameron. Pro: Cameron and Jon Landau. Ex Pro: Rae Sanchini. Co-Pro: Al Giddings, Grant Hill and Sharon Mann. Ph: Russell Carpenter; and Cameron, Caleb Deschanel. Pro Des: Peter Lamont. Ed: Cameron, Conrad Buff and Richard A. Harris. M: James Horner; 'My Heart Will Go On' sung by Celine Dion. Costumes: Deborah L. Scott. Sound: Christopher Boyes. Visual effects: Rob Legato. Special effects: Thomas L. Fisher. 'Old Rose' make-up effects: Greg Cannom. (Fox/Paramount/Lightstorm Entertainment–Fox.) Rel: 23 January 1998. 195 mins. Cert 12. USA. 1997.

Tomorrow Never Dies ★★★¹/₂

Tomorrow is the newspaper that delivers tomorrow's news today – but at a crippling price. In order to feed the growing appetite for lurid copy, media mogul Elliot Carver sets up an audacious scheme to activate World War Three. By overriding the satellite fix on a British frigate in the South China Sea – and then sinking the ship – Carver transfers the blame to the Chinese. Then he shoots down a Chinese MiG and moves in to scoop the story... As far as James Bond films can go within the straitjacket of their formula, this is

the wittiest, most ingenious and socially pertinent in decades. Even the mandatory car chase – filmed in London's Brent Cross, of all places – is given a nice twist as Bond becomes the ultimate back-seat driver (courtesy of a nifty remote control), while the one-liners are nowhere near as limp as usual (Miss Moneypenny, interrupting Bond's exploration of a Danish tongue: 'You always were a cunning linguist, James'). And by presenting a thinly disguised Rupert Murdoch as the villain, the film wields a chilling satirical edge. Filmed in London, the French Pyrenees, Bangkok, Hamburg, Mexico and Florida.

Pierce Brosnan (*James Bond*), Jonathan Pryce (*Elliot Carver*), Michelle Yeoh (*Wai Lin*), Teri Hatcher (*Paris Carver*), Joe Don Baker (*Jack Wade*), Judi Dench (*M*), Ricky Jay (*Henry Gupta*), Gotz Otto (*Stamper*), Desmond Llewelyn (*Q*), Samantha Bond (*Miss Moneypenny*), Geoffrey Palmer (*Admiral Roebuck*), Vincent Schiavelli (*Dr Kaufman*), Colin Salmon, Terence Rigby, Julian Fellowes, Nina Young, Cecilia Thomsen, Bruce Alexander, Christopher Bowen, Andrew Hawkins, Michael Byrne, Pip Torrens, Eoin McCarthy, Rolf Saxon.
Dir: Roger Spottiswoode. Pro: Michael G. Wilson and Barbara Broccoli. Line Pro: Anthony Waye. Screenplay: Bruce Feirstein. Ph: Robert Elswit. Pro Des: Allan Cameron. Ed: Dominique Fortin and Michel Arcand. M: David Arnold; 'Tomorrow Never Dies' sung by Sheryl Crow. Costumes: Lindy Hemmings. (Eon Prods/United Artists/MGM–UIP.) Rel: 12 December 1997. 119 mins. Cert 12. USA. 1997.

Traveller ★¹/₂

North Carolina; today. Sticking closely to themselves, the travellers are Irish-American gypsies who live by conning the innocent and gullible. When young Pat O'Hara turns up in their midst for the funeral of his father, he is told to beat a hasty retreat. For by marrying a woman outside of the clan, Pat's father had broken the inviolable law of the traveller. However, smooth-talking Bocky Sherlock takes Pat under his wing, arguing that he can turn the boy into a valuable asset... Of all the films about conmen jamming the multiplexes, this has got to be the most boring. Deprived of a decent plot and interesting characters, the film ambles along with little direction for 90 minutes and then excuses itself with a highly unpleasant climax. In this instance, it is the audience who is conned.

Bill Paxton (*Bocky Sherlock*), Mark Wahlberg (*Pat O'Hara*), Julianna Margulies (*Jean*), James Gammon (*Double D*), Luke Askew (*Boss Jack*), Nikki Deloach (*Kate*), Danielle Wiener (*Shane*), Vincent Chase (*Joe Bimbo*), Michael Shaner, Andrew Porter, Jean Howard, Rance Howard, Jo Ann Pflug, John Paxton.
Dir and Ph: Jack N. Green. Pro: Bill Paxton, Brian Swardstrom, Mickey Liddell and David Blocker. Ex Pro: Robert Mickelson and Rick King. Screenplay: Jim McGlynn. Pro Des: Michael Helmy. Ed: Michael Ruscio. M: Andy Paley; numbers performed by Bete Noir, East 17, Beautiful South, Edwyn Collins, Boyzone, James, Lighthouse Family, etc. Costumes: Douglas Hall. Sound: Scott Wolf. (MDP Worldwide/October Films/Banner Entertainment–First Independent.) Rel: 30 January 1998. 100 mins. Cert 18. USA. 1997.

Trial and Error ★★

Occasional actor Richard Rietti (a specialist in Mafia roles) has been the best friend of lawyer Charles Tuttle since they were nine. However, when Rietti arranges an impromptu stag party for Tuttle the night before the latter's defence of an inveterate conman, their friendship is sorely tested. With his friend so wasted that he can barely stand,

Rietti decides to take his place in the courtroom just long enough for Tuttle to sober up. But Rietti soon finds that he has to give the performance of his life as Tuttle's increasingly desperate efforts to join in the proceedings are scuttled by the judge... Employing stock characters, pat homilies and mounting extremes of slapstick, *Trial and Error* engages the interest on the most basic of levels, but never rises to the comic heights it attempts to ascend. At best, it yields a couple of giggles and capitalises on the visual attributes of its female cast and picturesque Nevada setting.

Michael Richards (*Richard Rietti*), Jeff Daniels (*Charles Tuttle*), Charlize Theron (*Billie Tyler*), Jessica Steen (*Elizabeth Gardner*), Austin Pendleton (*Judge Paul Z. Graff*), Rip Torn (*Benny Gibbs*), Alexandra Wentworth (*Tiffany*), Jennifer Coolidge, Lawrence Pressman, Dale Dye, Max Casella, Ken Magee, Gerry Spence.
    Dir: Jonathan Lynn. Pro: Lynn and Gary Ross. Ex Pro: Mary Parent and Allen Alsobrook. Assoc Pro: Jane DeVries Cooper and Edward Lynn. Screenplay: Sara Bernstein and Gregory Bernstein, from a story by Sara and Gregory Bernstein, and Cliff Gardner. Ph: Gabriel Beristain. Pro Des: Victoria Paul. Ed: Tony Lombardo. M: Phil Marshall; numbers performed by Anders Osborne, Taj Mahal, The Fabulous Thunderbirds, Aretha Franklin, The Subdudes, Oscar Peterson, Dion, etc. Costumes: Shay Cunliffe. (New Line/Larger Than Life–Entertainment.) Rel: 14 November 1997. 98 mins. Cert 12. USA. 1997.

TwentyFourSeven ★★½

With little to give their lives focus or direction, a group of teenage discontents are persuaded to join a boxing club by Alan Darcy, a local social worker. If Darcy can get the 'lads' to suspend their bad habits for a while, maybe he can enrich their lives, for ever, for, 'If you've never had anything to believe in, you'll always be poor' ... Presenting a marvellous opportunity for Bob Hoskins to get to grips with a role that is neither East End tough nor slaphappy American, *TwentyFourSeven* makes a virtue of its difference. Shot in murky black and white and featuring a cast of unknown and non-professional actors, the film resolutely refuses to kowtow to the commercial exigencies of mainstream cinema. And yet, in spite of its downbeat nature, it does offer some delights: Hoskins taking his giddy Aunt Iris dancing, an engaging soundtrack of songs from Sun House and a poetic, penetrating voice-over. Filmed in and around Nottingham and the Peak District. FYI: *TwentyFourSeven* is slang for 'making the most out of your life' – working 24 hours a day, seven days a week.

Bob Hoskins (*Alan Darcy*), Matt Hand (*Fagash*), Dany Nussbaum (*Tim*), Bruce Jones (*Geoff, Tim's dad*), Annette Badland (*Pat, Tim's mum*), Justin Brady (*Gadget*), James Hooton (*Knighty*), Darren Campbell (*Daz*), Karl Collins (*Stuart*), Johann Myers (*Benny*), Jimmy Hynd (*Meggy*), Frank Harper (*Ronnie Marsh*), James Corden (*Tonka*), Jo Bell (*Jo*), Pamela Cundell (*Auntie Iris*), Gina Aris (*Sharon*), Anthony Clarke, Lord Dominic Dillon of Eldon, Ian Smith, Colin Higgins, Maureen O'Grady, Lord Shane Meadows of Eldon, Ginger Keane.
    Dir: Shane Meadows. Pro: Imogen West. Screenplay: Meadows and Paul Fraser. Ex Pro: Stephen Woolley & Nik Powell, George Faber & David Thompson. Line Pro: Sally French. Ph: Ashley Rowe. Pro Des: John-Paul Kelly. Ed: Bill Diver. M: Neill MacColl and Boo Hewerdine; numbers performed by Sun House, Van Morrison, The Charlatans, Paul Weller, etc.

Burned-out case: Danny Nussbaum rouses Bob Hoskins from the ashes in Shane Meadows' resolutely uncommercial *TwentyFourSeven* (from Pathe)

Costumes: Philip Crichton. Sound: Simon Gershon. (BBC Films/Scala–Pathe.) Rel: 27 March 1998. 96 mins. Cert 15. UK. 1997.

The Twilight of the Ice Nymphs ★

Following four years of imprisonment, Peter Glahn returns to the magical kingdom of Mandragora, where the sun never sets and downy spores choke the air. There, Peter immediately falls for the ethereal charms of the enigmatic Juliana, but instead beds the seductive Zephyr, bride of the forest... Filmed entirely inside a warehouse in Winnipeg, this highly personal vision from the esoteric Canadian director Guy Maddin is wilfully weird. Like some ghastly experimental play produced by an obscure sect, it is amateurish, very, very silly and an unforgivable waste of celluloid.

Pascale Bussieres (*Juliana Kossel*), Shelley Duvall (*Amelia Glahn*), Frank Gorshin (*Cain Ball*), Alice Krige (*Zaphyr Eccles*), R.H. Thomson (*Dr Isaac Solti*), Ross McMillan (*Matthew Eccles*) and (*uncredited*) Nigel Whitmey (*Peter Glahn*).
    Dir: Guy Maddin. Pro: Ritchard Findlay. Ex Pro: Derek Mazur and Charlotte Mickie. Screenplay: George Toles. Ph: Michael Marshall. Pro Des: Rejean Labrie. Ed: Reginald Harkema. M: John McCulloch. Costumes: Donna Szoke. (Alliance Communications/Marble Island/Telefilm Canada/Manitoba Film, etc.–Alliance Releasing.) Rel: 10 April 1998. 91 mins. No cert. Canada. 1997.

The Ugly ★★★

First-time New Zealand writer-director Scott Reynolds delivers a classy and chilling horror movie that cleverly fills the void between art-house picture and video nasty. A serial killer (Rotondo) is interrogated by a beautiful and self-possessed psychiatrist (Hobbs), observed through a two-way mirror by the creepy boss of a forbidding mental asylum (that would be Dickensian if it didn't look so sixties). Rotondo is, of course, *The Ugly*, an abused child, both at home by his mom and at school by bullies. Naturally, Doctor Hobbs appears to make progress with Rotondo and, against the strongest advice to the contrary, orders him to be unhandcuffed... The protracted interview sequences are intercut with flashbacks to Rotondo's past and the suspenseful, dangerous-seeming film proceeds menacingly, atmospherically and teasingly. Both

Honey, I've Made a Comeback: Peter Fonda in his award-winning role as apiarist Ulysses Jackson, in Victor Nunez's contemplative and poetic *Ulee's Gold* (from Feature Film Co.)

main stars give effective, convincing performances and the rather gory film is imaginatively developed, using ideas from *Silence of the Lambs*-type staples of the genre, but managing to side-step most of the clichés and carve out a pretty compelling niche of its own. [*Derek Winnert*]

Paulo Rotondo (*Simon Cartwright*), Rebecca Hobbs (*Karen Schumaker*), Jennifer Ward-Lealand (*Evelyn, Simon's mother*), Roy Ward (*Dr Marlowe*), Vanessa Byrnes (*Julie, aged 25*), Darien Takle (*Marge*), Cath McWhirter, Aaron Buskin, Chris Bailey, Yvonne Dudman, Michael Dwyer, David Baxter.
    Dir and Screenplay: Scott Reynolds. Pro: Jonathan Dowling. Ph: Simon Raby. Pro Des: Grant Major. Ed: Wayne Cook. M: Victoria Kelly. Costumes: Emily Carter. Sound: Dave Whitehead. (The New Zealand Film Commission/Essential Prods–Metrodome.) Rel: 27 February 1998. 93 mins. Cert 18. New Zealand. 1996.

Ulee's Gold ★★★½

Ulysses Jackson is a beekeeper in the tupelo swampland of Florida. Still traumatised by the death of his wife six years ago, Ulee likes to keep himself to himself and is never happier than when tending his bees. But with his son in prison and his daughter-in-law run off to Orlando, Ulee is forced to bring up his two granddaughters by himself. Then his son asks him a very, very big favour... Above all, *Ulee's Gold* is a gentle, low-key character study illuminated by a remarkably dedicated performance from Peter Fonda. Looking more like his father than ever, the actor conveys with commendable economy the discomfort of a man forced to confront the messy exigencies of his life. For academics, the allusions to Homer's *Odyssey* are there, but this is best taken as a contemplative, poetic fable in its own right. FYI: Peter Fonda's own father, Henry, was a keen beekeeper.

Peter Fonda (*Ulysses 'Ulee' Jackson*), Patricia Richardson (*Connie Hope*), Jessica Biel (*Casey Jackson*), J. Kenneth Campbell (*Sheriff Bill Floyd*), Christine Dunford (*Helen Jackson*), Steven Flynn (*Eddie Flowers*), Dewey Weber (*Ferris Dooley*), Tom Wood (*Jimmy Jackson*), Vanessa Zima (*Penny Jackson*), Traber Burns, Ryan Marshall, Chad Fish.
    Dir, Pro, Screenplay and Ed: Victor

Nunez. Ex Pro: Edward Saxon, John Sloss and Valerie Thomas. Co-Pro: Sam Gowan and Peter Saraf. Line Pro: Stewart Lippe. Ph: Virgil Mirano. Pro Des: Pat Garner. M: Charles Engstrom; numbers performed by Juster, Billie Holiday, Morphine, Suicidal Tendencies, Van Morrison, etc. Costumes: Marilyn Wall-Asse. Sound: Pete Winter. (Jonathan Demme/Nunez-Gowan/Clinica Estetico–Feature Film Co.) Rel: 3 April 1998. 113 mins. Cert 15. USA. 1997.

Under the Skin ★★★★

Carine Adler's insightful and compelling film touches on sibling jealousies, but it is mainly concerned with the effect that a mother's death has on her two daughters. Rose, being married and pregnant, has a life of her own to fall back on, but 19-year-old Iris cannot cope emotionally and seeks escape in sexual promiscuity. Told with absolute conviction, superb acting (Samantha Morton's is the perform-ance of the year) and a striking sense of cinema, *Under the Skin*, if not quite flawless, is undoubtedly outstanding. It's also an example of a woman filmmaker achieving unusual frankness in portraying sex scenes, but the film's honesty is such that this is an observation and not a criticism, a matter of integrity not of sensationalism. [*Mansel Stimpson*]

Samantha Morton (*Iris Kelley*), Claire Rushbrook (*Rose Kelley*), Rita Tushingham (*Mum*), Stuart Townsend (*Tom*), Christine Tremarco (*Vron*), Matthew Delamere (*Gary*), Mark Womack, Clare Francis, Daniel O'Meara, Crissy Rock, Joe Tucker.
    Dir and Screenplay: Carine Adler. Pro: Kate Ogborn. Ex Pro: Ben Gibson. Ph: Barry Ackroyd. Pro Des: John-Paul Kelly. Ed: Ewa J. Lind. M: Ilona Sekacz; numbers performed by The Aloof, The Castle Singers, Massive Attack, and Samantha Morton. Costumes: Frances Tempest. (BFI/Channel Four/Strange Dog/Rouge Films–BFI.) Rel: 28 November 1997. 83 mins. Cert 18. UK. 1997.

Unforgettable ★★★★

Seattle; the present. Discovering that vital memories are stored in the cerebral spinal fluid, timid neurobiologist Martha Briggs unwittingly becomes involved with a medical examiner accused of his wife's murder. Although officially acquitted of the latter crime (on a technicality), forensic pathologist

David Krane is still a marked man. Covertly submitting himself as a human guinea pig in Martha's research into memory transfer, Krane injects the fluid from his late wife's spine into his own bloodstream in order to recall her death... Constantly casting off new strands of narrative that wrap around the central premise, *Unforgettable* is a complex, skilfully fashioned thriller that, if not worthy of Hitchcock, certainly recalls Brian De Palma at his peak. Consistently atmospheric (and intriguingly lit by Jeffrey Jur), the film manages to make its far-fetched concept surprisingly credible on its own terms. From the deftly staged (and suspenseful) chase scene in which Krane trails a chief suspect, to Krane's whispered confession to Martha, the film is an object lesson in how to bypass cliché.

Ray Liotta (*David Krane*), Linda Fiorentino (*Martha Briggs*), Peter Coyote (*Don Bresler*), Christopher McDonald (*Stewart Gleick*), David Paymer (*Curtis Avery*), Duncan Fraser (*Michael Stratton*), Kim Cattrall (*Kelly*), Stellina Rusich (*Mary Krane*), Kim Coates (*Eddie Dutton*), Caroline Elliott,

Memories are made of this: Linda Fiorentino trapped in the moral ambiguities of her own scientific research in John Dahl's provocative *Unforgettable* (from Fox)

Colleen Rennison, Suzy Joachim, Garwin Sanford, Jena Forryane, Nathaniel Deveaux, Dwight McFee, Tong Lung.
Dir: John Dahl. Pro: Dino De Laurentiis and Martha De Laurentiis. Ex Pro: Andrew Lazar, Rick Dahl and William Teitler. Line Pro: Lucio Trentini. Screenplay: Bill Geddie. Ph: Jeffrey Jur. Pro Des: Rob Pearson. Ed: Eric L. Beason and Scott Chestnut. M: Christopher Young;

A star unleashed: Gena Rowlands in *Unhook the Stars* (from Artificial Eye), directed by her son Nick Cassavetes

'Unforgettable' sung by Nat King Cole. Costumes: Terry Dresbach and Glenne Campbell. (MGM/Spelling Films– Fox.) Rel: 11 July 1997. 117 mins. Cert 15. USA. 1996.

Unhook the Stars ★★★★★
Mildred Hawks is a woman in her early sixties with an enormous gift for life who, until now, has primarily functioned for her family. A recent widow, she presently lives with her defiant 23-year-old daughter who, suddenly, decides to leave. Faced with the prospect of empty days, Mildred gratefully turns her attention to the six-year-old boy dumped on her by her capricious neighbour, Monica, whose life is falling apart. But even now Mildred is living her life through the dependence of another... A compassionate, observant portrait of a woman caught at an emotional crossroads in her life, *Unhook the Stars* is an extraordinarily mature piece of cinema illuminated by peerless performances. Gena Rowlands is simply wonderful in a

Music makes their day: Adrian Lester, Clare Cathcart, Amy Robbins, Daniel Ryan and Billy Carter in Simon Moore's feel-good *Up On the Roof* (from Rank-Castle Rock/Turner)

role written specially for her by her son – Nick Cassavetes – who makes his directorial debut here with accomplished finesse. Gerard Depardieu, an ardent fan of the films of John Cassavetes, produces this Franco-American co-production and brings unexpected charm to his role as a French-Canadian truck driver with an eye for Mildred. And Marisa Tomei, as the latter's emotional, volatile neighbour, has never been better.

Gena Rowlands (*Mildred Hawks*), Marisa Tomei (*Monica Warren*), Gerard Depardieu (*Big Tommy*), Jake Lloyd (*JJ Warren*), Moira Kelly (*Ann Mary Margaret Hawks*), David Thorton (*Frankie Warren*), David Sherrill (*Ethan Hawks*), Bridgette Wilson (*Jeannie Hawks*), Bobby Cooper, Clint Howard, Dave Rowlands, Tom Proctor.

Dir: Nick Cassavetes. Pro: Rene Cleitman. Ex Pro: Bernard Bouix. Screenplay: Cassavetes and Helen Caldwell. Ph: Phedon Papamichael. Pro Des: Phedon Papamichael Snr. Ed: Petra Von Oelffen. M: Steven Hufsteter; 'Country Feedback' performed by REM; other numbers performed by Shrine, Flood, Cyndi Lauper, Buddah Heads, Counting Crows, Richard Thompson, Richard Harris, etc. Costumes: Tessa Stephensen. (Hachette Premiere / Cie / Gerard Depardieu–Artificial Eye.) Rel: 4 July 1997. 105 mins. Cert 15. France/USA. 1996.

Up 'n' Under ★½

West Yorkshire; today. Nursing a life-long grudge against his wife's former lover, born loser Arthur Hoyle makes a bet with his nemesis that he lives to regret. In a moment of pique, he stakes his life's savings on a wager that says he can train the Wheatsheaf Arms rugby team to defeat the mercenary, unbeaten Cobblers Arms. The trouble is, the Wheatsheaves are only five men and would rather 'eat shit' than face the most vicious team in Rugby League history... Taking the tired old formula of a group of losers battling impossible odds, *Up 'n' Under* pads out its underdeveloped scenario with endless scenes of exercise and trips to the pub. Predictable, contrived and truly uninspired, the film is about as appetising as a scrum on a rainy Sunday morning. Filmed in and around Cardiff, Wales.

Gary Olsen (*Arthur Hoyle*), Neil Morrissey (*Steve*), Samantha Janus (*Hazel Scott*), Tony Slattery (*Reg Welsh*), Ralph Brown (*Phil*), Adrian Hood (*Tommy*), David MacCreedy (*Tony*), Richard Ridings (*Frank*), Brian Glover (*Jack*), Griff Rhys-Jones (*Ray Mason*), Jane Clifford-Thorton (*Doreen*), Susan Tully (*June*), John Thomson (*Stan*), Nick Lane, Jenny Jules, Maria Pastel, Mark Thomas, Elizabeth Godber.

Dir and Screenplay: John Godber. Pro: Mark Thomas. Ex Pro: David Ball. Line Pro: Clive Waldron. Ph: Alan M. Trow. Pro Des: Hayden Pearce. Ed: Chris Lawrence. M: Thomas; numbers performed by Bete Noire, Bruise, East 17, Edwyn Collins, Cast, Beautiful South, etc. Costumes: Pamela Moore. (Touchdown / Lluniau Llivv–Entertainment.) Rel: 23 January 1998. 98 mins. Cert 12. UK. 1997.

Up On the Roof ★★★

Hull; 1979 / Buckinghamshire; 1985; the South of France; 1994. While majoring in such diverse subjects as geology, politics, music, art and anthropology, five Hull University students are united by their love of singing. Performing under the name of The Roof Club, the quintet specialise in a cappella harmonies of popular seventies songs. However, over the ensuing years their paths diverge and their lives take surprising and dramatic turns. Yet, whenever they are reunited, their mutual chemistry absolves the pain of their mistakes... Ignited by five terrific performances from a cast of talented unknowns, *Up On the Roof* is a fresh, energetic and feel-good diversion that just misses the mark. In spite of a welcome refusal to spell out the obvious, the film suffers from the contrived nature of its conception and by a cheesy wholesomeness that doesn't entirely ring true. Still, Simon Moore's stylish direction and the musical numbers themselves are a real bonus.

Billy Carter (*Tim*), Clare Cathcart (*Angela*), Adrian Lester (*Scott*), Amy Robbins (*Bryony*), Daniel Ryan (*Keith*), Lavinia Bertram (*Bryony's mother*), Robin Herford (*Gavin*), Mary Healey (*Angela's mother*), Sylvester Morand, Chris Sanders.
   Dir: Simon Moore. Pro: Jane Prowse, Pippa Cross and Brian Eastman. Ex Pro: Humphrey Barclay. Co-Pro: Sarah Williams. Assoc Pro: Lars MacFarlane. Screenplay: Prowse and Moore. Ph: Nic Morris. Pro Des: Tim Hutchinson. Ed: Peter Hollywood. M: Alan Parker; Richard Strauss. A capella arrangements: Tot Taylor. Costumes: Charlotte Holditch. Sculptures: Sophie Dickens. (Rank / Granada Film / Carnival Films / Production Line–Rank-Castle Rock / Turner.) Rel: 7 November 1997. 101 mins. Cert 15. UK. 1997.

U.S. Marshals ★ ½

Chicago / Kentucky / Pennsylvania / New York; the present. When suspected government assassin Mark Sheridan escapes from a plane crash on his way to prison, US Marshal Sam Gerard determines to catch him at any cost. But what Gerard can't grasp is, if Sheridan is meant to be such a ruthless butcher, how come he keeps on escaping without killing anyone? For a chase movie to work, one needs either to care for the character on the run or to be baying for his blood. Here, the fugitive is a nebulous fellow with no personal background other than a Swiss chick on the side (a pitifully underemployed Irene Jacob). A follow-up to 1993's *The Fugitive*, *U.S. Marshals* moves Tommy Lee Jones to centre stage (repeating his Oscar-winning role), but when he is first encountered on a stake-out in a chicken costume any hope of integrity is blown out the window. Sloppy editing, artless plotting and hollow dialogue don't help either.

Tommy Lee Jones (*U.S. Marshal Sam Gerard*), Wesley Snipes (*Mark Sheridan*), Robert Downey Jr (*John Royce*), Joe Pantoliano (*Deputy Marshal Cosmo Renfro*), Kate Nelligan (*U.S. Marshal Walsh*), Irene Jacob (*Marie*), Daniel Roebuck (*Deputy Marshal Biggs*), Tom Wood (*Deputy Marshal Newman*), LaTanya Richardson (*Deputy Marshal Cooper*), Patrick Malahide (*Lamb*), Michael Paul Chan (*Chen*), Rick Snyder, Johnny Lee Davenport, Donald Li, Don Gibb, James Sie, Tracy Letts, Ray Toler.
   Dir: Stuart Baird. Pro: Arnold Kopelson and Anne Kopelson. Ex Pro: Keith Barish and Roy Huggins. Co-Pro: Stephen Brown. Co-Ex Pro: Wolfgang Glattes. Screenplay: John Pogue. Ph: Andrzej Bartkowiak. Pro Des: Maher Ahmad. Ed: Terry Rawlings. M: Jerry Goldsmith. (Warner / Kopelson Entertainment / Keith Barish–Warner.) Rel: 24 April 1998. 133 mins. Cert 12. USA. 1998.

U-Turn ★★

On his way to pay off a debt in Las Vegas, Bobby Cooper is stranded in a nowhere town in Arizona when the radiator hose on his Mustang blows. Shortly afterwards, he loses his entire stash of $30,000 when he's involved in a shoot-up at a local grocery store. Now virtually penniless, Bobby goes to greater and greater extremes to get the hell out of Dodge before his past catches up with him... Despite its spooky resemblance to John Dahl's far superior *Red Rock West*, Oliver Stone's noir western is remarkable for its 'bad boy' cast. Sean Penn, who took over the lead from Bill Paxton at seven days' notice, gives his loser an effective hard-boiled edge, while Nolte, Thornton and Voight display wicked transformations. But this being an Oliver Stone film, the arty distractions the director throws in the path of the narrative (arbitrary close-ups, flashbacks, speeded-up film, distorted camera angles, etc.) just irritate the hell out of the story. FYI: The film's original title, *Stray Dogs*, was changed at the request of Akira Kurosawa, director of *Stray Dog* (1949).

Sean Penn (*Bobby Cooper*), Jennifer Lopez (*Grace McKenna*), Nick Nolte (*Jake McKenna*), Powers Boothe (*Sheriff Virgil Potter*), Claire Danes (*Jenny*), Joaquin Phoenix (*Toby N. Tucker*), Billy Bob Thornton (*Darrell*), Jon Voight (*blind man*), Julie Hagerty (*Flo*), Abraham Benrubi, Bo Hopkins, Valery Nikolaev, Richard Rutowski, Aida Linares, Sean Stone, Brent Briscoe, Sheri Foster, Laurie Metcalf, Liv Tyler (*girl in bus station*).
   Dir: Oliver Stone. Pro: Dan Halsted and Clayton Townsend. Ex Pro and Screenplay: John Ridley, based on his book *Stray Dogs*. Co-Pro: Richard Rutowski. Ph: Robert Richardson. Pro Des: Victor Kempster. Ed: Hank Corwin and Thomas J. Nordberg. M: Ennio Morricone; numbers performed by Peggy Lee, Sammi Smith, Ditch Croaker, Pedro Fernandez, Gloria Lynne, Johnny Cash, Patsy Cline, Mahalia Jackson, Ricky Nelson, R. Crumb & The Cheap Suit Serenaders, etc. Costumes: Beatrix Aruna Pasztor. (Phoenix Pictures / Illusion Entertainment / Clyde Is Hungry / Canal Plus, etc.– Columbia TriStar.) Rel: 24 April 1998. 124 mins. Cert 18. USA / France. 1997.

Volcano ★★★★

While the residents of Los Angeles have learned to live with the prospect of earthquakes, fires, mud slides and drive-by shootings, nobody suspected the city's susceptibility to the onslaught of an unstoppable lava flow. But, following a 'small to moderate earthquake' one morning, a stream of scalding magma is unleashed from the cherished tourist attraction of the La Brea Tar Pits in LA's Westside. Spewing forth deadly lava bombs and showering the city with a blizzard of ash, the torrid tide pushes its inexorable way through the congested streets of the Wilshire Boulevard district, incinerating everything in its path. Dispensing with exposition and character development, *Volcano* is like a male counterpart to the entirely more feminine, thoughtful *Dante's Peak*, ramming home its relentless thrills with no-nonsense machismo. Yet, with the help of some frighteningly credible special effects, *Volcano* does make terrible sense. Where Pierce Brosnan managed to drive his jeep through molten lava in the first film, here car tyres explode on impact with the stuff. Only the ludicrously improbable ending lets the side down. FYI: Executives at Twentieth Century Fox insisted that the film's budget climbed no higher than $90 million, but insiders revealed that the figure was closer to $135 million.

Tommy Lee Jones (*Mike Roark, director of the Office of Emergency Management*), Anne Heche (*Dr Amy Barnes*), Gaby Hoffman (*Kelly Roark*), Don Cheadle (*Emmil Reese*), Keith David (*Lt Ed Fox*), Jacqueline Kim (*Dr Jaye Calder*), John Corbett (*Norman Calder*), John Carroll Lynch (*Stan Olber*), Laurie Lathem (*Rachel*), James G. MacDonald (*Terry Jasper*), Dayton Callie (*Roger Lapher*), Michael Rispoli, Marcello Thedford, Bert Kramer, Bo Eason, Michael

The coast is toast: Tommy Lee Jones and Anne Heche in Mick Jackson's no-nonsense *Volcano* (from Fox)

Cutt, Kevin Bourland, Lou Myers, Richard Schiff, Mother Love.

Dir: Mick Jackson. Pro: Neal H. Moritz and Andrew Z. Davis. Ex Pro: Lauren Shuler Donner. Screenplay: Jerome Armstrong and Billy Ray. Ph: Theo van de Sande. Pro Des: Jackson DeGovia. Ed: Michael Toronik and Don Brochu. M: Alan Silvestri; 'I Love L.A.' written and performed by Randy Newman. Costumes: Kirsten Everberg. Sound: Christopher Boyes. Visual effects: Mat Beck. Consulting volcanologist: Rick Hazlett. Cloud tank chief: Mark L. Hartman. (Fox 2000 Pictures/Shuler Donner/Donner/Moritz Original–Fox.) Rel: 3 October 1997. 104 mins. Cert 12. USA. 1997.

Les Voleurs – Thieves ★★★★

Starting with the death of a criminal, this drama, ably served by its stars, moves back and forth in time with admirable clarity. Its purpose is less to tell a strongly plotted tale than to thread together a view of various relationships. Auteuil's cop has been in sibling rivalry with his criminal brother and is also involved in an unusual romantic triangle (Deneuve's lesbian philosophy professor is part of it); the criminal's bereaved child resents his mother's new lover. But what links these elements is the suggestion that most emotions pass all too quickly. The exception to this – one lover who cares deeply – provides the unsentimental and touching heart to this well-judged picture, one of André Téchiné's best. (*Mansel Stimpson*)

Catherine Deneuve (*Marie*), Daniel Auteuil (*Alexandre Noel*), Laurence Cote (*Juliette Fontana*), Fabienne Babe (*Mireille Noel*), Ivan Desny (*Victor Noel*), Julien Riviere, Benoit Magimel, Didier Bezace, Didier Raymond.

Dir: André Téchiné. Pro: Alain Sarde. Line Pro: Jean-Jacques Albert. Screenplay: Téchiné and Gilles Taurand. Ph: Jeanne Lapoire. Pro Des: Ze Branco. Ed: Martine Giordano. M: Philippe Sarde; Mozart; numbers performed by Les Negresses Vertes, Liza Minnelli, The Archies, etc. Costumes: Elisabeth Tavernier. (Les Films Alain Sarde/Canal Plus/Studio Images, etc.–Metro Tartan.) Rel: 27 March 1998. 116 mins. Cert 18. France. 1996.

Wag the Dog ★★★

When it's revealed that the US president has molested a girl scout in the Oval Office two weeks before his re-election, a PR guerrilla is called in to fix the damage. Teaming up with a Hollywood producer ('war is show business'), the spin doctor invents a declaration of hostilities with Albania in order to distract the electorate's attention... A topical, razor-sharp script by Hilary Henkin and David Mamet is what keeps this wicked exposé humming, even when it fails to convince. Released in the US immediately prior to the Clinton/Lewinsky scandal, the film gained considerable satirical traction at the time, even though it was hardly ploughing new ground (in the 1995 satire *Canadian Bacon*, the US president declares war on the Canucks to bolster his popularity in the run-up to re-election). Still, the film's sense of humour is ruthless and its absurdities contain a disturbing ring of truth.

Dustin Hoffman (*Stanley Motss*), Robert De Niro (*Conrad Brean*), Anne Heche (*Winifred Ames*), Denis Leary (*Fad King*), Willie Nelson (*Johnny Green*), Woody Harrelson (*Sgt William Schumann*), Andrea Martin (*Liz Butsky*), Michael Belson (*The President*), Suzanne Cryer (*Amy Cain*), Suzy Plakson (*Grace*), John Michael Higgins, Kirsten Dunst, Jason Cottle, Sean Masterson, William H. Macy, Pops Staples, Drena De

Niro, Michelle Levinson, Merle Haggard, James Belushi, George Gaynes, Cliff Howard, Jay Leno (himself, of course), and (*uncredited*) Craig T. Nelson (*Senator John Neal*).

Dir: Barry Levinson. Pro: Jane Rosenthal, Robert De Niro and Levinson. Ex Pro: Michael De Luca, Claire Rudnick Polstein and Ezra Swerdlow. Screenplay: Hilary Henkin and David Mamet, from the novel *American Hero* by Larry Beinhart. Ph: Robert Richardson. Pro Des: Wynn Thomas. Ed: Stu Linder. M: Mark Knopfler; numbers performed by Maurice Chevalier, Willie Nelson, Pops Staples, Merle Haggard and The Strangers, Huey Lewis, Mark Knopfler, etc. Costumes: Rita Ryack. Technical advisor: Dale Dye. (New Line Cinema / TriBeca / Baltimore Pictures / Punch Prods–Entertainment.) Rel: 13 March 1998. 97 mins. Cert 15. USA. 1997.

The War at Home ★

An obvious adaptation from the stage set in Texas in 1972, this comment on the horrors of wars in general deals specifically with the post-Vietnam traumas of a son (Estevez) who has returned home. But anyone who admired the subtlety and intelligence of *Regeneration* is hardly likely to take to this schmaltzy treatment, which is equally overheated and banal in its portrait of a dysfunctional family. Wobbling from drama to comedy and back, the film floors Martin Sheen and Kathy Bates as the parents, and even weakens its seemingly anti-war stance by revealing that the son's real trauma lies in his wish to kill his father. Only essential viewing if you must hear 'Fur Elise' played by the film's director / star – or if you're family. [*Mansel Stimpson*]

Kathy Bates (*Maureen Collier*), Martin Sheen (*Bob Collier*), Kimberly Williams (*Karen Collier*), Emilio Estevez (*Jeremy Collier*), Carla Gugino (*Melissa*), Corin Nemec (*Donald*), Geoffrey Blake, Ann Hearn, Penny Allen, Renee Estevez, Paloma Estevez.

Dir: Emilio Estevez. Pro: Estevez, Brad Krevoy, Steve Stabler and James Duff. Ex Pro: Tracie Graham Rice. Screenplay: Duff, based on his play Homefront. Ph: Peter Levy. Pro Des: Eve Cauley. Ed: Craig Bassett. M: Basil Poledouris; Vivaldi; numbers performed by Crosby, Stills, Nash & Young, Kathy Bates, Martin Sheen, Emilio Estevez, etc. Costumes: Grania Preston. (Touchstone / Avatar Entertainment / Motion Picture

Corp–Metrodome.) Rel: 26 June 1998. 118 mins. Cert 15. USA. 1996.

Warriors of Virtue ★★

When lame teenager Ryan Jeffers falls into a water tank he finds himself magically transported to the Land of Tao. There, a quintet of kangaroos – the Warriors of Virtue – struggle to maintain the status quo, drawing on the five virtues of nature. Their adversary is the tyrannical warlord Komodo, who is keeping Tao's life-giving 'zubrium' all to himself. Yet unbeknownst to Ryan, it is his own *Book of Legend* – given to him by a Chinese chef – that holds the true key to the salvation of Tao... Ruthlessly borrowing from such adolescent outings as *Teenage Mutant Ninja Turtles*, *Mortal Kombat* and *The Karate Kid*, *Warriors of Virtue* could have been so much worse. While it's tempting to chuckle at the sight of kick-boxing kangaroos, Hong Kong director Ronny Yu handles the action scenes rather well, frequently drawing the attention away from a risible script. In addition, sumptuous sets and an unconventional charm almost make up for the cast's tendency to play to the gods. [*Ewen Brownrigg*]

Wings of the mouse: Jennifer Jason Leigh as Catherine Sloper in Agnieszka Holland's bumpy *Washington Square* (from Buena Vista)

Angus Macfadyen (*Komodo*), Mario Yedidia (*Ryan Jeffers*), Marley Shelton (*Elysia*), Chao-Li Chi (*Master Chung*), Dennis Dun (*Ming*), Jack Tate (*Yun*), Doug Jones (*Yee*), Don Lewis (*Lai*), J. Todd Adams (*Chi*), Adrienne Corcoran (*Tsun*), Michael John Anderson, Tom Towles, Lee Arenberg.

Dir and Co-Pro: Ronny Yu. Pro: Dennis, Ronald, Christopher and Jeremy Law, and Patrica Ruben. Ex Pro: Joseph Law. Co-Pro: Yu and Peter Pau. Screenplay: Michael Vickerman and Hugh Kelley. Ph: Pau. Pro Des: Eugenio Zanetti. Ed: David Wu. M: Don Davis; numbers performed by Wade Hubbard, Clannad, Speech, Charlie Sexton, and Richie Havens. Costumes: Shirley Chan. Sound: Irving Mulch and Kerry Uchida. (IJL Creations / Law Brothers / Four Brothers–Entertainment.) Rel: 25 July 1997. 103 mins. Cert PG. USA / China. 1996.

Washington Square ★★

21 Washington Square, New York; the 1850s. When the plain, socially graceless Catherine Sloper is courted by the penniless, handsome Morris Townsend, she experiences a happiness and sense of self-worth until now denied her. However, her wealthy father, who has never forgiven her for the death of his wife in childbirth, opposes the relationship as he cannot believe any man could want his daughter for anything other than her inheritance...
For all the recent efforts to make Henry James the next Jane Austen, the writer's interior, complex novels

Nice Year For a White Wedding: Adam Sandler sings 'You Spin Me Around (Like a Record)' in Frank Coraci's sweet and engaging *The Wedding Singer* (from Entertainment)

do not translate well to cinema. Both *The Portrait of a Lady* and *The Wings of the Dove* suffered from the process of force-feeding cinema into the mouth of the novelist's intimate prose. Here, director Agnieszka Holland attempts to have her cake and eat it, confining the action to facial close-ups and small, claustrophobic rooms and then whisking the camera about in a frenzy of compensatory movement. Unfortunately, the result creates a wrenching variegation of tone, like armchair theatre acted out on the deck of a storm-tossed ship. Uneven performances (Jennifer Jason Leigh doing her Stanislavsky bit, Maggie Smith playing it for laughs) further distance the viewer from any emotional involvement.

Jennifer Jason Leigh (*Catherine Sloper*), Albert Finney (*Dr Austin Sloper*), Ben Chaplin (*Morris Townsend*), Maggie Smith (*Aunt Lavinia Penniman*), Judith Ivey (*Mrs*

Elizabeth Almond), Jennifer Garner (*Marian Almond*), Betsy Brantley (*Mrs Montgomery*), Arthur Laupus, Robert Stanton, Nancy Daly, Peter Maloney.

Dir: Agnieszka Holland. Pro: Roger Birnbaum and Julie Bergman Sender. Ex Pro: Randy Ostrow. Screenplay: Carol Doyle. Ph: Jerzy Zielinski. Pro Des: Allan Starski. Ed: David Siegel. M: Jan A.P. Kaczmarek; Donizetti. Costumes: Anna Sheppard. Choreography: Elizabeth Aldrich. Horticultural consultant: Jay Price Stump. (Hollywood Pictures/ Caravan Pictures–Buena Vista.) Rel: 29 May 1998. 116 mins. Cert PG. USA. 1997.

The Wedding Singer ★★★★

The funniest, most charming and uplifting wedding singer in town, Robbie Hart dotes on his job because he believes in love and white weddings. But when he's jilted at the altar of his own nuptials, he subsides into a state of bitterness, belting out 'Love Stinks' at one reception and then resorting to bar mitzvahs. However, the romantic, dewy-eyed Julia Sullivan wants Rob to MC her upcoming event and will not take 'no' for an answer... Brandishing its time frame – 1985 – like a banner, *The Wedding Singer* is like a social document wrapped in

candy floss. Constant references to the silliness of yesterday (break dancing, Rubik's cube, Boy George, *Miami Vice*) guarantee easy laughs, but the film's story of lost love and dashed hopes is timeless. As the thoroughly likeable Mr Nice Guy, Adam Sandler has never been more appealing, while still displaying a wry edge to his humour (dig deeper and you could be offended). The film itself is sweet, utterly charming, strangely old-fashioned and very funny. And the soundtrack is classic.

Adam Sandler (*Robbie J. Hart*), Drew Barrymore (*Julia Sullivan*), Christine Taylor (*Holly*), Allen Covert (*Sammy*), Angela Featherstone (*Linda*), Matthew Glave (*Glen Gulia*), Alexis Arquette (*George*), Ellen Albertini Dow (*Rosie*), Billy Idol (*himself*), Frank Sivero, Christina Pickles, Jodi Thelen, Patrick McTavish, Carmen Filpi, Jason Cottle, Steve Buscemi (*David*), Jon Lovitz (*Jimmie Moore*).

Dir: Frank Coraci. Pro: Robert Simonds and Jack Giarraputo. Ex Pro: Brad Grey and Sandy Wernick. Co-Pro: Ira Shuman. Co-Ex Pro: Brian Witten and Richard Brener. Screenplay: Tim Herlihy. Ph: Tim Suhrstedt. Pro Des: Perry Andelin Blake. Ed: Tom Lewis. M: Teddy Castellucci; numbers performed by Adam Sandler, Alexis Arquette, After the Fire, Ellen Dow, Billy Idol, Nena, Musical Youth, The Cure,

Pricking the conscience with a pneumatic drill: Stephen Dillane is asked for his fare in Michael Winterbottom's shocking *Welcome to Sarajevo* (from Film Four)

The Thompson Twins, Kajagoogoo, Lionel Richie, The Cars, Jon Lovitz, The Police, Hall & Oates, Elvis Costello, New Order, David Bowie, The B-52s, Psychedelic Furs, Jan Hammer, Huey Lewis and the News, Bruce Springsteen, The Smiths, Steve Buscemi, The Presidents of the United States of America, etc. Costumes: Mona May. (New Line Cinema– Entertainment.) Rel: June 5 1998. 97 mins. Cert 12. USA. 1998.

Welcome to Sarajevo ★★★★★

Sarajevo, Bosnia; 1992. On the road leading to the capital of Bosnia and Herzegovina, a sign reads 'Welcome to Sarajevo'. Beneath it lies the body of a man with half his face missing. It is here, where civilians are routinely shot dead queuing for bread and water, that ITN war correspondent Michael Henderson (based on real-life reporter Michael Nicholson) is covering his 14th war. Coincidentally, the UN has declared Sarajevo the 14th most dangerous place on earth, an announcement that hardly displays a grasp of the real facts. Meanwhile, Henderson's professional reserve is beginning to buckle... Expertly blending fabricated newsreel footage with the real thing, *Welcome to Sarajevo* evokes an immediacy that is both exhilarating and horrifying. Like *The Killing Fields*, the film focuses a spotlight on a country ravaged by war as seen from the perspective of the international press corps, whose job, as one cameraman puts it, is not to help, but to report. Still, it was through the shocking images that these professionals risked their lives to capture that the reality of Bosnia was brought to the rest of the world. This film, which courageously keeps sentimentality in check, extends the message that *this must never happen again*.

Stephen Dillane (*Michael Henderson*), Woody Harrelson (*Flynn*), Marisa Tomei (*Nina*), Emira Nusevic (*Emira*), Kerry Fox (*Jane Carson*), Goran Visnjic (*Risto*), Emily Lloyd (*Annie McGee*), James Nesbitt (*Gregg*), Gordana Gadzic (*Mrs Savic*), Juliet Aubrey (*Helen Henderson*), Igor Dzambazov, Drazen Sivak, Vesna Orel, Kerry Shale, Frank Dillane.

Dir: Michael Winterbottom. Pro: Graham Broadbent and Damian Jones. Line Pro: Paul Sarony. Screenplay: Frank Cottrell Boyce, based on the book *Natasha's Story* by Michael Nicholson. Ph: Daf Hobson. Pro Des: Mark Geraghty. Ed: Trevor Waite. M: Adrian Johnston; numbers performed by Stereo MC's, Happy Mondays, Bobby McFerrin, Blur, Groupa Dollar, Teenage Fanclub, Stone Roses, The Rolling Stones, Massive Attack, House of Love, Bob Marley and The Wailers, Van Morrison, etc. Costumes: Janty Yates. (Channel Four Television/ Miramax/Dragon Pictures–Film Four.) Rel: 21 November 1997. 101 mins. Cert 15. UK/USA. 1997.

Western ★★★

Male-bonding in Brittany is the subject of this award-winning comedy. The odd couple are suitably contrasted and well played: Paco (Lopez) is an amorous Spanish salesman, while Nino from Russia (Bourdo) lacks his knack with women. Early on, Paco agrees when his latest girl (Vitali) suggests that he prove his sincerity by returning in three weeks if his feelings are unchanged. This gives writer-director Manuel Poirier every opportunity to depict episodic

Born to be Wilde: Stephen Fry as Oscar with Jude Law as Lord 'Bosie' Douglas in Brian Gilbert's articulate and daring *Wilde* **(from PolyGram)**

misadventures during Paco's time away with Nino and, since Paco is soon drawn to another woman, it's difficult to care about the final outcome. An atmospheric music score and genuine charm are assets, but 134 minutes is much too long for so slight a tale. Somewhere inside, a better, shorter film is trying to get out. [*Mansel Stimpson*]

Sergei Lopez (*Paco*), Sacha Bourdo (*Nino*), Elisabeth Vitali (*Marinette*), Marie Matheron (*Nathalie*), Daphne Gaudefroy D, Melanie Leray, Basile Siekoua, Helene Moreau.
   Dir: Manuel Poirier. Pro: Maurice Bernart and Michel Saint-Jean. Screenplay: Poirier and Jean-Francois Goyet. Ph: Nara Keo Kosal. Pro Des: Roland Mabille. Ed: Yann Dedet. M: Bernado Sandoval. Costumes: Sophie Dwernicki. (Salome-Diaphana/Canal Plus,

etc.–Artificial Eye.) Rel: 8 May 1998. 134 mins. Cert 15. France. 1997.

Wilde ★★★★★
1882-1898; Colorado/England/Italy. Returning from a hugely successful lecture tour of the United States and Canada, Oscar Wilde does the 'done thing' and marries the well-connected Constance Lloyd – and gives her two sons. Meanwhile, his notorious novel *The Picture of Dorian Gray* – not to mention his inimitable wit – makes him the toast of London society. But his meeting with Robbie Ross, a young Canadian homosexual, and his subsequent infatuation with the beautiful, arrogant Lord Alfred Douglas, sows the seeds for his eventual undoing... As Madonna was destined to play Evita and Geoffrey Rush to represent David Helfgott, so Stephen Fry was born to be Wilde. Besides sharing an uncanny facial resemblance to the writer, Fry is also an educated man, a writer of some regard and an

unapologetic homosexual, while his fastidious mode of expression perfectly mirrors that of the celebrated dilettante. He is perfectly brilliant. Moreover, the writer Julian Mitchell (*Another Country*) has avoided the habitual pitfalls of film biography (flashbacks, captions, historical compression) and has gone for the essence rather than the curriculum vitae of his subject. In short, this is an articulate, daring, stylish, funny and extremely moving study of a man destroyed by the paradoxes of his genius. FYI: Oscar Wilde was previously portrayed on film by Robert Morley and Peter Finch (both in 1960), and on television by Michael Gambon.

Stephen Fry (*Oscar Fingal O'Flahertie Wills Wilde*), Jude Law (*Lord Alfred 'Bosie' Douglas*), Vanessa Redgrave (*Lady Speranza Wilde*), Jennifer Ehle (*Constance Wilde*), Gemma Jones (*Lady Queensberry*), Judy Parfitt (*Lady Mount-Temple*), Michael Sheen (*Robert Ross*), Zoe Wanamaker (*Ada Leverson*), Tom Wilkinson (*The Marquess of Queensberry*), Ioan Gruffudd (*John Gray*), Matthew Mills (*Lionel Johnson*), Jason Morell (*Ernest Dowson*), Peter Barkworth (*Charles Gill*), David Westhead (*Edward Carson*), Robert Lang, Philip Locke, Benedict Sandiford, Mark Letheren, Michael Fitzgerald, Bob Sessions, Robin Kermode, Avril Elgar, Judi Maynard, Edward Laurie, Arthur Whybrow.
   Dir: Brian Gilbert. Pro: Marc Samuelson and Peter Samuelson. Ex Pro: Michiyo Yoshizaki, Michael Viner, Deborah Raffin, Alan Howden and Alex Graham. Screenplay: Julian Mitchell, based on the biography *Oscar Wilde* by Richard Ellmann. Ph: Martin Fuhrer. Pro Des: Maria Djurkovic. Ed: Michael Bradsell. M: Debbie Wiseman. Costumes: Nic Ede. Title design: John Goodison (with apologies to Aubrey Beardsley). (Samuelson Entertainment/Pony Canyon/NDF International/Dove International/Pandora Film/BBC Films/The Greenlight Fund/Wall-to-Wall Television/British Screen/National Lottery–PolyGram.) Rel: 17 October 1997. 117 mins. Cert 15. UK/USA/Japan/Germany. 1997.

Wild Man Blues ★★★
Paris/Madrid/Venice/Bologna/Milan/Vienna/London/New York; 1997. Documentary following Woody Allen and his New Orleans-style jazz band on their 18-concert, European tour. An affectionate and funny if conventional look at the guarded life

of a private man, the film actually reveals less about its subject than Woody's own comic fictions. Still, the extensive footage of Woody performing his beloved clarinet should delight jazz enthusiasts. [*Charles Bacon*]

With Woody Allen, Soon-Yi Previn, Letty Aronson (*Woody's sister*), Jean Doumanian, John Doumanian, Nettie Konigsberg (*Woody's mothe*r), Martin Konigsberg (*Woody's father*), and the band: Dan Barrett (*trombone*), Simon Wettenhall (*trumpet*), John Gill (*drums*), Cynthia Sayer (*piano*), Greg Cohen (*bass*), Eddy Davis (*banjo*).
   Dir: Barbara Kopple. Pro: Jean Doumanian. Ex Pro: J.E. Beaucaire. Assoc Pro: Kathleen Bambrick Meier. Ph: Tom Hurwitz. Ed: Lawrence Silk. (Magnolia Prods/Sweetland Films/Cabin Creek Films–Feature Film Co.) Rel: 8 May 1998. 105 mins. Cert 12. USA. 1997.

Miami spice: Matt Dillon acts as sex counsellor in John McNaughton's outrageously entertaining, post-modern satire *Wild Things* (from Entertainment)

Wild Things ★★★★
Blue Bay, Coconut Grove, Florida; the present. The recipient of a trophy for 'educator of the year', Sam Lombardo is a handsome, womanising sex counsellor at an upmarket high school. Then, when a female student accuses him of rape, he finds himself excluded from the society he has tried so hard to infiltrate... Dispensing with the gritty netherworld of his first three films (*Henry: Portrait of a Serial Killer*, *Mad Dog and Glory* and *Normal Life*), director John McNaughton launches into the slick tide of the mainstream with gusto. Utilising a pulsating percussion and guitar score, widescreen vistas of Miami and the sawgrass plains of the Florida Everglades and a roster of cosmetically friendly bodies, McNaughton sets the scene like some R-rated take on *Beverly Hills 90210*. Interestingly, prior to this, producer Kevin Bacon starred in *Telling Lies in America* from the semi-autobiographical screenplay by Joe Eszterhas. Yet *Wild Things*, with its slick sex and slippery plot, is the best thing Joe Eszterhas never wrote.

Kevin Bacon (*Ray Duquette*), Matt Dillon (*Sam Lombardo*), Neve Campbell (*Suzie Toller*), Theresa Russell (*Sandra Van Ryan*), Denise Richards (*Kelly Van Ryan*), Daphne Rubin-Vega (*Gloria Perez*), Robert Wagner (*Tom Baxter*), Bill Murray (*Ken Bowden*), Carrie Snodgress (*Ruby*), Jeff Perry (*Bryce Hunter*), Cory Pendergast (*Jimmy Leach*),

Jennifer Bini (*Barbara Baxter*), Marc Macaulay, Toi Svane, Dennis Neal, Victoria Bass, Leonor Anthony.
   Dir: John McNaughton. Pro: Rodney Liber and Steven A. Jones. Ex Pro: Kevin Bacon. Screenplay: Stephen Peters. Ph: Jeffrey L. Kimball. Pro Des: Edward T. McAvoy. Ed: Elena Maganini. M: George S. Clinton; numbers performed by Tito Puente, The Miracles, Smash Mouth, Barry White, Sugar Ray, Johnny Rivers, Iggy Pop, Morphine, etc. Costumes: Kimberly A. Tillman. (Mandalay Entertainment–Entertainment.) Rel: 15 May 1998. 111 mins. Cert 18. USA. 1998.

Will It Snow for Christmas? – Y'aura t'il de la Neige à Noël? ★★★½
Struggling against the insensitivity and arrogance of her husband, a woman strives to raise seven children while managing a farm in the south of France... Children play in the tunnels formed by bales of hay. Boats are improvised from hollowed out marrows and launched in the flooded furrows of a field. Leeks, onions, beetroot, parsley, pumpkins, cabbages and marrows are prepared for market. There is nothing wrong in luxuriating in the detail of everyday lives, but Sandrine

Veysset's lack of a cinematic eye makes the routine drudgery of this rural hell seem like routine drudgery. Only Dominique Reymond's performance as the long-suffering mother gives this tedious exercise any resonance.

Dominique Reymond (*the mother*), Daniel Duval (*the father*), Jessica Martinez, Alexandre Roger, Eric Huyard, Loys Cappatti.
   Dir: Sandrine Veysset. Ex Pro: Humbert Balsan. Screenplay: Veysset and Antoinette De Robien. Ph: Hélène Louvart. Pro Des: Jacques Dubus. Ed: Nelly Quettier. M: Henri Ancillotti. Costumes: Nathalie Raoul. (Ognon Pictures/Canal Plus, etc.–Artificial Eye.) Rel: 7 November 1997. 91 mins. Cert 12. France. 1996.

The Wings of the Dove ★★½
A pearl in the crown of the English aristocracy, Kate Croy finds herself torn between her social standing and her love for an impoverished journalist. At the mercy of her Aunt Maude, Kate knows that if she succumbs to the demands of her heart she will lose her position in society and threaten the modest allowance paid to her opium-addicted father. When a beautiful American heiress courts her friendship, Kate devises a way out of her dilemma, albeit at the risk of losing the love of her life... Seething with subtext, *The Wings of the Dove* serves the moral integrity of Henry

James's 1902 novel, but lacks the cinematic dash to tear itself from the page and on to the screen. Filmed at a number of distinguished landmarks (Knebworth House, Luton Hoo, Syon House, all over Venice), the film is an exceptionally handsome production if ultimately a rather dull ride. As the romantic linchpin, Linus Roache perfectly conveys the scrupulous character of Merton Densher, but lacks the ineffable charisma that would put so much at risk.

Helena Bonham Carter (*Kate Croy*), Linus Roache (*Merton Densher*), Alison Elliott (*Millie Theale*), Elizabeth McGovern (*Susan*), Michael Gambon (*Kate's father*), Alex Jennings (*Lord Mark*), Charlotte Rampling (*Aunt Maude*).
   Dir: Iain Softley. Pro: Stephen Evans and David Parfitt. Ex Pro: Bob Weinstein, Harvey Weinstein and Paul Feldsher. Line Pro: Mark Cooper. Screenplay: Hossein Amini. Ph: Eduardo Serra. Pro Des: John Beard. Ed: Tariq Anwar. M: Edward Shearmur. Costumes: Sandy Powell. (Miramax/Renaissance Films–Buena Vista.) Rel: 2 January 1998. 102 mins. Cert 15. USA/UK. 1997.

The Winner ★★

When a mysterious innocent finds that he is unable to lose at the gambling tables of Las Vegas, a myth quickly builds round him. So do the number of seedy characters who attempt to take a bite of his easily

Wet kiss: An award-laden Helena Bonham Carter with Linus Roache in Iain Softley's dull and pretty *The Wings of the Dove* (from Buena Vista)

won money. And when a good-time girl and hustler called Louise turns the Midas Boy's head, the stakes really begin to climb... While director Alex Cox and writer Wendy Riss introduce some neat touches (not to mention one of the most audacious endings in cinema history), *The Winner* cannot shake off the shackles of its unwieldy contrivance. Slick, superficial and gimmicky, the film should take a look at Paul Thomas Anderson's *Hard Eight* to see how one can rise above the limitations of the high-stakes gambling genre.

Rebecca DeMornay (*Louise*), Vincent D'Onofrio (*Phillip*), Richard Edson (*Frankie*), Saverio Guerra (*Paulie*), Delroy Lindo (*Frank Kingman*), Michael Madsen (*Johnny 'Wolf'*), Billy Bob Thornton (*Jack*), Frank Whaley (*Joey*), Sy Richardson, Bill Yeager, Alex Cox (*Gaston*).
   Dir: Alex Cox. Pro: Kenneth Schwenker. Ex Pro: Mark Damon and Rebecca DeMornay. Co-Ex Pro: Andrew Pfeffer. Co-Pro: Jeremiah Samuels and Wendy Riss. Screenplay: Riss, based on her play *A Darker Purpose*. Ph: Denis Maloney. Pro Des: Cecilia Montiel. Ed: Carlos Puente. M: Daniel Licht; numbers performed by Rebecca DeMornay, Pray For Rain, The Feminine Complex, and Joey Altruda with The Cocktail Crew. Costumes: Nancy Steiner. (Village Roadshow/Clipsal Films–

Feature Film Co.) Rel: 23 January 1998. 89 mins. Cert 15. USA/Australia. 1996.

The Winter Guest ★★★

The village of Pittenweem, Fife, Scotland; the present. Determined to combat the onslaught of old age, Elspeth trudges through the snow to visit her daughter, Frances, who is struggling to face life after the death of her husband. Meanwhile, Frances's 15-year-old son strives to come to terms with his own burgeoning manhood, brought into relief by an encounter with a local girl... As Gary Oldman's directorial debut was a raw, visceral autopsy of his father, so Alan Rickman's is largely a studied, lyrical view of a mother. And, as that, it is as feminine in texture as Oldman's film was posturingly macho. It was Rickman who was instrumental in jump-starting the play on which the film is based, when he introduced the dramatist Sharman Macdonald to his colleague Lindsay Duncan, suggesting that the history of the latter's relationship with her mother would make an intriguing dramatic premise. Macdonald wrote the play and Rickman directed its inaugural run in Leeds and then in London, before collaborating with Macdonald on the screenplay. The cinematic outcome is beautifully observed in Phyllida Law's expressively pronounced performance and is luminously photographed by Seamus McGarvey. Yet while Rickman is to be commended for plumbing the secrets expressed in his actors' faces, he has failed to shake the drama free from its theatrical roots and has produced a work that borders on the precious.

Phyllida Law (*Elspeth*), Emma Thompson (*Frances*), Gary Hollywood (*Alex*), Arlene Cockburn (*Nita*), Sheila Reid (*Lily*), Sandra Voe (*Chloe*), Douglas Murphy (*Sam*), Sean Biggerstaff (*Tom*), Tom Watson (*the minister*).
   Dir: Alan Rickman. Pro: Ken Lipper and Edward R. Pressman. Co-Pro: Steve Clark-Hall. Assoc Pro: Alan J. 'Willie' Wands. Screenplay: Rickman and Sharman Macdonald. Ph: Seamus McGarvey. Pro Des: Robin Cameron Don. Ed: Scott Thomas. M: Michael Kamen. Costumes: Joan Bergin. (Capitol Films/Fine Line Features/Channel Four/Scottish Arts Council Lottery Fund–Film Four.) Rel: 16 January 1998. 104 mins. Cert 15. USA/UK. 1996.

Becoming mothers: Phyllida Law and Emma Thompson in Alan Rickman's lyrical *The Winter Guest* (from Film Four)

Wishmaster ★

Chaos reigns when an evil genie pops out of an old statue and demands three wishes from the woman who has released him from his detention... A rather novel conceit (dreamed up by former Disney executive Clark Peterson) is supplied with the standard gore quotient, but Kurtzman's sluggish direction deprives the exercise of either shivers or giggles. Talk about a death wish. [*Ewen Brownrigg*]

Tammy Lauren (*Alexandra Amberson*), Andrew Divoff (*The Djinn/Nathaniel Demerest*), Tony Todd (*Johnny Valentine*), Kane Hodder (*Merritt's guard*), Robert Englund (*Raymond Beaumont*), Angus Scrimm (*narrator*), Ari Barak, Ted Raimi, Danny Hicks, Chris Lemmon, Ashley Power, Jenny O'Hara, Gretchen Palmer, Betty McGuire.
   Dir: Robert Kurtzman. Pro: Pierre David, Clark Peterson and Noel A. Zanitsch. Ex Pro: Wes Craven. Co-Pro: David Tripet. Screenplay: Peter Atkins. Ph: Jacques Haitkin. Pro Des: Dorian Vernaccio and Deborah Raymond. Ed: David Handman. M: Harry Manfredini. Costumes: Karyn Wagner. Sound: Phil Seretti. Make-up effects: Kurtzman, Greg Nicotero and Howard Berger. (LIVEfilm/Mediaworks–First Independent.) Rel: 29 May 1998. 90 mins. Cert 18. USA. 1997.

The Woodlanders ★★

Set in the woodland community of Little Hintock, Thomas Hardy's favourite novel centres on Grace Melbury, daughter of an affluent timber merchant, and Giles Winterbourne, a simple, solid cider-maker devoted to Grace since childhood. However, when Grace is sent away to finishing school her social aspirations are fostered and her liaison with the upwardly mobile Dr Edred Fitzpiers hotly cultivated by her father. And, in spite of her initial misgivings, Grace agrees to marry the icy, fickle doctor... Marking the feature debut of documentary filmmaker Phil Agland (*Baka – The People of the Rainforest*), *The Woodlanders* is strong on *mise en scène* but weak on passion (subliminal or otherwise). In fact, this timid adaptation of Hardy's 1887 novel tries so hard to translate the author's prose into visual terms that it neglects the fundamentals of audience involvement. The wide-screen photography is lovely and Emily Woof's open face the sort a man can drown in, but the acting is stilted and the pace decidedly leaden. Filmed on location in Hampshire, Dorset and Wiltshire.

Rufus Sewell (*Giles Winterbourne*), Polly Walker (*Felice Charmond*), Jodhi May (*Marty South*), Tony Haygarth (*George Melbury*), Cal MacAninch (*Dr Edred Fitzpiers*), Emily Woof (*Grace Melbury*), Sheila Burrell (*Grammer Oliver*), Walter Sparrow, Michael Culkin, Amanda Ryan, Robert Blythe, William Chubb.
   Dir: Phil Agland. Pro: Agland and Barney Reisz. Screenplay: David Rudkin. Ph: Ashley Rowe. Pro Des: Andy Harris. Ed: David Dickie. M: George Fenton. Costumes: Susannah Buxton. (Channel Four/Pathe/National Lottery, etc.–Pathe.) Rel: 6 February 1998. 97 mins. Cert PG. UK. 1997.

Of fair and clear complexion: Emily Woof as Thomas Hardy's favourite heroine - in *The Woodlanders* (from Pathe)

Video Releases

Compiled by Charles Bacon

Additional reviews by
James Cameron-Wilson

(*from July 1997 through to June 1998*)

❑ : denotes films released theatrically
  in the US
✳ : denotes films of special merit

All Dogs Go to Heaven 2 – Charlie's New Adventures ❑

Now firmly ensconced in heaven, the rakish but loveable alsatian Charlie (voiced by Charlie Sheen, taking over from Burt Reynolds) is bored out of his mind and so opts to chase a spy from hell back to earth. The latter is old Carface (Ernest Borgnine), a bulldog who has stolen Gabriel's Horn from the angels, thus jamming the Pearly Gates. Meanwhile, back on earth, Charlie is waylaid by a sexy singing pooch (Sheena Easton), but is unable to profess his undying love as he's invisible... While lacking the lush production values of the original, this sequel to the 1989 cartoon still displays much good-natured fun. However, the diabolical powers displayed by a feline Satan seem unnecessarily frightening for younger viewers. [JC-W]

Other voices: Dom DeLuise, George Hearn, Bebe Neuwirth, Adam Wyle. Dirs: Paul Sabella and Larry Leker. Songs: Barry Mann and Cynthia Weil. U. July 1997 (Warner).

The Beautician and the Beast ❑

Daft reworking of *The Sound of Music* and *Beauty and the Beast* in which a queen's beautician ends up tutoring the children of an Eastern European despot. More dumb than oddball.

With Fran Drescher, Timothy Dalton, Ian McNeice, Patrick Malahide, Lisa Jakub, Michael Lerner, Phyllis Newman, Todd Graff. Dir: Ken Swapis. Screenplay: Todd Graff (he who wrote *Used People* and *Angie*). M: Cliff Eidelman. PG. June 1998 (CIC).

Beauty and the Beast: The Enchanted Christmas

Serviceable sequel to Disney's Oscar-nominated cartoon, in which the Enchanted Objects recall the time that Belle attempted to bring Christmas back to the beast's castle. Five new songs and a villainous organ (voiced by Tim Curry) contribute to the tale, which boasts splendid animation and a few good lines (Cogsworth to crystal goblets: 'Don't whine, glasses'). [JC-W]

With the voices of Paige O'Hara, Robby Benson, Jerry Orbach, David Ogden Stiers, Bernadette Peters, Angela Lansbury, Paul Reubens, Frank Welker. Dir: Andy Knight. M: Rachel Portman; songs: Portman, Don Black. U. December 1997 (Walt Disney).

Before Women Had Wings

Adapted by Connie May Fowler from her own novel, this is the first of Oprah Winfrey's TV movies developed by her production company Harpo Films, an accomplished and well acted, if somewhat simplistic, drama. Ellen Barkin is particularly impressive as an alcoholic piece of white trash, and is well matched by Tina Majorino as her vivacious nine-year-old daughter. Lloyd Kramer directs well, too, but the subject matter is a real downer.

Also with Oprah Winfrey, Julia Stiles, John Savage, Burt Young. 15. March 1998 (Odyssey).

Beverly Hills Ninja ❏

Puerile, embarrassing farce in which Chris Farley plays an unlikely and ungainly Ninja warrior on a rescue mission in Rodeo Drive. Pathetic.

Also with Nicolette Sheridan, Robin Shou, Nathaniel Parker, Chris Rock. Dir: Dennis Dugan. M: George S. Clinton. 12. March 1998 (Columbia TriStar).

Bogus ❏

Orphaned when his mother is killed in a car wreck, a seven-year-old boy picks up an imaginary friend (a Gallicly charming Gerard Depardieu) when he goes to stay with his hard-working aunt in New York. Old-fashioned and whimsical, *Bogus* strives for charm and naturalism but is a little too pat for its own good. Thank heavens, then, for Depardieu.

Also with Whoopi Goldberg, Haley Joel Osment, Nancy Travis, Ute Lemper, Sheryl Lee Ralph. Dir and Pro: Norman Jewison. Screenplay: Alvin Sargent. M: Marc Shaiman. PG. July 1997 (Warner).

A Brooklyn State of Mind

Underwhelming visit to the crime-scarred streets of Brooklyn, with the familiar tale of a local Godfather (Danny Aiello, no surprise) and the young hoodlum who works for him (Vincent Spano). While the atmosphere is well evoked, the story is rather tired and predictable.

Also with Maria Grazia Cucinotta, Abe Vigoda, Tony Danza, Morgana King, Ricky Aiello. Dir: Frank Rainone. 18. February 1998 (Mosaic).

Bullet ❏

Turgid, incoherent shambles in which a vicious gangster-cum-Tony Curtis fan is released from prison only to continue his reign of terror. A surprisingly nasty piece of work from Julien Temple, director of *Absolute Beginners* and *Earth Girls Are Easy*.

With Mickey Rourke, Tupac Shakur, Ted Levine, Adrien Brody. 18. December 1997 (First Independent).

Beauty and the Beast: *The Enchanted Christmas* (from Walt Disney)

Bulletproof ❏

Formulaic, derivative actioner in which undercover cop Damon Wayans comes under fire after a sting backfires. No amount of crude asides or large bangs can disguise the fact that this is just a sketchy re-hash of *Midnight Run*.

Also with Adam Sandler, James Caan, Kristen Wilson, James Farentino, Bill Nunn, Xander Berkeley. Dir: Ernest Dickerson. M: Elmer Bernstein. 18. November 1997 (CIC).

Cold Heart

Yet another heist-gone-wrong crime thriller-cum-road movie, and no amount of brisk pacing can compensate for trite characters and lack of suspense. US title: *Cold Around the Heart*.

With David Caruso, Kelly Lynch, Stacey Dash, Chris Noth, John Spencer, Pruitt Taylor Vince. Dir and Screenplay: John Ridley. M: Mason Daring. 18. March 1998 (Hi-Fliers).

Commandments

When his life collapses around him (loss of wife, job, dog, etc.), Seth Warner concocts his revenge on God by setting out to break all ten commandments. A nice idea is served by a good cast but hardly by a tenable screenplay.

With Aidan Quinn, Courtney Cox, Anthony LaPaglia, Pat McNamara, Tom Aldredge, Joanna Going. Dir and Screenplay: Daniel Taplitz. 18. February 1998 (CIC).

Dead Heart ❏ ✳

Gritty, creditable outback drama in which Bryan Brown plays a down-to-earth cop investigating the mysterious murder of a young Aborigine. Exploring the on-going

Bryan Brown takes his best shot in Nicholas Parsons' gripping *Dead Heart* (from Hi-Fliers)

clash between whites and Aborigines in contemporary Australia, *Dead Heart* speaks volumes with a clear, powerful – and gripping – voice. And the photography of Central Australia's arid wilderness is ace.

Also with Ernie Dingo, Angie Milliken, Lewis FitzGerald, David Gulpilil. Dir and Screenplay: Nicholas Parsons, from his play. 18. June 1998 (Hi-Fliers).

Dead Silence
Timely HBO drama with James Garner an FBI hostage negotiator wrangling with three escaped cons who've taken a busload of deaf children hostage. Besides some silliness in the latter stages, the film does hit a number of home runs.

Also with Kim Coates, Marlee Matlin, Charles Martin Smith, Lolita Davidovich, Kenneth Welsh. Dir: Daniel Petrie Jr. Screenplay: Donald Stewart, from the novel *A Maiden's Grave*. 15. November 1997 (Mosaic).

Dear God ❏
Another inspired comic conceit from the pen of Warren Leight (*The Night*

We Never Met), in which a conman is challenged to hold down a job for a year. Relegated to the 'dead letter office' of the post office, Tom Turner (Gregg Kinnear) responds to letters addressed to Santa, Elvis and God and sets off an epidemic of good deeds among his peers. A delightful, loopy cast enters into the spirit of the daft concept, but the schmaltz ladled on by director Garry Marshall rapidly smothers the film in treacle.

Also with Laurie Metcalf, Tim Conway, Hector Elizondo, Roscoe Lee Browne, Jon Seda, Donal Logue, Nancy Marchand, Larry Miller, Rue McLlanahan, Jack Klugman, Garry Marshall. PG. September 1997 (CIC).

Fire Down Below ❏
Taking on where he left off in the ecologically sensitive 1994 thriller *On Deadly Ground*, a pony-tailed Steven Seagal plays an environmental protection agent who locks horns with toxic waste-dumping industrialists in Kentucky's Appalachians. Plenty of colourful locations, handsome stunts and boo-hissable villains go some way in making up for the predictable plot and cringe-making preachiness. Incidentally, this tosh was previously earmarked for Bruce Willis.

Also with Marg Helgenberger, Harry Dean Stanton, Stephen Lang, Kris Kristofferson, Levon Helm, Brad Hunt, Richard Masur, Randy Travis. Dir: Felix Enriquez Alcala. Screenplay: Jeb Stuart. M: Nick Glennie-Smith. 18. May 1998 (Warner).

The Garden of Redemption
In war-torn Italy, 1944, a mild-mannered priest pines for a village beauty as he struggles with his conscience over whether or not to help her people undermine the local Nazi presence. A good cast struggles valiantly to overcome the implausibilities of a muddled script, while the Portuguese locations (doubling for Tuscany) almost win the day.

With Anthony LaPaglia, Embeth Davidtz, Dan Hedaya (as an Italian partisan), Peter Firth (a Nazi commandant), James Acheson, Bernice Stegers. Dir and Screenplay: Thomas Michael Donnelly. M: John Altman. 12. January 1998 (CIC).

Getting Away With Murder ❏
Truly excruciating black comedy in which a professor of moral philosophy (Dan Aykroyd) discovers that his neighbour is a Nazi war criminal (Jack Lemmon, of all people). Unforgivable.

Also with Lily Tomlin, Bonnie Hunt, Brian Kerwin, Andy Romano. Dir: Harvey Miller. 15. August 1997 (PolyGram).

Gold in the Streets
Arriving in New York with his head full of visions of the American Dream, young Liam of Ballykelly, Northern Ireland, quickly falls in with a crowd of disillusioned Irish immigrants. 'You've come to the right place,' offers a wiseacre bartender. 'New York is the homeless capital of the world.' However, Liam is determined to make the most of his lot, even if his new circle of friends fail to share his optimism... A slice-of-life drama based on Janet Noble's play *Away Alone*, *Gold in the Streets* strives to bring authenticity to a facet of New York life little explored by the cinema. Unfortunately, even as the film wears its dramatic integrity on its sleeve, a number of the relationships fail to ring true. Paddy's unlikely fling with an

attractive socialite is only sketchily realised (if that), while one of the more interesting characters, Breda, is never allowed to develop beyond a series of mysterious reaction shots. The film's strength lies in its atmosphere, but then you can get that down at the local. [JC-W]

With Ian Hart, Jared Harris, Louise Lombard, Aiden Gillen, Karl Geary, Lorraine Pilkington, Andrea Irvine, James Belushi. Dir: Elizabeth Gill. 15. September 1997 (PolyGram).

Gone Fishin' ❏
Genuinely dire, predictable comedy in which a pair of dumb anglers get hooked up with two women on the trail of a deadly conman in Florida.

With Joe Pesci, Danny Glover, Rosanna Arquette, Lynn Whitfield, Willie Nelson, Nick Brimble. Dir: Christopher Cain. M: Randy Edelman. 12. April 1998 (Hollywood).

Grand Isle
Good-looking but uninvolving 1899 drama about a married woman who casts off the shackles of convention after an encounter with a bohemian artist. Stilted dialogue and stiff performances hardly help this self-consciously leisurely adaptation of Kate Chopin's novel *The Awakening*.

With Kelly McGillis, Jon DeVries, Adrian Pasdar, Ellen Burstyn, Glenne Headly, Julian Sands. Dir: Mary Lambert. Pro: McGillis. Ph: Toyomichi Kurita. M: Elliot Goldenthal. October 1997 (Warner).

The Heidi Chronicles
Well-acted version of Wendy Wasserstein's keenly observed, trenchantly humorous Tony-winning play about coming of age in the feminist era. Jamie Lee Curtis is excellent in a difficult role, but ultimately the film suffers from stilted direction and an uninspired adaptation (by Wasserstein herself).

Also with Tom Hulce, Peter Friedman, Kim Cattrall, Roma Maffia, Shari Belafonte. Dir: Paul Bogart. M: David Shire. 12. October 1997 (Warner).

Hollow Point
An incongruous trio (unstable DEA commando Thomas Ian Griffith,

seductive FBI agent Tia Carrere and carefree hitman Donald Sutherland) join forces to combat a power-hunger government traitor (John Lithgow). Hammy and derivative this may be, but thanks to a choice cast it's also rather fun.

Dir: Sidney J. Furie. 18. February 1998 (Hi-Fliers).

House Arrest ❏
On the day of their surprise wedding anniversary party for Mom and Dad, Grover (Kyle Howard), 14, and Stacy (Amy Sakasitz), 10, are told that their parents are separating. Refusing to face a one-parent future (in spite of the prospect of twice as many presents for Christmas and on his birthday), Grover locks his parents in the basement to sort out their differences. This prescription is met with such approval by Grover's school mates that they bring along their own dysfunctional guardians to share quality time in the communal cellar... Overflowing with sentimentality and sitcom formula, *House Arrest* is a reasonable idea packaged in that unbearable style of American comedy in which lots of songs, dancing and shouting fill in for wit. Not the worst farce of the year, but these days that's not saying much. [JC-W]

With Jamie Lee Curtis, Kevin Pollak, Jennifer Tilly, Christopher McDonald, Ray Walston, Wallace Shawn, Caroline Aaron, Jennifer Love Hewitt, Sheila McCarthy, Colleen Camp. Dir: Harry Winer. M: Bruce Broughton. PG. March 1998 (Entertainment).

Idiot Box ✳
A corrosive Australian satire in *Trainspotting* vein, this is one heist comedy that delivers in spades. A couple of TV-reared thugs think they can rob a bank just because they've seen it done on the telly... Funny, unsettling and very smart.

With Ben Mendelsohn, Jeremy Sims, Robyn Loau. Dir and Screenplay: David Caesar. 18. December 1997 (Hi-Fliers).

I'm Not Rappaport ❏
A not entirely successful adaptation of Herb Gardner's award-winning play, let down by an insistence to dilute the original's magic with an

uneasy dose of cinematic naturalism. Still, Walter Matthau is perfect as the embittered Nat Moyer and the dialogue is choice.

Also with Ossie Davis, Amy Irving, Martha Plimpton, Craig T. Nelson, Boyd Gaines, Guillermo Diaz, Elina Lowensohn, Ron Rifkin. Dir and Screenplay: Herb Gardner. Ph: Adam Holender. 12. December 1997 (CIC).

Inside
A two-tiered drama, *Inside* is the story of a brutal Afrikaner colonel (Nigel Hawthorne) who persecutes a white activist (Eric Stoltz) and is then cross-examined himself ten years later by a black representative of the Truth Commission (Louis Gossett Jr). While the claustrophobic atmosphere is well maintained by director Arthur Penn, Bima Stagg's screenplay misses a number of prime opportunities, refusing to offer any new prognosis of an old wound. Bruising viewing, none the less, with a consummate turn from Hawthorne as the compassionless interrogator.

18. January 1998 (Entertainment).

A Kid in King Arthur's Court ❏
Reasonably serviceable Disney yarn in which a contemporary American boy is magiced back to Camelot when Merlin botches a time-travelling spell. There, the kid must do battle with Art Malik's dastardly usurper and win the hand of the Princess Katey – just with the aid of his teenage guile and a Swiss Army knife.

Also with Thomas Ian Nicholas, Joss Ackland, Paloma Baeza, Kate Winslet, Ron Moody, Daniel Craig. Dir: Michael Gottlieb. PG. July 1997 (Disney).

Kull the Conqueror ❏
Sword-and-sorcery hokum from the pen of *Conan*'s Robert E. Howard, with Kevin Sorbo as the titular hunk who searches for a magic weapon to help him get his kingdom and his crumpet back. Plodding and hackneyed.

Also with Tia Carrere, Thomas Ian Griffith, Karina Lombard, Litefoot, Harvey Fierstein. Dir: John Nicolella. PG. May 1998 (CIC).

Last Stand at Saber River ✳

A handsome, thoughtful and exceptionally well-acted Western with Tom Selleck as the mustang rancher who tries to pick up the pieces after returning – disillusioned – from the Civil War. Adapted from the novel by Elmore Leonard.

Also with Suzy Amis, Keith Carradine, David Carradine, Tracey Needham, Harry Carey Jr, David Dukes, Rex Linn. Dir: Dick Lowry. Ex Pro: Selleck. Ph: Ric Waite. M: David Shire. 12. August 1997 (Warner).

Lewis & Clark & George ❑

Old ingredients are given a fresh flourish in this stylish dish of film noir in which three improbable low-lives – and a snake – team up to find a gold mine.

With Rose McGowan (*as George, a mute, sexy femme fatale*), Salvator Xuereb, Dan Gunther, Art LaFleur, James Brolin, Paul Bartel. Dir and Screenplay: Rod McCall. 18. April 1998 (Hi-Fliers).

Louisa May Alcott's Little Men ❑

Gushingly sentimental, pedestrian version of the 1871 novel in which two troublesome street kids are taken in by the school run by Jo Bhaer (formerly Jo March) and her husband Fritz.

A golden opportunity: Salvator Xuereb and Dan Gunther make conversation with James Brolin – in Rod McCall's fresh and stylish *Lewis & Clark & George* (from Hi-Fliers)

With Michael Caloz (*Nat Blake*), Mariel Hemingway (*Jo*), Ben Cook (*Dan*), Chris Sarandon (*Fritz Bhaer*). Dir: Rodney Gibbons. PG. June 1998 (First Independent).

Mandela and De Klerk ✳

An illustrious reunion for Sidney Poitier and Michael Caine (who co-starred together in *The Wilby Conspiracy*) as, respectively, the imprisoned ANC activist and the South African president – prior to Mandella's release from prison in February 1990. A creditable and riveting docudrama that reminds us what a fine, dignified actor Poitier still is.

Dir: Joseph Sargent. 15. January 1998 (Entertainment).

The Man in the Iron Mask ❑

Definitely not to be confused with the Leonardo DiCaprio version of the Dumas novel, this listless, low-budget 'romp' brings the oft-filmed classic to a new low.

With Edward Albert (*Athos*), Dana Barron, Timothy Bottoms, Meg Foster, James Gammon, Dennis Hayden (*D'Artagnan*), William Richert (*Aramis*), R.G. Armstrong. Dir and Screenplay: William Richert. 15. June 1998 (Film 2000).

McHale's Navy ❑

Puerile, pointless update of the 1962-66 sitcom in which Lt Commander Quinton McHale (Tom Arnold) is dragged out of retirement to do battle with 'the second best terrorist in the world'.

Also with David Alan Grier, Dean Stockwell, Ernest Borgnine (who played McHale on TV), Debra Messing, Tim Curry, Bruce Campbell, Tommy Chong. Dir: Bryan Spicer. PG. June 1998 (CIC).

Meet Wally Sparks ❑

Tiresome farce in which a blue talkshow host (Rodney Dangerfield) scrambles to hoist his ratings at the expense of the Governor of Georgia (David Ogden Stiers). Crude, predictable and ugly.

Also with Debi Mazar, Cindy Williams, Burt Reynolds, Alan Rachins, Tony Danza, Tim Allen, Roseanne, Jay Leno, Gilbert Gottfried. Dir: Peter Baldwin. Screenplay: Dangerfield and Harry Basil. 15. August 1997 (First Independent).

Mistrial

Disappointing, talky HBO thriller in which a cop takes a judge and jury hostage when a suspected cop killer is exonerated.

With Bill Pullman, Robert Loggia, Blair Underwood. Dir: Heywood Gould. Ex Pro: Renny Harlin, Geena Davis. 15. August 1997 (Entertainment).

Monty Python's Fliegender Zirkus – The Missing Films

Long overdue release of classic material shot on location in Germany in 1971 and 1972 featuring many familiar items with a fresh twist (such as 'The Lumberjack Song' sung by the Austrian border police). There are also a number of brand-new sketches, including the Python's own version of a traditional German fairy tale called *The Princess with the Wooden Teeth* (this mini-feature alone is worth the price of the video). An absolute must for all Python fans.

With Graham Chapman, John Cleese, Terry Gilliam, Eric Idle, Terry Jones, Michael Palin, Connie Booth. Dir Ian MacNaughton. 15. June 1998 (Guerilla Films).

Mother ❑ ✳

Los Angeles/San Francisco; today. Just divorced from his second wife, science fiction novelist John Henderson (Albert Brooks) decides to tackle his problem with women head on: he moves back with Mother. Claiming back his old room, he hangs up his posters of *2001* and *Barbarella* and attempts to mend fences with his maternal unit. He reasons that if he can return to his adolescence, he may be able to pinpoint his current romantic difficulties. However, his mother is less sure about this so-called 'experiment'... Employing his characteristic wit, writer-director Brooks aims an affectionate, insightful spotlight on the whole mother-son conundrum. The joy of the film is its compassionate accuracy in highlighting the little irritants that real mothers are prone to, beautifully delineated by Debbie Reynolds in her first starring role for 27 years. While the film may prove too leisurely for some viewers (the story *is* on the weak side), this is a gentle valentine that should strike a chord with anybody who's ever known their mother. [JC-W]

Also with Rob Morrow, Lisa Kudrow, Isabel Glasser, Peter White. M: Marc Shaiman. PG. December 1997 (CIC).

Murder in Mind
Nifty, gripping little thriller in which hypnotherapist Nigel Hawthorne burrows into the mind of suspected spouse-butcherer Mary-Louise Parker to uproot some startling revelations.

Also with Jason Scott Lee, Jimmy Smits. Dir: Andy Morahan. 18. September 1997 (Marquee).

My Fellow Americans ❏
Blatantly contrived farce in which two antagonistic ex-presidents (Jack Lemmon, James Garner) find themselves forced to team up in order to clear their names and expose corruption in the Oval Office. Repetitive, bland and obvious.

Also with Dan Aykroyd, John Heard, Sela Ward, Wilford Brimley, Everett McGill, Bradley Whitford, Lauren Bacall, James Rebhorn, Esther Rolle, Conchata Ferrell. Dir: Peter Segal. 12. July 1997 (Warner).

National Lampoon's Vegas Vacation ❏
Not without its moments, this fourth instalment of the Griswold's hapless holiday excursions sees the dysfunctional numskulls trying their luck in Vegas. There, the strains of material temptation take their toll, while Wayne Newton takes a shine to Ellen (Beverly D'Angelo). You have to snigger.

Also with Chevy Chase, Randy Quaid, Ethan Embry, Marisol Nichols, Miriam Flynn, Wallace Shawn, Sid Caesar, Julia Sweeney, Christie Brinkley. Dir: Stephen Kessler. PG. September 1997 (Warner).

The Near Room ❏
Visually arresting but somewhat unconvincing drama in which a Glaswegian reporter probes a child pornography racket. Good performances abound, although elocution lessons would have helped.

With Adrian Dunbar, David O'Hara, David Hayman, Julie Graham, Tom Watson, James Ellis, Robert Pugh. Dir: Hayman. 18. December 1997 (Fox Pathe).

Never Too Late
Drawing on the OAP flavour of *Cocoon*, this agreeable dramatic comedy gives wonderful opportunities for its veteran cast who play a gaggle of golden oldies investigating a financial scam at the Sunshine Manor retirement home. Cloris Leachman, as a lesbian paraplegic, is particularly memorable.

Also with Olympia Dukakis, Jan Rubes, Corey Haim, Matt Craven. Dir: Giles Walker. PG. September 1997 (First Independent).

The Pallbearer ❏
Occasionally winning, if familiar, romantic comedy in which David Schwimmer is pursued by the mother of a deceased friend from high school that he can't remember. Another old scholar, Gwyneth Paltrow, can't remember Schwimmer, but, in turn, is pursued by him. Evoking obvious comparisons to *The Graduate*, this low-key vehicle for the *Friends* star is no classic, but it does have its moments (like Gwyneth Paltrow, for one).

Also with Barbara Hershey, Michael Rapaport, Carol Kane, Toni Collette, Corey Parker. Dir: Matt Reeves. M: Stewart Copeland. 12. January 1998 (Buena Vista).

Graham Chapman in *Monty Python's Fliegender Zirkus – The Missing Films* (from Guerilla Films)

The Pest ❏
Vanity project for the indisputably talented John Leguizamo who plays a con artist with an uncanny ability to transform himself. Leguizamo is good, but the film's farcical excesses and low, low taste is not.

Also with Jeffrey Jones, Freddy Rodriguez, Joe Morton. Dir: Paul Miller. Co-Pro and Co-Screenplay: Leguizamo. 12. February 1998 (Columbia TriStar).

Power of Attorney
When an attorney (Elias Koteas) joins a law firm he discovers that his new boss is the Mafia kingpin he once tried to have convicted. Good acting (especially from Koteas and Danny Aiello) goes a long way in papering over the cracks of this somewhat contrived if occasionally gripping Canadian thriller.

Also with Rae Dawn Chong, Nina Siemaszko. Dir: Howard Himelstein. 18. July 1997 (Hi-Fliers).

Rasputin ✳

Award-winning TV movie about Russia's Mad Monk with Alan Rickman on fine form as the drunken healer. The facts may be a little off, but the conjecture is fascinating and even shocking.

Also with Greta Scacchi, Ian McKellen (*as Tsar Nicholas*), David Warner, John Wood, James Frain. Dir: Uli Edel. 15. August 1997 (Mosaic).

Rebound

Convincingly rendered if somewhat depressing tale of Earl 'The Goat' Manigault, whose illustrious career as a basketball giant was cut short by heroin addiction. Made for cable. Full title: *Rebound: The Legend of Earl 'The Goat' Manigault.*

With Don Cheadle, James Earl Jones, Michael Beach, Loretta Devine, Clarence Williams III, Eriq LaSalle, Forest Whitaker, Glynn Turman, Ronny Cox. Dir: Eriq LaSalle. 15. April 1998 (Warner).

Riders of the Purple Sage ✳

Fifth screen version of Zane Grey's 1912 novel, with Ed Harris the stranger who rides into town looking for the killer of his sister. Atmospheric direction from the actor Charles Haid, exemplary performances from Harris and Amy Madigan (the latter's wife) and the stunning Utah scenery mark this out as one of the best TV westerns in recent memory.

Also with Henry Thomas, Robin Tunney, G.D. Spradlin. Pro: Harris, Madigan. 12. July 1997 (Warner).

The Sixth Man ❏

A bizarre, sentimental slapstick comedy in which an inseparable pair of basketball-playing brothers are parted by death. But, heh, when did an unscheduled fatality ever get in the way of winning? Some inspired mugging from Marlon Wayans and Kadeem Hardison (the latter as a zany poltergeist) goes some way to sweetening this chaotic free-for-all.

Also with David Paymer, Kevin Dunn. Dir: Randall Miller. 12. April 1998 (Touchstone).

Steel ❏

When a former colleague steals a top secret military weapon, steel expert John Henry Irons (basketball behemoth Shaquille O'Neal) dons steel-plated armour and steels himself for vengeance. Yet another fantasy hero plundered from the pages of DC comics, *Steel* proves to be a suitably entertaining creation, while the film has enough humour, in-jokes and comic-strip violence to keep fans happy.

Also with Judd Nelson, Annabeth Gish, Richard Roundtree, Irma P. Hall. Dir and Screenplay: Kenneth Johnson. 12. February 1998 (Warner).

That Old Feeling ❏

Falling for the romantic overtures of her straight-arrow boyfriend, Molly warns him that her 'parents hate each other with a nuclear capability'. And, sure enough, on the wedding day Molly's father and mother meet for the first time in 14 years and immediately carry on where they left off. But where there's passion, music and champagne... Soon, the combative duo are discovering other forgotten feelings for each other and Molly finds her own honeymoon upstaged by the embarrassing courtship of her parents... A middle-aged domestic romantic comedy, *That Old Feeling* tackles a novel war zone for its battle of the sexes and exploits it unremittingly. Breathlessly paced by director Carl Reiner and played to the gods by Bette Midler, the film makes up in energy what it lacks in wit and subtlety. Broad, sentimental, fuzzy, formulaic – with lots and *lots* of squabbling. [JC-W]

Also with Dennis Farina, Paula Marshall, Gail O'Grady, David Rasche, Danny Nucci. M: Patrick Williams. On-set chanteuse: Estelle Reiner. 12. March 1998 (CIC).

'Til There Was You

Gwendolyne Moss and Nick Dawkan both grew up in small-town California and both were reared on the icky sitcom *One Big Happy Family* (not a million miles removed from *The Brady Bunch*). Fuelled by the fantasy of her parents' ideal marriage, Gwen always believed that, one day, she would find her predestined partner. And, as their respective paths increasingly entwine, Gwen

and Nick begin to alter each other's lives – without even knowing it. They haven't even met, but they are obviously perfect for each other... Borrowing what I call the Claude Lelouch premise (so superbly realised by the director in his 1974 *And Now My Love*), *'Til There Was You* is a shamelessly sentimental, schematic romance that will boil the vitriol in cynics' veins. Yet, in spite of the absence of any real wit or credibility, this beautiful people fable just about coasts by on its sweetness and charm. Jeanne Tripplehorn, who played Matthew Broderick's ex in the similarly themed *The Night We Never Met*, is not really up to the material and is frequently strident and bug-eyed when she should be calm and confused. Still, there's a host of excellent support (particularly from Alice Drummond as Gwen's sweet, nonsensical neighbour) and a delightful piano-driven score from Miles Goodman and Terence Blanchard. [JC-W]

Also with Dylan McDermott, Sarah Jessica Parker, Jennifer Aniston, Ken Olin, Craig Bierko, Nina Foch, Christine Ebersole, Michael Tucker, Patrick Malahide, Karen Allen. Dir: Scott Winant. 12. April 1998 (CIC).

To Gillian On Her 37th Birthday ❏

Earnest, well-acted adaptation of Michael Brady's play in which a family falls apart following the death of a young mother (Michelle Pfeiffer) in a boating accident. Nobody seems able to come to grips with their loss, which gets a bit much at times, although Claire Danes – as Gillian's introspective daughter – is sensational.

Also with Peter Gallagher, Kathy Baker, Wendy Crewson, Bruce Altman. Dir: Michael Pressman. M: James Horner. 15. August 1997 (Columbia TriStar).

Top of the World!

A framed cop, crooked casino owner and the New York Mafia collide head-on in this daft but entertaining crime thriller with an eye for some spectacular set pieces.

With Peter Weller, Tia Carrere, Dennis Hopper, Peter Coyote, Joe Pantoliano. Dir: Sidney J. Furie. 18. January 1998 (Marquee).

The Trigger Effect ❑

All hell's let loose when a gargantuan power cut triggers social chaos and marital disharmony in this contemplative, taut but occasionally muddled psychological thriller.

With Kyle MacLachlan, Elisabeth Shue, Dermot Mulroney, Richard T. Jones, Michael Rooker. Dir and screenplay: David Koep. M: James Newton Howard. 15. January 1998 (CIC).

12 Angry Men ✳

A powerful, intelligent update of Sidney Lumet's award-winning 1957 film, itself based on the 1954 TV play. Here, Jack Lemmon takes the Henry Fonda role as the sole member of an all-male jury who expresses reasonable doubt as to the guilt of a young man accused of killing his father.

Also with George C. Scott, William Petersen, Courtney B. Vance, Ossie Davis, Armin Mueller-Stahl, Dorian Harewood, James Gandolfini, Tony Danza, Hume Cronyn, Mykelti Williamson, Edward James Olmos, Mary McDonnell. Dir: William Friedkin. Screenplay: Reginald Rose (adapted from his own original script). 12. May 1998 (MGM).

Underworld ❑

Insipid, heavy-handed comedy-thriller in which a hood (Denis Leary) ekes out his revenge for the murder of his father. Armed with a degree in psychotherapy (which he acquired in prison), Leary intends to sort out the psychological motives of his victim before blowing him away... Still, there's some nice dialogue to wile away the *longueurs*.

Also with Joe Mantegna, Annabella Sciorra, Larry Bishop, Abe Vigoda, Traci Lords. Dir: Roger Christian. Screenplay: Bishop. 18. November 1997 (Hi-Fliers).

Vegas Vacation

See *National Lampoon's Vegas Vacation*.

A Very Brady Sequel ✳

In spite of their eye-opening adventures in *The Brady Bunch Movie* (1995), the quintessential 1970s family are still entrenched in their formica-enhanced, polyester-adorned groovy world – or, as one character puts it, they are just as 'decade impaired'. Opening with a scene straight out of *Raiders of the Lost Ark*, this superior sequel quickly leaps back into the cosy universe of the happily inane household. Marcia is as self-centred as ever, Greg is enjoying some funky new threads and Jan has decided to invent a boyfriend. But of greater moment is the arrival of Carol's first husband, Roy, who is quickly absorbed into the Brady bosom, in spite of dispensing some extremely unsavoury advice to the kids, like (to Jan), 'The only way you'll get a boyfriend is to make one up' and (to Peter), 'Put yourself up for adoption.' A lot of the jokes are as time-worn as their subject, but the introduction of an Afro-American family just as naff and a sub-plot involving Brady incest keep things rolling. And the players' consistently straight-faced delivery makes this just as fun as the first film – if not more so. Out of sight. [JC-W]

With Shelley Long, Gary Cole, Tim Matheson, Henriette Mantel, Christopher Daniel Barnes, Christine Taylor, Zsa Zsa Gabor (*as herself*), Rosie O'Donnell, Adam Sandler, Barbara Eden. Dir: Arlene Sanford. 12. September 1997 (CIC).

Weapons of Mass Distraction

Yet another satire on the media pitches two avaricious tycoons in a ruthless, unethical clash to acquire a professional football team, the Tucson Titans. Larry Gelbart's script is not exactly subtle, but it's served by two towering performances from Gabriel Byrne and Ben Kingsley, who temper the film's tendency to play to the gods. The fact that Rupert Murdoch was attempting to buy the Los Angeles Dodgers at the time was purely coincidental.

Also with Mimi Rogers, Jeffrey Tambor, Illeana Douglas, Chris Mulkey, Paul Mazursky, Kathy Baker, R. Lee Ermey, Jason Lee. Dir: Steve Surjik. 15. January 1998 (Entertainment).

Zeus and Roxanne ❑

Impossibly sappy and infantile romance about a single marine biologist (Kathleen Quinlan) and her widowed neighbour (Steve Guttenberg) who are engineered into a romance by their kids. Then Guttenberg's dog Zeus and Quinlan's dolphin Roxanne get in on the act!

Also with Arnold Vosloo (*the baddie*), Miko Hughes, Dawn McMillan. Dir: George Miller (of *Andre* fame). U. April 1998 (Entertainment).

Other Video Releases

Alibi. Thriller with Tori Spelling, Rae Dawn Chong. 15. September 1997 (CIC).

Any Place But Home. Thriller with Joe Lando, Dale Midkiff. 12. August 1997 (CIC).

Armageddon. Thriller with Mark Dacascos, Rutger Hauer. Dir: Tibor Takacs. 18. March 1998 (Marquee).

Asylum. Conventional medical thriller with Robert Patrick, Sarah Douglas, Malcolm McDowell, Henry Gibson. Dir: James Seale. 18. October 1997 (BMG).

Back in Business. Standard cops 'n' robbers fare with Brian Bosworth, Joe Torry, Brion James. Dir: Philippe Mora. 18. October 1997 (PolyGram).

Bad Moon. Horror film with Mariel Hemingway, Michael Pare. 18. July 1997 (Warner).

Bad to the Bone. Thriller with Kristy Swanson, Jeremy London. 15. May 1998 (CIC).

Below Utopia. Ponderous action-thriller with Justin Theroux, Alyssa Milano, Ice T, Tommy 'Tiny' Lister. Dir: Kurt Voss. 18. November 1997 (First Independent).

Black Mask. Above-average Hong Kong actioner with Jet Li. Dir: Daniel Lee. 18. May 1998 (BMG).

Blackwater Trail. Dull Australian crime drama with Judd Nelson, Dee Smart, Mark Lee, Peter Phelps. Dir: Ian Barry. 18. July 1997 (Hi-Fliers).

Blast. Awful action-thriller with Rutger Hauer, Linden Ashby, Andrew Divoff, Tim Thomerson. Dir: Albert Pyun. 18. July 1997 (BMG).

Blaze of Glory. True story with Lori Loughlin, Bruce Campbell, Brad Sullivan, Bradley Whitford. Pro and Dir: Dick Lowry. 15. July 1997 (Odyssey).

Bloodhounds 2. Thriller with Corbin Bernsen, Nia Peebles, Amy Yasbeck. 15. July 1997 (CIC).

The Boys Club. Rather dull Canadian drama with Chris Penn. Dir: John Fawcett. 15. July 1997 (Hi-Fliers).

Breaking the Surface. True story with Mario Lopez, Michael Murphy, Bruce Weitz. Dir: Steven Hilliard Stern. 12. August 1997 (Odyssey).

Buried Alive II. Enjoyable supernatural thriller with Ally Sheedy, Stephen Caffrey, Tim Matheson. Dir: Matheson. 15. October 1997 (CIC).

Business For Pleasure. Thriller with Gary Stretch, Joanna Pacula, Jeroen Krabbe. 18. October 1997 (Hi-Fliers).

Casualties. Intriguing thriller with Caroline Goodall, Mark Harmon, Michael Beach. Dir: Alex Graves. 18. August 1997 (Hi-Fliers).

Catherine's Grove. Psychological thriller with Jeff Fahey, Maria Conchita Alonso, Priscilla Barnes, Michael Madsen. Dir: Rick King. 18. March 1998 (Hi-Fliers).

A Change of Heart. Legal drama with Andrew McCarthy, Michael Learned, Teri Polo, Shirley Knight. Dir: Alan Metzger. 15. June 1998 (Odyssey).

Contagious. Engagingly old-fashioned medical drama with Lindsay Wagner, Elizabeth Pena. Dir: Joe Napolitano. 12. November 1997 (CIC).

Cosa Nostra: The Last Word. Gangster thriller with Richard Dreyfuss, Timothy Hutton, Joe Pantoliano, Chazz Palminteri, Michelle Burke, Tony Goldwyn, Cybill Shepherd, Jimmy Smits. Dir: Tony Spiridakis. 18. April 1998 (Marquee).

Criminal Pursuit. David Chokachi, Athena Massey, Cyril O'Reilly, Timothy Busfield. 18. July 1997 (Medusa).

Critical Choices. Abortion drama with Betty Buckley, Diana Scarwid, Pamela Reed, Brian Kerwin. Dir: Claudia Weill. 15. January 1998 (CIC).

Dallas: JR Returns. With Larry Hagman, Patrick Duffy, Linda Gray, Ken Kercheval, Tracy Scoggins. 15. July 1997 (Warner).

Dark Drive. Sci-fi with Ken Olandt. 18. August 1997 (Marquee).

Diary of a Serial Killer. Mildly diverting action-thriller with Michael Madsen, Gary Busey, Arnold Vosloo. Dir: Alan Jacobs. 18. April 1998 (Xscapade).

The Disappearing Act. Drama with Patty Duke, Kelly Rowan. 15. November 1997 (Odyssey).

Divided By Hate. Thriller with Dylan Walsh, Tom Skerritt. Dir: Skerritt. PG. August 1997 (CIC).

DNA. Risible, old-hat sci-fi with Mark Dacascos, Jurgen Prochnow. Dir: William Mesa. 15. November 1997 (BMG).

The Don's Analyst. Godfather parody with Kevin Pollak, Robert Loggia, Joseph Bologna, Angie Dickinson, Sherilyn Fenn. 12. March 1998 (CIC).

Double Take. Illogical thriller with Craig Sheffer, Costas Mandylor, Brigitte Bako. Dir: Mark L. Lester. 18. January 1998 (Hi-Fliers).

Ed's Next Move. Sweet and enchanting comedy with Matt Ross. 15. July 1997 (Film 2000).

The Eighteenth Angel. Run-of-the-mill sci-fi horror film with Christopher McDonald, Maximilian Schell, Rachel Leigh Cook, Wendy Crewson, Stanley Tucci. Dir: William Bindley. 15. April 1998 (Entertainment).

Elmore Leonard's Gold Coast. Romantic thriller with David Caruso, Marg Helgenberger. Dir: Peter Weller. 18. April 1998 (CIC).

Escape From Atlantis. Wildly disjointed fantasy with Jeff Speakman, Tim Thomerson. 12. June 1998 (CIC).

Evil Ed. Horror film with John Rubeck. 18. October 1997 (Film 2000).

Evil Instinct. Rough-and-ready but highly engaging sexploitational take-off of *Basic Instinct* – with Carrie Ng, Pan Dang. 18. May 1998 (Hong Kong Classics).

Exception to the Rule. Bemused erotic

Brian Dennehy, star and director of *A Father's Betrayal* **(from Odyssey)**

thriller with Kim Cattrall, Sean Young, William Devane. Dir: David Winning. 18. July 1997 (Medusa).

Executive Target. Thriller with Michael Madsen, Roy Scheider, Angie Everhart, Keith David. Dir: Joseph Merhi. 18. October 1997 (PolyGram).

Fall Into Darkness. True story with Tatyana M. Ali, Jonathan Brandis. Dir: Mark Sobel. 15. July 1997 (Odyssey).

Family Plan. Witless comedy with Leslie Nielsen, Judge Reinhold. PG. March 1998 (First Independent).

A Father's Betrayal. Drama with Brian Dennehy, Reed Diamond, Lynn Redgrave, Alice Krige. Dir: Dennehy. 15. January 1998 (Odyssey).

The Fiancé. Thriller with Lysette Anthony, William R. Moses. 18. October 1997 (First Independent).

Fifteen and Pregnant. Lucid and enlightening domestic drama with Kirsten Dunst, Park Overall, David Andrews. 12. April 1998 (Odyssey).

Firehouse. Shambolic drama with Richard Dean Anderson, Lillo Brancato Jr, Morris Chestnut, Edie Falco, Burt Young. Dir: Alan Smithee. 15. November 1997 (Entertainment).

First Kid. Comedy with Brock Pierce, Sinbad, Robert Guillaume, Timothy Busfield. PG. October 1997 (Buena Vista).

First Time Felon. True-life penal drama with Omar Epps, William Forsythe, Rachel Ticotin, Delroy Lindo. Dir: Charles S. Dutton. 15. May 1998 (Columbia TriStar).

For Hire. Sluggish and familiar thriller with Rob Lowe, Joe Mantegna. Dir: Jean Pellerin. 18. May 1998 (Xscapade).

For the Future. True story with Marilu Henner, Linda Lavin. Dir: David Jones. 15. August 1997 (Odyssey).

Foxfire. Clumsy adaptation of Joyce Carol Oates' female-bonding saga with Hedy Burress, Angelina Jolie, Jenny Lewis, Chris Mulkey. Dir: Annette Haywood-Carter. 18. September 1997 (Entertainment).

From Beyond the Grave. Thriller with David Keith, Martin Kove, Thomas Ian Nicholas. Dir: John Eyres. 18. October 1997 (Marquee).

Ghost Fever. Lamentable comedy with Sherman Hemsley. PG. May 1998 (CIC).

Gold Coast See *Elmore Leonard's Gold Coast.*

Goodbye America. Boring war movie with Corin Nemec, Rae Dawn Chong, Alexis Arquette, Wolfgang Bodison, Michael York, James Brolin. Dir: Thierry Notz. 18. October 1997 (Medusa).

Gunfighter's Moon. Western with Lance Henriksen, Kay Lenz. 12. May 1998 (Entertainment).

Haemoglobin: It's in the Blood. Incest and cannibalism with Rutger Hauer, Jackie Burroughs. Dir: Peter Svatek. 18. February 1998 (Hi-Fliers).

Heist. Thriller with Robert Pastorelli, Daniel Benzali, James Russo, Glenn Plummer, Brion James. Dir: Peter Rossi. 18. May 1998 (Film 2000).

Homeboyz. Risible cop melodrama with Marc Singer, Steve Railsback. Dir: Chuck Bail. 18. September 1997 (Marquee).

Hollywood Confidential. Action-drama with Edward James Olmos, Ricky Aiello. 15. February 1998 (CIC).

Honey, We Shrunk Ourselves! OK sci-fi comedy with Rick Moranis, Robin Bartlett. Dir: Dean Cundey. PG. July 1997 (Buena Vista).

Hostile Intent. Action-thriller with Rob Lowe, Sofia Shinas, John Savage, Saul Rubinek. Dir: Jonathan Heap. 18. February 1998 (BMG).

In Dark Places. Erotic thriller with Joan Severance. 18. April 1998 (Hi-Fliers).

The Invader. Irrational sci-fi with Sean Young, Ben Cross, Daniel Baldwin, Nick Mancuso. Dir: Mark Rosman. 15. December 1997 (Mosaic).

Invasion of Privacy. Cynically satirical thriller with Jonathan Schaech, Mili Avital, Naomi Campbell, Charlotte Rampling, David Keith. Dir: Anthony Hickox. M: Angelo Badalamenti. 18. November 1997 (BMG).

Joyride. Thriller with Tobey Maguire, Amy Hathaway, Benicio Del Toro, Adam West. Dir: Quinton Peeples. 18. December 1997 (Hi-Fliers).

The Killing Grounds. Gripping outdoors thriller with Priscilla Barnes, Courtney Gains, Cynthia Geary, Rodney A. Grant, Anthony Michael Hall, Charles Rocket. Dir: Kurt Anderson. 18. January 1998 (First Independent).

Killing Time. Violent thriller with Craig Fairbrass, Kendra Torgan.

Dir: Bharat Nalluri. 18. May 1998 (Columbia TriStar).

Kounterfeit. Thriller with Bruce Payne, Corbin Bernsen, Hilary Swank, Michael Gross. Dir: John Mallory Asher. 18. December 1997 (Hi-Fliers).

Last Lives. Sci-fi opus with C. Thomas Howell, Jennifer Rubin, Judge Reinhold, Billy Wirth. Dir: Worth Keeter. 18. October 1997 (Hi-Fliers).

Let It Be Me. Romantic drama with Campbell Scott, Jennifer Beals, Yancy Butler, Patrick Stewart, Leslie Caron. Dir: Eleanor Bergstein. 12. May 1998 (Entertainment).

Livers Ain't Cheap. See *The Real Thing.*

Lookin' Italian. Hackneyed drama with Matt Le Blanc, Jay Acovane, Lou Rawls. Dir: Guy Magar. 18. November 1997 (Marquee).

Love in Another Town. Romantic drama from the Barbara Taylor Bradford bestseller, with Victoria Principal, Mary Kay Place, Adrian Pasdar. 12. February 1998 (Odyssey).

Love to Kill. Black comic thriller with James Russo, Michael Madsen, Tony Danza, Amy Locane, Louise Fletcher. Dir: James Bruce. 15. June 1998 (Xscapade).

Magenta. Arid erotic thriller with Julian McMahon. 18. July 1997 (Marquee).

Magic in the Water. Cluttered family yarn with Mark Harmon, Harley Jane Kozak. Dir: Rick Stevenson. PG. July 1997 (Columbia TriStar).

Melanie Darrow. Legal soap with Delta Burke. PG. May 1998 (CIC).

Murder at My Door. With Judith Light, R. H. Thomson, Grace Zabriskie, Johnny Galecki. Dir: Eric Till. 15. October 1997 (Odyssey).

My Very Best Friend. Thriller with Jaclyn Smith, Jill Eikenberry, Tom Irwin. PG. March 1998 (CIC).

Narrow Escape. True-life drama with Richard Thomas, Eve Gordon. 15. December 1997 (Odyssey).

National Lampoon's Dad's Week Off. Comedy with Henry Winkler, Olivia d'Abo. Dir: Neal Israel. 12. September 1997 (CIC).

National Lampoon's The Don's Analyst. Gangster satire with Kevin Pollak, Robert Loggia, Sherilyn Fenn, Angie Dickinson, Joseph Bologna. Dir: David Jablin. 15. May 1998 (CIC).

No Strings Attached. Thriller with

Vincent Spano, Cheryl Pollak. 18. November 1997 (Hi-Fliers).

The Occultist. Low-budget horror exploitation with Rick Gianasi. 18. April 1998 (Allied).

Path to Paradise. Terrorist drama with Peter Gallagher, Marcia Gay Harden, Art Malik. 15. June 1998 (Warner).

Payback. True story with Mary Tyler Moore, Edward Asner, Denis Arndt. Dir: Ken Cameron. 15. September 1997 (Odyssey).

The Peacekeeper. Canadian action-thriller with Dolph Lundgren, Roy Scheider, Michael Sarrazin. Dir: Frederic Forestier. 18. October 1997 (Marquee).

Perfect Crime. True-life thriller with Mitzi Kapture, Jasmin Guy. 15. February 1998 (CIC).

The Perfect Daughter. With Tracey Gold. 15. August 1997 (CIC).

Portraits of Innocence. Thriller with Jennifer Grey, Michael Ironside, Costas Mandylor. Dir: Bill Corcoran. 18. August 1997 (Marquee).

Quicksilver Highway. Horror double bill from stories by Clive Barker and Stephen King, with Christopher Lloyd, Matt Frewer, Missy Crider. Dir: Mick Garris. 15. January 1998 (Hi-Fliers).

Ratchet. Taut thriller with Tom Gilroy, Margaret Welsh, Mitchell Lichtenstein. Dir: John S. Johnson. 18. October 1997 (PolyGram).

Ravager. Sci-fi with Bruce Payne, Yancy Butler, Juliet Landau. Dir: James D. Deck. 15. January 1998 (BMG).

The Real Thing. Violent noir thriller with James Russo, Emily Lloyd, Gary Busey, Rod Steiger, Esai Morales. Dir: James Merendino. Aka *Livers Ain't Cheap*. 18. May 1998 (Hi-Fliers).

Red Shoe Diaries: Girl On a Bike. Three-part slice of erotica with David Duchovny, Robbi Chong. 18. March 1998 (Vision Replays).

Red Shoe Diaries: Laundrymat. Three more tales of the erotic with David Duchovny. 18. March 1998 (Vision Replays).

Red Shoe Diaries: The Picnic. Three-part erotica with David Duchovny, Kira Reed. 18. March 1998 (Vision Replays).

Rescuers: Stories of Courage. Dramatic double-bill with Elizabeth Perkins,

Sela Ward. 12. March 1998 (CIC).

Retroactive. Violent time-travelling thriller with James Belushi, Kylie Travis, Frank Whaley, Jesse Borrego, M. Emmet Walsh. Dir: Louis Morneau. 18. June 1998 (Hi-Fliers).

Robo Warriors. Sci-fi with James Remar. 18. January 1998 (PolyGram).

Rude. Distinctive, powerful drama with Maurice Dean Wint, Rachel Crawford. Dir: Clement Virgo. 18. July 1997 (Hi-Fliers).

Runaway Car. True story with Judge Reinhold, Nina Siemaszko, Leon. Dir: Jack Sholder. PG. August 1997 (Odyssey).

The Shadow Men. Sci-fi thriller with Eric Roberts, Sherilyn Fenn, Dean Stockwell, Andrew Prine. Dir: Timothy Bond. 15. March 1998 (Mosaic).

Shiloh. Family fun with Rod Steiger, Michael Moriarty, Scott Wilson, Bonnie Bartlett. Dir: Dale Rosenbloom. U. January 1998 (Warner).

The Shining – Parts 1 & 2. Highly effective horror opus with Rebecca De Mornay, Steven Weber, Melvin Van Peebles. 18. November 1997 (Warner).

Sin and Redemption. Drama with Richard Grieco, Cynthia Gibb. 18. May 1998 (CIC).

Sins of the Mind. Thriller with Jill Clayburgh. 15. February 1998 (CIC).

Snowboard Academy. Comedy with Corey Haim, Jim Varney, Brigitte Nielsen. PG. February 1998 (Columbia TriStar).

Solo. Sci-fi action with Mario Van Peebles, William Sadler. 18. September 1997 (Columbia TriStar).

Stag. Well-acted stag night thriller with Mario Van Peebles, Andrew McCarthy, Kevin Dillon, Taylor Dayne, William McNamara, Jerry Stiller, Ben Gazzara. Dir: Gavin Wilding. 18. June 1998 (Fox).

The Stepsister. Thriller with Rena Sofer, Bridgette Wilson, Linda Evans. 12. November 1997 (CIC).

Stranger in the House. Thriller with Michele Green, Steve Railsback. 15. July 1997 (First Independent).

Suspicious Minds. Thriller with Patrick Bergin, Gary Busey. Dir:

Alain Zaloum. 18. September 1997 (Hi-Fliers).

Swearing Allegiance. True-life murder with Holly Marie Combs and David Lipper. 15. April 1998 (Odyssey).

Taken Away. True-life thriller with Michael Tucker, Jill Eikenberry, James Marsden. Dir: Jerry Jameson. 15. September 1997 (Odyssey).

Target For Rage. Real-life inspired drama with Rick Schroder, Henry Winkler. 18. February 1998 (Odyssey).

The Three Lives of Karen. Corkscrew thriller with Gail O'Grady, Dennis Boutsikaris, Tim Guinee. 12. March 1998 (CIC).

The Ticket. Chase thriller with Shannen Doherty, James Marshall. Dir: Stuart Cooper. 12. January 1998 (CIC).

Trojan War. Condom-seeking comedy with Will Friedle, Jennifer Love Hewitt, Anthony Michael Hall. Dir: George Huang. 12. May 1998 (Warner).

Twilight Man. Thriller with Tim Matheson, Dean Stockwell. Dir: Craig R. Baxley. 15. July 1997 (CIC).

Twists of Terror. Three-part Canadian chiller with Jennifer Rubin, Nick Mancuso. Dir: Douglas Jackson. 18. April 1998 (CIC).

Ultimate Revenge. Thriller with Lou Diamond Phillips, Ralph Waite, Melinda Dillon, Salli Richardson. Dir: Lou Diamond Phillips. 15. August 1997 (Medusa).

An Unexpected Family. Predictable domestic drama with Stockard Channing, Stephen Collins, Christine Ebersole. Dir: Larry Elikann. PG. July 1997 (CIC).

Victim of the Haunt. Haunted house thriller with Beau Bridges, Sharon Lawrence. 15. September 1997 (Hi-Fliers).

Welcome to Planet Earth. Sci-fi farce with George Wendt, Shanna Reed. Dir: Lev. L. Spiro. 18. September 1997 (Film 2000).

When Husbands Cheat. Insipid true-life drama with Patricia Kalember, Tom Irwin, Brenda Vaccaro. 15. May 1998 (Odyssey).

The Widow. Thriller with Shannon Tweed. 18. July 1997 (Marquee).

Wounded. Thriller with Madchen Amick, Graham Greene, Adrian Pasdar. 18. February 1998 (Hi-Fliers).

Movie Quotations of the Year

'The only way that girl is coming back to you is if a blast of semen catapults her across the street and through the window.'

Meg Ryan, rubbing salt into the broken heart of a pining Matthew Broderick, in *Addicted to Love*

'I don't know what I like, but I know what art is.'

Nick Nolte, showing his appreciation for the paintings of Lara Flynn Boyle, in *Afterglow*

'I may be on the devil's hit list, but I'm on God's mailing list.'

Robert Duvall in *The Apostle*

'I never knew there was so much world in the world.'

Arrietty Clock (Flora Newbigin) as she takes her first eyeful of the great outdoors – in *The Borrowers*

'To die in our prime is our right.'

Noble swordsman Vincent Perez in *Le Bossu*

Jack Nicholson, overhearing couple in a restaurant: 'I think people who talk in metaphors ought to shampoo my crotch.'

In *As Good As It Gets*

Jack Nicholson, in answer to how he manages to write about women so well: 'I think of a man [pause] – and I take away reason and accountability.'

In *As Good As It Gets*

Jack Nicholson, to gay, self-pitying neighbour Greg Kinnear: 'Nelly, you're a disgrace to depression.'

In *As Good As It Gets*

'You make me want to be a better man.' Jack Nicholson's ultimate compliment to Helen Hunt.

In *As Good As It Gets*

'She's evicted me from my life.' Jack Nicholson acknowledging Helen Hunt's power over him.

In *As Good As It Gets*

'Come in - and try not to ruin everything by being "you".' Helen Hunt inviting Jack Nicholson into her apartment.

In *As Good As It Gets*

'That's my daughter Tuesday. She was born on Saturday but her mother's bonkers.'

Andy Serkis proudly showing off a photograph of his child, in *Career Girls*

'I'm just not strong enough to be as vulnerable as you.'

Katrin Cartlidge to Lynda Steadman in *Career Girls*

'I'm not an idiot, you know. I'm like an idiot savant. I just haven't found my savant yet.'

A socially impaired Mark Benton in *Career Girls*

'I'm not against technology. I'm against the men who deify it at the expense of truth.'

Matthew McConaughey in *Contact*

'Don't ever fuck with a guy looking for heads.'

A formidable Joe Pesci in *8 Heads in a Duffel Bag*

'The most beautiful phrase in the English language is not "I love you" – it's "it's benign"'.

A hypochondriac Woody Allen in *Deconstructing Harry*

'Do you know the best way to make your dream come true? You wake up.'

A profound Benicio Del Toro in *Excess Baggage*

'Your life is something I'd be ashamed to rent.'

Billy Crystal on the sexual escapades of Robin Williams, in *Father's Day*

Robin Williams: 'How did you get him to talk?'
Billy Crystal: 'I head-butted him.'
Williams: 'How Joe Pesci of you.'

From Father's Day

'You are the one thing I never knew I always wanted.'

Matthew Perry to Salma Hayek in *Fools Rush In*

'Nevada is a sandbox for adults with too much money.'

Jon Tenney in *Fools Rush In*

'Two and two can add up to five. It's our classroom.'

Corrupt cop James Belushi in *Gang Related*

'He's pregnant.'

Matthew Broderick delivering his bombshell regarding a certain over-sized lizard – in *Godzilla*

'Sometimes I wish I had never met you. Because then I could go to sleep at night not knowing there was someone like you out there.'

Stellan Skarsgard to Matt Damon in *Good Will Hunting*

'She is not perfect. You are not perfect. The question is whether or not you are perfect for each other.'

Robin Williams in *Good Will Hunting*

'You'd be lucky to get the surfing gig in Kansas.'

TV anchorman Alan Alda on rival Dustin Hoffman's professional chances – in *Mad City*

A lovesick Matthew Perry

'I long for the day when somebody says, "who is Madonna?"'

Jason Alexander in *Love! Valour! Compassion!*

'I have to say that in two-and-a-half centuries America has turned out almost as many poofters as England has in a thousand years.'

John Glover, in *Love! Valour! Compassion!*

'I hate opera. I don't know why I bother being gay.'

John Benjamin Hickey in *Love! Valour! Compassion!*

'This is how I look. Love me, love my love handles.'

A naked, unabashed Jason Alexander in Love! Valour! Compassion!

'My perfect partner is me – with breasts.'

Would-be womaniser Rufus Sewell in *Martha – Meet Frank, Daniel and Laurence*

'It's you I want to make love to, not eight pints of lager with an erection."

Emily Watson to her intoxicated husband (Christian Bale), in *Metroland*

'Cardiac arrest: the medical term for dying in the arms of a 25-year-old cocktail waitress.'

Kevin Spacey in *Midnight in the Garden of Good and Evil*

'Am I a cunt or am I a cunt?'

A complacently obstreperous Ray Winstone in *Nil By Mouth*

'Love is like a flame. When it burns, it is visible to all.'

Jennifer Ehle in *Paradise Road*

'Sometimes God reaches down and pulls the wings off his butterflies.'

German Jew and POW Frances McDormand, in *Paradise Road*

'How do you know when a lawyer's lying? When his lips are moving.'

Matt Damon in *The Rainmaker*

'What's the difference between a lawyer and a hooker? A hooker won't screw you after you're dead.'

Matt Damon in *The Rainmaker*

Sound reason, hhmmmphh: Billy Bob

'I don't reckon I've got any reason to kill anybody.'

> Billy Bob Thornton in *Sling Blade*

'They could fuck the human race to extinction.'

> Blustering general George Dzundza regarding the unchecked libido and reproductive acumen of two deadly aliens – in *Species II*

'I'm a young virgin in Italy and I want my sexual awakening and I want it now!'

> Georgina Cates in *Stiff Upper Lips*

'If you've never had anything to believe in, you'll always be poor.'

> Bob Hoskins, in *TwentyFourSeven*

'There's nothing wrong with letting the ladies know that you're money and you wanna party.'

> Vince Vaughn exercising his hip lingo in *Swingers*

'All I do is stare at their mouths and wrinkle my nose, and I turn out to be a sweetheart.'

> Vince Vaughn in *Swingers*

'I don't want you to be like the guy in the PG-13 movie who everyone's really pulling for. I want you to be like the guy in the R-rated movie.'

> Vince Vaughn to unlucky-in-love Jon Favreau, in *Swingers*

Mira Sorvino: 'I hate throwing up in public.' Lisa Kudrow (happily incredulous): 'Me too!'

> From Romy and Michelle's *High School Reunion*

'This dress exacerbates the genetic betrayal that is my legacy.'

> Janeane Garofalo rejecting the sartorial elegance of her frock – in Romy and Michelle's *High School Reunion*

Anne Heche, to older man Harrison Ford: 'I'm not sure I trust your equipment.' Ford, taking up the sexual innuendo: 'We may be old, but we're sturdy.'

> From *Six Days, Seven Nights*

'I've decided my life is too simple. I want to complicate the hell out of it.'

> Harrison Ford wooing Anne Heche in *Six Days, Seven Nights*

'We're dealing with very determined stuff here.'

> Seismologist Anne Heche understating the obvious – in *Volcano*

'We're not here to help, we're here to report.'

> Cameraman James Nesbitt in *Welcome to Sarajevo*

Woody Harrelson: 'Only two good things ever came out of England: America and The Beatles.' Stephen Dillane: 'The Beatles aren't from England. They're from Liverpool.'

> From *Welcome to Sarajevo*

'Remember – alcohol equals puke equals smelly mess equals nobody likes you.'

> Adam Sandler admonishing a young boy on his drinking habits in *The Wedding Singer*

'It's perfectly awful how people say things behind your back that are absolutely true.'

> Stephen Fry as *Oscar Wilde*

'Anything worth learning can't be taught.'

> Stephen Fry as *Oscar Wilde*

'Give a man a mask and he'll tell you the truth.'

> Stephen Fry as *Oscar Wilde*

'I find that alcohol taken in sufficient doses can bring about all the effects of drunkenness.'

> Stephen Fry as *Oscar Wilde*

'You've got beautiful bone structure. You get that from me. I'll make a beautiful skeleton when the time comes.'

> Phyllida Law to her daughter Emma Thompson in *The Winter Guest*

'There's nothing wrong with anger. It's better than Australia.'

> Phyllida Law in *The Winter Guest*

The Gospel According To Al Pacino
(in *Devil's Advocate*)

'Some people, you squeeze them, they focus; others, they fold.'

'The worst vice is advice.'

'Look – but don't touch. Touch – but don't taste. Taste – but don't swallow.'

'God is an absentee landlord!'

'Biologically, love is the equivalent of eating large amounts of chocolate.'

Quotes, off-screen

(*that is, notable lines not scripted*)

'Where I romanticise it [pornography] could have gone was a place where acting, storytelling and camerawork got better. With interesting characters where you also had the luxury to show them fucking. We can't see Forrest Gump fuck Jenny Curran, to make that kid. But God, wouldn't that be a great scene? Not just because I want to get off watching Tom Hanks fuck Robin Wright, but think what can be told about Gump through watching him have sex.'

Paul Thomas Anderson, writer-director of *Boogie Nights*

'After you stop moaning about being stereotyped as a horror guy, you can say, "I'm employed doing interesting movies that can be called, in some sense, auteur work." Nobody's telling me what to do, I have final cut and there's virtually no limitation except my imagination, and I have to stay within a certain subject matter. But you can put as much comedy as you want in the movie, as much romance or philosophy; anything, as long as you scare the bejesus out of people six or ten times.'

Horror guy **Wes Craven**

'He [co-star Billy Connolly] originally wanted Bob Hoskins to play Queen Victoria and I'm just delighted to have been Bob Hoskins' understudy.'

Judi Dench, accepting her BAFTA award for *Mrs Brown*

'I played a girl who doesn't get thin by the end of the movie; she remains true to herself. Then there's me. I lose weight and become successful. There's a deep irony in that that's not lost on me.'

Minnie Driver

'He's wearing my glasses. That's my suit...my haircut... I'm magnificent in this film!'

Producer **Robert Evans** on Dustin Hoffman's impersonation of him in *Wag the Dog*

'Late in the game – principal photography might have been over – I started to understand what I believe the picture to be about. "That which makes us safe imprisons us." I felt very good when I finally understood what the movie was about.'

James L. Brooks, talking about his fourth picture as director, *As Good As It Gets*

'I feel I was smarter than the young Tibetans who played me, but they spoke better English.'

The Dalai Lama, after seeing *Kundun* and *Seven Years in Tibet*

'If you asked any of my leading ladies they would tell you that they loved me. They should, because they have all given the best performances of their life opposite me.'

An irresistible **Michael Douglas**

'Anything I say about the media would be associated with this terrible event, and that is something I really do not want to do. I think it would almost trivialise it to discuss both issues at the same time – her death and the impact of the media.'

Jodie Foster refusing to let her own problems with the paparazzi overshadow the tragedy of Princess Diana's death

'If you were making *On the Waterfront* now, the executives would be thinking, "Does it have any kind of merchandising potential? Can it be a video game?"'

Barry Levinson

'I actually find [Princess] Diana really nauseating... and half crazy, poor thing. She has an unbearable stress and pressure, the likes of which we can't really comprehend. Especially because she has no mental resources to deal with it. She's incredibly stupid, to start off with.'

Helen Mirren, prior to Diana's death

'Lust. And respect. And forgiveness. And persistence.'

Paul Newman on the secret of his 40-year-marriage to Joanne Woodward

'Our generation are the new old. I remember what someone of 60 looked like when I was a kid. They didn't look like me.'

Jack Nicholson, 60

A desireable Micheal Douglas

'If Scorsese knocks on my door, I won't drop everything to work with him. I'll ask, 'How much does he pay?'

Gary Oldman

'As long as he is on top of political issues, I don't care who's on top of him.'

Gary Oldman, on Bill Clinton

'I'm a big fan of body doubles. Whether it's a nude scene or a stunt, I just say, "Bring 'em in – I'll be in my trailer.'

Gwyneth Paltrow, body beautiful

'Make them hate you. If too many people like you, you're doing something wrong.'

Sean Penn dispensing advice to his assistant on the set of U-Turn

'I'll tell you what I think of Woody Allen. I think he is the worst human being on the planet. I think he is the worst human being I have ever heard of, read of or been able to imagine. And let's just leave it at that.'

Andre Previn, former husband of Mia Farrow

'Nobody wanted me. I couldn't get arrested. Now my phone rings. Nice. All I hope is that I can accept this new phase graciously and not make wisecracks that inevitably backfire.'

Burt Reynolds, the new Comeback Kid

'I love Drew. Everybody loves Drew. My mother loves her – even the birds in my backyard love her.'

Adam Sandler on his The Wedding Singer co-star Drew Barrymore

'I think Leonardo is our Brando, our Mozart, our special, magical, mystical talent... Leonardo just has it. He doesn't reach for it, he doesn't have to go learn it, he just has it.'

Sharon Stone, not talking about Leonardo Da Vinci, but young Mr DiCaprio, her co-star from The Quick and the Dead

'I hope it is as controversial and popular as Crash. Being compared with Cronenberg is a wonderful compliment.'

Writer-director **Lynne Stopkewich**, talking about her film Kissed

'Japan is a country where it is not customary and can even be embarrassing to be seen out at a social function with your spouse. Married couples keep communication to a minimum and the assumption is that implicit understanding is better than talking. We don't have customs like hugs of greeting or goodnight kisses.'

Masayuki Suo, director of Shall We Dance?, explaining the shocking nature of ballroom dancing in Japan

'I'm not going to do another one [an Alien sequel]. I can't because Ripley [her character] can't and it's as simple as that. They can offer $10 million but I couldn't do another one. I don't want to go through it all again.'

Sigourney Weaver in 1992, four years before accepting $11 million to star in Alien Resurrection

'I don't have any plastic surgery, I don't have colonic irrigation and I burp.'

Kate Winslet, setting a few facts straight

'Violence in the movies is like drugs. The more of it you have, the more you want.'

Wim Wenders

And, some of the year's most memorable tag lines:

(those blurbs dreamed up by marketing people to put on movie posters)

'A comedy from the heart that goes for the throat.'

As Good As It Gets

'Her life was in their hands. Now her toe is in the mail.'

The Big Lebowski

'She didn't believe in angels until she fell in love with one.'

City of Angels

'Even a hit man deserves a second shot.'

Grosse Pointe Blank

'Size does matter.'

Godzilla

'Two's company. Three's a crowd. Four's a catastrophe.'

Martha – Meet Frank, Daniel and Laurence

'What went down on the way to the top.'

Primary Colors

'The Blonde Leading The Blonde.'

Romy and Michele's High School Reunion

'There are worse crimes than killing a person.'

Six Ways To Sunday

'The story of a lifetime.'

The Truman Show

Faces of the Year

Joey Lauren Adams

Joey Lauren Adams was given a gift of a part in *Chasing Amy*. Written and directed by her real-life boyfriend Kevin Smith, the film was an astonishing about-turn for the man who brought us the rough-and-ready *Clerks* and the lifeless, banal *Mallrats*. Here was a rounded, daring, intelligent, insightful and blisteringly funny film that wriggled into parts of the consciousness that cinema has seldom braved before. Conjuring up the image of a sassy, earth-bound cross between Ellen Barkin and Cameron Diaz, Adams was sensational as the lesbian pursued by Ben Affleck, spewing forth torrents of PMT-fuelled rage tempered with buckets of good humour. It was a performance that captured the eye and heart and secured Adams a Golden Globe nomination for best actress but, alas, no Oscar counterpart. It should also be noted that Adams helped considerably with reshaping the script of *Chasing Amy* herself, bringing her character into sharp relief. 'It was a very personal project for me,' she clarified.

Born: 6 January 1971 in Little Rock, Arkansas
Film debut: Simone, the two-timed girlfriend of Jason London's 'Pink' Floyd, in *Dazed and Confused* (1993)
First line on celluloid: 'I'm headed this way' (the very first words spoken in *Dazed and Confused*)
Next up: John N. Smith's small-town drama *A Cool Dry Place* with Vince Vaughn and Monica Potter
The other films: *The Program, Coneheads, Sleep With Me, The Pros & Cons of Breathing, SFW, Mallrats, Drawing Flies, Bio-Dome, Michael*
Significant others: Writer-director Kevin Smith
Amazing fact: She lost the role of Dorothy Boyd in *Jerry Maguire* to her friend Rene Zellweger (whom she met on the set of *Dazed and Confused*)
Penetrating quote: 'I long to play a character who wears pantyhose'

Ben Affleck

Ben Affleck was fine-tuning his script for *Good Will Hunting* in the trailer of his friend and co-writer, Matt Damon. They were on the lot of *The Rainmaker*, in which Damon was starring, and both Danny DeVito and Francis Ford Coppola walked past the window. Affleck recalls saying something like, 'Wow, even if we're panhandling a year from now, we'll have some things to show our grandchildren – we weren't always complete degenerates.'

As it happens, 18 months later Matt and Ben were the recipients of an Oscar each and were dating Winona Ryder and Gwyneth Paltrow respectively. *Good Will Hunting* had grossed more than $200 million worldwide and, after his starring role in the critically acclaimed *Chasing Amy*, Affleck was fielding offers from all over the shop. In his next film, *Armageddon*, the 25-year-old actor was starring opposite Bruce Willis, an asteroid and a budget that was spiralling off the map (conservative estimates put it in the $100m range).

Six foot two inches tall and blessed with regular guy good looks, Affleck is not too handsome not to play the nerd. A naturalistic and laid-back actor, he knows how to let his lines deliver the joke, rather than any exaggerated gesture on his part. Thus, he was a splendid straight man to Joey Lauren Adams' wailing lesbian siren in *Chasing Amy* and his measured delivery in *Good Will Hunting* certainly made its mark. He's also a terrific writer and observer of human nature, which comes from having worked with the cream of America's independent cinema (Richard Linklater, Kevin Smith, Gus Van Sant).

Born: 15 August 1972 in Berkeley, California

Breakthrough cinematic moment: When, in *Dazed and Confused*, he beats the pulp out of Wiley Wiggins with a cricket bat

The other films: *Hands of a Stranger* (for TV), *Daddy* (TV), *School Ties*, *Mallrats*, *Going All the Way*, *Phantoms*, *Big Helium Dog*, *200 Cigarettes* (cameo), *Dogma*, *Shakespeare in Love* (with Gwyneth)

Next up: *Forces of Nature*, a romantic comedy in which he plays a New Yorker prevented from keeping a date with his fiancée by a series of natural phenomena and Sandra Bullock; then Jordan Brady's *The Third Wheel*; and then *Halfway House*, from his and Damon's own screenplay set in a lunatic asylum

Significant other: Gwyneth

Penetrating quote: 'If I ever woke up with a dead hooker in my hotel room, Matt would be the first person I'd call'

Cate Blanchett

Like every great screen actress, Cate Blanchett can look quite plain one minute and extraordinarily beautiful the next. She also owns a face that can be moulded into virtually any century – which to date has served her rather well. She has been a Second World War POW in Bruce Beresford's *Paradise Road*, a

nineteenth-century heiress in Gillian Armstrong's *Oscar and Lucinda* and the 'Virgin' Queen herself in Shekhar Kapur's controversial biography *Elizabeth I*. Ms Blanchett also displays an intelligence and spirit that backs up her chameleonic looks to devastating effect. And, then, as if to undermine a perfectly good critic's hard-earned judgment, she will play the sweet girl-next-door with throwaway charm.

Inundated with theatre awards and critical laurels in her native Australia (for *Kafka Dances*, David Mamet's *Oleanna*, her Ophelia in *Hamlet* and Miranda in *The Tempest*), Cate was a star barely out of drama school (The National Institute of Dramatic Art). Absurd hyperbole has already been written about her, but, thankfully, she's taking it all in her stride. The hype, she says, 'is so dangerous, so volatile,' adding, 'It's very important to be earthed. There's so much static electricity surrounding you, you'd explode otherwise.'

Born: 1969 in Melbourne

Film debut: *Paradise Road*

TV: *Heartland*, *Bordertown*, *G.P.*, *Police Rescue*

Next up: Mike Newell's *Pushing Tin*, a comedy about air-traffic controllers with John Cusack and Billy Bob Thornton; Anthony

Ben Affleck and Joey Lauren Adams in Kevin Smith's audacious, moving and very, very funny *Chasing Amy*

Minghella's adaptation of the Patricia Highsmith novel *The Talented Mr Ripley*, with Matt Damon and Gwyneth Paltrow; and a new adaptation of Oscar Wilde's

Cate Blanchett as the coquettish Lucinda Leplastrier in Gillian Armstrong's *Oscar and Lucinda*

Neve Campbell

An Ideal Husband with Minnie Driver and Rupert Everett
Latest gong: The Best Supporting Actress Award from the Australian Film Institute – for *Thank God He Met Lizzie*
Other half: Assistant director Andrew Upton, whom she met on the set of the romantic black comedy *Thank God He Met Lizzie*
Penetrating quote: 'I've always found the concept of being an actor slightly indulgent. There's a war within me about whether to do it or not'

Neve Campbell

Tagged the model teenager of American TV – thanks to her role as the virtuous, loveable Julia Salinger in *Party of Five* – Neve Campbell turned the tables on her persona when she took on the movies. Besides her part as the fist-throwing Sidney Prescott in Wes Craven's slasher hits *Scream* and *Scream 2*, she played a high-school witch in *The Craft* and a trashy, devious heroin addict in the steamy *Wild Things* (complete with lesbian sex scene).

Next, she plays a soap opera diva opposite Mike Myers in *54*.

The second child of showbusiness parents (who divorced when she was a baby), Neve (rhymes with 'Bev') left home at 15 to join the Toronto cast of *Phantom of the Opera*, subsequently dancing her way through 800 performances. At 17 she moved in with a bartender, married him five years later and divorced him two years after that. Still only 24, Neve is a veteran of theatre, TV, film and, indeed, life, although she insists, 'I find youthful characters very interesting because they haven't got it together yet, and they don't know exactly what life is about.' Hmmm.

Born: 3 March 1973 in Guelph, Ontario, Canada
Film debut: *Web of Deceit* (1993), a domestic drama starring Corbin Bernsen and Amanda Pays
The other films: *Paint Cans*, *The Dark*, *Northern Passage* (aka *Baree*) (TV), *I Know My Son is Alive* (TV), *The Forget-Me-Not Murders* (TV), *Love Child*, *The Canterville Ghost* (TV), *Simba's Pride* (voice only), *Hairshirt* (co-starring her brother Christian Campbell)
Next up: *Three to Tango* with Matthew

Perry and Dylan McDermott vying for her attentions
Ex-husband: Actor/ex-bartender Jeff Colt (1995-97)
Significant other: Matthew Lillard who, as Stuart, tried to kill her in *Scream*
Amazing fact: Having posed for a swimsuit catalogue, she was amazed to see her scantily clad body on a Toronto billboard
What they say: 'The way she's grown as an actress has astonished me. She's incredibly versatile, incredibly composed. She's not flighty. There's a lovely calm to her.' Amy Lippman, co-creator of *Party of Five*. 'Neve has such a great heart, she makes me want to hug her.' Courteney Cox, co-star of *Scream* and *Scream 2*
Penetrating quote: 'I really don't believe that anything is negative. Any kind of experience, whether it seems to be negative or positive, if you learn from it and you grow from it and you are aware of where you are within it, then you've made it positive somehow.' And: 'As long as I touch people through my acting, nothing else matters'

Robert Carlyle

Regardless of the fact that Robert Carlyle is the star of the most profitable film of all time, he would still have made these pages. Because while his appearances on the big screen have been relatively few, the standard of his films – and his participation in them – has been exceptional. Ignoring his small part in Bill Forsyth's embarrassing era-jumping saga *Being Human* (Robin Williams should take the blame for that), Carlyle has had a remarkable run. He was the sensitive gay lover of Linus Roache in Antonia Bird's *Priest*, one of the most courageous and moving films of 1994, and in *Trainspotting* he was unrecognisable as the psychotic, beer-swilling, knife-wielding Begbie. In Ken Loach's powerful and strangely underrated *Carla's Song* he was both funny and touching as the Glaswegian bus driver sucked into the troubles in Nicaragua. In Antonia Bird's *Face*, the best British gangster film since *The Long Good Friday*, he was the mildly sociopathic leader of a gang of London criminals. And then there was this film called *The Full Monty*.

Small, sinewy and far from conventionally handsome, Carlyle has enough versatility in his left ear lobe to have attracted admirers from across the board. Directors and critics love him for the selfless dedication he applies to his work (he has been compared to a Caledonian De Niro). Female viewers have been seduced by the down-to-earth charm he exuded as both the vulnerable Scottish policeman in TV's *Hamish Macbeth* and by the enterprising steel worker in *The Full Monty*. And then of course there is the gallery of rogues he has played on screen – both big and small – which has made him popular with the boys. A good all-round egg, then, with a future of incontestable stardom ahead. Let's just hope he can hang on to that integrity.

Born: 14 April 1961 in Glasgow, Scotland
Film debut: The prison officer 'Big Woodsy' in David Hayman's *Silent Scream* (1989)
First starring role: Stevie, ex-con and builder in Ken Loach's *Riff-Raff* (1990)
TV: *Cracker* (as a football-mad serial

killer), *Hamish Macbeth* (as a gentle, hash-smoking copper), *Go Now* (as a football-mad plasterer with multiple sclerosis), *Looking After Jo Jo* (as a hard-nosed drug dealer)
Next up: The role of a legendary highwayman in the period action-adventure *Plunkett and Macleane* (co-starring Jonny Lee Miller and Liv Tyler); and *Ravenous*, in which he is united with director Antonia Bird for the fourth time to play a flesh-eating psychotic – opposite Guy Pearce and David Arquette
Significant other: Make-up artist Anastasia Shirley, whom he married in December 1997
Amazing fact: He cried for half an hour when Scotland's Gary McAllister missed a penalty shot in Euro 96
Second amazing fact: He begged on the streets of London for five days to prepare for his role as a homeless man in Antonia Bird's *Safe*
Third amazing fact: He turned down parts in *Rob Roy* and *Braveheart*
What they say: 'In a way he is not like an actor. He's a proper person. There is a great warmth and generosity to him.' Director Antonia Bird
Penetrating quote: 'I cannot possibly sit here and say I am still a working-class guy. [But] inside my head I still have that *raison d'être*. My whole fucking reason for being is that'

Matt Damon as *Good Will Hunting*

Matt Damon

Endowed with an athletic physique and a mischievous, impish grin, Matt Damon vaulted his way from anonymous young blade to Oscar-winning pin-up in less than twelve months. Having had good roles in *School Ties*, *Geronimo: An American Legend* and *Courage Under Fire*, he landed the lead in Francis Ford Coppola's starry adaptation of John Grisham's *The Rainmaker*, beating out fellow contenders Stephen Dorff and Edward Norton. Next, he held out for the title role in *Good Will Hunting*, from a script he had co-written with childhood friend Ben Affleck (qv) while still at Harvard. Miramax finally bought the property for $1 million plus and agreed to let Damon and Affleck play their own roles – with Robin Williams brought in for some box-office ballast. The film was an enormous commercial and critical success, won Damon an Oscar nomination for best actor and got him and Affleck the statuette for Best Original Screenplay (Damon's acceptance speech was largely shanghaied by Affleck). Since then,

Robert Carlyle (with William Snape) in *The Full Monty*

Damon has played Private Ryan in Steven Spielberg's *Saving Private Ryan* and starred in John Dahl's gambling drama *Rounders*, with Edward Norton, John Turturro and John Malkovich.

Born: 8 October 1970 in Cambridge, Massachusetts
Real name: Matthew Paige Damon
Film debut: Steamer Winsor, younger brother of Adam Storke's Charles Winsor (who's romancing Julia Roberts), in Donald Petrie's *Mystic Pizza* (1988)
First line on celluloid: 'Mom, do you want my green stuff?'
The other films: *The Good Mother* (extra), *Rising Son* (for TV), *The Good Old Boys* (TV), *Glory Daze*,

Stephen Dillane with Sophie Marceau in *Firelight*

Chasing Amy (cameo), *Dogma*, *Planet Ice* (voice only)
Next up: Tom Ripley in Anthony Minghella's *The Talented Mr Ripley*, co-starring Gwyneth Paltrow and Jude Law; and then the lead in Billy Bob Thornton's *All the Pretty Horses*, from the novel by Cormac McCarthy
Significant others: Claire Danes, Minnie Driver, Winona Ryder… who next?
Amazing fact: Having lost 45 lbs to play a heroin-addicted Gulf War veteran in *Courage Under Fire*, Damon still requires daily medication to combat the side effects of what was a ruthless dieting regime
Penetrating quote: 'I'm surrounded by people I love and trust who will not hesitate to knock me down if they see me getting arrogant'

Stephen Dillane

He has been packed into the pigeonhole of the next Ralph Fiennes, but Dillane's recent catalogue of lost, humourless souls suggests an actor more akin to a marginally younger Jeremy Irons. Besides his lugubrious and naked *Hamlet* in the acclaimed Peter Hall production, he has played the battle-scarred war correspondent Michael Henderson in *Welcome to Sarajevo*, the soulful soul mate of Henry Jaglom's screen wife in *Déjà Vu* and the tormented secret lover of Sophie Marceau in William Nicholson's *Firelight*. Conventionally handsome in an excessively English way, Dillane has fought against his good looks, seeking the interior motive of his characters rather than adopting any physical swagger.

According to Nicholson, when he was casting his intensely passionate romance, he was 'looking for the thinking woman's crumpet. Not a hunk, not a pretty boy, but someone who could convey sexual power and the Victorian sense of obsessive duty and moral anguish.' Well, he found his man.

A theatre actor to the marrow, Dillane has suddenly found himself in demand as a screen presence. In *Sarajevo*, an intelligent and ferocious study of the Bosnian conflict, he headed an international cast that included Woody Harrelson, Marisa Tomei and Kerry Fox. He was in equally good company in Jaglom's *Déjà Vu* (supported by Vanessa Redgrave, Michael Brandon and Noel Harrison), even if he's none too keen on recalling the experience. And he's the lead in *Firelight*, an exceptionally well sustained romantic drama that activates the brain cells as it manipulates the heart strings. Like it or not, Dillane is heading for major stardom.

Born: 1957 in London
Film debut: Horatio in Zeffirelli's *Hamlet* (1990)
First line on celluloid: 'Hail to your Lordship!'
The other films: *La Chance, Two If By Sea* (aka *Stolen Hearts*)
TV: *The Secret Garden, The One Game, An Affair in Mind*, Dennis Potter's *Christabel, Heading Home, Frankie's House, You Me + It, The Rector's Wife, Hostages*
Next up: *Love and Rage*, a nineteenth-

century drama of revenge with Greta Scacchi and Daniel Craig

Significant others: The actress Naomi Wirthner, by whom he has two children

Amazing fact: After reading an interview with Trevor Eve he gave up his job as a reporter for a South London newspaper and enrolled at the Bristol Old Vic drama school

Penetrating quote: 'I don't really like watching people act. I want to be affected by the play, and the best acting is the sort that doesn't get in its way'

Minnie Driver

Director Barry Levinson calls her '*very* versatile'. Ex-boyfriend John Cusack thinks she's 'unbelievably intuitive'. Americans think she is American. Whatever else she is, Minnie Driver is outspoken, dedicated and a very, very fine actress. Whether playing an Irish pudding in Pat O'Connor's affecting *Circle of Friends* (for which she piled on 25 lbs of flab) or the svelte 'Noo Joisy' girlfriend of Stanley Tucci in *Big Night*, she is totally convincing in the part at hand. For her performance as Skylar, the forthright, fun-loving Harvard medical student in *Good Will Hunting*, she was nominated for an Oscar. She says, 'I have to prove that I'm in the great tradition of whoredom, that I can be whatever

they want me to be. People don't really know if I'm English, Irish, Russian or American. They don't know if I'm 5'10" or 5'2" [she's the former]. We're going for the unbranded brand. "Minnie Driver Question Mark".'

Furthermore, the actress tends to get her own way. When, in sixth grade, she was cast as a tree, she ended up playing a fairy. 'I created the part for myself,' she explains. 'If there's not a part for you, create your own.' Minnie Driver is certainly creating a stir on both sides of the Atlantic.

Born: 31 January 1971 in Barbados

Real name: Amelia Driver, nicknamed 'Minnie' by her sister, the model Kate 'Lori' Driver

Film debut: Irina, the tone-deaf Russian singer in *GoldenEye* who has an eye for Robbie Coltrane and no ear for Country & Western music

The other films: *Sleepers, Grosse Pointe Blank, Hard Rain, Tarzan* (the voice of Jane), *The Governess*

TV: *God on the Rocks, Murder Most Horrid, The Day Today, Peak Practice, Mr Wroe's Virgins, The Beast in Man, That Sunday, The Politician's Wife*

Turned down: The title role in Granada TV's *Moll Flanders*; the Gwyneth Paltrow part in *Sliding Doors*

Next up: *An Ideal Husband*, Oliver Parker's film version of the Oscar Wilde play, also starring Cate

Minnie Driver

Blanchett, Rupert Everett, Julianne Moore and Jeremy Northam

Significant others: Aaron, a lawyer; Matt LeBlanc; John Cusack; Matt Damon; Foo Fighters drummer Taylor Hawkins

Most recent date: Robert Downey Jr

Amazing fact: She boxes in her spare time

Penetrating quote: 'I don't come from the grand tradition of British theatre. I come from the grand tradition of crappy TV'

Catherine McCormack

She has the fair skin and bone structure of an aristocratic socialite. Yet with her elegant curves and penetrating hazel eyes, she suggests something entirely more physical. And with her poise and slow-burning talent she should be headed down the same road graced by

Catherine McCormack

In the money: Vince Vaughn as the hip-talkin' Trent in Doug Liman's *Swingers*

Jacqueline Bisset, Charlotte Rampling and Kristin Scott Thomas.

In the low-budget and generally lambasted *Loaded* she played a paranoid virgin, a performance that caught the attention of Mel Gibson. At that time he was casting *Braveheart* and, following an interview made up largely of an exchange of jokes, he chose her to play the ill-fated wife of William Wallace in his Oscar-winning film. Her fiery performance – capped by her long chestnut tresses – was one of the movie's finer points, and Ms McCormack waited for the offers to roll in.

Considering her lack of experience, it was understandable that she took the female lead in *North Star*, if only to be torn between the hearts of Christopher Lambert and James Caan. She fared much better in David Leland's World War II drama *Land Girls*, in which she played a farm volunteer in love with a naval officer. Taking top billing over a choice ensemble cast, she exhibited the stuff of star charisma and proved that, with the right role, she could be around for a long time to come.

Born: 1972 in Alton, Hampshire, England

The other films: *Dangerous Beauty* and Pat O'Connor's *Dancing at Lughnasa*

Next up: David Kane's bittersweet romantic comedy *This Year's Love*, co-starring Kathy Burke, Ian Hart and Jennifer Ehle

Penetrating quote: 'Snogging Mel Gibson is fun'

Vince Vaughn

Unlike Brendan Fraser, Matt Damon, Chris O'Donnell and Ben Affleck, Vince Vaughn wasn't in *School Ties*. And unlike Matthew McConaughey, Ben Affleck, Parker Posey and Joey Lauren Adams, he wasn't in *Dazed and Confused* either. But he did audition for both movies – he just didn't get the roles. He then thought his luck had changed when he landed a fairly substantial part in the football drama *Rudy*. However, most of his contribution ended up on the cutting-room floor. His one solace was that he made a friend out of co-star Jon Favreau, another struggling young actor caught up in the Hollywood maelstrom.

Six-foot-four, baby-faced and strong on charm, Vaughn originally believed he had made it when he landed a national TV ad for Chevrolet. It certainly convinced his parents to let him off the college hook. But Vaughn's career refused to take off. He landed another film, the Aids drama *At Risk*, but nobody saw

it. And there was talk of his friend Favreau writing a script with Vaughn pencilled in for the role of a swingin', hyper-cool out-of-work actor. Great.

Well, Favreau wrote the script, a pathetic budget of $250,000 was scraped together and the picture got shot. Embraced by the critics, the film – *Swingers* – was a considerable commercial success and Vaughn's hip poser, Trent, became something of a cult icon, with lines like 'You're so money and you don't even know it' enthusiastically adopted by fans. There was a scene in the movie in which Vaughn swoops down on to an unsuspecting 'honey' that just cried out for the accompaniment of the two-note theme from *Jaws*. In order to give his permission for the music's use, Steven Spielberg viewed an early video of *Swingers* and was struck by Vaughn's screen presence. Ironically, the actor was making out with Spielberg's wife (Kate Capshaw) in *The Locusts* when the filmmaker cast him in the major role of Nick Van Owen, the wildlife photographer in *The Lost World: Jurassic Park*. The latter movie grossed a phenomenal $100 million in its first six days of release and Vaughn was suddenly on his way to major money.

Born: 28 March 1970 in Minneapolis, Minnesota

Next up: *Clay Pigeons* with Joaquin Phoenix and Georgina Cates, a thriller about a young man framed for murder (Phoenix) and 'the world's nicest serial killer'(Vaughn). He'll then play a struggling young lawyer in *A Cool Dry Place* with Joey Lauren Adams and Monica Potter; star opposite Anne Heche and Joaquin Phoenix in the human drama *Return to Paradise*; and take on the Norman Bates role in Gus Van Sant's remake of Hitchcock's *Psycho*, with Anne Heche in the Janet Leigh part. After that he will team up with Jon Favreau in the western *The Marshal of Revelation*, which the friends will write and direct together

What they say: 'Vince Vaughn is an American icon to be.' Steven Spielberg

Penetrating quote: 'I never liked dancing so much. I'm more into sitting, having some drinks, some conversation…'

Film World Diary

July 1997 - June 1998

James Cameron-Wilson

Neve Campbell: an early divorce

July 1997

After ten months of marriage, **Lauren Holly** files for divorce from **Jim Carrey**, citing 'irreconcilable differences'. The actress is reportedly now snuggling up to **Edward Burns**, director and co-star of her new movie, *Long Time, Nothing New* ✳ Chancellor Gordon Brown's new budget introduces 100 per cent tax relief on British films costing less than £15 million ✳ Having failed to sell her ailing hotel and casino in Las Vegas, property tycoon, mother and sometime actress **Debbie Reynolds** files for bankruptcy ✳ *The Lost World: Jurassic Park* grosses $300 million worldwide ✳ **Joan Cusack** and her husband, lawyer Dick Burke, are the proud parents of a baby boy, Dylan John ✳ In the US, *Men in Black* grosses $100m in its first eight days ✳ Arrested near the home of **Steven Spielberg** in Pacific Palisades, Los Angeles, stalker Jonathan Norman is found in possession of several pairs of handcuffs, tape, a knife and a diary containing the names of Spielberg's family and business associates. Norman admits to police that he was planning to rape the filmmaker and, had Spielberg's wife, **Kate Capshaw**, been at home, he'd 'have tied her up, handcuffed her and made her watch' ✳ **Kirstie Alley** and her actor husband of 14 years, **Parker Stevenson**, sign their divorce papers ✳ **Dudley Moore**'s estranged wife, Nicole Rothschild, files a $10 million lawsuit against him, claiming that he abused her, forced her to take drugs and made her 'dance' for him ✳ **Antonio Banderas** consents to a £5 million divorce settlement with his ex-wife Ana Leza. He also agrees to hand over the marital pile in Madrid, worth about £2m ✳ **Joely Richardson** and her producer husband Tim Bevan (*Four Weddings and a Funeral*, *Dead Man Walking*, *Bean*, etc.) separate ✳ **Will Smith**'s asking price goes up to $20m per picture, making him the first black star to join the elite ranks of the Exorbitant Eleven: **Jim Carrey**, **Kevin Costner**, **Tom Cruise**, **Michael Douglas**, **Harrison Ford**, **Mel Gibson**, **Tom Hanks**, **Arnold Schwarzenegger**, **Sylvester Stallone**, **John Travolta** and **Bruce Willis** ✳ *Batman and Robin* grosses $100m in the US ✳ **Julia Roberts** is back: *My Best Friend's Wedding* grosses $100m in the US ✳ **Bruce Willis** and **Demi Moore** sue the *Star* for $5 million after the tabloid newspaper reports 'their marital split' ✳ **Neve Campbell**, 23, co-star of *The Craft* and *Scream*, splits from her husband of two-and-a-half years, actor Jeff Colt ✳ *Men in Black* grosses $200m in the US.

August 1997

Jennifer Flavin, wife of **Sylvester Stallone**, suffers a miscarriage ✻ Rumours insist that **Barbra Streisand** and **James Brolin** are tying the conjugal knot at a Rhode Island resort this weekend (9 August) ✻ Following in the footsteps of salad dressing tycoon **Paul Newman**, **Clint Eastwood** launches his own beer label, Pale Rider Ale. All profits will go to charity ✻ Director **James Cameron** (*The Terminator*) and his long-term girlfriend **Linda Hamilton** (*The Terminator*) finally tie the knot at a Hawaii-style wedding in Malibu. Their four-year-old daughter, Josephine, presides as flower girl ✻ **Christian Slater** is arrested in Los Angeles after attacking a female friend, biting a man in the stomach and kicking a police officer down the stairs. The actor admits that he was under the influence of cocaine ✻

Kelsey Grammer ties the knot with *Playboy* model Camille Donatacci before embarking on a Caribbean honeymoon ✻ Divorce proceedings begin between **Anthony Quinn** and his wife of 35 years, Iolanda. The latter filed for separation when her husband openly conducted an affair with his personal secretary, Kathy Bevin ✻ *Face/Off* grosses $100m in the US ✻ *Air Force One* grosses $100m in the US – in under three weeks ✻ **Geena Davis** files for divorce from her husband of four years, **Renny Harlin**, the Finnish director of *Die Hard 2*, *Cliffhanger* and *The Long Kiss Goodnight*. The actress cites 'irreconcilable differences' ✻ After eight weeks at the US box office, *Men in Black* conquers *The Lost World: Jurassic Park* to become the top-grossing movie of 1997 – so far.

September 1997

Steven Seagal: would you trust your soul to this man?

The Lost World: Jurassic Park grosses $500m worldwide ✻ *Air Force One* grosses $150m in the US – in seven weeks ✻ *Con Air* grosses $100m in the US ✻ A Buddhist monastery proclaims that **Steven Seagal** is the reincarnation of a venerable Tibetan lama ✻ *George of the Jungle* grosses $100m in the US ✻ **Patrick Stewart**, 57, announces his engagement to Wendy Neuss, 39, a producer on the *Star Trek* series ✻ **Robin Givens**, 32, ties the knot with the Yugoslav-born tennis coach Svetozar Marinkovic, 30, in California ✻ **Dudley Moore** undergoes open-heart surgery ✻ Media mogul **Ted Turner** donates one billion dollars to the United Nations. He admits that he has more money than he knows what to do with, adding, 'I just hope this giving thing is contagious' ✻ Actor **Donovan Leitch**, son of the singer **Donovan** and brother of actress **Ione Skye,** marries Chanel model Kirsty Hume in a traditional Scottish wedding ✻ **Julianne Moore** and her boyfriend, writer-director **Bart Freundlich** (*The Myth of Fingerprints*), are expecting ✻ **Harry Connick Jr** and his model wife, Jill Goodacre, are the proud parents of a bouncing baby girl, Sara Kate.

October 1997

Brigitte Bardot is fined 10,000 francs by a French court for inciting racial hatred. The animal rights campaigner and former sex goddess was convicted after criticising the Muslim ritual of slaughtering sheep ✳ *Contact* grosses $100m at the US box office ✳ After 14 years of cohabitation with her lover **Kurt Russell**, **Goldie Hawn** reveals that they are to marry. Apparently, it was the ghost of Goldie's mother – who, the actress claims, materialised in her bathroom – that suggested they should finally secure the knot ✳ *Men in Black* grosses $500m worldwide ✳ **Angela Bassett** and **Courtney B. Vance** tie the knot ✳ **Quentin Tarantino**, whose screenplay for *Natural Born Killers* was extensively rewritten, lands a series of blows on the face of **Don Murphy**, producer of the said film, in a Los Angeles restaurant. After Miramax co-chairman **Harvey Weinstein** manages to pacify Tarantino, the latter confides, 'I really think I slapped some respect into the guy.' Murphy, while obviously rattled, decides not to press charges ✳ **Robert Downey Jr** is in trouble again after his wife, Deborah Lynn Falconer, almost dies from a cocaine overdose. Having promised to clean up his own drug habit, Downey could face three years behind bars for abusing his terms of probation ✳ *Men in Black* becomes the tenth highest grossing film in global history ✳ **Beatrice Dalle** is caught kissing the French football icon and aspiring actor **Eric Cantona** (*Le Bonheur*) at the Atlantic Bar in London ✳ **David Aukin**, the man who built Channel Four into the most potent force in British cinema, forms Hal Films, his own UK studio under the auspices of Miramax Films. Joining fellow Channel Four alumnus **Colin Leventhal** and American executive **Trea Hoving**, Aukin will have $50 million at his disposal to produce five or six major features a year. Aukin notes that, 'It's the first time a US company has made a significant investment in film production here and left the control of that money in the hands of a British management team.' Aukin was previously responsible for such hits as *Four Weddings and a Funeral*, *Trainspotting*, *The Madness of King George* and *Secrets and Lies* and will now be able to develop, produce, co-produce, finance and acquire feature films with the backing of a principal Hollywood studio ✳ 'Go ahead, make my day' is replaced by 'Sweetie, did you floss?' as the new catchphrase linked to **Clint Eastwood**. As revealed in the autobiography of **Sondra Locke**, Clint's live-in lover for 17 years, his signal for whoopee was this dental reference ✳ Pizza entrepreneur Richie Palmer, 37, ditches girlfriend **Cathy Moriarty** (Oscar nominee for *Raging Bull*), 37, for **Raquel Welch**, 57 ✳ *Face/Off* grosses $200m worldwide ✳ It's official: **Marisa Tomei** and **Dana Ashbrook** are an item ✳ **Richard Gere** organises mass demonstrations in protest of President Clinton's open-armed welcome to Chinese president Jiang Zemin. An emphatic sympathiser with the fate of Tibet, which has been subjugated by China since 1950, Gere rounded up the public support of fellow celebrities **Harrison Ford** and **Uma Thurman** ✳ **Ralph Fiennes** and **Alex Kingston** are officially divorced.

November 1997

Thirty-eight years after it was made, Michael Powell's *Peeping Tom* is finally granted a showing on British television ✳ **Joel Schumacher**, director of *Falling Down*, *The Client* and *Batman and Robin*, is 'outed' by a security guard who claims that the filmmaker gave him $280 to buy the services of a male escort. Not surprisingly, Schumacher denies the allegation ✳ *Liar Liar* grosses $300m worldwide ✳ Having contracted flu, **Julia Roberts** postpones her Thanksgiving wedding to fitness guru Pat Manocchia. This is a shame as the couple's last wedding day – 14

February 1997 – was also postponed. No stranger to cancelled nuptials, Ms Roberts pulled out of her 14 June 1991 wedding to **Kiefer Sutherland** just one week before the occasion ✳ **William Shatner** marries for the third time ✳ In an effort to demonstrate his undying love and win back the adoration of his wife, **Mickey Rourke** cuts off a finger in front of her. Unfortunately, Mrs Rourke – top model **Carre Otis** – is unimpressed and her impaired husband dashes off to hospital with his digit on ice ✳ The body of **Yves Montand** – who died in 1991 – is exhumed in order to establish the star's paternity of one Aurore Drossart, 23 ✳ **Kevin Costner** reveals in *Premiere* magazine that he was in talks with **Princess Diana** to co-star with her in a sequel to *The Bodyguard.* 'She wanted to talk,' the actor revealed. 'She wanted the right to reinvent herself' ✳ *The Lost World: Jurassic Park* grosses $600m worldwide ✳ Production on Universal's Bosnian drama *The Age of Aquarius* collapses when **Harrison Ford** abandons ship. That leaves Ford's leading lady, **Kristin Scott Thomas**, high and dry.

Woody Allen: old lover and new son-in-law of Mia Farrow

December 1997

Robert Downey Jr is sentenced to six months in prison after ignoring a court order to stay off drugs and alcohol. The actor begs the Malibu judge for leniency, but is told that he has run out of chances ✳ According to the *Express*, **Don Johnson** leaves his 18-year-old fiancée **Jodi O'Keefe** for a 72-year-old millionairess, Denise Hale. Interestingly, O'Keefe has remained 18 in the media's eyes for at least two years now ✳ Producer **Jonathan Krane**, 45, leaves his wife of 19 years, actress **Sally Kellerman** (*M*A*S*H, Prêt-à-Porter*), 60, for **Nastassja Kinski**, 36 ✳ **Christian Slater**, 28, is sentenced to three months in prison after pleading guilty to possession of cocaine and heroin. He is also reprimanded for assaulting a police officer ✳ *Hercules* grosses $200m worldwide ✳ According to *People* magazine, **Julia Roberts** is now dating the actor **Benjamin Bratt** (from TV's *Law and Order*) ✳ **Robert Carlyle** marries make-up artist Anastasia Shirley, whom he met on the set of TV's *Cracker* ✳ Following the October announcement of **David Aukin**'s relocation to Miramax Films, **Michael Jackson**, chief executive of Channel Four, appoints **Paul Webster** as the new head of film. Webster, who, ironically, most recently served as senior executive VP in charge of worldwide production for Miramax, will take over the new post in January ✳ Nominated vice-president of the National Rifle Association, **Charlton Heston** publicly declares his support for the pro-gun lobby. 'The first act of a dictator is to disarm the people,' he argues. 'Fidel Castro, Hitler, Stalin, Mao – the first thing they do is take away private arms' ✳ **Helen Mirren** and her boyfriend of 11 years, American director **Taylor Hackford** (*An Officer and a Gentleman, Devil's Advocate*), finally tie the knot – near Inverness in Scotland ✳ **Larry Hagman** breaks six ribs after being hurled off his motorbike ✳ **Woody Allen** marries Soon-Yi Previn in Venice, Italy, thus making himself the son-in-law of **Mia Farrow,** his ex-girlfriend ✳ **Will Smith** and **Jada Pinkett** tie the knot in a lavish $3 million wedding on New Year's Eve. Jada, who's currently playing a college scaredy-cat in *Scream 2*, is pregnant with their first child.

January 1998

Michael Gambon, star of *The Cook, The Thief, His Wife and Her Lover* and *The Gambler*, is bestowed with a knighthood in the New Year's Honours ✳ British cinema admissions for 1997 climb to 138.9 million, 8.9 million more than 1996, setting a 21-year record ✳ After 20 years in the US, **Lynn Redgrave** is granted American citizenship ✳ *Titanic* grosses $100m in the US ✳ *Tomorrow Never Dies* grosses $100m in the US ✳ **Woody Harrelson** marries Laura Louie, the mother of his three children, in Costa Rica ✳ *Titanic* grosses $200m in the US ✳ *Air Force One* grosses $300m worldwide ✳ Having filed for divorce from his fifth wife, Oscar-winning actor **Rod Steiger** is reportedly in love again – with Oscar-winning actress **Elizabeth Taylor** ✳ *Titanic* grosses $250m in the US – in a record six weeks ✳ It's public: **Ethan Hawke** and **Uma Thurman** are expecting their first child ✳ **Vivica A. Fox** (*Independence Day*, *Set It Off*) announces her engagement to the rapper **Sixx-Nine**. They are to be married in December, two years – to the day – after they first met ✳ **Jane Fonda**, 60, whose last film was *Stanley & Iris* nine years ago, announces her retirement from acting ✳ Two British photographers reject counts of reckless driving and false imprisonment in a court case in Santa Monica, California. According

to **Arnold Schwarzenegger,** one of the reporters rammed his car into the star's Mercedes, while the other stopped to take photographs. Schwarzenegger's wife, Maria Shriver, was with him and was shouting and screaming, while Schwarzenegger feared for his life. The previous week the actor had undergone cardiac valve surgery and had been told that if his blood pressure rose above 100 he would be in grave danger ✳ **Leonardo DiCaprio**, 23, is dating the model **Amber Valletta**, one year his senior ✳ *The Full Monty* becomes the top-grossing movie in Britain of all time, beating out such films as *Jurassic Park*, *Independence Day* and *Men in Black* ✳ *Titanic* grosses $300m in the US, making it the eighth all-time highest grosser in North America ✳ Strapped in a harness, **Christopher Reeve** takes his first steps for 34 months.

February 1998

To celebrate her 51st birthday, **Farrah Fawcett** splashes out on a new, 'softer' look, having her breasts, eyes, eyelids, nose and forehead fine-tuned under the surgeon's knife ✳ Kim Tannahill, the former nanny employed by **Bruce Willis** and **Demi Moore**, files a lawsuit in Los Angeles claiming damages from the celebrity couple for civil rights violations, deceit, fraud, invasion of privacy, stalking, false imprisonment and assault ✳ **Brad Pitt** is dating **Claire Forlani**, the actress who played Sean Connery's daughter in *The Rock* ✳ **Tony Blair** announces at the White House that **Bob Hope** is to receive an honorary knighthood ✳ **Nicole Kidman** undergoes two hours of surgery to remove a benign ovarian cyst ✳ **Jack Nicholson** receives his *eleventh* Oscar nomination as the Academy unveils its 1997 shortlist and snubs *The Boxer*, *The Ice Storm*, *My Best Friend's Wedding* and *Oscar and Lucinda* ✳ **Robert De Niro** is at the centre of a row concerning the 15-month-old investigation into an international prostitution racket. Apparently, his name was discovered in an address book seized by French authorities. He is subsequently

escorted from his Paris hotel by ten policemen and interrogated about his relationship with three call girls. The star abruptly files a legal complaint against Frederic N'Guyen, the investigating magistrate, for 'breaking the rules of judicial secrecy' and for using his name to bring publicity to the inquisition ✳ A 'close friend' of **Daniel Day-Lewis** reveals that the Oscar-winning star has decided to retire from acting – in spite of denials from his agent ✳ **Sharon Stone** marries Phil Bronstein, the executive editor of *The San Francisco Examiner*, on St Valentine's Day ✳ After 16 hours of labour, **Elle Macpherson** gives birth to her first child, Arpad Flynn Busson, on St Valentine's Day ✳ *Titanic* becomes the highest grossing film in initial release in US history ✳ *As Good As It Gets* grosses $100m at the US box office ✳ *Titanic* grosses $400m in the US ✳ **Paul Hogan** and **Linda Kozlowski** are expecting their first child ✳ **Burt Reynolds**, 62, announces plans to marry his girlfriend, ex-waitress Pam Seals, 38. She will be his third wife ✳ According to the *Mirror*, **Tom Cruise** and **Nicole Kidman** have acquired a Gulfstream

Nicole Kidman: disposing of an ovarian cyst and acquiring a Gulfstream IV

IV to ferry them between their homes in Los Angeles and Britain. The jet, which cost Cruise £21 million, comes complete with a cinema, jacuzzi and children's play area ✳ Following nine hours of interrogation by French investigators, **Robert De Niro** returns his *Legion d'Honneur*, saying, 'I'm never coming back to France. I couldn't give a damn about the Cannes Film Festival' ✳ **Robert Downey Jr** is hospitalised after being beaten up by two fellow prisoners ✳ The two British photographers who forced **Arnold Schwarzenegger**'s Mercedes off the road in order to take pictures of him are charged with false imprisonment and reckless driving. They are sentenced to three months and two months in prison, respectively ✳ *Titanic* pockets $915m worldwide, making it the biggest grossing film in history. However, taking inflation into account, *Gone With the Wind* is still the box-office champ ✳ Officials in Downing Street deny allegations of a 'smear campaign' against **Sean Connery** because of the actor's affiliations with the Scottish National Party. Plans set in motion by the Conservative government to bestow a knighthood on Connery were apparently blocked by **Donald Dewar**, the Scottish Secretary.

March 1998

Jodie Foster confirms that she is pregnant – but will not reveal the identity of the father (nor the 'method' of fertilisation). Because of this she has to bail out of the movie *Double Jeopardy*, for which she was to receive $15 million, the highest sum ever paid to an actress ✳ *Titanic* becomes the first film in history to gross more than $1 billion ✳ *Good Will Hunting* grosses $100m in the US ✳ **Lesley-Anne Down**, 44, gives birth to her first child for 15 years, George Edward Fauntleroy ✳ **Greg Kinnear** announces his engagement to the British-born Helen Labdon ✳ **Robert De Niro** and his wife, Grace Hightower, are the proud parents of a baby boy. It is the actor's fifth child, although the first in his latest marriage ✳ **Gary Oldman** announces his retirement from acting – again ✳ In an interview with *Vogue*, **Emma Thompson** reveals that she suffered a miscarriage in 1995, the year she broke up with **Kenneth Branagh** ✳ It's official: **Don Johnson** has split from his fiancée **Jodi O'Keefe**, 19 ✳ **Alain Delon**, the French star of such films as *Le Samourai*, *Borsalino* and *Notre Histoire*, announces his retirement from the cinema ✳ **Christian Slater** is released from jail after serving 59 days ✳ The Screen Actors' Guild braces itself for an all-out strike ✳ The average cost of a studio film is estimated to be a phenomenal $75.6 million ✳ **Robert De Niro** and **Balthazar Getty** are to be called as defence witnesses of a man accused of the multiple rape of two underage girls ✳ **Winona Ryder** publicly admits that she is the new girlfriend of serial dater **Matt Damon** ✳ *Titanic* grosses $500m in the US ✳ **Macaulay Culkin**, 17, announces his engagement to the actress Rachel Miner, 17.

April 1998

Dame Judi Dench announces that she will no longer be doing any interviews. Her last words to the press were recorded in the *Radio Times*, Britain's top-selling magazine ✳ *Lost in Space* becomes the first film to snatch the number one spot at the US box office since *Titanic* set sail on 19 December last year ✳ A Los Angeles judge rules that **Dudley Moore**, following four strokes and open-heart surgery, is too ill to meet the financial demands of his fourth wife, Nicole Rothschild ✳ The *News of the World* claims that **Emma Thompson** spent a night of 'passion, caressing and laughter' with the Swedish singer **Michaela de la Cour**.

According to de la Cour, the paper says, 'I felt like a schoolgirl who had had her first kiss' ✳ In order to persuade the world that her ex-boyfriend **Leonardo DiCaprio** is not gay, the model Kristen Zang informs the American *Star* tabloid that nookie with the actor was 'like having a glorious fantasy – even better than his millions of female fans have imagined it' ✳ **Rik Mayall** is hospitalised in a coma after falling off his four-wheel motorbike and striking his head ✳ Karina Hoffman-Birkhead, 32, the adopted daughter of **Dustin Hoffman**, is ordered to pay £3,600 compensation and £70 court costs for embezzling more than £5,000 from her former employers. She is also instructed to complete 180 hours of community service after stealing from a friend ✳ **Don Johnson** is in love again, this time with the affluent socialite Kelley Phleger, 30. Johnson's previous 'dalliance', the 72-year-old Denise Hale, insists that 'it's a really big romance' ✳ **David Schwimmer** proposes to his girlfriend, Israeli actress **Mili Avital** (*Polish Wedding*, *Kissing a Fool*), with a diamond engagement ring from Tiffanys ✳ As *Titanic* grosses $550m in the US, the film earns an extra billion dollars at the overseas box office ✳ After six years together and a wedding last August, **James Cameron** and **Linda Hamilton** go their separate ways. According to press reports, Cameron is now dating the actress **Suzy Amis** and Hamilton is in love with another woman.

May 1998

With the birth of baby Julian Murray Stern, **Lisa Kudrow** becomes the first star of the phenomenally successful *Friends* sitcom to be a parent. **Courteney Cox**, who plays Monica Geller in the series, was there at the birth ✳ Lions Gate Films announce that they are paying **Leonardo DiCaprio** $21m to star as Patrick Bateman in *American Psycho*, making him the highest paid actor of all time ✳ **Gerard Depardieu** is treated for a fractured left leg after crashing his motorcycle outside Paris. With five times the legal limit of alcohol in his blood, the French star could face imprisonment for drunk driving ✳ In Manhattan Criminal Court, **Michael Rapaport** pleads guilty to aggravated harassment of his former girlfriend, **Lili Taylor**, star of *The Addiction* and *I Shot Andy Warhol*. Rapaport is ordered by Judge Arlene Goldberg to visit a therapist twice a month for a year and to keep his distance from the actress ✳ Could it be true? Reports in the press indicate that **Julia Roberts** and her lover, actor **Benjamin Bratt**, have married in private ✳ **Carol Channing**, 77, files for divorce from Charles Lowe, 87, her husband of 41 years. She claims that Lowe only had sex with her twice, the last time when President Eisenhower was still in office ✳ **Diahann Carroll**, 62, undergoes surgery to remove a 'very small' cancerous growth from her breast ✳ **Tommy Lee**, drummer for Motley Crue, is jailed for six months for beating up his wife **Pamela (Lee) Anderson** ✳ **Charlie Sheen**, who is on probation for attacking a former girlfriend, is rushed to hospital after collapsing from a suspected drug overdose. After having his stomach pumped he is declared 'stable but serious' ✳ *Scream 2* grosses $100m in the US ✳ American tabloid latest: **Brad Pitt** and **Jennifer Aniston** are in love ✳ Arriving in Cannes to promote *Lulu On the Bridges*, **Mira Sorvino** reveals that she has split from boyfriend **Quentin Tarantino** ✳ **Brooke Shields** is detained by police and has her luggage searched at Cannes airport. The actress refuses to divulge why ✳ **Sharon Stone** raises more than $210,000 for Aids charities just by dancing at a celebrity auction in Cannes. Accompanied by **Elton John** on piano and **Ringo Starr** on drums, the actress undulated to 'Twist And Shout' and 'Great Balls Of Fire!' ✳ **Frank Sinatra** leaves his fourth wife, Barbara, $3.5 million in cash and three exclusive properties in Beverly Hills, Malibu and Nevada.

Jennifer Aniston: the new love of Brad Pitt

His three children (by his first marriage) receive $200,000 each ✳ **Leonardo DiCaprio** denies having accepted $21m to star in *American Psycho*. If he decides to take the role, the film's original star – **Christian Bale** – will have to walk ✳ Under the influence of anti-depressant drugs, alcohol and cocaine, the wife of comic actor **Phil Hartman** – Brynn – shoots her husband in the head and neck before turning the gun on herself ✳ *Deep Impact* becomes the first 1998 movie in the US to gross $100m.

June 1998

Godzilla grosses $100m in the US – in two weeks ✳ In court to testify against Warner Brothers for dumping his live-action *Pinocchio* project, **Francis Ford Coppola** breaks down in tears on the stand ✳ **Julie Walters** goes public regarding her secret marriage to Grant Roffey, the father of her ten-year-old daughter, Maisie. Apparently, she and Grant – who is eight years her junior – got hitched in New York last year ✳ It's true: **James Cameron** goes public with his new girlfriend, actress **Suzy Amis** (seen in *The Usual Suspects*, *Titanic*) ✳ According to *The New York Post*, **Minnie Driver** has been dumped by her boyfriend **Taylor Hawkins**, the drummer for Foo Fighters ✳ **Leonardo DiCaprio** is now offered $22 million by **Aurelio Di Laurentiis** to star in a new film version of Ernest Hemingway's *A Farewell to Arms*, topping the previous record of $21m offered to DiCaprio to star in *American Psycho*. However, the 23-year-old actor isn't signing anything yet ✳ Genetic tests carried out on the seven-year-old corpse of **Yves Montand** prove that he is not the father of Aurore Drossart, 23, whose mother had an affair with the French star ✳ **Ian Holm** receives a knighthood in the Queen's birthday honours list ✳ **Daniel Day-Lewis** and his actress wife **Rebecca Miller** are the proud parents of a baby boy ✳ **Macaulay Culkin** and **Rachel Miner** marry in Connecticut. They are still just 17 years old, which means they would have required parental permission to exchange their wedding vows ✳ Word has it that **Brad Pitt** and **Jennifer Aniston** are already planning *their* wedding. According to the *National Enquirer*, the superstar couple are contemplating a 'Greek-Buddhist ceremony' ✳ Following constant denials that their marriage was in trouble, **Bruce Willis** and **Demi Moore** publicly announce plans for divorce. They were wed in November of 1987 and splashed out on a second wedding a month later ✳ **Sylvester Stallone** and his wife Jennifer Flavin are the proud parents of a 7lb 6oz girl, Sistine Rose ✳ *The Truman Show* becomes the third 1998 release to gross $100 million in the US.

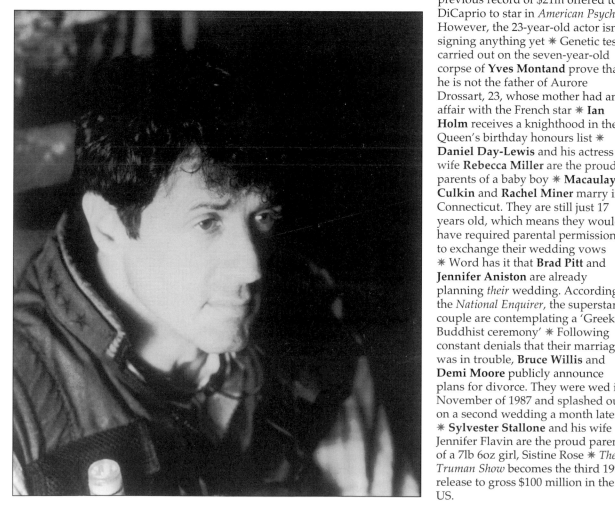

Sylvester Stallone: one of the Exorbitant Eleven and a proud dad

Film
Soundtracks

I so wanted to include the music of *The Boxer, Kundun* and *Wilde* in my round-up of the year's best soundtracks. But, as often as I listened to the scores, they just didn't seem special enough to merit inclusion, regardless of the prizes heaped on them. In keeping with my theme in the last edition of this annual, the finest soundtrack of the year was written by an Eastern European, namely Poland's **Jan A.P. Kaczmarek**. Until now best known in film circles for his music to Agnieszka Holland's dismal *Total Eclipse* (starring someone called Leonardo DiCaprio), Kaczmarek outdoes himself with Holland's subsequent feature, *Washington Square*, creating a work as complex, delicate and penetrating as many a classical composition.

Talking of DiCaprio, the actor starred in a film which produced something of a miracle in soundtrack circles. With just Celine Dion's hit song – 'My Heart Will Go On' – to give it commercial credence, **James Horner**'s score for *Titanic* surfaced at No. 1 in the album charts – and stayed there. Not since the reign of **Vangelis**'s *Chariots of Fire* in 1981 has a soundtrack of incidental music so impinged itself on the public consciousness. It is a shame, then, that Horner's score was not more distinguished (see review).

Conversely, it seemed odd that so many *lacklustre* pictures produced such exceptional CDs. In my round-up of the year, *Keep the Aspidistra Flying, Mojo, Stiff Upper Lips, This World, Then the Fireworks,* *TwentyFourSeven* and *Washington Square* all came some way to redeeming themselves with hugely satisfactory scores. Contrarily, the music to such outstanding pictures as *As Good As It Gets, Mrs Brown* and *Wilde* were all on the disappointing side. In fact, it was not a good year for the orchestral score. Not one work came close to the potency of *The English Patient* or *The Portrait of a Lady*. So it was the flourishing phenomenon of the pop-fuelled compilation that kept the soundtrack world a-buzzing. Still, if a song can capture – or promote – the right spirit of the material, it can fulfil its proviso just as well as any worked-up orchestra. It's when a track is used by a corporation to push an up-and-coming contracted player that the whole shebang becomes a charade. And the growing number of soundtracks featuring songs 'inspired' by a film is an insult to the fan.

But for every tacky shopping list there is a compilation that works dividends, with the likes of *The End of Violence, Great Expectations, Grosse Pointe Blank, Mojo* and *My Best Friend's Wedding* falling into the latter camp. Who can envision the last-named without picturing Rupert Everett breaking out into 'Say A Little Prayer' or recall *Grosse Pointe Blank* without reviving the image of John Cusack making his first kill to the strains of Johnny Nash's innocuous 'I Can See Clearly Now'? Or, for that matter, think of *Butch Cassidy and the Sundance Kid* without recalling 'Raindrops Keep Fallin' On My Head'?

Soundtracks of the Year

Amy Foster
John Barry's music has always sounded the same to me, but his graceful, mesmeric score for this Joseph Conrad story of maritime obsession seems to be a propitious meeting of minds. Nobody writes for the sea better than Barry (sorry Mr Horner), and this is the film that's been waiting to capitalise on his symphonic ebb and flow.

Anastasia
Agreeably slick animated musical from **Lynn Ahrens** and **Stephen Flaherty**, lyricist and composer of *Ragtime*, with lashings of variety, lush orchestration and a sterling vocal cast headed by the radiant Liz Callaway as Anastasia (singing for Meg Ryan). The lyrics certainly have their moments: 'Paris holds the key to *l'amour*/ And not even Freud knows the cure.'

The Apostle
Inspirational collection of grassroot songs and traditional ballads from 'and inspired' by Robert Duvall's marvellous film, with class acts from Lyle Lovett, Rebecca Lynn Howard, the Gaither Vocal Band, Johnny Cash and even Duvall himself, teamed with Emmylou Harris.

Blues Brothers 2000
Terrific, all-star rhythm and blues compilation that matches if not exceeds the magic of the first soundtrack. Aretha, B.B. King, James Brown, Wilson Pickett and Taj Mahal are all here plus Dan Aykroyd, John Goodman, Blues Traveler...

Cinema's Classic Romances
A choice collection of timeless melodies from 15 classy films, including *The English Patient*, *Emma*, *Sense and Sensibility*, *Far From the Madding Crowd* and Franco Zeffirelli's *Romeo and Juliet*. An exceptional compilation from the ever-dependable Silva Classics.

City of Angels
Probably the top-selling film soundtrack after *Titanic*, this is a genuine treat. We not only have 20 minutes of the seductive, ethereal score from **Gabriel Yared**, but some standout numbers from Paula Cole, John Lee Hooker, Sarah McLachlan, Goo Goo Dolls, U2 and, presenting her first song since her smash-hit debut album, Alanis Morissette at her soulfully gritty best.

The End of Violence
Jazzy, smoky and atmospheric score from **Ry Cooder**, continuing his fruitful collaboration with Wim Wenders (cf. *Paris, Texas*). Here, Cooder not only supplies his characteristic slide guitar but makes good use of the piano (on the divine track 'Pourquoi?') and supplies some sublime bass sax and accordion. The companion CD, featuring the likes of Tom Waits, U2 and Michael Stipe, isn't half bad either.

Gattaca
Another masterly, hypnotic composition from **Michael Nyman**, maestro of the melodic drone. His first for a Hollywood film, too.

George and Ira Gershwin in Hollywood
Glorious, nostalgic wallow in the songs and melodies of the great Gershwin brothers featuring a host of their most celebrated interpreters (Jolson, Astaire, Ella, even Bob Fosse) – and many very rare recordings. A double-barrelled treasure chest, complete with a handsome, informative booklet.

Good Will Hunting
A genuinely pleasing album, this, with **Elliott Smith**'s mellow, Art Garfunkelesque songs interspersed with old and new numbers from Al Green, Gerry Rafferty, The Dandy Warhols and those excellent Waterboys.

Great Expectations
Sterling example of a compilation soundtrack that works for a film, with new songs establishing and reflecting the movie's tone. With standout tracks from Mono, Pulp and Stone Temple Pilot's Scott Weiland, the album is also a great listen on its own terms.

Grosse Pointe Blank
Hard-edged, exceedingly hip collection of acts, including Violent Femmes, The Clash, Guns 'N' Roses, The Specials, etc., tempered by Johnny Nash exclaiming 'I Can See Clearly Now' (played during John Cusack's first kill). However, the crowning glory – Los Fabulosos Cadillacs' 'El Matador' – should have done for LFC what *Pulp Fiction* did for the surf guitar.

The Hanging Garden
For anybody who caught and cared about this extraordinary film, the soundtrack is a real must – an unusual, haunting and poetic mixture of the schmoozy, lyrical and ironic performed by traditional Canadian acts.

The Ice Storm
Anything by **Mychael Danna** is fine by me, but his arresting, Eastern-influenced score only lasts for eleven and a half minutes, leaving the rest of the soundtrack to David Bowie, Free, Sammi Smith, Jim Croce and the like. So one can't exactly complain.

Keep the Aspidistra Flying
One of the unexpected finds of the year, this, an elegant, melodic and charming score that sidesteps the irritations of the movie it supports. And all this refined honey from **Mike Batt**, the man who once urged us to 'Remember You're A Womble'.

L.A. Confidential

A sublimely glitzy, brassy, heart-soaring collection of golden classics from the 1950s, with sterling hits such as Kay Starr's 'Wheel Of Fortune' and Joni James's 'How Important Can It Be?' mixed in with rare recordings from Johnny Mercer and Dean Martin. Nostalgic ecstasy – and a perfect reflection of the themes of a terrific movie.

The Leading Man

Irresistible smorgasbord of good sounds, combining the old (Peter Sarstedt) and new (Gary Barlow), the exotic (Beausoleil) and provincial (Dubstar), with **Edward Shearmur**'s accomplished, arresting score evenly distributed throughout. Now *that's* how a soundtrack should work.

Midnight in the Garden of Good and Evil

A soaring tribute to the songs of Johnny Mercer, this irresistible concoction features a prestigious cast (k.d. lang, Joe Williams, Paula Cole, Rosemary Clooney, Cassandra Wilson, Alison Krauss, Tony Bennett) and some startling cameos (Clint Eastwood used to be a singer?). The real surprise, though, is Kevin Spacey, who brings real melody and feeling to Mercer and Harold Arlen's 'That Old Black Magic'.

Mojo

Hated the movie, loved the soundtrack, a roster of schmoozy, toe-tapping oldies reinvented by the likes of Marc Almond, The Stone Cold Strollers and the oh-so-sensual St Etienne. And the new numbers composed specially for the film all sound like they should have been hits before we were born.

My Best Friend's Wedding

One of the year's most enjoyable soundtracks, a collection of joyful, upbeat numbers garnished with Ani DiFranco's magnificently straight-faced pisstake 'Wishin' And Hopin'' and Rupert Everett's very own rendition of 'Say A Little Prayer'.

Oscar and Lucinda

In spite of his prodigious output and knack for an engaging melody, **Thomas Newman** has never really broken out of the shadow of his more famous colleagues. Yet his lush scores for *Fried Green Tomatoes*, *Little Women* and *Red Corner* represent some of the most captivating film music around. Here, aided by the heart-flipping sound of The Paulist Boy Choristers of California, Newman displays his mettle, producing a nuanced, seductive and varied work.

Paradise Road

Exquisite collection of classical pieces of vocal orchestra music performed by the Malle Babbe Women's Choir. Based on the actual arrangements made by Margaret Dryburgh and Norah Chambers while incarcerated in a Japanese POW camp, the music is uplifting and inspirational, a tribute to the haunting power of the human voice.

Sondheim at the Movies

A collector's wet dream, this, rare works by **Stephen Sondheim** composed specifically for the cinema, including his music for *Stavisky* and *Reds*, four songs from *Dick Tracy*, two numbers from the unproduced film musical *Singing Out Loud* and two more written for *The Birdcage* (only one of which, in fractured form, survived in the film). Yet this is all vintage Sondheim, vividly performed by an enthusiastic, polished cast.

Stiff Upper Lips

Yet another example of a wonderful soundtrack born from a terrible film – a lively, melodic mix of classics and original (albeit knowingly derivative) music from **David A. Hughes** and **John Murphy**. So I threw away the cover and slipped the CD into the case for *Howards End* and nobody noticed.

The Sweet Hereafter

Blending the mesmeric drone of ancient instruments with the exotic sound of the East, Canada's **Mychael Danna** has produced a score of singular distinction, proving again that film music doesn't have to be symphonic wallpaper. In addition, Sarah Polley (who plays Nicole in the film) contributes five sweet, dreamlike songs.

This World, Then the Fireworks

A bit of a discovery, this, a smoochy, smoky, breezy and moody collection of jazz tracks by **Pete Rugolo** culled from the dreadful film noir stiff starring Billy Zane. Every film has its redemption.

Titanic

It won the Golden Globe, it climbed to the top of the US pop charts, but **James Horner**'s pretty, Celtic-tinged score is not the equal of his last film, *The Devil's Own*.

TwentyFourSeven

One of the year's more unexpected delights, a varied rock-folksy collection of tracks (notable cuts from Van Morrison, Beth Orton, Primal Scream, Tim Drake, The Charlatans) plus brief snatches of Boo Hewerdine and Neill MacColl's likeable score.

Washington Square

Why is it that the novels of Henry James inspire such poor movies and such wonderful film music? Following Wojciech Kilar's magnificent score for the woefully misconceived *The Portrait of a Lady* comes **Jan A.P. Kaczmarek**'s richly melancholic, densely melodic composition.

The Wedding Singer

Another prime compilation, with the peerless sounds of The Thompson Twins, Billy Idol, Culture Club... and Adam Sandler belting out 'Somebody Kill Me'.

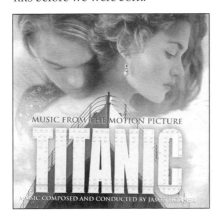

Bookshelf

James Cameron-Wilson

Elliott's Guide to Home Entertainment, by John Elliott; Aurum Press; £12.99; 954 pages.

By my last count, there are *fourteen* A-Z movie/video guides on the market. So what does *Elliott's* have that the others don't? Well, for a start it features TV mini-series, TV dramas, a lot of video dross and fairly extensive cast lists. Thus, you can look up *Inspector Wexford: Kissing the Gunner's Daughter* and discover that the good detective is unapproving of his daughter's new boyfriend. You can also find out that Don Fischer is 15th down the cast list of that 1992 classic *Sex, Love and Cold Hard Cash.* Furthermore, *Can I Do It 'Til I Need Glasses?* is, apparently, as bad as it sounds. However, what you won't find is (for instance) Ingmar Bergman's 1953 Expressionist landmark *Sawdust and Tinsel*, nor the Oscar-winning box-office hit *Call Me Madam.* This is because, to quote the book's author, 'The emphasis is now very firmly directed towards titles produced within the past ten years.' Nevertheless, the real classics are included (*Casablanca* is described as 'by no means a perfect film') as are the foreign hits (*Borsalino, Antonia's Line*). So, this will not only appeal to those who don't give a rat's ass for the forgotten gems of Hitchcock or Astaire, but will also strengthen the case for the cinema of Don 'The Dragon' Wilson and Eric Roberts. For reference buffs, it is perhaps an essential complement to *Maltin's Movie & Video Guide.* Now, you must excuse me while I go and look up Bob Clark's *Fudge-a-Mania.*

Final Curtain, by Everett Grant Jarvis; Biblios/Citadel Press; £17.99; 411 pages.

This has got to be one of the weirdest and certainly the most macabre film reference books of the year. Yet what is truly unsettling is that this is the *eighth* edition of the work. Nothing more than a series of tables, *Final Curtain* is plainly the product of a man severely afflicted by a desire to compile lists. Jarvis obviously sat down at his computer and jiggled inventories for the sheer hell of it. But what the author has failed to do is to provide a practical use for his obsession. Here, he provides an interminable register of film and TV personalities, arranged in order of death (from 1912 to 1996), with the cause of and/or location of their expiration listed alongside. So, should you wish to find out how Lillian 'Red Wing' St Cyr (who she?) shuffled off her mortal coil, you will have to know that she passed away in 1974 in order to learn that she 'died in New York, NY', aged 100. A number of entries don't even have a cause or location, which is a bit of a cheat (so why include them?). But fear not, Jarvis has incorporated a second register, in which his dead are arranged alphabetically, which sort of defeats the purpose of the first 125 pages. Then there's a table that breaks down the data of the first two sections, revealing that only one personality died in 1912, but 255 expired in 1995, which is less an indication of a growing fatality rate than of the names Jarvis has seen fit to include in any given year. He also enthrals us with the knowledge that 25 of his entries perished from lymphatic disease, 213 from Aids, 1,120 from cancer, eight from ulcers, and so on. The book's fourth zone comprises a list of cemeteries (complete with address and telephone number), followed by a chapter supplying a select, alphabetical list of stars and their place of rest (e.g. Joan Crawford can be found at Ferncliff Cemetery and Maus. in Hartsdale, New York, in unit 8, alcove E, crypt number 42). Undoubtedly all this will appeal to some readers, but then, from page 317, the book takes a dramatic U-turn by embracing the living. Here we have another list of film and TV personalities (dead and alive), arranged alphabetically, with their given name listed alongside. Huh? Jump to page 361 and Jarvis plies us with more lists in which he groups together famous spouses, fathers and sons, mothers, brothers, sisters, aunts and so on. There's more, including a totally pointless table of stars and the year they received Oscar nominations (but no film titles), which reveals a severe lack of direction. Pick from it what you will.

Hollywood: The New Generation,
by James Cameron-Wilson; Batsford; £15.99; 224 pages.

As a general rule I don't tend to write up my own books, but then I couldn't find anybody cheap enough to review it for me – besides, review copies were hard to come by. The purpose of the book is to plug a gap in the market (in some cases, to quench an insatiable craving) for serious information on the next generation of stars following in the grease stains of Costner, Willis and Ford. While newsagents' shelves are straining under the weight of fanzines, posters, postcards and other paraphernalia pertaining to the Brad Pitts and DiCaprios of this world, there was – until now – no reference that surveyed the stars in any beneficial depth. Thus, *Hollywood: The New Generation* was written to provide the filmographies, birthdays,

gossip, background, career assessments, film breakdowns, awards, personal idiosyncrasies and photographs of everybody from Tom Cruise to Will Smith via Claire Danes. One critic carped that nobody from the *Scream* films was included, but then the first *Scream* hadn't been released when the book was delivered to the publishers. And, as tempting as it may seem now to spend 14-hour days researching the lives of David Arquette and Rose McGowan, who is to say that they won't be reduced to taking cameos in *Dawson's Creek* two years hence? As for the book's literary merits – I just couldn't say.

Leonard Maltin's 1998 Movie & Video Guide;
Penguin; £8.99; 1,620 pages.

As the unfailing champion of all works of movie reference, *Maltin's* gets yet another mention here if only because there are still people out there who don't know about it. The same price it was last year (and three pages thicker), this guide may not have Matt Damon's birthday, but it reviews over 19,000 movies and includes comprehensive filmographies of major stars and directors. Besides the essential credits – star ratings, certificates, video and laserdisc availability, sequel information, running times (plus allusions to edited and censored versions), alternative titles, extensive cast listings, star cameos (credited or otherwise) and screen formats – the book boasts a thrifty wit (*Defcon 4* 'sounds like an industrial-strength roach killer, and it could use one'). Again, Maltin himself waxes conscientious in his engaging and informative intro, setting the record straight that Kristin Scott Thomas has no hyphen in her name and that Geoffrey Rush made his film debut in Gillian Armstrong's *Starstruck* and not *Shine*. Regarding the filmographies at the back of the book, the range embraces the likes of Abbott and Costello, Christopher Lee and Brad Pitt and boasts new entries on Leonardo DiCaprio, Nicole Kidman and George Lucas.

That's Sexploitation!, by Eddie
Muller and Daniel Faris; Titan Books; £14.99; 160 pages.

Subtitled 'The Forbidden World of "ADULTS ONLY" Cinema', this orgy of arcane information and tantalising illustration tackles a subject given little or no space by other film reference books. Well written and exhaustively researched, *That's Sexploitation!* (known as *Grindhouse* in the US) explores the history of celluloid smut from the cautionary independent films of Florence Reid (the wife of silent star Wallace Reid) to the proliferation of today's hardcore videos (the authors calculate that there are an average of 537,600 taped sexual acts available in the average American city). If one is to criticise this captivating volume, then it must be to question the tone adopted by it. In his erudite introduction, Geoffrey O'Brien refers to the punters of such forbidden material as being 'so desperate as scarcely to care whether the product delivers'. He has a point, but it seems an odd view to air in a book that is soliciting the prurient interest of those he condemns. The authors themselves are at pains to point out that they 'do not spend all their time watching Adults Only movies'. So, if they feel so guilty about it, why write the book? Be that as it may, their material does actually deliver.

The Ultimate Encyclopedia of Science Fiction, edited by David
Pringle; Carlton; £19.99; 304 pages.

As this handsome tome points out, science fiction has become the most dominant form of fiction in the twentieth century. The most globally popular TV series? Why, *Star Trek*, of course. The most famous radio drama? Orson Welles' revolutionary *The War of the Worlds*. The most significant novel? Orwell's *1984*, with its prescient warnings of Big Brother, doublethink and the thought police. And, pre *Titanic*, the top-grossing film of all time? *E.T. The Extra-Terrestrial*. And all this postulation prior to the release of *Independence Day* and *Men in Black*. With the accent on gloss rather than comprehensiveness, this well-rounded volume is an attractive starting point for budding sci-fi buffs. Spreading its net to include all aspects of the genre – genesis, themes, personalities, novels, film, TV, radio and magazines – it is nothing if not ambitious. In fact, because of its broad scope, film buffs may be disappointed, but then this is by no means a film book (the ultimate encyclopaedia of science fiction cinema is published by Aurum). Here, though, you will find chapters devoted to the wider manifestations of sci-fi (or sf, as this book prefers to call it). Thus, in the chapter 'Astounding Stories', you can find articles on 'future cities', 'genetic engineering' and 'inner space' – and even such thematic tangents as 'steampunk' and 'sex wars'. In the chapter 'They Came From Hollywood', key films are chronologically listed – from the Russian *Aelita* (1924) to *Waterworld* – with a variety of sidebars covering parallel themes (Disney, paranoia, 'the great apes'). And then there are sections on TV, radio, prominent personalities (Isaac Asimov, Gerry Anderson, Steven Spielberg), fictional characters (Captain America, Winston Smith) and, finally, a brief glossary.

Variety International Film Guide 1998, edited by Peter Cowie; Andre Deutsch; £14.99; 432 pages.

I've always liked this book. In a tide of repetitive annuals, this informed, intelligent survey of world cinema explores areas unheard of by other publications. It's comforting to know that after the 34 years since its genesis, there's still a journal dedicated to unearthing the joys of Armenian, Estonian and Zimbabwean cinema. Indeed, each country is afforded its own chapter, complete with comment, news, a breakdown of the major films, plus – wherever realisable – photographs, awards and box-office statistics. Who, for instance, would have guessed that *The Hunchback of Notre Dame* was the top-grossing film in France during the 1996-7 period (where the cartoon was publicly reviled), or that *Michael Collins* made more money in Ireland than *Independence Day* (there's national

pride for you)? Even stranger is that *Jingle All the Way* out-grossed *Mission: Impossible* in Peru, and that Bosnia and Herzegovina staged the Sarajevo Film Festival, supported by the likes of Ingmar Bergman, Francis Ford Coppola and Martin Scorsese. Stretching out to 432 pages, the guide also offers supplementary sections on animation, international film magazines and bookshops, archives, film schools, festivals and much, much more, You can't really overestimate the usefulness of the thing.

VideoHound's Golden Movie Retriever 1998, edited by Martin Connors and Jim Craddock; Visible Ink; £15.50; 1,711 pages.

First published in 1991 and now available in its seventh edition, this massive tome is as zestful, irreverent and action packed as ever. Priding itself on being the only guide to include all new video titles, the *Golden Movie Retriever* is as useful as it is a fun browse. Indeed, its range is formidable and sometimes close to inconceivable. Besides the traditional coverage of video titles (with review, credits, rating, etc.), the book packs in a list of alternative titles, awards and nominations (including Sundance, the Cesars and Golden Raspberries), a table of foreign titles (comprising features from Algeria to Yugoslavia), filmographies of stars, character actors, directors, scenarists, cinematographers and composers, plus guides to distributors and web sites. However, my own favourite is the extensive table of themes, which runs the gamut from 'Africa', 'Aids' and 'air disasters' to 'dates from hell', 'killer appliances' (cf. *Microwave Massacre*) and 'revealing swimwear' (cf. *Best Buns on the Beach*). A real find and a must for all film fans (and, considering the amount of material packed into its 1,711 pages, the best value film reference on the market). N.B. All titles cited (including those featured in the filmographies and awards section) are only listed if available on video in America and, ergo, in the main portion of the book.

VideoHound's Independent Film Guide, by Monica Sullivan; Visible Ink; £14.00; 558 pages.

With the emergence of independent cinema as an acknowledged commercial force, the timing of this book could not be more germane. Citing the independent feature as an 'audacious, risk-taking and original movie made outside of the Hollywood system', the publication embraces 800 titles, providing generous commentary, adequate credits and, where applicable, lists of awards. Indeed, the book's range is formidable. *The English Patient*, *Fargo* and *Four Weddings and a Funeral* share equal billing with *Brief Encounter*, *The Manchurian Candidate* and *My Life as a Dog*, while even such suspect efforts as *Confessions of a Window Cleaner*, Franco Zeffirelli's *Jane Eyre*, *Princess and the Goblin* and *Silent Tongue* get a look-in. Notwithstanding, too many omissions are conspicuous by their absence. While inane soft porn like *Emmanuelle* is given due space, such seminal, cutting-edge ventures as *Freaks*, *Reefer Madness*, *Shadows*, *Shock Corridor*, *El Topo*, *Eraserhead*, *Bad Taste* and even John Waters' quintessentially independent *Pink Flamingos*, are all AWOL. Still, Monica Sullivan's prose is chatty and informative and her compilation goes some way in redressing a cinematic imbalance.

VideoHound's Soundtracks, edited by Didier C. Deutsch; Visible Ink; £19.00; 1,024 pages.

So, you want to find out which movies have featured the songs of Terence Trent D'Arby? Simple: *Beverly Hills Cop III*, *The Fan* and *Prêt-à-Porter*. Well, then, what films has David Arnold scored? Again, simple: *Stargate*, *Last of the Dogmen* and *Independence Day*. OK, so on which soundtrack will one find the song 'Johnny B. Goode'? Answer: *American Graffiti* and *Back to the Future*. Whatever your musical film question, this magnificent tome can serve up the answer in seconds. With the interest in soundtracks growing by the month, VideoHound's latest compendium is a gift to enthusiasts of cinema and music alike. The downside is that an undertaking like this, by its very nature, has to be selective. Thus, where the book cites eleven albums featuring the inimitable voice of Aretha Franklin, it overlooks such soundtracks as *The First Wives Club*, *Miracle on 34th Street* and *Sister Act 2*. Besides, David Arnold also wrote the music for *The Young Americans* (prior to such post-deadline scores as *A Life Less Ordinary*, *Tomorrow Never Dies* and *Godzilla*). But *VideoHound's Soundtracks* doesn't profess to be a comprehensive directory. None the less, it does include over 2,000 entries on the most 'significant' soundtracks you'd want to put money down for, whether it be Bernard Herrmann's celebrated score to *Psycho*, the pop-infested compilation of *Forrest Gump*, the original Broadway recording of *Carousel* (or the 1965 and 1994 revivals), Carl Davis's music for the BBC's *Pride and Prejudice* or a compilation like *Gotta Dance!: The Best of Gene Kelly* and *Country Goes to the Movies*. Still, you'd think there would have been room for *The Blues Brothers* or *That's Entertainment!*

Anyway, each album is reviewed by an expert in his field and is accompanied by track listings, running times, artists, dates and various essential credits. The reviews themselves are informed and accessible, if occasionally on the brief side. And then there's the invaluable cross-referencing at the back of the book, with lists of titles, composers, producers, orchestras, conductors, artists and songs. I mean, you do really have to buy the thing immediately.

Other notable books:

The BFI Companion to Crime, edited by Phil Hardy; Cassell.
Cagney, by John McCabe; Aurum.
Close Up: Martin Scorsese – The Making of His Movies, by Andy Dougan; Orion.
Close Up: Oliver Stone – The Making of His Movies, by Chris Salewicz; Orion.
Don't Tell Dad: A Memoir, by Peter Fonda; Simon and Schuster.
Film Posters of the 60s, edited by Tony Nourmand and Graham Marsh; Aurum.
The Films and Career of James Stewart, by Tony Thomas; Carol via Biblios.
Fritz Lang: The Nature of the Beast, by Patrick McGilligan; Faber.
The Hammer Story, by Marcus Hearn and Alan Barnes; Titan Books.
Harvey Keitel: The Art of Darkness, by Marshall Fine; HarperCollins.
High Concept: Don Simpson and the Hollywood Culture of Excess, by Charles Fleming; Bloomsbury.
Hong Kong Babylon, by Fredric Dannen; Faber and Faber.
Hurrell's Hollywood Portraits, by Mark A. Vieira; Abrams.
Imagining Reality: The Faber Book of Documentary, by Kevin Macdonald and Mark Cousins; Faber.
James Cameron's Titanic, the 'story of the film' edited by W. Marsh; Boxtree.
Killer Instinct; Jane Hamsher's record of her involvement on the making of *Natural Born Killers*; Orion.
Kiss Kiss Bang Bang! The Unofficial James Bond Film Companion, by Alan Barns and Marcus Hearn; Batsford.
Making Mischief: The Cult Films of Pete Walker, by Steve Chibnall; FAB Press.
The Making of Joel and Ethan Coen's The Big Lebowski, by William Preston Robertson; Faber.
Me and Hitch, by Evan Hunter (aka Ed McBain); Faber and Faber.
Meat is Murder! An Illustrated Guide to Cannibal Culture, by Mikita Brottman; Creation.
Monty Python Encyclopedia, by Robert Ross; Batsford. Everything you wanted to know about TV's greatest comedy team.
The Movie Book of the Western, Ian Cameron and Douglas Pye; Studio Vista.
Nosferatu in Love; Jim Shepard's novelisation of the life of F.W. Murnau; Faber and Faber.
Paul Verhoeven, by Rob van Scheers, translated by Aletta Stevens; Faber.
A Personal Journey with Martin Scorsese Through American Movies, by Martin Scorsese and Michael Henry Wilson; Faber and Faber.
Peter Cook, A Biography, by Harry Thompson; Hodder & Stoughton.
Peter Greenaway: Museums and Moving Images, by David Pasco; Reaktion.
Picture; Lillian Ross on the making of John Huston's *The Red Badge of Courage*; Faber and Faber.
Pornocopia: Porn, Sex, Technology and Desire, by Laurence O'Toole; Serpent's Tail.
Projections 8: Film-makers on Film-making, edited by John Boorman and Walter Donhoe; Faber and Faber.
Robert Bolt: Scenes From Two Lives, by Adrian Turner; Hutchinson.
Special Effects in Film and Tele-vision, by Jake Hamilton; Dorling Kindersley.
Stanley Kubrick: A Biography, by John Baxter; HarperCollins.
Stars, Stars, Stars...Off the Screen, Edward Quinn; Scalo.
Star Wars: The Annotated Screen-plays, by Laurent Bouzereau; Boxtree.
Tender Comrades: A Backstory of the Hollywood Blacklist, by Patrick McGilligan and Paul Buhle; St Martin's Press.
Travolta: The Life, by Nigel Andrews; Bloomsbury.
The Undeclared War: The Struggle For Control of the World's Film Industry, by David Puttnam and Neil Watson; HarperCollins.
VideoHound's Video Premiers, by Mike Mayo; Visible Ink; £14.00; 431 pages.
Weirdsville USA: The Obsessive Universe of David Lynch, by Paul A. Woods; Plexus.
Wes Craven's Last House on the Left: The Making of a Cult Classic, by David A. Szulkin; FAB Press.

In Memoriam

James Cameron-Wilson

Sonny Bono

Born: 16 February 1935 in Detroit, Michigan.
Died: 5 January 1998 in South Lake Tahoe, Nevada.
Real name: Salvatore Bono.

Sonny Bono was best known as the short one in the singing/bickering Sonny and Cher partnership on TV and in the charts (remember 'I Got You Babe' and 'The Beat Goes On'?). Later, he became almost as well known as the mayor of Palm Springs, memorably starting up a local film festival and banning the wearing of G-strings in public. He did, however, also appear in a few films, including *Good Times* (with Cher, his then-wife), *Escape to Athena, Airplane II: The Sequel*, John Waters' *Hairspray* and *Under the Boardwalk*. He was killed when he ski'd into a tree on the slopes of the Heavenly Ski Resort.

Lloyd Bridges

Born: 15 January 1913 in San Leandro, California.
Died: 10 March 1998 'of natural causes' in Los Angeles.

A contract player at Columbia in the 1940s, Bridges laboured in supporting roles in forgettable B-movies until landing the lead in the forgettable *She's a Lady Too* (1944). He remained a relative non-entity for another eight years, when he won the part of Gary Cooper's disloyal deputy in *High Noon* (1952). His fortunes improved on TV when he played underwater adventurer Mike Nelson in the series *Sea Hunt*, which ran from 1957 to 1961 and flourished in syndication. He followed this with *The Lloyd Bridges Show* (1962-63) and became a familiar face on the small screen in a slew of TV movies. In 1980 his career enjoyed an enormous boost when he took on the role of an eccentric air traffic controller in *Airplane!* (and its 1982 sequel) and he became a reliable character actor in a number of high-profile films, including *Hot Shots!, Blown Away* and *Jane Austen's MAFIA!* His two sons, Beau and Jeff, have also done rather well in the acting business.

Saul Chaplin

Born: 19 February 1912 in Brooklyn, New York.
Died: 15 November 1997 at the Cedar-Sinai Medical Center, following injuries sustained in a fall.
Real name: Saul Kaplan.

A celebrated composer, arranger, musical director and producer, Chaplin will be best remembered for his collaboration on the Oscar-winning orchestration and scoring of *An American in Paris* (1951), *Seven Brides for Seven Brothers* (1954) and *West Side Story* (1961). A product of Tin Pan Alley, he was writing songs at the age of 20 and via vaudeville and Broadway went on to help score such films as *Cover Girl* (1944), *The Jolson Story* (1945), *On the Town* (1949), *Kiss Me Kate* (1953) and

High Society (1956). Then, in 1957, he turned his hand to associate production, working on such projects as *Les Girls* (1957), *Can-Can* (1960) and *The Sound of Music* (1965). He was also the credited producer of the disastrous Julie Andrews musical *Star!* (1968). His autobiography, *The Golden Age of Movie Musicals and Me*, was published in 1994.

Rosalie Crutchley

Born: 4 January 1921 in London.
Died: 28 July 1997.

An imposing character actress, Ms Crutchley was never afraid to take on unsympathetic roles, which her dark colouring and gaunt visage rather encouraged. A noted stage actress (who perhaps did her best work with John Gielgud at London's Haymarket Theatre, 1944-45), Crutchley distinguished such films as *Quo Vadis?* (1951), *The Spanish Gardener*, *A Tale of Two Cities*, *Sons and Lovers*, *Freud*, *Man of La Mancha*, *Mahler*, *A World Apart*, *Little Dorrit*, *The Fool* and *Four Weddings and a Funeral*. Ironically, her second former husband, the actor and director Peter Ashmore, died two days before she did.

Lloyd Bridges (right) with Murray Hamilton in the 1971 TV movie *A Tattered Web*

John Denver

Born: 31 December 1943 in Roswell, New Mexico.
Died: 13 October 1997 when the single-engined home-built plane he was piloting (without a valid licence) crashed into the water of Monterey Bay, northern California.
Real name: Henry John Deutschendorf Jr.

A Country & Western singer-songwriter best known for the hits 'Take Me Home, Country Roads', 'Rocky Mountain High', 'Annie's Song' and 'Thank God I'm A Country Boy', Denver also dabbled in acting. He played the assistant manager of a supermarket who becomes a messenger for The Almighty in *Oh, God!* (1977) and was then involved with the ghost of Hume Cronyn in the award-winning TV movie *Foxfire* (1987).

John Derek

Born: 12 August 1926 in Hollywood.
Died: 22 May 1998 in Santa Maria, California, following heart surgery.

Following his role as a juvenile delinquent defended by Humphrey Bogart's reluctant lawyer in *Knock On Any Door* (1949), the conventionally handsome Derek graduated to leading man status in a chain of

B-movies and costume dramas. However, in his later years he became better known as a photographer and as the husband of his naked subjects, Ursula Andress, Linda Evans and Bo Derek. He also turned to directing, churning out soft-focus erotic vehicles for his wives: *Once Before I Die* (with Andress), *Childish Things* (with Evans), *Tarzan the Ape Man*, *Bolero* and *Ghosts Can't Do It* (all with Bo).

Billie Dove

Born: 14 May 1900 in New York City.
Died: 31 December 1997 of pneumonia in Woodland Hills, California.
Real name: Lillian Bohney.

Such was the popularity of Billie Dove in her day that the post office in Los Angeles was forced to take on extra employees just to deal with her fan mail. A Ziegfeld showgirl, Ms Dove got her break in the 1921 *Get-Rich-Quick-Wallingford* (directed by future husband Irving Willat) and went on to star in many silent and early sound films, winning the sobriquet of 'The American Beauty'. She also enjoyed a celebrated fling with Howard Hughes, before retiring in 1932 as the wife of a prosperous rancher.

Chris Farley

Born: 15 February 1964 in Madison, Wisconsin.
Died: 18 December 1997 in Chicago of a drug overdose.

A stout, rambunctious comic from the *Saturday Night Live* stable, Chris Farley secured some success in the films *Tommy Boy* and *Black Sheep*, enough to establish a $6 million payday for *Beverly Hills Ninja*, another hit. Much compared to John Belushi for his unrestrained lifestyle and fondness for food, alcohol and drugs, Farley was an unapologetic fan of the late comic, citing Belushi as the reason he entered comedy in the first place. He reportedly knew every Belushi skit off by heart and even thought about playing him in a screen biography. As it happens, he was due to play another tragic fat comic, Fatty Arbuckle – from a script

Chris Farley (right) with friend and colleague David Spade – in *Tommy Boy*

by David Mamet – when he died, aged 33, the same age that Belushi passed away from a drug overdose. He was last seen in *Dirty Work* and *Almost Heroes*.

Alice Faye

Born: 5 May 1912 in 'Hell's Kitchen', New York City.
Died: 9 May 1998 of cancer in Rancho Mirage, California.
Real name: Alice Jeanne Leppert.

A sunny, peachy blonde singer, dancer and actress, Alice Faye brightened the lives of countless fans even though she was never fully appreciated by the critics. Leaving school at 14, she joined the Chester Hale Dance Group and then danced her way into the 'George White's Scandals' revue. It was in the chorus of the latter that she was discovered by Rudy Vallee and subsequently cast in the 1934 film version when the original star, Lilian Harvey, walked off the project. Fox came running with a contract and Faye

starred opposite Spencer Tracy in the taut melodrama *Now I'll Tell*, but she didn't display her real talent until ten films later when she starred in a trio of effervescent musicals, *Wake Up and Live*, *You Can't Have Everything* and *You're a Sweetheart* (all 1937). Her other major successes included *In Old Chicago*, *Alexander's Ragtime Band* (both 1938), *Rose of Washington Square*, *Hollywood Cavalcade* (both 1939), *Lillian Russell* (1940) and *Hello Frisco Hello* (1943). She married the singer and bandleader Phil Harris in 1941 and after her part in *Fallen Angel* (1945) was severely reduced, she argued with producer Darryl F. Zanuck and called it quits. She returned to films 17 years later, playing Pamela Tiffin's mother in the disastrous remake of *State Fair* and a friendly singing waitress in the 1978 *The Magic of Lassie*.

Dodi Fayed

Born: 1955 in Egypt.
Died: 31 August 1997 in a car crash in Paris.

Known less for his films than for his string of famous female escorts (Britt Ekland, Winona Ryder, Brooke Shields, Koo Stark, Princess Stephanie of Monaco), Dodi hit the headlines in earnest when he started courting Diana, the Princess of Wales. Heir to the Harrods empire ruled over by his father, Mohamed

Al Fayed, Dodi earned credits as a producer on such films as *Breaking Glass*, *Chariots of Fire*, *F/X*, *F/X2 – The Deadly Art of Illusion*, *Hook* and *The Scarlet Letter*. However, in Hollywood he was better known for pulling finance *out* of movies.

Samuel Fuller

Born: 12 August 1911 in Worcester, Massachusetts.
Died: 30 October 1997 'of natural causes' in the Hollywood Hills.

A genuine character who honed his world view while riding freight trains, penning pulp fiction and fighting in North Africa during the Second World War, Fuller was seldom recognised as a distinctive filmmaker in his day. Yet in retrospect his amoral, kinetic low-budget features have attained a cult following – and the unstinting praise of such directors as Godard and Wenders. Breaking into movies in 1936 with his script for *Hats Off*, Fuller directed his first feature, *I Shot Jesse James* – from his own screenplay – in 1949. His subsequent pictures included *The Steel Helmet* (1951), *Underworld USA* (1961), *Shock Corridor* (1963), *The Naked Kiss* (1964), *The Big Red One* (1980) and the banned *White Dog* (1982). His

Alice Faye (extreme right) with Jack Haley and Shirley Temple in Irving Cummings' 1936 *Poor Little Rich Girl*

rugged, irascible personality – stamped with ubiquitous cigar – was used to fine effect in such films as *The Last Movie, Hammett, La Vie de Boheme* and Wenders' *The American Friend* and *The State of Things*. In fact, Fuller's cameo in Godard's *Pierrot le Fou* (1965) summed up the director's whole attitude to cinema when his character stressed 'a film is like a battleground: love, hate, action, violence, death – in a word: emotion!'

Brian Glover

Born: 2 April 1934 in Sheffield, South Yorkshire.
Died: 24 July 1997 from a brain tumour.

A distinctive character actor recognisable by his bald pate and rotund appearance, Brian Glover was best known as rough and ready working-class types. A former wrestler, he was teaching English and French when a fellow tutor suggested he play the autocratic games master – Sugden – in Ken Loach's *Kes*, based on the tutor's own novel, *A Kestrel For a Knave*. The film was a success and the rookie thespian, 35 at the time, never looked back. Since then he added his rough, singular brand of menace and comedy to such films as *O Lucky Man!, Brannigan, Jabberwocky, An American Werewolf in London, Britannia Hospital, Laughterhouse, Alien 3, Leon the Pig Farmer* (as Yorkshire pig farmer Brian Chadwick), *Stiff Upper Lips* and *Snow White – A Tale of Terror*. He also dabbled in TV scriptwriting and lent his voice to the 'gaffer' in the Tetley tea commercials.

Phil Hartman

Born: 24 September 1948 in Brantford, Canada.
Died: 28 May 1998 in Los Angeles from several gunshot wounds to the neck and head.

The longest running member of TV's *Saturday Night Live* (he appeared in 153 episodes), Hartman was an Emmy-winning writer of the show and a highly adept comic actor. Frequently stealing films from his more famous co-stars, he was a past

William Hickey

Born: 19 September 1927 in Brooklyn, New York.
Died: 29 June 1997 in New York City from complications of emphysema and bronchitis.

One of Hollywood's most singular character actors, William Hickey resembled a gnarled willow with advanced bronchitis and was adept at playing doddery capos, moribund priests and irritable uncles. Although he made his film debut in the 1957 *A Hatful of Rain*, Hickey was better known as a drama coach with the HB Studios in Greenwich Village, New York, and tutored such future stars as Barbra Streisand, Steve McQueen, George Segal and Christine Lahti. However, at the age of 57, his performance as the infirm, wise old Don Corrado Prizzi in John Huston's *Prizzi's Honor* earned him an Oscar nomination and belated offers of work. Since then he made memorable contributions to *The Name of the Rose, Bright Lights Big City, Da, Sea of Love, National Lampoon's Christmas Vacation, My Blue Heaven, Forget Paris* and, his last film, *MouseHunt*.

Juzo Itami

Born: 15 May 1933 in Kyoto, Japan.
Died: 20 December 1997 in Japan of suicide.
Real name: Yoshihiro Ikeuchi.

A director best known for the international hits *Tampopo* and *A Taxing Woman*, Itami was generally considered to be the finest satirist of the Japanese New Wave. He is survived by his wife Nobuko Miyamoto, the star of his two best-known films. Accused by the

master at straight-faced playing, enlivening such features as *CB4, So I Married an Axe Murderer* (as a stony Alcatraz warden called Vicky), *Greedy, Houseguest, Sgt Bilko, Jingle All the Way* and *Small Soldiers*. He is also remembered as the designer of the Crosby, Stills and Nash logo. He was shot dead in bed by his wife, Brynn, who later turned the gun on herself. They left behind two children: a nine-year-old boy and six-year-old girl.

Brian Glover

Japanese tabloid *Flash* of having an extramarital affair, Itami denied the allegations in a note before jumping off the roof of an eight-storey building.

Stubby Kaye

Born: 11 November 1918 in New York City.
Died: 14 December 1997 in Rancho Mirage of lung cancer.

A rotund, ebullient comic, singer and actor, Stubby Kaye started out in vaudeville at the age of 21, played

Phil Hartman as he appeared in *Jingle All the Way*

Nicely-Nicely Johnson in the original 1950 Broadway production of *Guys and Dolls* and made his film debut three years later in the Gregory Ratoff-directed comedy *Taxi*. Since then, he lit up a number of comedies and musicals with his effervescent presence, notably singing 'Sit Down You're Rockin' The Boat' in the film version of *Guys and Dolls* (1955) and 'I Love To Cry At Weddings' in *Sweet Charity* (1968). He also played Marvin Acme, head of the biggest gag company in Toontown, in *Who Framed Roger Rabbit* (1988).

Andrew Keir

Born: 3 April 1926 in Scotland.
Died: 5 October 1997.

An imposing Scottish character actor, Andrew Keir graduated from picturesque comedies like *The 'Maggie'* (1953) to a string of costume dramas and war films. Then, abruptly, he made his name as Professor Quartermas in Hammer's *Quatermas and the Pit* (1967). Other credits include *Tunes of Glory*, *Greyfriar's Bobby*, *Cleopatra*, *Lord Jim*, *Dracula Prince of Darkness*, *Daleks – Invasion Earth 2150 AD*, *Blood From the Mummy's Tomb* and Michael Caton-Jones' *Rob Roy*, in which he played the Duke of Argyll.

Jean-Claude Lauzon

Born: 29 September 1953 in Montreal, Quebec.
Died: 10 August 1997 in a plane crash in northern Quebec.

Along with David Cronenberg, Atom Egoyan and Denys Arcand, Lauzon was one of an elite cadre of film-makers celebrated outside of their native Canada. Following work as a taxi driver and scuba diver, Lauzon attended the University of Quebec and made his first feature, *Night Zoo*, in 1987. A fairly unpleasant drama about an ex-con attempting to organise a hunting trip with his father, the film collected an unprecedented 13 Genie awards at the Canadian Oscars. Then, five years later, Lauzon directed the disturbing and unforgettable *Leolo*, the stunningly visual exploration of a boy's inner fantasy life (largely drawn from the director's own).

Something of a recluse who preferred to hunt in the Canadian tundra and shoot commercials, Lauzon recently committed to his third feature – and his first in English. He was killed alongside his girlfriend Marie-Soleil Tougas, a popular star of Quebec TV.

Jack Lord

Born: 30 December 1930 in New York City.
Died: 21 January 1998 in Honolulu of congestive heart failure.
Real name: John Ryan.

Forever associated with his jaw-jutting performance as Steve McGarrett in TV's long-running *Hawaii Five-O* (1968-80), Jack Lord appeared in a few films. Of these, his role as Felix Leiter in *Dr No* (1962) is probably the best known. Latterly, he had been suffering from Alzheimer's disease.

Daniel Massey

Born: 10 October 1933 in London.
Died: 25 March 1998 of heart failure in London.

A charismatic character actor, Daniel Massey was the son of the Canadian film star Raymond Massey and sister of the actress Anna Massey. Spreading his talents evenly across the stage, screen and TV, he made his film debut aged eight in *In Which We*

Burgess Meredith (left) seen here with Gene Hackman and Teri Garr in Peter Masterson's *Full Moon in Blue Water*

Serve (1942), the World War II classic co-directed by his godfather, Noel Coward, and David Lean. Twenty-six years later he received an Oscar nomination for playing Coward opposite Julie Andrews in *Star!*, Robert Wise's big-budget biography of Gertrude Lawrence. Other film credits included *The Entertainer*, *The Amorous Adventures of Moll Flanders*, *Mary Queen of Scots* (as Robert Dudley), *The Incredible Sarah*, *Bad Timing*, *Scandal* and *In the Name of the Father*. His marriages to the actresses Adrienne Corri and Penelope Wilton both ended in divorce.

Burgess Meredith

Born: 16 November 1907 in Cleveland, Ohio.
Died: 9 September 1997 in Malibu, California.

An irascible character actor, Burgess Meredith could cut quite a formidable figure in spite of his diminutive stature. Although he made his film debut as long ago as 1936 (in *Winterset*), he kept on resurrecting his career, refusing to disappear into TV stock. He was the lead in Lewis Milestone's *Of Mice and Men* (1939) – as George – and made a memorable impression as the war correspondent Ernie Pyle in *The Story of G.I. Joe* (1945). He also notched up starring roles in *San Francisco Docks*, *Street of Chance* and *Mine Own Executioner* and starred in and directed the suspenseful psychological thriller *The Man on the Eiffel Tower* (1949). After a brush with the House Un-American Activities

Committee in the 1950s (he was considered an unfriendly witness), he fell out of view for a while but, in 1962, returned in Otto Preminger's powerful denouncement of McCarthyism, *Advise and Consent* (ironically playing an informing witness). He became a household name as the eccentric Penguin in the *Batman* TV series (1966-68) and landed his first Oscar nomination as Harry, the down-at-heel vaudevillian, in John Schlesinger's *The Day of the Locust* (1975). He secured a second nomination – and a renewed burst of fame – as the tough-as-nails trainer, Mickey, in *Rocky* (1976), and was again unforgettable as Jack Lemmon's horny, foul-mouthed 94-year-old father in *Grumpy Old Men* (1993). His fourth marriage (1944-49) was to the actress Paulette Goddard, and he penned his autobiography, *So Far, So Good*, in 1994.

Toshiro Mifune

Born: 1 April 1920 in Tsingtao, China.
Died: 24 December 1997 in Mitaka, Japan, of 'organ failure'.

Not only was Toshiro Mifune the biggest star of the Japanese cinema, he was one of the most globally recognisable faces of Japan. The son of a doctor, he joined the army, then won a studio talent contest that led to a series of small movie roles. He was given the lead in *Snow Trail* (1947), then starred as a crook with tuberculosis in *Drunken Angel*, for Akira Kurosawa. The latter was immediately taken with the mercurial, budding star, noting, 'His reactions are extraordinary. If I say one thing, he understands ten. He reacts very quickly to the director's intentions.' Kurosawa and Mifune were to make a symbiotic team and when the actor starred in the filmmaker's *Rashomon* (1950) he became an internationally recognisable name. The subsequent success and cult following of Kurosawa's *Seven Samurai* (1954) cemented Mifune's stardom, which he backed up with parts in the director's *Throne of Blood*, *The Lower Depths*, *Yojimbo* and *Red Beard*. Best known for his warrior roles, Mifune was actually an extremely versatile

A rather young Robert Mitchum

actor, playing detectives, truck drivers, businessmen, admirals and even a Mexican peasant. Occasionally, he made appearances in American films, including *Grand Prix*, *Hell in the Pacific*, *Paper Tiger*, *Midway*, *Inchon!*, *1941* and, in 1993, *Shadow of the Wolf*.

Robert Mitchum

Born: 6 August 1917 in Bridgeport, Connecticut.
Died: 1 July 1997 (in his sleep) of emphysema and lung cancer, in Santa Barbara, California.

Famous for his tough guy persona, heavy drinking and sleepy, heavy-lidded gaze, Robert Mitchum was the ultimate anti-star, a man who once swore, 'I've never been an actor – and I've got 70 movies to prove it.' The son of a railroad switchman, Mitchum was just two when his father was crushed to death between two carriages, leaving his mother seven months' pregnant with her third child. At 16, Mitchum was arrested for vagrancy and served seven days on a Georgia chain gang where he almost lost his left leg. Later, he worked at a variety of jobs, including dishwasher, ditch-digger, nightclub bouncer and astrologist's publicist and, as a professional boxer, was a veteran of 27 fights. He had a

bit as a villain in the Hopalong Cassidy western *Border Patrol* (1943) and went on to make another 22 movies in the first 18 months of his film career. 'I was getting a hundred bucks a week plus all the horse manure I could take home,' he reasoned. The size of his parts increased until, in 1945, his role as Lt Walker in *The Story of G.I. Joe* earned him an Oscar nomination and universal raves. Overall, he made more than 100 pictures, most notably *Out of the Past*, *The Big Steal*, *River of No Return* (opposite Marilyn Monroe), *The Night of the Hunter* (in which he played Harry Powell, a homicidal preacher with 'love' and 'hate' tattooed on his knuckles), *Heaven Knows Mr Allison* (his own favourite), *The Sundowners*, *Cape Fear*, *El Dorado*, *Farewell My Lovely*, *The Friends of Eddie Coyle* and his last film, Jim Jarmusch's *Dead Man*. In the words of David Lean (who directed him in *Ryan's Daughter*): 'Mitchum can, simply by being there, make almost any other actor look like a hole in the screen.'

Jeanette Nolan

Born: 30 December 1911 in Los Angeles.
Died: 5 June 1998 in Los Angeles, following a stroke.

Jeannette Nolan started her film career somewhat inauspiciously as

She Jane: Maureen O'Sullivan in her most famous incarnation – in *Tarzan and His Mate*, with Johnny Weissmuller

Lady Macbeth in Orson Welles' 1948 film, but recovered to become a staple in westerns. She was also the ungrieving widow Bertha Duncan in Fritz Lang's *The Big Heat* (1953) and was a regular in the TV series *Hotel de Paree*, *The Richard Boone Show*, *The Virginian* (as Holly Grainger) and *Dirty Sally* (as Sally). At 85 she played Ellen Booker, mother to Robert Redford, in *The Horse Whisperer*. She was married to the character actor John McIntire (who died in 1991) and was the mother of actor Tim McIntire (who died of heart failure in 1986).

Maureen O'Sullivan

Born: 17 May 1911 in Boyle, County Roscommon, Ireland.
Died: 23 June 1988 in the suburbs of Phoenix, Arizona, of a heart attack.

Typecast as virginal ingenues, Maureen O'Sullivan will forever be associated with her part as Jane in the six Tarzan films she starred in with Johnny Weissmuller. Discovered at Dublin's International Horse Show by Frank Borzage, she was cast in the director's 1930 soap opera *Song o' My Heart* and subsequently landed good roles in *A Connecticut Yankee* and

Payment Deferred. In 1932 she played Jane in *Tarzan, the Ape Man* and went on to appear in such films as *The Barretts of Wimpole Street*, *David Copperfield*, *Anna Karenina* and *A Day at the Races*. She retired in 1942 to play house with her husband, the film director John Farrow, but returned in 1948 as the wife of Ray Milland in Farrow's *The Big Clock*. Her later films included *Bonzo Goes To College*, *Never Too Late*, *Hannah and Her Sisters* and *Peggy Sue Got Married*. The mother of Mia Farrow, she accused Woody Allen – her daughter's ex-lover – of being 'a desperate and evil man'.

Denver Pyle

Born: 11 May 1920 in Bethune, Colorado.
Died: 23 December 1997 in Los Angeles, of lung cancer.

A rangy, hard-working character actor, Denver Pyle will be best remembered in his autumnal years for playing wise ol' Uncle Jesse in the TV series *The Dukes of Hazzard*. A regular in westerns, Pyle hid his distinctive features behind a beard in his later films, although his more notable credits include the earlier *Johnny Guitar*, *The Alamo* and *The Man Who Shot Liberty Valance*. He was notable as the irate sheriff in *Bonnie and Clyde* and, on television, played Caleb in *Gunsmoke* and Mr Darlin' on *The Andy Griffith Show*.

Gene Raymond

Born: 13 August 1908 in New York City.
Died: 3 May 1998 of pneumonia in Los Angeles.
Real name: Gene Guion.

A former child actor, Gene Raymond was a leading man in the 1930s but is still probably best known as the husband of Jeanette MacDonald from 1937 to her death in 1965. His films included *Red Dust*, *Zoo in Budapest*, *Flying Down to Rio* (co-starring Fred Astaire and Ginger Rogers), Hitchcock's *Mr and Mrs Smith* and, in 1964, *The Best Man*. In 1948 he directed himself in the Hawaii-set mystery *Million Dollar Weekend*.

Bill Shine

Born: 20 October 1911 in London.
Died: August 1997.
Real name: Wilfred William Dennis Shine Jr.

A ubiquitous presence in British films from 1929 to the 1960s, Shine was a dependable character actor who cut an aristocratic if absent-minded figure with his gangly build and omnipresent handlebar moustache. In all, he appeared in 164 films, including *The Scarlet Pimpernel*, *Under the Greenwood Tree*, *Father Brown*, *Richard III*, *Blue Murder at St Trinian's* and *The Jigsaw Man*.

Frank Sinatra

Born: 12 December 1915 in Monroe Street, Hoboken, New Jersey.
Died: 14 May 1998 of a heart attack in Los Angeles.
Nicknames: Ol' Blue Eyes, Chairman of the Board, The Voice.

Described as the entertainer of the century, Frank Sinatra was a Grammy-winning balladeer, Oscar-winning actor, womaniser, teen idol, serial husband, father, tycoon, drinker, film director and philanthropist, as well as a friend of presidents and the Mafia. The son of a boxer and nurse, both Italian immigrants, he was an ardent admirer of Bing Crosby and quit school at 16 to sing at local nightclubs on the weekend. For money, he loaded delivery trucks for the *Jersey Journal*, was promoted to sports writer and dallied in local amateur singing contests. With three colleagues he formed The Hoboken Four, who, after winning a radio talent show, toured with the Major Bowes Amateur Hour and thus Sinatra's radio career began to take off. By 1939 he had cut his first record (uncredited) and two years later had a number one hit with 'I'll Never Smile Again'. The same year he made his film debut in *Las Vegas Nights* (singing 'I'll Never Smile Again') and in 1943 he was starring opposite Michele Morgan and Jack Haley in the RKO musical *Higher and Higher*. During his career as a singer he recorded over 100 albums, turned the hits 'My Way' and 'New York New York' into personal anthems and appeared in a number of outstanding films, including *Anchors Aweigh*, *On the Town*, *From Here to Eternity* (for which he won the Oscar as Best Supporting Actor), *Guys and Dolls*, *The Man With the Golden Arm*, *High Society*, *Pal Joey*, *Some Came Running* and *The Manchurian Candidate*. In 1965 he directed the war drama *None But the Brave* and made his last film appearance in the awful Burt Reynolds vehicle *Cannonball Run II* (1984). He was married four times, to Nancy Barbato (1939-1951), Ava Gardner (1951-1957), Mia Farrow (1966-1968) and Barbara Marx, the widow of Zeppo (1976-), and was briefly engaged to Juliet Prowse. As for his seemingly effortless talent for knocking out a good song, the jazz critic Benny Green once said: '[Sinatra] is not simply the best popular singer of his generation, but the culminating point in an evolutionary process which has refined the art of interpreting words set to music.' Marlon Brando had a different spin: 'Frank is the kinda guy that, when he dies, is going up to heaven to give God a bad time for making him bald.' Sinatra himself admitted that, 'I'm for anything that gets you through the night, be it prayer, tranquillisers or a bottle of Jack Daniels.' His very last words, according to Artie Funair, his former assistant, were: 'Oh dear Lord, oh mother.' However, according to his daughter Nancy, his last words were: 'I'm losing.'

Red Skelton

Born: 18 July 1910 in Vincennes, Indiana.
Died: 17 September 1997 in Palm Springs, California, following a prolonged illness.
Real name: Richard Bernard Skelton.

Red Skelton was an immensely durable, red-headed comic who prospered first on radio, then in film and finally on his own long-running TV show (1951-71). The son of an impoverished circus clown (who died before he was born), Skelton was just 14 when he started performing his own comedy routines on Mississippi showboats. In 1938 he made an auspicious film debut in the Ginger Rogers comedy *Having Wonderful Time*, which led to

a successful career at MGM for whom he starred in *Whistling in the Dark*, *Whistling in Dixie*, *Panama Hattie*, *Whistling in Brooklyn*, *DuBarry Was a Lady*, *Bathing Beauty* and so on. However, MGM weren't sure how to handle Skelton's slapstick and he was seldom given the opportunity to make a film his own. By the early 1950s his popularity at the cinema was replaced by his phenomenally successful TV showcase, *The Red Skelton Show*. In the late 1960s he returned to the vaudeville format of his youth and at the age of 80 was performing his schtick at Carnegie Hall.

Dawn Steel

Born: 1946 in Manhattan, New York.
Died: 20 December 1997 in Los Angeles of a brain tumour.
Real Name: Dawn Spielberg.

The first woman ever to head a major Hollywood studio, Dawn Steel lived up to her name as she doggedly worked her way from secretary to merchandising director of *Penthouse* magazine to president of production at Paramount to the main muscle behind Columbia TriStar Pictures. More recently she formed Atlas Pictures with her husband Charles Roven, producing such movies as *Twelve Monkeys* and *City of Angels*. In the words of fellow Hollywood executive Jeffrey Katzenberg, Ms Steel 'was a determined tornado with a lot of passion and no room in her life for the words "no" or "it can't be done". She titled her autobiography *They Can Kill You, But They Can't Eat You.*

James Stewart

Born: 20 May 1908 in Indiana, Pennsylvania.
Died: 2 July 1997 in Beverly Hills.

It's hard to think of a figure in the Hollywood firmament who was as much loved as James Stewart. With his gangling physique and inimitable drawl, he brought integrity, humanity and a down-to-earth humour to the screen that worked equally well in comedy, thriller or western. The eldest of three children, he was brought up in an atmosphere of music and learning

Frank Sinatra

and regularly attended the local Presbyterian church where his mother played the organ. Studying architecture at Princeton University, he was persuaded to join the University Players by fellow student Joshua Logan and was firmly bitten by the acting bug. Bit parts on Broadway quickly followed and for a time he shared a cramped apartment with another aspiring actor, Henry Fonda. Together, they moved to Hollywood in 1935, where Stewart secured the small part of a reporter (called 'Shorty'!) in the Spencer Tracy vehicle *The Murder Man*. A year later he was another reporter in *Next Time We Love*, this time wed to Margaret Sullavan, a friend from the University Players. He was the lead in *Speed* (1936), just one of eight features he made that year, and he then landed his first real break with *Born to Dance* (in which he sang Cole Porter's 'Easy To Love'). W.S. Van Dyke II's screwball comedy *It's a Wonderful World* (1939) was an even

James Stewart

bigger success, spearheading a string of popular star vehicles, starting with *Mr Smith Goes to Washington* – which won the actor his first Oscar nomination. The classic western *Destry Rides Again*, with Marlene Dietrich, followed, as did Ernst Lubitsch's *The Shop Around the Corner*, before Stewart won the Oscar for George Cuckor's immortal *The Philadelphia Story* (1940). During the war, the actor signed up as a bomber pilot and flew 20 missions over Germany, earning him the Distinguished Flying Cross. After the war his film career flourished and he went on to make *It's a Wonderful Life*, *Rope*, *Harvey*, *Winchester '73*, *Broken Arrow*, *The Glenn Miller Story*, *Rear Window*, *The Man Who Knew Too Much*, *The Spirit of St Louis*, *Vertigo*, *Anatomy of a Murder*, *The Man Who Shot Liberty Valance*, *The Flight of the Phoenix*, *The Shootist* and, with Bette Davis, the TV movie *Right of Way* (1983). Besides the astonishing number of classic films that bore his name above the title, Stewart went down

in history for being the first star to acquire a percentage of his box-office gross. While his fans preferred to think of him as the social conscience of America, a star like Jack Nicholson (who earned $60 million from *Batman*) must have regarded Stewart as a financial godsend. Incidentally, it was President Harry S. Truman who declared, 'If Bess and I had a son, we'd want him to be just like Jimmy Stewart.' However, there is no more fitting epitaph than the line spoken by Henry Travers' avuncular angel (to Stewart's character, George Bailey) in *It's a Wonderful Life*: 'Strange, isn't it? Each man's life touches so many other lives – and, when he's not around, it leaves an awful hole, doesn't it?'

Richard Vernon

Born: 7 March 1925 in Reading, Berkshire.
Died: 4 December 1997.

An inimitable character actor of British stage, TV and film, Vernon specialised in distinguished types clouded by an air of mild

bemusement. A prolific and familiar face, the actor was a minimal but always welcome presence in films, including *The Navy Lark*, *Village of the Damned*, *The Servant*, *Goldfinger*, *A Hard Day's Night*, *The Early Bird*, *Goodbye Mr Chips* (1969), *Evil Under the Sun*, *Gandhi* and many, many others.

James Villiers

Born: 29 September 1933 in London.
Died: 18 January 1998.

A lofty, lazy-eyed and omnipresent character actor, James Villiers cornered the market in snooty aristocrats and heartless cads.

J.T. Walsh

Born: 28 September 1943 in San Francisco.
Died: 27 February 1998 in La Mesa, near San Diego, California, of a heart attack.
Born: James Patrick Walsh.

A ubiquitous character actor, J. T. Walsh excelled at playing suspect figures of authority and seedy cops. Stockier of late, he was beginning to resemble George Kennedy in his late middle-age. His numerous film credits include *House of Games*, *Good Morning Vietnam*, *Tin Men*, *Things Change*, *Tequila Sunrise*, *Red Rock West*, *A Few Good Men*, *Hoffa*, *Needful Things*, *National Lampoon's Loaded Weapon 1*, *The Last Seduction*, *The Client*, *Miracle on 34th Street*, *Executive Decision*, *Sling Blade*, *Persons Unknown*, *Breakdown* and *The Negotiator*.

Richard Warwick

Born: 24 April 1945 in Dartford, Kent.
Died: 16 December 1997 of Aids.

Best known for his role as Wallace – Malcolm McDowell's guitar-strumming accomplice – in Lindsay Anderson's momentous *if...* (1968), Richard Warwick never capitalised on the film's success, in spite of his boyish good looks. He had the lead in the 1970 *The Breaking of Bumbo* (as an officer of the guards) and played Justin in Derek Jarman's *Sebastiane* (1976), but in his later years he was struggling to find work.

Awards and Festivals

The 70th American Academy of Motion Picture Arts and Sciences Awards ('The Oscars') and Nominations for 1997, Los Angeles, 23 March 1998

Best Film: *Titanic*. Nominations: *As Good As It Gets*; *The Full Monty*; *Good Will Hunting*; *L.A. Confidential*.

Best Director: James Cameron, for *Titanic*. Nominations: Atom Egoyan, for *The Sweet Hereafter*; Peter Cattaneo, for *The Full Monty*; Curtis Hanson, for *L.A. Confidential*; Gus Van Sant, for *Good Will Hunting*.

Best Actor: Jack Nicholson, for *As Good As It Gets*. Nominations: Matt Damon, for *Good Will Hunting*; Robert Duvall, for *The Apostle*; Peter Fonda, for *Ulee's Gold*; Dustin Hoffman, for *Wag the Dog*.

Best Actress: Helen Hunt, for *As Good As It Gets*. Nominations: Helena Bonham Carter, for *The Wings of the Dove*; Julie Christie, for *Afterglow*; Judi Dench, for *Mrs Brown*; Kate Winslet, for *Titanic*.

Best Supporting Actor: Robin Williams, for *Good Will Hunting*. Nominations: Robert Forster, for *Jackie Brown*; Anthony Hopkins, for *Amistad*; Greg Kinnear, for *As Good As It Gets*; Burt Reynolds, for *Boogie Nights*.

Best Supporting Actress: Kim Basinger, for *L.A. Confidential*. Nominations: Joan Cusack, for *In & Out*; Minnie Driver, for *Good Will Hunting*; Julianne Moore, for *Boogie Nights*; Gloria Stuart, for *Titanic*.

Best Original Screenplay: Ben Affleck and Matt Damon, for *Good Will Hunting*. Nominations: Mark Andrus and James L. Brooks, for *As Good As It Gets*; Paul Thomas Anderson, for *Boogie Nights*; Woody Allen, for *Deconstructing Harry*; Simon Beaufoy, for *The Full Monty*.

Best Screenplay Adaptation: Brian Helgeland and Curtis Hanson, for *L.A. Confidential*. Nominations: Paul Attanasio, for *Donnie Brasco*; Atom Egoyan, for *The Sweet Hereafter*; Hilary Henkin and David Mamet, for *Wag the Dog*; Hossein Amini, for *The Wings of the Dove*.

Best Cinematography: Russell Carpenter, for *Titanic*. Nominations: Janusz Kaminski, for *Amistad*; Roger Deakins, for *Kundun*; Dante Spinotti, for *L.A. Confidential*; Eduardo Serra, for *The Wings of the Dove*.

Best Editing: Conrad Buff, James Cameron and Richard A. Harris, for *Titanic*. Nominations: Richard Francis-Bruce, for *Air Force One*; Richard Marks, for *As Good As It Gets*; Pietro Scalia, for *Good Will Hunting*; Peter Honess, for *L.A. Confidential*.

Best Original Score (musical or comedy): Anne Dudley, for *The Full Monty*. Nominations: Stephen Flaherty (music), Lynn Ahrens (lyrics) and David Newman (orchestral score), for *Anastasia*; Hans Zimmer, for *As Good As It Gets*; Danny Elfman, for *Men in Black*; James Newton Howard, for *My Best Friend's Wedding*.

Best film of the year? Kate Winslet and Leonardo DiCaprio star in James Cameron's Oscar-laden *Titanic*

Best Original Score (dramatic): James Horner, for *Titanic*. Nominations: John Williams, for *Amistad*; Danny Elfman, for *Good Will Hunting*; Philip Glass, for *Kundun*; Jerry Goldsmith, for *L.A. Confidential*.
Best Original Song: 'My Heart Will Go On', from *Titanic*, music by James Horner, lyrics by Will Jennings. Nominations: 'Go The Distance', from *Hercules*, music by Alan Menken, lyrics by David Zippel; 'How Do I Live', from *Con Air*, music and lyrics by Diane Warren; 'Journey To The Past', from *Anastasia*, music by Stephen Flaherty, lyrics by Lynn Ahrens; 'Miss Misery,' from *Good Will Hunting*, music and lyrics by Elliott Smith.
Best Art Direction: Peter Lamont (art direction), Michael Ford (set decoration), for *Titanic*. Nominations: Jan Roelfs (art), Nancy Nye (set), for *Gattaca*; Dante Ferretti (art), Francesca Lo Schiavo (set), for *Kundun*; Jeannine Oppewall (art), Jay R. Hart (set), for *L.A. Confidential*; Bo Welch (art), Cheryl Carasik (set), for *Men in Black*.

Best Costume Design: Deborah L. Scott, for *Titanic*. Nominations: Ruth E. Carter, for *Amistad*; Dante Ferretti, for *Kundun*; Janet Patterson, for *Oscar and Lucinda*; Sandy Powell, for *The Wings of the Dove*.
Best Sound: Gary Rydstrom, Tom Johnson, Gary Summers and Mark Ulano, for *Titanic*. Nominations: Paul Massey, Rick Kline, D.M. Hemphill and Keith A. Wester, for *Air Force One*; Kevin O'Connell, Greg P. Russell and Arthur Rochester, for *Con Air*; Randy Thom, Tom Johnson, Dennis Sands and William B. Kaplan, for *Contact*; Andy Nelson, Anna Behlmer and Kirk Francis, for *L.A. Confidential*.
Best Sound Effects Editing: Tom Bellfort and Christopher Boyes, for *Titanic*. Nominations: Mark P. Stoeckinger and Per Hallberg, for *Face/Off*; Mark Mangini, for *The Fifth Element*.
Best Make-Up: Rick Baker and David LeRoy Anderson, for *Men in Black*. Nominations: Lisa Westcott, Veronica Brebner and Beverly Binda, for *Mrs Brown*; Tina Earnshaw, Greg Cannom and Simon Thompson, for *Titanic*.
Best Visual Effects: Robert Legato, Mark Lasoff, Thomas L. Fisher and Michael Kanfer, for *Titanic*.

Nominations: Dennis Muren, Stan Winston, Randal M. Dutra and Michael Lantieri, for *The Lost World: Jurassic Park*; Phil Tippett, Scott E. Anderson, Alec Gillis and John Richardson, for *Starship Troopers*.
Best Animated Short Film: *Geri's Game*. Nominations: *Famous Friend*; *La Vieille Dame et Les Pigeons* (*The Old Lady and the Pigeons*); *The Mermaid*; *Redux Riding Hood*.
Best Live Action Short Film: *Visas and Virtue*. Nominations: *Dance Lexie Dance*; *It's Good to Talk*; *Sweethearts?*; *Wolfgang*.
Best Documentary Feature: *The Long Way Home*. Nominations: *Ayn Rand: A Sense of Life*; *Colors Straight Up*; *4 Little Girls*; *Waco: The Rules of Engagement*.
Best Documentary Short: *A Story of Healing*. Nominations: *Alaska: Spirit of the Wild*; *Amazon*; *Daughter of the Bride*; *Still Kicking: The Fabulous Palm Springs Follies*.
Best Foreign-Language Film: *Character* (The Netherlands). Nominations: *Beyond Silence* (Germany); *Four Days in September* (Brazil); *Secrets of the Heart* (Spain); *The Thief* (Russia).
Career Achievement Award: Stanley Donen.

The 39th Australian Film Institute Awards, Melbourne, November 1997

Best Film: *Kiss or Kill*.
Best Actor: Richard Roxburgh, for *Doing Time for Patsy Cline*.
Best Actress: Pamela Rabe, for *The Well*.
Best Supporting Actor: Andrew S. Gilbert, for *Kiss or Kill*.
Best Supporting Actress: Cate Blanchett, for *Thank God He Met Lizzie*.
Best Director: Bill Bennett, for *Kiss or Kill*.
Best Original Screenplay: Santo Cilauro, Tom Gleisner, Jane Kennedy and Rob Sitch, for *The Castle*.
Best Screenplay Adaptation: Laura Jones, for *The Well*.
Best Cinematography: Andrew Lesnie, for *Doing Time for Patsy Cline*.
Best Production Design: Michael Philips, for *The Well*.
Best Editing: Henry Dangar, for *Kiss or Kill*.
Best Music: Peter Best, for *Doing Time for Patsy Cline*.
Best Costumes: Louise Wakefield, for *Doing Time for Patsy Cline*.
Best Sound: Wayne Pashley and Toivo Lember, for *Kiss or Kill*.
Best Foreign Film: *Secrets and Lies*, by Mike Leigh (UK–France).
The Byron Kennedy Award: actor John Polson (for encouraging young filmmakers with his annual Tropicana short film festival).
The Raymond Longford Award: Jan Chapman (producer of *Love Serenade* and *The Piano*).

The 48th Berlin International Film Festival, 22 February 1998

Golden Bear for Best Film: *Central Station* (Brazil–France).
Silver Bear, Special Jury Prize: *Wag the Dog* (USA).
Silver Bear for Best Director: Neil Jordan, for *The Butcher Boy* (USA–Ireland).
Silver Bear, Best Actor: Samuel L. Jackson, for *Jackie Brown* (USA).
Silver Bear, Best Actress: Fernanda Montenego, for *Central Station*.
Silver Bear for Outstanding Single Achievement: Matt Damon, star and writer of *Good Will Hunting* (USA).

Silver Bear for Lifetime Contribution to the Art of Cinema: Alain Resnais.
Blue Angel Prize: Jeroen Krabbe, for *Left Luggage* (The Netherlands–Belgium–USA).
Alfred Bauer Prize: *Hold You Tight* (Hong Kong).
Golden Bear for Best Short Film: *I Move So I Am* (The Netherlands).
Silver Bear for Best Short Film: *Cinema Alcazar* (Nicaragua).
Ecumenical Jury Prizes:
Competition: *Central Station*.
Panorama Prize: *Sue* (USA).
International Forum: *Homesick Eyes* (Taiwan).
Special Mentions: Isabella Rossellini, for *Left Luggage*.
Young Actor: Eamonn Owens, for *The Butcher Boy*.
Cinematographer: Slawomir Idziak, for *I Want You* (UK).
FIPRESCI Prizes (International Film Critics' Association):
Best Film: *Sada* (Japan).
Panorama: *Sue*.
International Forum: *Fragments * Jerusalem* (Israel).
Special Mention: *In That Land* (Russia).
UNICEF Prize: *The Climb* (France–New Zealand).
Pierrot Prize For Young European

Cinema: *Love Tangles* (France–Switzerland–Spain).
Wolfgang Staudte Prize: *Xiao Wu* (China).
CICAE (international confederation of art cinemas): *The Kid From Chaaba* (France).
Gay Teddy Bear Awards:
Best Feature: *Hold You Tight*.
Documentary: *The Brandon Teena Story* (USA).
Special Jury Prize: *The Man In Her Life* (Philippines).
Special Mention: *Uncut* (Canada).
Peace Film Prize: *In That Land*.
Caligari Film Prize: *Kasaba* (Turkey).
NETPAC (network for the promotion of Asian cinema) Award: *Xiao Wu*.
International Federation of Film Societies Prize: *Thirteen* (USA).

President of the jury: Ben Kingsley

The 1997 British Academy of Film and Television Arts Awards ('BAFTAs'), 19 April 1998

Best Film: *The Full Monty*.
David Lean Award for Best Direction: Baz Luhrmann, for *William Shakespeare's Romeo + Juliet*.
Best Original Screenplay: Gary Oldman, for *Nil by Mouth*.
Best Adapted Screenplay: Craig Pearce and Baz Luhrmann, for *William Shakespeare's Romeo + Juliet*.
Best Actor: Robert Carlyle, for *The Full Monty*.

Frances O'Connor and Matt Day star in Bill Bennett's *Kiss or Kill*, winner of the Best Film award from the Australian Film Institute

Best Actress: Judi Dench, for *Mrs Brown*.

Best Supporting Actor: Tom Wilkinson, for *The Full Monty*.

Best Supporting Actress: Sigourney Weaver, for *The Ice Storm*.

Best Cinematography: Eduardo Serra, for *The Wings of the Dove*.

Best Production Design: Catherine Martin, for *William Shakespeare's Romeo + Juliet*.

Best Editing: Peter Honess, for *L.A. Confidential*.

The Anthony Asquith Award for Best Music: Nellee Hooper, Craig Armstrong and Marius de Vries, for *William Shakespeare's Romeo + Juliet*.

Best Costumes: Deirdre Clancy, for *Mrs Brown*.

Best Sound: Terry Rodman, Roland Thai, Kirk Francis, Andy Nelson, Anna Behlmer, and John Leveque for *L.A. Confidential*.

Best Special Visual Effects: Mark Stetson, Karen Goulekas, Nick Allder, Neil Corbould, Nick Dudman, for *The Fifth Element*.

Best Make-up/Hair: Sallie Jaye and Jan Archibald, for *The Wings of the Dove*.

Alexander Korda Award for Best British Film: *Nil by Mouth*.

Best Foreign Language Film: *L'Appartement*.

Best Short Film: *The Deadness of Dad*.

Best Animated Short: *Stage Fright*.

BAFTA Fellowship: Sean Connery.

The 18th Canadian Film Awards ('Genies'), Toronto, 14 December 1997

Best Film: *The Sweet Hereafter*.

Best Director: Atom Egoyan, for *The Sweet Hereafter*.

Best Actor: Ian Holm, for *The Sweet Hereafter*.

Best Actress: Molly Parker, for *Kissed*.

Best Supporting Actor: Peter MacNeill, for *The Hanging Garden*.

Best Supporting Actress: Seana McKenna, for *The Hanging Garden*.

Best Screenplay: Thom Fitzgerald, for *The Hanging Garden*.

Best Cinematography: Paul Sarossy, for *The Sweet Hereafter*.

Best Editing: Susan Shipton, for *The Sweet Hereafter*.

Best Music: Mychael Danna, for *The Sweet Hereafter*.

Best Original Song: Luc Plamondon and Francois Dompierre, for the theme song to *L'Homme Ideal*.

Best Make-Up: Pierre Saindon, for *Karmina*.

Claude Jutra Award for Best First Feature: *The Hanging Garden*.

Best Feature-length Documentary: *Tu As Crie, Let Me Go*, by Anne-Claire Poirier.

The Golden Reel Award for Box-Office Performance: *Air Bud*.

The 51st Cannes Film Festival Awards, 24 May 1998

Palme d'Or for Best Film: *Eternity and a Day*, by Theo Angelopoulos (Greece).

Grand Prix du Jury: *Life is Beautiful*, by Roberto Benigni (Italy).

Best Actor: Peter Mullan, for *My Name is Joe* (UK).

Best Actress (shared): Elodie Bouchez and Natacha Regnier, for *The Dream Life of Angels* (France).

Best Director: John Boorman, for *The General* (Ireland–UK).

Best Screenplay: Hal Hartley, for *Henry Fool* (USA).

Palme d'Or for Best Short: *The Interview*, by Xavier Giannoli (France).

Jury Prize: *The Class Trip*, by Claude Miller (France); and *Celebration*, by Thomas Vinterberg (Denmark).

Jury Prize for Best Short: *Horseshoe*, by David Lodge (UK); and *Gasman*, by Lynne Ramsay (UK).

Camera d'Or for First Feature: *Slam*, by Marc Levin (USA).

Prix de la Jeunesse (the youth prize): *Last Night*, by Don McKellar (Canada).

Grand Prix Technique: Vittorio Storaro, cinematographer of *Tango* (Argentina–Spain).

Fipresci International Critics' Award: *The Hole*, by Tsai Mingliang (France–Taiwan).

Out of competition: *Happiness*, by Todd Solondz (USA).

Best Artistic Contribution: *Velvet Goldmine*, by Todd Haynes (USA).

Ecumenical Prize: *Eternity and a Day*.

Jury: Martin Scorsese (president); Alain Corneau, Chen Kaige, Chiara Mastroianni, Lena Olin, Winona Ryder, MC Solaar, Sigourney Weaver, Michael Winterbottom, Zoe Valdes

The 23rd Deauville Festival of American Cinema, 14 September 1997

Grand Prix for Best Film: *Sunday*, by Jonathan Nossiter.

Jury Prize shared by: *In the Company of Men*, by Neil LaBute; and *Ulee's Gold*, by Victor Nunez.

Prix du Public: *The Myth of Fingerprints*, by Bart Freundlich.

Youth Jury Award shared by: *In the Company of Men*; and *The House of Yes*, by Mark Waters.

President of the jury: Sophie Marceau

The 10th European Film Awards ('The Felixes'), Berlin, 6 December 1997

Best European Film: *The Full Monty* (UK), by Peter Cattaneo.

Best Actor: Bob Hoskins, for *TwentyFourSeven* (UK).

Best Actress: Juliette Binoche, for *The English Patient* (USA).

Best Screenplay: Alain Berliner and

Ariane Ascaride, voted Best Actress by the French Academy for her gritty, enchanting performance in *Marius et Jeannette*

Chris Vander Stappen, for *Ma Vie en Rose* (France–Belgium–UK).
Best Cinematography: John Seale, for *The English Patient*.
Discovery of the Year (Fassbinder Award): Bruno Dumont, director of *La Vie de Jesus* (France).
Best Documentary (Prix Arte): *Gigi, Monica … & Bianca*.
European Critics' Award: *Journey to the Beginning of the World* (Portugal–France).
People's Award for Best Film: *The Full Monty*.
Best Actor: Javier Bardem.
Best Actress: Jodie Foster.
Life Achievement Award: Jeanne Moreau.
The Screen International Five Continents Award: *Hana-Bi*, by Takeshi Kitano (Japan).
Achievement in World Cinema: Milos Forman.

The 23rd French Academy ('Cesar') Awards, 7 March 1998

Best Film: *On Connait la Chanson* (*Same Old Song*).
Best Director: Luc Besson, for *The Fifth Element*.
Best Actor: Andre Dussollier, for *On Connait la Chanson*.
Best Actress: Ariane Ascaride, for *Marius et Jeannette*.
Best Supporting Actor: Jean-Pierre Bacri, for *On Connait la Chanson*.
Best Supporting Actress: Agnes Jaoui, for *On Connait la Chanson*.
Most Promising Young Actor: Stanislas Merhar, for *Nettoyage à Sec*.
Most Promising Young Actress: Emma de Caunes, for *Frère*.
Best First Film: *Didier*.
Best Screenplay: Jean-Pierre Bacri and Agnes Jaoui, for *On Connait la Chanson*.
Best Photography: Thierry Arbogast, for *The Fifth Element*.
Best Production Design: Dan Weil, for *The Fifth Element*.
Best Editing: Herve de Luze, for *On Connait la Chanson*.
Best Music: Bernardo Sandoval, for *Western*.
Best Costumes: Christian Gasc, for *Le Bossu*.
Best Sound: Pierre Lemoir and Jean-Pierre Laforce, for *On Connait la Chanson*.

Best Foreign Film: *Brassed Off*.
Honorary Cesars: Jean-Luc Godard, Clint Eastwood, Michael Douglas.

The 55th Hollywood Foreign Press Association ('Golden Globes') Awards, 18 January 1998

Best Film – Drama: *Titanic*.
Best Film – Comedy or Musical: *As Good As It Gets*.
Best Actor – Drama: Peter Fonda, for *Ulee's Gold*.
Best Actress – Drama: Judi Dench, for *Mrs Brown*.
Best Actor – Comedy or Musical: Jack Nicholson, for *As Good As It Gets*.
Best Actress – Comedy or Musical: Helen Hunt, for *As Good As It Gets*.
Best Supporting Actor: Burt Reynolds, for *Boogie Nights*.
Best Supporting Actress: Kim Basinger, for *L.A. Confidential*.
Best Director: James Cameron, for *Titanic*.
Best Screenplay: Matt Damon and Ben Affleck, for *Good Will Hunting*.
Best Original Score: James Horner, for *Titanic*.
Best Original Song: 'My Heart Will Go On', music by James Horner, lyrics by Will Jennings, from *Titanic*.
Best Foreign Language Film: *Ma Vie en Rose* (France–Belgium–UK–Switzerland).
Best TV Film: *George Wallace* (TNT).
Cecil B. De Mille Award for Lifetime Achievement: Shirley MacLaine.

The 13th Independent Spirit Awards, Santa Monica, 21 March 1998

Best Film: *The Apostle*.
Best First Film: *Eve's Bayou*.
Best Director: Robert Duvall, for *The Apostle*.
Best Actor: Robert Duvall, for *The Apostle*.
Best Actress: Julie Christie, for *Afterglow*.
Best Supporting Actor: Jason Lee, for *Chasing Amy*.
Best Supporting Actress: Debbi Morgan, for *Eve's Bayou*.
Best Debut Performance: Aaron Eckhart, for *In the Company of Men*.

Best Screenplay: Kevin Smith, for *Chasing Amy*.
Best First Screenplay: Neil LaBute, for *In the Company of Men*.
Best Cinematography: Declan Quinn, for *Kama Sutra*.
Best Foreign Film: *The Sweet Hereafter*.
Best Documentary: *Soul in the Hole*, by Danielle Gardner; and *Fast, Cheap & Out of Control*, by Errol Morris.
Someone To Watch Award: Scott Saunders.

Host: John Turturro.

The 18th London Film Critics' Awards ('The Alfs'), The Dorchester, London, 5 March 1998

Best Film: *L.A. Confidential*.
Best Actor: Al Pacino, for *Donnie Brasco* and *Looking for Richard*; and Geoffrey Rush, for *Shine*.
Best Actress: Claire Danes, for *William Shakespeare's Romeo + Juliet*.
Best Director: Curtis Hanson, for *L.A. Confidential*.
Best Screenwriter: Brian Helgeland and Curtis Hanson, for *L.A. Confidential*.
Best British Film: *The Full Monty*.
Best British Producer: Uberto Pasolini, for *The Full Monty*.
Best British Director: Anthony Minghella, for *The English Patient*.
Best British Screenwriter: Simon Beaufoy, for *The Full Monty*.
Best British Actor: Robert Carlyle, for *The Full Monty*.
Best British Actress: Judi Dench, for *Mrs Brown*.
Best British Supporting Actress: Minnie Driver, for *Big Night*, *Grosse Pointe Blank* and *Sleepers*.
Best British Newcomer: Peter Cattaneo, director of *The Full Monty*.
Best Foreign Language Film: *Ridicule*, by Patrice Leconte (France).
Dilys Powell Award: Michael Caine.
Special Awards: Woody Allen, Paul Scofield, Martin Scorsese, Kevin Spacey.

Presenters: Christopher Tookey, James Cameron-Wilson, Paul Gambaccini, Marianne Gray, Tom Hutchinson, Richard Jobson, Karen Krizanovich, George Perry, Simon Rose, etc.

The Los Angeles Film Critics' Association Awards, December 1997

Best Film: *L.A. Confidential*.
Best Actor: Robert Duvall, for *The Apostle*.
Best Actress: Helena Bonham Carter, for *The Wings of the Dove*.
Best Supporting Actor: Burt Reynolds, for *Boogie Nights*.
Best Supporting Actress: Julianne Moore, for *Boogie Nights*.
Best Director: Curtis Hanson, for *L.A. Confidential*.
Best Screenplay: Brian Helgeland and Curtis Hanson, for *L.A. Confidential*.
Best Cinematography: Dante Spinotti, for *L.A. Confidential*.
Best Production Design: Peter Lamont, for *Titanic*.
Best Music: Philip Glass, for *Kundun*.
Best Foreign Film: *La Promesse* (Belgium).
Best Animated Feature: *Hercules*; and *Spirit of Christmas*.
Best Documentary: *Riding the Rails* (USA), by Michael Uys and Lexy Lovell.
Experimental/Independent Award: *Finished*, by William E. Jones.
New Generation Award: Paul Thomas Anderson, writer-director of *Boogie Nights*.
Special Honour: Peter Bogdanovich.

The National Board of Review of Motion Pictures, New York, 9 December 1997

Best Film: *L.A. Confidential*.
Best Actor: Jack Nicholson, for *As Good As It Gets*.
Best Actress: Helena Bonham Carter, for *The Wings of the Dove*.
Best Supporting Actor: Greg Kinnear, for *As Good As It Gets*.
Best Supporting Actress: Anne Heche, for *Donnie Brasco* and *Wag the Dog*.
Best Director: Curtis Hanson, for *L.A. Confidential*.
Best Directorial Debut: Kasi Lemmons, for *Eve's Bayou*.
Best Ensemble Cast: *The Sweet Hereafter*.
Best Documentary: *Fast, Cheap & Out of Control*, by Errol Morris.
Best Foreign Film: *Shall We Dance?* (Japan), by Masayuki Suo.

Breakthrough Performance: Bai Ling, for *Red Corner*.
Special Achievement in Filmmaking Award: Matt Damon and Ben Affleck, for their screenplay and appearance in *Good Will Hunting*.
Freedom of Expression Award: Director Jon Avnet and actor Richard Gere, for *Red Corner*.

The 63rd New York Film Critics' Circle Awards, 11 December 1997

Best Film: *L.A. Confidential*.
Best Actor: Peter Fonda, for *Ulee's Gold*.
Best Actress: Julie Christie, for *Afterglow*.
Best Supporting Actor: Burt Reynolds, for *Boogie Nights*.
Best Supporting Actress: Joan Cusack, for *In & Out*.
Best Director: Curtis Hanson, for *L.A. Confidential*.
Best Screenplay: Brian Helgeland and Curtis Hanson, for *L.A. Confidential*.
Best Cinematography: Roger Deakins, for *Kundun*.
Best Foreign Film: *Ponette* (France), by Jacques Doillon.
Best Non-Fiction Film: *Fast, Cheap & Out of Control*, by Errol Morris.
Best First Film: *In the Company of Men*, by Neil LaBute.
Special Tribute Award: Daniel Talbot of New Yorker Films.

The 14th Sundance Film Festival, Park City, Utah, 24 January 1998

The Grand Jury Prize (best feature): *Slam*, by Marc Levin.
The Grand Jury Prize (best documentary): *The Farm*, by Jonathan Stack and Liz Garbus; and *Frat House*, by Andrew Gurland and Todd Phillips.
Best Performance: Andrea Hart, for *Miss Monday*.
Best Direction: Darren Aronofsky, for *Pi*.
Best Direction (documentary): Julia Loktev, for *Moment of Impact*.
Best Cinematography: Declan Quinn, for *2 by 4*.
Best Cinematography (documentary): Tom Hurwitz, for *Wild Man Blues*.

Audience Award (best feature): *Smoke Signals*, by Chris Eyre.
Audience Award (best documentary): *Out of the Past*, by Jeff Dupre.
Filmmakers' Trophy (best feature): *Smoke Signals*.
Filmmakers' Trophy (best documentary): *Divine Trash*, by Steve Yeager.
Waldo Salt Screenwriting Award: Lisa Cholodenko, for *High Art*.
Freedom of Expression Award: *The Decline of Western Civilization Part III*, by Penelope Spheeris.
Latin American Cinema Award: *Who the Hell is Juliette?*, by Carlos Marcovich.
Special Recognition Award: *Snake Feed*, by Debra Granik.
Honourable Mention: *Human Remains*, by Jay Rosenblatt.

The 54th Venice International Film Festival Awards, September 1997

Golden Lion for Best Film: *Hana-Bi*, by Takeshi Kitano (Japan).
Special Jury Grand Prix: *Ovosodo*, by Paolo Virzi (Italy).
Best Actor: Wesley Snipes, for *One Night Stand* (USA).
Best Actress: Robin Tunney, for *Niagara, Niagara* (USA).
Best Screenplay: Gilles Taurand and Anne Fontaine, for *Dry Cleaning* (France).
Best Photography: Emmanuel Machuel, for *Ossos* (Portugal).
Best Music: Graeme Revell, for *Chinese Box*.
Gold Medal (for a film which emphasises civil progress and human solidarity): *The Thief* (Russia), by Pavel Chuchraj.
Fipresci Award: Histoire Milosne, by Jerzy Stuht; *TwentyFourSeven* (UK), by Shane Meadows. Special mention: *Gummo* (USA), by Harmony Korine.
Film critics' award: *Alors Voila*, by Michel Piccoli.
Ocic Jury Award: *The Winter Guest* (UK), by Alan Rickman. Special mentions: *Histoire Milosne*, and *Bent Famiglia*, by Nouri Bouzid.
Prix du Festival: *La Strana Storia di Banda Sonora*, by Francesca Arcibugi.

Jury: Jane Campion (president), Charlotte Rampling, Francesco Rosi.

Index